Global Migration and Education

Schools, Children, and Families

Global Migration and Education

Schools, Children, and Families

Edited by

Leah D. Adams
Eastern Michigan University

Anna Kirova
University of Alberta

LAWRENCE ERLBAUM ASSOCIATES, PUBLISHERS
2007   Mahwah, New Jersey   London

Lawrence Erlbaum Associates, Inc., Publishers
10 Industrial Avenue
Mahwah, New Jersey 07430
www.erlbaum.com

Cover design by Tomai Maridou

Library of Congress Cataloging-in-Publication Data

Adams, Leah.
Global migration and education : school, children, and families /
Leah D. Adams and Anna Kirova.
        p. cm.
Includes bibliographical references and index.
ISBN 0-8058-5837-7 (cloth : alk. paper) — ISBN 0-8058-5838-5
(pbk. : alk. paper)
        1. Children of immigrants—Education. 2. Home and school.
3. Multicultural education. 4. Emigration and immigration.
I. Kirova, Anna. II. Title.
LC3745.A33 2006
371.826'912—dc22
2006008679

Printed in the United States of America
10   9   8   7   6   5   4   3   2   1

This book is dedicated to Anna's son, Peter, whose experiences as an immigrant child inspired her research in this area and to the newly immigrated students and parents Leah worked with as a teacher, who infused her with a lifelong interest in global migration and education.

About the Editors

Leah D. Adams is Professor Emerita of Education at Eastern Michigan University. She holds a PhD in Educational Psychology from the University of Michigan, an MA in Human Development from Wayne State University, and a BS in Education from Ohio State University.

In addition to her writing and research, Dr. Adams has been an active leader in early childhood professional organizations at the national and international levels. She has visited schools and child care centers all over the world and has given invited addresses in such diverse locations as Argentina, Fiji, Jordan, Hungary, China, and Cuba. Her early teaching experiences in working with newly immigrated children and their families before multicultural education became a critical goal in public schools, inspired her long standing interest in their special needs.

Anna Kirova is Associate Professor of Education in the Department of Elementary Education at the University of Alberta, Edmonton, in Canada, and the Education Research Domain leader at the Prairie Centre of Excellence in Research in Immigration and Integration. She holds a PhD in Early Childhood Education from the University of Sofia, Bulgaria, and a PhD in Elementary Education from the University of Alberta. Prior to her present academic appointment, she taught at Oakland University, Rochester, Michigan.

Dr. Kirova has published numerous articles and book chapters on childhood loneliness, peer interactions and acceptance of immigrant children, identity formation and second language learning in ESL students, and the role of teachers in helping linguistically and culturally diverse students adjust to the school culture.

Contents

Preface   xiii
Acknowledgments   xvii

1. Introduction: Global Migration and the Education of Children   1
   Leah D. Adams, USA, and Anna Kirova, Canada

**PART I.   MULTIPLE GLOBAL ISSUES FOR IMMIGRANT
            CHILDREN AND THE SCHOOLS THEY ATTEND   13**
Introduction to Part I

2. Bringing Multicultural Education Into the Mainstream:
   Developing Schools for Minority and Majority Students   17
   Christian Horst and Anne Holmen, Denmark

3. Acculturation and Educational Achievement of Children With
   an Immigrant BackGround in German Primary Schools   35
   *Leonie Herwartz-Emden, and Dieter Küffner,
   Julia Landgraf, Germany*

4. Inclusion in Schools in Latin America and the Caribbean:
   The Case of Children of Haitian Descent in the
   Dominican Republic   53
   Rosa Blanco and Yuki Takemoto, Chile

5. Nutritional Challenges Among Immigrant Children and
   Youth in Norway   67
   Bernadette Kumar and Margareta Wandel, Norway

PART II.   THEY ARE HERE: NEWCOMERS IN THE SCHOOLS   83
Introduction to Part II

6. Teachers', Children's and Parents' Perspectives on
    Newly Arrived Children's Adjustment to Elementary School   87
    Leah D. Adams and Krista M. Shambleau, USA

7. The Role of Home and School in the Socialization
    of Immigrant Children in Israel: Fathers' Views   103
    Dorit Roer-Strier and Roni Strier, Israel

8. A Challenge of Transnational Migration: Young
    Children Start School   121
    Eva L. Vidali, Greece and Leah D. Adams, USA

PART III.   VIEWS AND VOICES OF IMMIGRANT CHILDREN   135
Introduction to Part III

9. Listening to Children: Voices of Newly Arrived
    Immigrants From the Chinese Mainland to Hong Kong   139
    Nirmala Rao and Mantak Yuen, Hong Kong

10. Immigrant Children's Understandings of Nonverbal Peer
    Interactions Through the Development of Visual Narratives   151
    Anna Kirova and Michael Emme, Canada

11. Talking Television Across Cultures: Negotiating Inclusion
    and Exclusion   169
    Liesbeth de Block, United Kingdom

12. Moving Childhoods: Young Children's Lived
    Experiences of Being Between Languages and Cultures   185
    Anna Kirova, Canada

PART IV.   FAR FROM HOME WITH FLUCTUATING HOPES   199
Introduction to Part IV

13. Transnational Displacement of Children: An Australian Perspective   203
    Ann Farrell, Australia

14. Exploring the Needs of Refugee Children in Our Schools   219
    Judit Szente and James Hoot, USA

15. Crossing Cultural Borders in the United States: A Case Study
    of a Sudanese Refugee Family's Experiences With
    Urban Schooling   237
    Guofang Li, USA

16. Refugee Families With Preschool Children: Adjustment
    to Life in Canada   251
    Darcey M. Dachyshyn, Canada

PART V.   SEARCHING FOR NEW WAYS TO BELONG   263
    Introduction to Part V

17. The Experiences of Third-Culture Children   267
    Marjory Ebbeck, and Valerie Reus, Australia

18. Children in Transition: Learning to Become Global Citizens   279
    Hilary Fabian, United Kingdom, and Cari Roberts, Germany

19. The Social Adaptation and Skills of Migrant Children
    Attending Primary School in Turkey   293
    Esra Ömeroğlu and Adalet Kandir, Turkey, Leah D. Adams, USA

20. Community-Based Education for Children of Migrant
    Peasant Workers   307
    Zhang Yan and Wei-Xiao Bing, China

21. Lessons Learned and Implications for the Future   321
    Anna Kirova, Canada, and Leah D. Adams, USA

Author Index   327
Subject Index   337

Preface

This book is committed to the understanding of children in schools all over the world, specifically those who are newly arrived from another nation or from a very different society and environment within the same nation. Globalization is both multifaceted in its operations and massive in its reach and implications for all aspects of life. Through the new considerable fissures as well as the new bridges it has created between societies and states, it has become an emblem of both hope and apprehension. As one of the most commonly found institutions and most commonly shared experiences, education is in the center of the social and cultural processes that result from and influence the economic and political changes. Although one of the goals of education can be seen by some as reproducing national culture and national identity, preparing the human capital as a force for future change is a goal shared by most education institutions in the world. However, with the increased diversification of the student body, rethinking the role of schools in general, and their moral and political responsibilities in contemporary societies in particular, has become essential to educational discourse. Issues of justice, questions of both opportunities in and outcomes of schooling, and tensions produced by the assertion of ethnicities and cultural identities within the educational landscape have challenged educators and policymakers around the globe.

The process of children moving from one context to another and the struggles of schools to both stabilize and enhance the result for those children are the focus of this book. This book is intended to help teachers, administrators, teacher educators, and all who are interested in the educational milieu and its populace to gain a deeper understanding of the related issues. Although it acknowledges that schools cannot take on all of societies' ills or assume full responsibility for providing all of the support services for all families in the community, this book engages the reader in exploring how the issues faced by immigrant children and their parents are addressed by educators as they interact in school settings. By providing a close look at some of the common challenges to, and successes in, educational institutions worldwide as they cope with these issues, we invite educators and others involved in these complex processes to see beyond the notion of *problems* created and experienced by recently arrived young children.

In this volume, we strive to offer many concrete examples of the diverse experiences of migration that families with young children have and the adjustments made by them as well as by the host countries. Individual chapters identify some specific problems related to newly immigrated children and families, the support services needed, and some of the ways that schools can assume their related responsibilities. Those who are seen as immigrants when they arrive in a new location may be the significant presence in the community in the future. The education of their children is important not only for the sake of these children's future but also for the sake of our shared future. The suggestions offered by the authors of the individual chapters are derived from the stories and voices of teachers, parents, and students. We hope that these stories will invite the reader to gain a deeper understanding of the complexity of the contexts in which they find themselves to be and to appreciate the opportunities given to all of us to learn form one another.

We believe that the works presented here will assist educators in addressing the challenges they may encounter in their work with newly arrived children, regardless of their racial, social, ethnic, and religious differences and individual capabilities. We also believe that the volume offers strong evidence that diversity is not an impediment to education. Rather, when understood, embraced, and supported, diversity can be a condition for learning that leads to rich learning opportunities for all involved that would not exist without diversity. As complexity theorists insist, complex systems such as societies, rely on diversity because novelty, creativity, change, and learning can rise only when there are differences that enable and compel departure from established patterns. Thus, the influx of students from diverse cultural, linguistic, ethnic, and religious backgrounds in the mainstream schools is an opportunity for educators and policymakers to develop new pedagogical approaches and ways of building communities of learners. All of the authors offer recommendations about educational policy and practices to address and ultimately improve the education of all children, including immigrant children.

In this book, we attempt to present the uniqueness as well as the similarity of the educational experiences of newly arrived people from the point of view of the children, their parents, and their teachers. We also present the multiple challenges faced by educators, schools, and school authorities around the world as they try to address the needs of the increasing number of children and families in transition, as well as some successes in easing this transition for parents and children. The book is organized around five themes that define each part of the book:

- Multiple Global Issues for Immigrant Children and the Schools They Attend
- They Are Here: Newcomers in the Schools
- Views and Voices of Immigrant Children
- Far From Home With Fluctuating Hopes
- Searching for New Ways to Belong

As with any division of materials, the placement of chapters was often a difficult or arbitrary decision reflecting both the commonalities and the individuality of the chapters. Introductions are provided for each part; these introductions both tie the part chapters together and offer insights as to why the particular focus of a chapter is vital to the overall content of the book.

We believe that this book—intended for researchers, students, school professionals, and educational policymakers and analysts around the world in the fields of multicultural education, child psychology, comparative and international education, educational foundations, educational policy, and cross-cultural studies—will be highly relevant as a text for courses in these disciplines. The content in the wide range of chapters may provide a look at a different reality for those who were less aware of situations in countries poles apart economically and culturally from their own. Thus, we feel that this book makes a notable contribution to understanding the experiences of immigrant children, their families, and teachers as they interact and strive to negotiate the shared space we call school and to identifying future directions in making school a better place for all.

Acknowledgments

We wish to acknowledge the 29 authors who have contributed their expertise, vast knowledge, and writing skills to make this book a reality. It is truly a collaborative effort of 31 of us from 14 nations with multifaceted experiences, complementary views, a wide range of professional experiences and life stories, and differing approaches to both life and research. Those 29 authors have our highest respect and lifelong gratitude. We all worked toward a common goal based on our mutual commitment to the smoothest transition possible and a quality education for all immigrant children, whoever they are and wherever they may be.

Our gratitude also goes to the entire staff at LEA especially Naomi Silverman and Erica Kica, expert handholders who offered unflagging support and encouragement. We would also want to acknowledge the assistance provided by Naomi Stinson, who has helped us tremendously with the editing of the chapters.

Most important of all, we must say thanks to our families and our colleagues for their tolerance of the effects of stress and hard work on our dispositions and on the time available to spend with those we care about.

Leah Adams, Ann Arbor, Michigan, USA
Anna Kirova, Edmonton, Alberta, Canada
January 2006

Chapter 1

Introduction: Global Migration and the Education of Children

Leah D. Adams
Eastern Michigan University, USA

Anna Kirova
University of Alberta, Canada

Migration is not new. Human beings have always migrated; much of the prehistoric and historic record focuses on the migration of people. Although the highest percentage of world population migration was between 1850 and 1910, when as much as 10% of the world population was on the move, the transitional displacement of people appears to have become endemic by the beginning of 21st century, with more people on the face of the globe then ever before and some 200 million living away from their country of birth (Global Commission on International Migration, 2005). Every nation is a sending, receiving, or transient nation for migrants, and there is every indication that international mobility and the challenges associated with transition will continue to affect future generations (Langford, 1998; RAND Corporation, 2000; Schiff & Özden, 2005). The trend has significant effects on the racial and ethnic composition of many of the world's schools (Rong & Preissle, 1998).

Although *transnational migration* is an increasingly recognized international term for people moving from one country to another, because of the international nature of this volume, the chapters and introductory sections use various terms for transnational migrants or for those who move from rural to urban locations. In many countries, particularly in North America, *immigration* is the term for the act of people moving from other nations to settle, and people who do so are termed *immigrants;* the term *migrants* is reserved for those who move within national borders. In Europe and in some other areas, new arrivals from other nations are sometimes referred to as *migrants,* and, in some instances, the terms *immigrants* and *migrants* are used interchangeably. In general, although the terms *immigrants, migrants,* and *newcomers* are used differently in various parts of the world, they typically refer to people who have left their places of birth by choice to settle in a new place either permanently or temporarily. The terms used to describe the people who have left their homes not by choice are *refugees, asylum seekers,* and *displaced people.* For the purposes of this book, we decided that readers would be able to cope with the interchanging of the terms and that it would be inappropriate to alter the authors' preferred terms. The semantics used to describe the phenomenon are not as important as the recognition of the magnitude of the global phenomenon of movement from one nation to another and the impact on societies, communities, and schools.

The particular focus of this volume is the factors that shape the lives of families with young children in transition as they experience schooling in their new location. We see these experiences as fundamental to the study of global migration of people, because they provide a glimpse into how schools might allow space for the expression of people's ideas, languages, social behaviors, ideologies, and ways of seeing the world. Educators and school environments are the key to facilitating the socialization and acculturation of immigrant children. It is in schools that children often first encounter in-depth contact with the host culture, which leads to school becoming a central part of life for the children (Hones & Cha, 1999; Trueba, Jacobs, & Kirton, 1990; Yale Center in Child Development and Social Policy, 2003). As Corson (1998) pointed out, schools are where most of a culture's dominant discourses are exchanged; most simple, everyday conventional acts are observed; and new ways of doing things are learned. The cultural capital valued in schools may not be equally available to the newcomer who brings another set of cultural conventions into the classroom (Suárez-Orozco & Suárez-Orozco, 2001). Events experienced by children and their families before entering the school system, as well as the experiences of schooling in the host country, to a large extent affect the kind of relationship children will develop with the new culture and how they will begin to shape their new identities.

In the past, the paths of migration were more predictable, that is, from less economically developed countries to more highly developed areas. Current global economic trends, the growth of global communication, and greater access to transportation have affected this pattern of migration. Although it can still be expected that most immigrant families struggle financially and that children in immigrant families are more likely to be poor and to live in crowded housing conditions (Children Now, 2004; Segal 1993), this is not true of all immigrants. Many highly skilled and well-educated workers, managers, and entrepreneurs are among those who migrate (Fix & Passel, 2003). This trend has challenged the traditional view of immigrants as people who are forced to move away from their countries of origin to survive economically. Migration of skilled workers is often referred to as a *brain drain* (Schiff & Özden, 2005), and some of the world's poorest countries have the highest incidence of this phenomenon. More than 50% of the university-educated professionals from many countries in Central America and the Caribbean live abroad; for some countries, this statistic is as high as 80%. Most college-educated emigrants from developing countries go to the United States, the European Union, Australia, and Canada. Canada and Australia have the largest percentage of educated migrants among the total number of migrants, and immigrants represent approximately 25% of the skilled labor force in Australia, Luxembourg, and Switzerland (Schiff & Özden, 2005).

Migration for the children of highly educated workers is not necessarily any less challenging. Educated migrants often fail to find work that matches their education levels; one of the main reasons is lack of fluency in the host language. The family may struggle to obtain enough income for basic necessities, and many new arrivals feel obliged to support family members in their home country. Although the question arises as to whether the brain drain has adverse effects on the sending nation, a World Bank report (Schiff & Özden, 2005) clearly shows that the remittances from migrants do help alleviate poverty in the home country. Sending remittances adds to the financial strain on immigrant families, but teachers should not assume that the parents of newly arrived children who live at or near the poverty line have limited education or skills.

Although the trend toward global movement among highly skilled workers and entrepreneurs still represents a small percentage of the overall number of people in transitional migration, it illustrates one aspect of global change that results in people considering themselves global citizens—comfortable living almost anywhere (Friedmann, 2002). Schools must be able to face the challenge of meeting the needs of students who are well prepared for the curriculum and already global citizens. It is important to consider that although importing culture, goods, and foods, along with global media and media products, may facilitate the process of becoming a global citizen, it also may lead to reduction in diversity through hybridization or even assimilation. Noddings (2005) reminded us that in our world of instant communication and swift travel, we have become keenly aware of our global interdependence. Along with this awareness, we ponder the question of global citizenship and how we can preserve diversity while seeking unity.

The forces behind international transitional migration cannot be reduced to economic factors. Intolerance and political exclusion and various forms of violence, including armed conflicts, civil wars, ethnic cleansing, or natural disasters, can and do force people away from their countries of origin to protect their own lives and those of their families. The United Nation High Commissioner for Refugees (UNHCR, 1994) estimated that more than half of any refugee population consists of children. Separation of families during flight (Boyden, de Berry, Feeny, & Hart, 2002); rape, abduction, and trafficking of refugee children; illness and malnutrition; loss of stability; and lack of education (Boyden et al., 2002; Tollefson, 1989) are among the traumas refugee families with children may experience before entering the host country. The multiple losses of the children and their families and the children's fears, confusion, sadness, loneliness, and alienation are carried with them to their new schools (Kirova, 2001). Thus, these premigration experiences present challenges to both the newcomers and the people and institutions that receive them in the new locations. Educators who work with immigrant and refugee children and their families must recognize the social, economic, health, and education hardships faced by these people. At the same time, educators need to recognize that many systemic challenges in education have yet to be overcome. The plight of the immigrant who is marginalized in the community through encountering xenophobia and economic, linguistic, or cultural barriers is a reality that needs the attention of all members of the international education community.

Although the reasons behind peoples' migration are multifaceted and usually involve a complex decision-making process that takes into consideration several factors, the process of settlement and establishing a new pattern of life in the new location after migration has some common elements for all transitional migrants. For example, regardless of their level of education, many migrants, especially those who are racially different from the dominant group, encounter varying degrees of prejudice, racism, rejection, or indifference (Li, 2001; Moreau, 2000; Nauck & Sattles, 2001). With regard to schools, recent studies (Gitlin, Buendía, Crosland, & Doumbia, 2003) in the United States have shown a discrepancy between what students, teachers, and administrators say about diversity and the exclusionary practices in place in schools that lead to marginalization of immigrant children. These experiences point to unresolved power issues among the cultural groups and indicate that the "mainstream population in the country of settlement is almost always more powerful than the migrating group" (van de Vijver & Phalet, 2004, p. 216). However, not all encounters with the dominant group are negative. Depending on their encounters with the dominant culture, newcomers may engage in "cultural frame switching," (Lafromboise, Coleman, & Gerton, 1993) which over time leads them to develop different relationships with the host culture.

The change in an individual or cultural group that results from contact with another culture is known as acculturation (McBrien, 2005). The process of acculturation, which once was seen as a unidimensional change in the direction of the mainstream culture, is now envisaged as bidimensional (Berry & Sam, 1997), an acknowledgment that immigrants increasingly choose options other than pursuing complete adjustment. For example, migrants who have positive relationships with the mainstream culture and consider it important to combine elements of it with their own integrate into the mainstream culture and become bicultural (Phalet & Hagendoorn, 1996; Phalet, Van Lotringen, & Entzinger, 2000). Terms such as *biculturalism, transculturalism,* and *additive assimilation* (McBrien, 2005) are used to indicate the processes through which, depending on the circumstances, people are able to move between cultures. Children of immigrants clustering around a bicultural style of adaptation (Trueba & Bartolome, 2000) typically emerge as *cultural brokers* who mediate the often-conflicting cultural currents of home and the host culture.

Immigrant groups who live in ethnic enclaves in the host country may gain sufficient momentum to develop and sustain their own culture through institutions such as schools (van de Vijver & Phalet, 2004) and may consider maintaining their own culture more important than establishing relationships with the host culture. This strategy is known as *separation* or *segregation.* The opposite strategy, which attempts complete absorption into the host culture and entails loss of the original culture, is known as *assimilation* (Berry & Sam, 1996; Gordon, 1964). Assimilation is associated with cultural dissonance, where children acquire the language and skills of their new culture, reject their parents' culture, and often join "oppositional structures of marginalized peers" (Gibson, 2001, p. 21). Trueba and Bartolome (2000) suggested that children in this pattern may develop either an "ethnic flight style" or "adversarial style" of adaptation. An ethnic flight style is expressed in the struggle of immigrant children and youth to mimic the dominant group and attempt to join in, thereby rejecting their own ethnic group—including parental authority, moral codes, values, and expectations—as anachronistic and not current in the new country. The adversarial style of adaptation is characterized by newcomer children's rejecting the institutions of the dominant culture, including school and the formal economy. The resultant school dropouts also tend to have significant problems with parents and relatives, because the culturally constituted function of parental authority often becomes severely corroded. It is from this situation, typically, that gangs emerge that exist on the margins of the dominant society and construct spaces of competence in the underground alternative economy or counterculture. Although these patterns are more often seen in second- or third-generation children of immigrants, recently arrived refugee children who lack a significant social support system are especially vulnerable to this negative pattern of acculturation, also known as *subtractive acculturation* (McBrien, 2005).

With the greater accessibility of technology, international transportation, and the magnitude of migration that facilitates the formation of social networks among ethnic groups after migration, more immigrants may choose to resist assimilation. Also, because the assimilation doctrine among mainstream cultures has largely been replaced by a climate of greater acceptance of migrants maintaining their culture of origin (van de Vijver & Phalet, 2004), transnational spaces created in the receiving countries allow immigrants to establish and maintain productive ties between their country of origin and the host country (Brittain, 2002).

Despite some current positive trends in overall societal acceptance of immigrants, educating children from diverse cultural, linguistic, ethnic, racial, or religious backgrounds is perceived as problematic. Bias and preconceived expectations on the part of educators are not limited to newly arrived children (Lee, 2002; McBrien, 2005; Suárez-Orozco, 1989; Trueba et al., 1990). The school's view of parents may be just as prejudiced and equally wrong. For example, the new community may hold false impressions about women from countries where a patriarchal culture predominates and strong cultural expectations influence the lives of women. Erel (2002) pointed out that migrant women from Turkey are generally perceived in an Orientalist manner as backward, oppressed, and passive, with the family unit perceived as the main site of sexist oppression. Her research reveals the self-representations of migrant women of Turkish background and provides a more complex view of mothering relations and migration than the stereotypical fixation on tradition. Further, the mothering relationships and the attainment of more autonomy may occur as a result of the migration process. Izuhara and Shibata (2002) studied Japanese migrant women in the United Kingdom and concluded that when removed from Japanese society, many appreciated the reduced pressure to conform to Japanese social norms. At the same time, it is essential for educators to recognize that reaching out to female members of an immigrant household demands different strategies than when looking to local residents for parental participation. Both sensitivity and cultural understanding are needed.

In addition to being accepting of immigrants, schools and communities must be prepared to adjust to the demographic changes that may accompany immigration (Bryceson & Vuorela, 2002; Segal, 1993; Yale Center, 2003). Although fertility rates are declining in all developed nations, those who immigrate to these countries may have larger families, and the women are more likely to be of child-bearing age (RAND Corporation, 2005), which will affect school enrolments in areas with high rates of immigration. Births in immigrant families accounted for 56% of the population growth in the United States in 2002 (Camerota, 2002). Female immigrants in the United States also may have more children than women in their home countries. For example, Mexican immigrant women have an average of 3.5 children, whereas women in Mexico average 2.4 children (Camerota, 2002). Friedmann (2002) pointed out that immigrants go primarily to urban areas, where they may place a strain on already stretched services and infrastructure. Urban schools may lack special comprehensive services needed to offer to newly arrived students to ease their adjustment to the new education system. Conversely, an increasing number of immigrants are now settling in rural areas (Bryceson & Vuorela, 2004; Segal, 1993). Rural communities and schools may lack experience with immigrant populations and have no community services in place to support the needs of new immigrants (Yale Center, 2003).

Some immigrant families arrive in locations where they have no personal contact with other newly arrived families. Others move by choice to a location where they know or have heard that other members of their national group reside. Newly arrived immigrant families may assume that they will be quickly integrated into an existing ethnic community, only to discover that they are not warmly welcomed. Conflicts may develop between newcomers and earlier arrivals when established immigrants see the newcomers as bringing competition for work and resources (Fong, 2004; Weirzbicki, 2004).

Regardless of the acculturation path the family takes or where the family finds itself in the continuum of acculturation, migration is a process that deeply transforms the family system. Studies suggest that there is a higher than usual incidence of domestic violence in immigrant homes, and many parents believe that they will lose control of their children once they become acculturated to life in the new country (Bryceson & Vuorela, 2004). The strain on newcomer parents may leave little time for attending to their children's need for special support. Several chapters in this book suggest that schools need to help immigrant families take advantage of all available community resources during their adjustment period and to advocate for services where none exist.

The factors involved in shaping the changing lives of immigrant children are complex. School and home are inextricably linked for all students, but they are especially so for immigrant children. Many immigrant families are separated for considerable periods when one or both parents move to the new location before their children can join them. Bryceson and Vuorela (2004) preferred the term *revitalizing* for the process that takes place when families reunite. Families can maintain contact when separated by long distances in various ways and also can handle the revitalization process in as many ways. The individual personalities, the particular family dynamics, the culture-driven behaviors, and the new host community milieu all contribute to how previously separated families renew their relationships. The time required for the family to settle into a reestablished unit altered by time and events may strongly affect a child's adjustment to school. The euphoria of a long-awaited and smoothly progressing revitalizing of a family unit will have a positive effect, whereas an unpleasant and struggling reunification cannot help but affect a child's mental well-being.

Children of immigrant backgrounds are strongly affected by their parents' attitudes toward the host society. This has implications not only for children's acculturation but also important cognitive ramifications such as learning a new language. Current theories of identity acknowledge that identities are negotiated in complex and dynamic ways in the multiple social, psychological, and cultural dimensions of everyday life (Pile & Thrift, 1995). From this point of view, immigrants are recognized as engaging in fragmented and multiple processes of identification that were in place before resettlement (Hebert, 2001). Thus, identities that are formed in the complex relationships between globalization, transnationalism, and transmigration remain fluid and open to transformation.

Immigrant children's identity formation is influenced by at least two distinct, and sometimes contradicting, cultural systems: the home culture and the school culture. As immigrant children begin to navigate the complex, often contradictory, territories of home and host culture, socially structured hierarchies of authority such as gender scripts, parental voice, values, and beliefs are often disrupted. The peer group can become not only the primary point of reference for values and tastes but also a source of social and emotional support, economic resources, and safety (De Vos, 1992). Because of the emotional relevance of the peer group, the interpersonal tone set by peers is an important variable in the adaptation of immigrant children. Trueba and Bartolome (2000) suggested that identity and agency are important factors in immigrant children's adaptation to the host culture.

Some common challenges revealed through the studies in this volume include appropriate assessment and grade placement. Immigrant children arriving in a school do not represent a homogeneous group and are usually difficult to categorize. Some may come from economically stable, urban backgrounds where they have been prepared from a young age for high-stakes, competitive academic tasks such as achievement tests. These children know how to study and know that their parents expect them to succeed (Bankston & Zhou, 2002). However, "doing well is not the same as being well" (Mosselson, 2002, p. 408); high academic achievement has been found to be negatively correlated with self-esteem and depression (Bankston & Zhou, 2002). Conversely, some children have entered the host country with little or no prior schooling. They lack prior group experiences or may have experienced strife and trauma, the memories of which impede their ability to function in school. The knowledge and experience of these children is not of an academic type and cannot be measured by the available standardized assessment tools (Ogilvie et al., 2005). As a result, teachers may give high priority to socially sensitive teaching and practice but may feel less competent to provide the adequate level of content to the newcomer children. Paired with lack of appropriate curriculum and curriculum materials, lack of proper information about the child's prior educational experiences, and poor assessment of general knowledge and skills, educators' day-to-day life in a classroom with these children is challenging. Children who have experienced multiple losses and trauma may need psychological counseling before they can be fully ready to concentrate on their schoolwork (Gonzales-Ramos & Sanchez-Nester, 2001). Language barriers; lack of support programs, proper identification, and assessment of needs; and family resistance to assessment and counseling may prevent full attention to the problems.

From the parents' point of view, assessments may have a different meaning based on their prior experiences. They may see assessments as offensive or frightening, and this could lead them to reject further testing if teachers express concerns about their child's performance level. Some parents may strongly object to individual testing or any suggestion that their child might need special services. Depending on culture, prior experiences, and individual personalities, parents may not speak openly to school personnel. They may see the teacher as deserving the highest respect and may believe that it is inappropriate for them to express an opinion or to question the teacher. Parents may have come from a country where the school authorities do not seek or listen to the opinions of parents. Such misunderstandings can result in a dysfunctional relationship between schools and parents and contribute to stereotyping of immigrant families and students.

Although some parents may strongly object to their children being tested or may not actively seek additional support if the child is not performing well in school, as Suárez-Orozco and Suárez-Orozco (2001) pointed out, immigrant families as a rule firmly believe in the importance of schooling. Research suggests (Portes & Rumbaut, 2001) that parents' involvement can increase the likelihood of academic success for immigrant students. However, studies also indicate that although parental support and interest in their children's education makes a difference to their success in school, this involvement may not be what teachers have come to expect from parents in the majority culture. Some immigrant parents may believe that as long as they send the child to school and see that homework is completed, they are involved in the child's schooling (Moosa, Karabenick, & Adams, 2001). Parents may view teachers as the education experts and so will not consider being involved in their children's education. Furthermore, they may have no frame of reference for understanding parent–teacher conferences (Timm, 1994; Trueba et al., 1990). Others who are highly skilled professionals may pressure their children to excel in school (Bankston & Zhou, 2002). By contrast, most North American parents, for example, often consider involvement as being actively present at school events and parent–teacher conferences and openly advocating or voicing demands about what the school should or should not do, particularly concerning their own children.

Some immigrant parents described in this book do advocate for their own children, using this advocacy to help their children achieve their high expectations for their future in the host country. As some of the chapters indicate, when educational programs are based in local communities and are flexible enough to accommodate the parents' work schedules and when parents are involved in both their children's and their own education, such parents become the main actors and agents in community education.

All the authors offer recommendations about educational policy and practices to address and ultimately improve the education of all children, including immigrant children. However, because of the international nature of the collection presented here, the recommended education policies and practices may not necessarily be of interest or apparent value to all readers. In addition, the wide range of approaches to analyzing problems and gathering information in each chapter reflects the authors' views of issues that are of a particular importance to them in their specific location and context and may not be immediately applicable in other contexts. As editors, we are aware that this book cannot offer resolutions to the many issues raised by the authors about the schooling of immigrants or suggest changes in the immigration policies in the 14 countries represented. It would be impossible to consider the myriad policies and problems related to immigration in all these countries. However, we believe that the volume presents a mosaic of issues that, viewed together, present a picture of the complex processes of adjustment of both migrant families and school systems, not only as problems and challenges but also as opportunities for a cross-fertilization of cultural views, beliefs, and expectations.

Many other important issues are not directly addressed in this volume, including questions of mental health and the well-being of those whose physical health was in jeopardy before emigration. The issues related to the recognition of foreign credentials of immigrants and the effect on their socioeconomic status, changes in family dynamics and parenting styles are also not addressed. From the inception of the book, our focus has been exclusively on the experiences of newly immigrated children of preschool through elementary school ages from the point of view of the children, their parents, and their teachers. We believe that because this volume is a unique collection of studies of all types of families with young children, including both voluntary and forced migrants, it offers the reader specific information about the needs, challenges, and successes of a particular group. It also offers an opportunity to identify some similarities and differences among and within these groups in terms of their educational experiences.

REFERENCES

Bankston III, C. L., & Zhou, M. (2002). Being well vs. doing well: Self-esteem and school performance among immigrant and non-immigrant racial and ethnic groups. *International Migration Review, 36,* 389–415.

Berry, J. W., Poortinga, Y. H., Pandey, J., Dasen, P., Saraswathi, T. S., Segall, M., & Kagitcibasi, C. (Eds.). *Handbook of Cross-Cultural Psychology* (2nd ed., Vol. 3, pp. 291–326). Boston, MA: Allyn & Bacon.

Berry, J. W., & Sam, D. L. (1997). Acculturation and adaptation. In J. W. Berry, M. H. Segall & C. Kagitcibasi (Eds) Handbook of Cross-cultural Psychology, Vol. 3: Social behaviour and Applications 2nd. ed., (pp. 291–326). Boston: Allyn & Bacon.

Boyden, J., de Berry, J., Feeny, T., & Hart, J. (2002). Childrten Affected by Conflict in South Asia: A Review of Trends and Issues Identified Through Secondary Research. RSC Working Paper No. 7. Oxford, UK: Refugee Studies Centre, University of Oxford. Retrieved September 6, 2005, from http://www.rsc.ox.ac.uk/PDFs/workingpaper7.pdf

Brittain, C. (2002). *Transnational Messages: Experiences of Chinese and Mexican Immigrants in American Schools.* New York: LFB Scholarly Publishing.

Bryceson, D., & Vuorela, U. (2003). Transnational families in the twenty-first century. In D. Bryceson & U. Vuorela (Eds.), *The Transnational Family: New European Frontiers and Global Networks* (pp. 3–30). Oxford Berg Press.

Camerota, S. A. (2002, November). *Immigrants in the United States—2002 A Snapshot of America's Foreign-Born Population.* Washington, DC: Center for Immigration Studies. Retrieved April 22, 2006, from http://www.cis.org/articles/2002/back1302.html

Children Now. (2004). *California Report Card: Focus on Children in Immigrant Families.* Oakland, CA: Author. Retrieved August 26, 2005 from http://publications.childrennow.org/publications/invest/reportcard_2004.cfm

Corson, D. (1998). *Changing Education for Diversity.* Milton Keynes, UK: Open University Press.

De Vos, G. (1992). *Social Cohesion and Alienation: Minorities in the United States and Japan.* Boulder, CO: Westview.

Erel, U. (2002). Reconceptualizing motherhood: Experiences of migrant women from Turkey living in Germany. In D. Bryceson & U. Vuorela (Eds.), *The Transnational Family: New European Frontiers and Global Networks* (pp. 127–146). New York: Oxford University Press.

Fix, M., & Passel, J. (2003, January). *U.S. Immigration—Trends and Implications for Schools.* Paper presented at the National Association for Bilingual Education NCLB Implementation Institute, New Orleans, LA.

Fong, R. (2004). *Culturally Competent Practice with Immigrant and Refugee Children and Families.* New York: Guilford.

Friedmann, J. (2002). *The Prospect of Cities.* Minneapolis, MN: University of Minnesota Press.

Global Commission on International Migration. (2005). *Migration at a Glance: Global Commission on International Migration.* Retrieved September 29, 2005, from www.gcim.org

Gibson, M. A. (2001). Immigrant adaptation and patterns of acculturation. *Human Development, 44,* 19–23.

Gitlin, A., Buendía, E., Crosland, K., & Dounbia, F. (2003). The production of margin and center: Welcoming–unwelcoming of immigrant students. *American Educational Research Journal, 40*(1), 91–122.

Gordon, M. M. (1964). *Assimilation in American Life: The Role of Race, Religion, and National Origin.* New York: Oxford University Press.

Gonzales-Ramos, G., & Sanchez-Nester, M. (2001). Responding to Immigrant Children's Mental Health Needs in the Schools: Project Mi Tierra/My Country. *Children and Schools, 23*(1), 49–63.

Hebert, Y. (2001). Identity, diversity, and education: A critical review of the literature. *Canadian Ethnic Studies, 33*(3), 155–186.

Hones, D. F., & Cha, C. S. (1999). *Educating New Americans: Immigrant Lives and Learning.* Mahwah, NJ: Lawrence Erlbaum Associates, Inc.

Izuhara, M., & Shibata, H. (2002). Breaking the generational contract? Japanese migration and old-age care in Britain. In D. Bryceson & U. Vuorela (Eds.), *The Transnational Family: New European Frontiers and Global Networks* (pp. 155–169)*.* New York: Oxford University Press.

Kirova, A. (2001). Loneliness in immigrant children: Implications for classroom practice. *Childhood Education, 77,* 260–267.

Lafromboise, T., Coleman, H. L. K., & Gerton, J. (1993). Psychological impact of biculturalism: Evidence and theory. *Psychological Bulletin,* 114, 395–412.

Langford, M. (1998). Global nomads, third culture kids and international schools. In M. Hayden & J. Thompson (Eds.), *International Education* (pp. 28–43)*.* London: Kogan Page.

Lee, S. (2002). Learning "America": Hmong American high school students. *Education and Urban Society, 34,* 233–246.

Li, P. (2001). The racial subtext in Canada's immigration discourse. *Journal of International Migration and Integration, 2*(1), 77–97.

McBrien, J. L. (2005). Educational needs and barriers for refugee students in the United States: A review of literature. *Review of Educational Research, 75,* 329–364.

Moosa, S., Karabenick, S. A., & Adams, L. (2001). Teachers' perceptions of Arab parent involvement in elementary schools. *School Community Journal, 11,* 1–23.

Moreau, G. (2000). Some elements of comparison between the integration policies of Germany, Canada, France, Great Britain, Italy and the Netherlands. *Journal of International Migration and Integration, 1*(1, Winter), 101–120.

Mosselson, J. (2002). Roots and routes: Reimagining the identity construction of Bosnian adolescent female refugees in the United States. *Dissertation Abstracts International, 63*(04), 1287. (UMO No. 3048196)

Nauck, B., & Sattles, B. H. (2001). Social capital, intergenerational transmission and intercultural contact in immigrant families. *Journal of International Migration and Integration, 32*(4), 465–488.

Noddings, N. (Ed.) (2005). *Educating Citizens for Global Awareness.* New York: Teachers College Press.

Ogilvie, L., Fleming, D., Burgess-Pinoto, E., Caufield, C., Chui, Y., Kirova, A., Linschoten, K., Martin, W., & Ortiz, L. (2005). *Examining culturally appropriate assessment practices in early childhood development (ECD) programs.* Unpublished manuscript.

Phalet, K., & Hagendoorn, L. (1996). Personal adjustment to acculturative transitions: The Turkish experience. *International Journal of Psychology, 31,* 131–144.

Phalet, K., Van Lotringen, C., & Entzinger, H. (2000). *Islam in de multiculturele samenleving* [Islam in multicultural society]. Utrecht, The Netherlands: University of Utrecht, European Research Centre on Migration and Ethnic Relations.

Pile, S., & Thrift, N. (Eds.) (1995). Mapping the Subject. In S. Pile and N. Thrift (Eds.), *Mapping the Subject: Geographies of Cultural Transformation* (pp. 13–57). London: Routledge.

Portes, A., & Rumbaut, R. (2001). *Legacies: The Story of the Immigrant Second Generation.* Berkeley, CA: University of California Press.

RAND Corporation. (2000). *Population Matters. Policy Brief.* Santa Monica, CA: Author.

Rong, X. L., & Preissle, J. (1998). *Educating Immigrant Students: What We Need to Know to Meet the Challenges.* Thousand Oaks, CA: Corwin Press.

Schiff, M., & Özden, C. (Eds.). (2005). *International Migration, Remittances, and the Brain Drain.* New York: Palgrave Macmillan.

Segal, A. (1993). *An Atlas of International Migration.* New Providence, NJ: Hans Zell.

Suárez-Orozco, C., & Suárez-Orozco, M. M. (2001). *Children of Immigration.* Cambridge, MA: Harvard University Press.

Suárez-Orozco, M. M. (1989). *Central American Refugees and the U.S. High School: A Psychological Study of Motivation and Achievement.* Stanford, CA: Stanford University Press.

Timm, J. T. (1994). Hmong values and American education. *Equity and Excellence in Education, 27*(2), 36–44.

Tollefson, J. (1989). *Alien Winds: The Reeducation of America's Indochinese Refugees.* New York: Praeger.

Trueba, E. T., & Bartolome, L. I., (2000). *Immigrant Voices: In Search of Educational Equity.* Boston, MA: Rowman & Littlefield.

Trueba, H. T., Jacobs, L., & Kirton, E. (1990). *Cultural Conflict and Adaptation: The Case of Hmong Children in American Society.* New York: Falmer.

United Nations High Commission for Refugees (UNHCR). (1994). *Refugee children: Guidelines and Protection.* Retrieved October 5, 2005, from http://www.unhcr.ch/cgi-bin/texis/vtx/protect/opendoc. pdf?tbl =PROTECTION&id=3b66c2aa10.

van de Vijver, F. J. R., & Phalet, K. (2004). Assessment in multicultural groups: The role of acculturation. *Applied Psychology: An International Review, 53,* 215–236.

Wierzbicki, S. (2004). *Beyond the Immigrant Enclave: Network Change and Assimilation.* New York: LFB Scholarly Publishing.

Yale Center in Child Development and Social Policy. (2003). *Portraits of Four Schools: Meeting the Needs of Immigrant Students and Their Families.* New Haven, CT: Author.

Introduction to Part I

Multiple Global Issues for Immigrant Children and the Schools They Attend

The process of globalization has been accompanied by social movements toward establishing just and egalitarian societies inspired by the human rights movement, the adoption of the United Nations Declaration of Human Rights (1948), and, more recently, by the adoption of the Declaration of Education for All (2000). The critical framework adopted in the works presented in part I is based on the human rights of equality in general and the right to equality in education in particular. More specifically, the chapters in this part touch on global issues of acculturation, multicultural education, attitudes toward inclusion or rejection of newcomers, and the health of children of immigrant backgrounds.

Assuring all children's access to quality education has become a concern to educators around the world as transnational migration brings changes in the demographics of student populations. As a result, education systems are faced with the need to change to respond to these trends. The curriculum, pedagogy, management of schools, expectations of teachers, and personal relationships are some of the factors that could either facilitate or impede students' learning in the educational context. Although the school environment has been identified as a key to socialization and acculturation (Yale Center, 2003; Trueba, Jacobs, & Kirton, 1990), findings from the studies on the academic underachievement of ethnic-minority students discussed in chapters 2 and 3 demonstrate that currently schools alone cannot break the social pattern of poverty for underprivileged children. Chapter 2 points to the limited success of a number of remedial measures taken by education authorities in Norway that have ignored the linguistic and cultural backgrounds of minority students and have resulted in insignificantly improved learning outcomes and, in general, only modest innovation in education. The authors emphasize the need for all students to see their own backgrounds reflected in the narratives of schools and to be able to make active use of their linguistic, cultural, and social resources in constructing new knowledge and developing skills and attitudes.

The relationships between acculturation, self-concept or self-esteem, gender, and school achievement are vital to the study presented in chapter 3. The authors offer a definition of performance of acculturation competence that has been found useful in studying immigrant children's academic achievement. This definition refers not only to learning the language of the host country but also to learning about new knowledge domains and integrating new values, norms, symbols, and behavior patterns into one's original value system. Thus, becoming acculturated is seen and interpreted as a synthesis of actions in various aspects of life that form a foundation for the successful development of a hybrid or bicultural identity. Rather than referring only to broadening one's competences to align oneself with the cultural expectations of the host country, acculturation designates a meta-competence that allows the individual to incorporate cultural differences productively. Deficiencies in attaining acculturation competence have an adverse effect on school achievement in general or on achievement in specific subject areas.

Research suggests that teachers and school personnel play a role in school practices that may lead to marginalization of immigrant and refugee students (Lee, 2002; McBrien, 2005; Suárez-Orozco, 1989; Trueba et al., 1990). Empirical data show that questions asked of students in the school setting, and the limited range of responses for which these allow, provide minority, immigrant, and aboriginal students with little opportunity to become active participants in classroom dialogue. This often leads to negative evaluations of students' abilities (Dei, James, Karumanchery, James-Wilson, & Zine, 2000; Gossetti & Rusch, 1995), thus affecting minority students not only emotionally but also cognitively. Ladson-Billings and Tate (1995) argued that race was the most important variable in the difference in students' achievement, which according to Steele (1997), is consistent at every level of schooling (prekindergarten–12). Even in the absence of formal discrimination against immigrants in a country's school system, the immigrant population typically has lower educational attainment levels than children of nonimmigrants and may be unable to close this gap (Conger et al., 2003).

When teacher preparation does not include sufficient training in cultural diversity, intercultural understanding, and multicultural education (chapter 2), teachers may misunderstand or misinterpret as culturally inappropriate children's attempts to succeed in their environments and either may not support or may reject such attempts (Hones, 2002; Lee, 2002; Trueba et al., 1990).

Although specific cases are presented in each chapter, the issues discussed have some degree of global application as they challenge readers to examine their own context critically. One such issue, for example, as discussed in chapter 4, is the need for a deep transformation of the organizational and educational practice of schools so that they might respond to the diversity of educational needs of all students, respecting their social and cultural origins and personal competence. The difficulties that Haitian immigrant children face in schools in the Dominican Republic, as discussed in chapter 4, offers a look at the reality of racial and ethnic discrimination. Haiti, which became the world's first independent Black republic in 1804, had little net emigration throughout the 19th century despite a subsistence economy and an isolated and despotic polity (Segal, 1993). However, massive waves of Haitians emigrated during the 20th century, although those seeking asylum, particularly in the United States, were often repatriated. The desperate economic conditions in an eroded and deforested land have driven many Haitians across the border into the Dominican Republic to seek employment despite deplorable working conditions and marginalization in society. The authors of chapter 4 advocate for the inclusion of all children, recognizing that the problem is not the child but rather the school as part of the system as a whole. Inclusive education is seen as an essential road toward eliminating social exclusion based on racial, social, ethnic, and religious differences or those of gender and individual capabilities. The enormous steps involved in changing attitudes—not only of teachers but also of the society that the teachers reflect—are not easily taken.

Bias toward and misunderstanding of immigrants is not limited to schools. Other community agencies are involved, and attention to the needs of immigrant families, including from community agencies that deal with health services, affects education. The effect of poor health education among immigrant communities in general, which results in a disproportionately high incidence of nutrition-related diseases among immigrant children, presents strong arguments in support of urgent changes. Countries that are affected by demographic transition are seeing a changing epidemiology at a time when children's nutrition is increasingly recognized as crucial for their present and future health (Tomkins, 2001) as well as for their school performance. According to Gracey (2004), many young migrants are refugees who have significant health needs and medical conditions (such as infectious diseases) and mental health problems cause by their original stressful living conditions. He suggests that pediatricians give the best possible care to such children and act as their advocates. Chapter 5, written by a pediatrician and a nutritionist, addresses the question of the diet and health of immigrant children in Norway, a nation that has experienced a significant increase in ethnic-minority migrants in recent times (Statistics Norway, 2005). Their study demonstrates that migration brings about changes in diet and lifestyle, including foods chosen, methods of eating and preparation, number of meals per day, time of eating, and size of portions. All this can have significant effects on the health of the immigrant families in general and on the children in particular. Their findings are similar to those in other countries, indicating the universality of the problem (Ghaemii-Ahmadi, 1992).

The authors advocate for an increased understanding of the interwoven influences of cultural attributes to health-related behaviors through stronger emphasis on health education, which should focus especially on nutrition and physical activity. They encourage educators to counsel about the negative aspects of changing to a more Westernized diet, as well as to point out instances in which a change in dietary habits may bring nutritional benefits. It is also important to find culturally acceptable ways to suggest nutritional improvements.

Schools cannot shoulder the entire responsibility for communicating acceptance, tolerance, and recognition of human rights; avoiding bias in community attitudes toward newcomers; and assisting with all aspects of acculturation, including providing health information for new arrivals. However, educators can squarely face the issues in the schools, do as much as is feasible in the school setting, and thus set an example for the entire community. The chapters in this opening part show the need for this to take place.

REFERENCES

Conger, D., Schwartz, A. E. & Stiefel, L. (2003) Who are Our Students? A Statistical Portrait of Immigrant Students in New York City Elementary and Middle Schools. New York: Wagner Graduate School of Public Service, New York University.

Dei, G. J. S., James, I. M., Karumanchery, L. L., James-Wilson, S., & Zine, J. (2000). *Removing the Margins: The Challenges and Possibilities of Inclusive Schooling*. Toronto, ON: Canadian Scholars' Press.

Ghaemii-Ahmadi, S. (1992). Attitudes toward breast-feeding and infant feeding among Iranian, Afghan, and Southeast Asian immigrant women in the United States: Implications for health and nutrition education. *Journal of American Dietetics Association, 92,* 354–355.

Gossetti, P. P. & Rusch, E. (1995). Reexamining educational leadership: Challenging assumptions. In D. M. Dunlap & Patricia A. Schmuck (Eds.) *Women leading in education* (pp. 11–35). Albany State University of New York Press.

Gracey, M. (2004). Caring for the health and medical and emotional needs of children of immigrants and asylum seekers. *Acta Paediatrica, 93*(11), 1423–1426.

Hones, D. F. (2002). *American Dreams, Global Visions: Dialogic Teacher Research with Refugee and Immigrant Families.* Mahwah, NJ: Erlbaum.

Ladson-Billings, G. & Tate, W. F. (1995). Toward a Critical Race Theory of Education. *Teachers College Record, 97*(1), 47–68.

Lee, S. (2002). Learning "America": Hmong American high school students. *Education and Urban Society, 34,* 233–246.

McBrien, J. L. (2005). Educational needs and barriers for refugee students in the United States: A review of literature. *Review of Educational Research, 75,* 329–364.

Segal, A. (1993). *An Atlas of International Migration.* New Providence, NJ: Hans Zell.

Statistics Norway. (2005). *Immigrants From 200 Countries in Norway.* Oslo, Norway: Author. Retrieved April 22, 2006, from http://www.ssb.no

Steele, T. (1997). *The Emergence of Cultural Studies: Adult Education, Cultural Politics, and the 'English' Question.* London: Lawrence & Wishart.

Suárez-Orozco, M. M. (1989). *Central American Refugees and the U.S. High Schools: A Psychosocial Study of Motivation and Achievement.* Stanford, CA: Stanford University Press.

Tomkins, A. (2001). Vitamin and mineral nutrition for the health and development of the children of Europe. *Public Health Nutrition 4*(1a), pp. 101–107.

Trueba, H. T., Jacobs, L., & Kirton, E. (1990). *Cultural Conflict and Adaptation: The Case of Hmong Children in American Society.* New York: Flamer Press.

Yale Center in Child Development and Social Policy. (2003). *Portraits of Four Schools: Meeting the Needs of Immigrant Students and Their Families.* New Haven, CT: Author.

Chapter 2

Bringing Multicultural Education Into the Mainstream: Developing Schools for Minority and Majority Students

Christian Horst and Anne Holmen
The Danish University of Education Denmark

Within the last 20 years, the number of children with ethnic-minority background in the Danish *folkeskole* (municipal primary and lower secondary schools) has increased from 13,457 in 1986–1987 to 57,523 in 2003–2004 (Ministry of Education, 2004; Ministry of the Interior, 1998), making up approximately 10% of all pupils. We use the term *ethnic-minority children* as synonymous with the term *bilingual children.* Over time, the terminology has shifted a number of times reflecting inclusiveness or exclusiveness. For example, in 1976, the official definition was *foreign-language-speaking children.* Today the legally binding definition is "Bilingual children are children who have another mother tongue than Danish and who will learn Danish when coming in contact with the surrounding society or in school" (*Law About the Danish Folk School,* Section 4a, 1.2, 1995).

The increase in bilingual children in Denmark reflects a change in the ethnic composition of the population similar to that of other European nation states because of postwar migration and reception of refugees. A growing awareness of the academic underachievement of minority students has brought about a number of remedial measures. However, because these measures tend to ignore the linguistic and cultural background of minority students, they hardly improve the learning outcomes of minority students and in general bring only modest innovation into education. As an alternative, supported by the growing internationalization of society, there is a need for multicultural development in schools for all students. In this chapter, we report on the initial years of an ongoing study based on the transformation process of schools in Aarhus, the second largest city in Denmark, which has 51 public schools.

MULTICULTURAL EDUCATION: INTERACTION BETWEEN EDUCATIONAL TRADITION AND NATIONAL IDENTITY

The rooting of democratic society in universal values raises the question of how linguistic, social, and cultural diversity is being addressed in social institutions. To what extent does the educational system reflect the diversity of the country, and are there signs of change? Countries that have recognized complexity in their educational systems, for some years, have been in the process of developing a new basis for changes in curriculum and school organization (Banks, 1997; Brisk, 1998; Hyltenstam, 2003; Miramontes, Nadeau, & Commins, 1997; Østerk, 2003).

In Danish schools, changes are now called for, inspired by modern educational thinking combined with reflections on equity based on universal values. According to this perspective, equal access to education is a major concern, but of high priority is also the question of how schools must be organized for their students to profit the most. One important goal is for all students to be able to see their own background reflected in the narratives of school and to be able to make active use of their linguistic, cultural, and social resources in taking up new knowledge and developing skills and attitudes.

To fully grasp the scope of this development, one may make a comparison to the effect on Danish educational thinking brought about by the recent change from separating children according to test results toward teaching all children in the same classroom. This has meant a stronger emphasis on child development and on the adjustment of teaching to students' background rather than shaping students to a given educational content and form.

Throughout the 20th century, the struggle for equality has extended individual rights and created an awareness of socioeconomic, gender, and cultural rights in the value systems of schools. As a parallel, ethnic and linguistic complexity is being recognized and secured through international conventions and national legislation (Batelaan & Coomans, 1999). This has engendered a conflict between the dominant culture of the nation–state, which has traditionally had a homogenizing function in the educational system, and the recognition of ethnic complexity as a prerequisite to learning (Horst, 2003). One may ask how in an ethnically complex

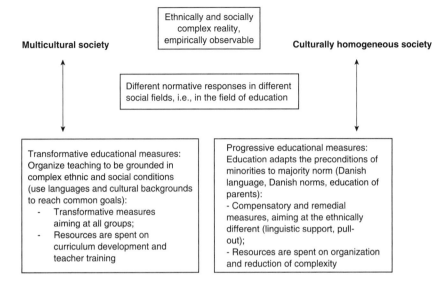

Figure 1.   Normatives Response to Social Change

society such as Denmark education can be transformed to give the same weight to the linguistic, cultural, and family background of all children. In other words, how can schools achieve Klafki's (2000) "double opening": opening the curriculum for children as well as children for curriculum? And what role does the introduction of intercultural education as a general approach play in transforming a specific school system?

THEORETICAL POSITION

In a study of the politics of the multicultural society, Parekh (2000) focused on how decision makers conceptualize ethnically and socially complex realities. As varying conceptualizations structure the description and interpretation of social problems, normative responses will differ, as shown in Figure 1. Parekh echoes Bourdieu and Wacquant's (1996) understanding of the double life of social structures, first as a distribution of material resources and second as a system of classification.

When viewing the relationship between conceptualization and normative response from a culturally homogeneous position, one tends to take measures to maintain this interpretation when facing a complex social reality. Accordingly, ethnic minorities are seen as different from naturalized cultural or national norms, and the social and political legacy from the nation states tends to confirm this position.

As social problems in ethnic-minority groups are seen as related to their ethnicity, the ethnic majority will make the minorities the object of democratic decisions, which will eventually make them the social problem per se. In educational settings, the underachievement of ethnic-minority children will be interpreted as a result of their lack of proficiency in the majority language and culture. This deficit view leads to a natural development of remedial interventions to further the minorities' competence in the majority language and culture. To achieve a reduction of ethnic complexity in the individual school, local systems of "fair" distributions of the "social problem" develop like busing arrangements and quotas (e.g., a maximum of 25% of children of ethnic-minority background in each school in a given municipality). Thus, social problems in an ethnic group become an inherent part of ethnic identity.

When a complex ethnic and social reality is interpreted in terms of a multicultural society founded on democratic values, one realizes that institutions in the culturally homogeneous society are incapable of serving varying ethnic groups with the same standards as the ethnic majority. In education, one consequence is a transformation of institutional practice to make schools more inclusive and to open the curriculum for all students. Among the tools used is the development of teaching materials that reflect ethnic complexity and the beginnings of appropriate in-service training for teachers. Thus, languages and cultures become new resources in education, and they are brought into the curriculum as reflections of both local and international complexity.

DEVELOPING MULTICULTURAL EDUCATION IN SCHOOLS

With the intention of making multicultural education an integral part of mainstream education, school authorities in Aarhus initiated their project as part of a larger school development plan (School Authorities of Aarhus, 2002). The initiative was motivated by pressure to strengthen the internationalization of schools and by growing social and ethnic segregation of schools in Aarhus.

The project not only focuses on ethnic-minority children but also includes all children in a wider framework with the intention that "All children in the schools of Aarhus will meet the international dimension as part of curriculum, which means that they will know about and learn to respect cultural diversity by recognizing their own resources." To achieve this goal, schools adhere to the following objectives:

- To develop school culture and values
- To develop intercultural didactics (in the German sense, based on theories of Bildung, Klafki, 2000) and teaching
- To develop intercultural competence in students, teachers, and principals

Type of site	Agent	General Frame	Data type
Political level	Mayor for schools	Political program	Politically visionary texts
Administrative level	Civil servants	Public administrative regulations (national, local)	Policy texts (interpretation of political texts related to thematic professionalism). Interview, dialogue.
School level	School board/ parent groups	Elected representatives	School policy texts
	Head-teacher	School leadership	Survey, interview, dialogue. Development plans
	Teachers	Colleagues Classroom	Survey, interview, dialogue. Sparring
	Pupils	Classroom, playground	Observation

Figure 2.   Data Collection Sites

The project was started in eight schools in 2002, was extended to six more schools in 2003, and was expanded to another five in 2004 (all schools are public *folkeskole*). According to the project plan, all 51 schools in Aarhus will take part by 2006.

THE RESEARCH PROJECT

The development of multicultural education in Aarhus schools is being studied in a research project based on data collected from various levels or sites in the transformation process (Fig. 2). The sites are seen as interrelated in a Bourdieu-based model for field research and analysis inspired by Mathiesen (2002).

The project was designed as action or dialogue research (Læssøe & Baungaard Rasmussen, 1989; Reason, 1994). Researchers cooperated in planning the project and interpreting the resultant changes with various agents who also interact. This was done along a vertical line, where dialogue could be initiated from a bottom-up as well as a top-down perspective, and along a horizontal line, where schools, groups of teachers from various schools, or other professionals could make contact with one another around a theme.

As researchers, our roles included those of consultants; sparring partners in project planning; interviewers and dialogue partners in evaluating the process; and the more traditional role of conducting observation, surveys, and so forth in the various sites. This design included the well-known tension between researchers maintaining analytic distance from the research sites and being involved in the progress of the project.

To enable us to identify various kinds of change during the project period, we decided to determine the status of the initial situation. This followed the strong wishes of principals and teachers to be evaluated on their own terms and not compared with general standards. To respect this position, we constructed a survey for teachers and principals on general and specific school features, profiles, attitudes, and practices related to diverse core elements in multicultural education.

Survey data from the first eight schools, with a focus on ambivalences and contradictions in the initial situation seen through teachers' and principals' answers to questions about their training, attitudes, and previous experience with developing multicultural and bilingual education, are presented here. The picture presented here is related to international research on the schooling of minority children, as well as to recent critical voices about the quality and efficiency of Danish schools in general, for example, as expressed in the analysis of the Programme for International Student Assessment (PISA) results (Organization for Economic Cooperation and Development [OECD], 2002).

Data on Teacher Training and Experience

To create a school profile of their qualifications before entering the school development project, we asked teachers about their basic education, in-service training, continued certified education, and previous professional experience.

A total of 268 teachers from the eight schools completed the survey. Only one in four reported having encountered the topic of multicultural education in their basic training. More than four in five teachers had had hardly any or no in-service training on teaching bilingual children, and few had finished a certified education. Only 15 teachers had studied Danish as a second language. Taken together, the formal qualifications of the teachers for entering the specific school project were remarkably weak.

We are aware that the multicultural perspective is new in Danish educational professions. We do not include this part of the survey to expose the lack of relevant training among Aarhus teachers but rather to link the project to the overall situation of minority children in Danish schools. In general, multicultural education has no independent position as a specific subject area in teaching guidelines and legislation. Danish as a second language (DSL) has been recognized as an independent discipline, and its position is being increasingly strengthened in teacher training colleges. However, it still has a limited remedial function in most schools and is seen as a part of special education for individual children rather than as a general dimension of the school development of linguistic minority

TABLE 1

Experience in Teaching Bilingual Pupils (Only one mark in each row)

	None	*1–2 years*	*3–5 years*	*More than 5 years*
In reception classes	59%	18%	7%	16%
As pull-out; in support centers; special needs education	38%	24%	8%	30%
In MTE	89%	3%	–	8%
In mainstream classrooms	12%	19%	14%	54%

children (Kristjansdottir, 2004). Mother-tongue education (MTE), a modest extracurricular activity for minority children, has recently lost state support (Horst, 2003). However, some municipalities continue to offer it, and a few school projects seek to integrate minority children's mother tongue into core activities. In general, languages are not seen as resources in the schooling of minority children but as problems. Cultural diversity is treated similarly.

It is our impression that the multicultural dimension is treated as optional in basic teacher training, as is further development for the experienced teacher. From students in teacher training colleges we know that the dimension is prescribed only by teacher educators who have a personal interest in the field; from schools all over Denmark, we know that in-service training in multicultural education is given low priority by most schools leaders. Thus, educational issues of multiculturalism are in the same marginalized position as ethnic minorities in other social domains.

To establish the nature and extent of the Aarhus teachers' experience with ethnic-minority children, we asked them to specify the kinds of teaching that they had previously done. The responses to the question "What is your experience in teaching bilingual pupils?" are shown in Table 1.

Table 1 shows that most of the 268 teachers had had bilingual children in their classrooms; only 12% having had no such contact. A smaller number of teachers had been involved in various kinds of nonmainstream teaching, in reception (kindergarten) classes, in pull-out measures and support centers (mainly as DSL), and in MTE. As this was done with little formal training, the teachers must have undertaken extensive self-teaching. The teachers in this survey were fully aware of the untenableness of the situation, and more than four in five agreed that multicultural education should be developed in teacher training colleges.

Fifty-three teachers reported having participated in earlier development projects related to multicultural education or having taught bilingual pupils. According to the principals, three of the eight schools had not participated in any development project in this field, whereas this was the case for only one school according to the teachers. The mismatch may be because of a recent change of principals or to a highly decentralized structure of development in schools that gave responsibility to the individual teachers rather than to the school. In any case, the mismatch shows that principals do not always give high priority to multicultural issues.

The projects reported varied in content and time span from a few weeks to 10 years. They included projects on local teacher training in DSL, development of teaching materials for bilingual students, projects about how to combine MTE with ordinary teaching, language and science, parent collaboration, and so forth. However, only a few projects were of longer duration, and most did not focus on issues of teaching and learning in formal situations but on cultural and social activities outside the classroom.

Positions on School Achievement

When we combine the Aarhus data on teacher qualifications with the general educational position of minority children in Danish schools, it is hardly surprising to find that ethnic minorities (both first and second generation) underachieve substantially in the school system (according to PISA results, OECD, 2002; Egelund, 2003). In most OECD countries, this is the case for minority students of the first generation (recent migrants) but not for second-generation students. Only in Denmark and Belgium do these students perform at the same low level in the areas covered by PISA (reading, mathematics, and science). Another finding is that Danish students in general perform below expected levels. A recent examiners' report on the Danish primary and lower secondary school (OECD, 2004) pointed out that achievement in Danish schools is relatively low compared with the investment in Danish education and compared with the general impression that Danish schools produce both quality education and equal access to further education. In questioning both dimensions, the OECD report cited widespread complacency in Danish schools. Conversely, it is emphasized that students in Danish schools are relatively happier and more satisfied with their school life than students in most other OECD countries.

To gain insight into the general priorities of Danish schools, we asked the teachers about possible causes of differentiated school achievement. We listed eight options that were related either to the individual characteristics of the child, to activities in school, or to the child's family situation (all factors well known from studies of why children's achievement differs in schools). We asked the teachers to rank the eight options in order of importance according to their personal experience (1 being the most important factor and 8 the least).

Table 2 gives an overview of the relative priority given to each factor, with a focus on ratings 1–3. For example, the number 61 in the line Family background means that a total of 61 teachers checked Family background as first, second, or third factor.

TABLE 2

Teachers' Interpretation of Background Factors for School Success

	Rated first	Rated second	Rated third	Total	Rank order
Home					
Family background	22	19	20	61	1
Social differences	13	15	12	40	4
Cultural background	5	15	11	31	6
School					
Well-being	26	15	13	54	3
Instruction	3	8	10	21	7
Teachers' expectations	0	2	3	5	8
Child					
Language	23	17	18	58	2
Intellectual capacity	13	11	15	39	5

In general it is difficult, if not impossible, to identify single factors that explain why children's achievement in school varies. It is well known that the answer must lie in a combination of factors: children's qualifications and abilities, conditions in the school, and family situation. However, in the survey it is remarkable that family background, language, and well-being of the children were ranked higher than the main activity of the school: instruction (and the other important variable *teacher expectations*).

We realize that the age and gender of the teachers might affect their opinion on school success. However, we found no clear rating difference related to these factors. Probably the effects of age or gender differences are reduced by the effect of a strong national identity that penetrates and dominates traditionally strong social boundaries when people face the presence of new ethnic minorities. Thus, the rating results may be guided by the bipolar theme of "*us versus them*" reflected in public discourse and thus rooted in the culturally homogeneous earlier position.

This interpretation is supported by responses to the survey of principals about development of their school profiles and planning for the initiation of the intercultural education project. When asked if they had considered giving their school a multicultural public profile (e.g., on the school's home page), principals of three of eight schools confirmed that they would, two refused, and another three were ambivalent or undecided. When asked if they intended to develop DSL as a general competence for all teachers, only two schools mentioned in-service training. All but two schools employed bilingual teachers, but the total number was limited, and they were mainly engaged in remedial activities. Four of the schools had ethnic-minority parents on their school boards, but only one had deliberately planned to involve minority parents in school democracy.

Probably the Aarhus schools resemble other Danish schools in representing a strong national identity, which is supported by a high degree of consensus across the political scene in defending Denmark as a monocultural society.[1] This is expressed in common policies and attitudes about a number of issues (e.g., dispersal of ethnic minorities through busing and housing policy, restrictions to family reunification). However, it is clear that the ratings in Table 2 are not only the result of issues of national identity. There is also a complex interaction with educational tradition, values, and priorities of the school in general, on which we comment here.

The Role of Well-Being for School Achievement

The high rating of the school factor *well-being* is compatible with the results of PISA 2000, in which it was reported that Danish children in general are satisfied with their school life. Children's positive response to being at school is hardly contestable, but the high priority given to this and the low priority given to the quality of instruction raises the question of whether the general objective is more focused on social issues—that is, socially sensitive teaching practices—than on developing the quality of teaching across the curriculum. This interpretation is supported by the fact that development projects in the Aarhus schools tend to focus on extracurricular issues, as reported earlier.

The ranking order shown in Table 2 resembles the findings of an earlier study in which teachers from eight schools in Copenhagen were asked the same question (Gimbel, Holmen, & Jørgensen, 2000). The priorities may reflect a dichotomized trend in educational discourse with socially sensitive education on one side and increased subject learning (e.g., "back to basics") on the other. The two positions are often mediated in discussions about content learning and the teaching of skills in developing more effective schools (Sammons, Thomas, & Mortimore, 1997).

However, when according high priority to the well-being of ethnic-minority children in school, the issue becomes more complex, evoking the Parekh (2000) dichotomy of normative responses to a multicultural reality presented above

---

[1]"Under no circumstances will I put up with a multicultural society in the sense of a society where cultures are treated equally," Karen Jespersen, Minister of the Interior (the social–democratic–liberal government 1998–2001), Berlingske Tidende, September 6, 2000. "Everyone talks about cultural equality and the need for ethnic equality. No, this should not be so.… In Denmark, Danishness must have a preference. Of course. Anything else would be to disregard culture. A culturally based policy cannot be founded on equality between the Danish and the foreign. It must necessarily be a policy which favours the Danish," Bertel Haarder, Minister of Refugees, Immigrants and Integration (in the present liberal and conservative government), Kristeligt Dagblad, December 7, 2001.

(Miramontes et al., 1997). From the position of the culturally homogeneous society, ethnic-minority students' well-being is understood as adapting each child to given national or local school standards. From the position of the multicultural society, well-being is achieved through the schools' ability to recognize the pre-conditions of each child in organizing learning activities—that is, recognizing the bilingual and bicultural resources of the child.

The Role of Language for School Achievement

Probably the strong rating for language reflects the difficult linguistic situation that ethnic-minority students face in education. Official state policy has abandoned support for mother-tongue instruction and favors all-Danish initiatives. Minority languages are seen as a problem and only rarely as a resource (Holmen, 2002; Horst, 2003). In the current situation, the children's mother tongues can be applied as a medium of instruction only occasionally and not systematically.

At the local level, this emphasizes an already existing ambivalence between a *general* acceptance of children's background and abilities and the *actual use* of the languages and cultural backgrounds in the teaching situation. How to mediate between these positions as a teacher can be seen in responses to a series of questions in the Aarhus study that reflect attitudes to the teaching of ethnic-minority students. In the survey, teachers were asked to mark their degree of agreement with 24 statements on a 5-point scale from *fully agree* to *disagree strongly.*

The overwhelming majority of the teachers agreed with the statement *Schools should integrate children's cultural and linguistic preconditions* and disagreed with the statement *Mother tongue teaching in ethnic-minority languages should be completely abolished.* We see this as an expression of a positive attitude toward ethnic-minority languages based on general educational theory.

However, more specific questions about the educational value of minority languages are met with either the opposite view or strong ambivalence. Thus, three of four teachers disagreed with the statement *Math can be taught in the children's mother tongue,* and they were divided on the following statements: *Other languages than Danish can be successfully used for instructional purposes* and *Pupils should be allowed to use other languages than Danish.*

The Role of Family and Cultural Background for School Achievement

In educational discourse, *social differences* holds a strong position in explaining differences in school achievement. Why has this otherwise forceful factor been reduced (to fourth position) but not as far as *cultural background* (sixth position), and why is *family background* given the highest rating?

In general, family background refers to the composition of the family (e.g., couple or single-parent household, number of siblings, parents' education).

A main focus on family background will necessarily lead to an individualized view in which cultural resources that exist in all ethnic groups are ignored. The low rating of cultural background may thus be rooted in a devaluation of collective cultural resources. This prevents teachers from recognizing the presence of ethnic groups in their own right and from valuing cultural resources irrespective of socioeconomic conditions.

The importance given to family background reproduces the asymmetrical dichotomy of *us* and *them* used by the Danish ethnic majority as a framework to interpret interethnic relationships. Thus a focus on family background might lead to the social construction of a *them* consisting of aggregated individual family problems, colonizing the concept of specific ethnic identities such as Somalis or Turks when interacting with the local Danish community (and teachers).

If the cultural background of students were fully recognized, it might lead to a change in the understanding of the school's practices. In relation to parents' cooperation, focus would then shift from individual problems to questions of parental involvement and dialogue in which the presence of differing cultures and the use of other languages would be integral parts of the negotiation of a common future. In relation to teaching, children's cultural and linguistic backgrounds would then be viewed as resources, and it would be relevant to develop a language policy that would combine mother-tongue and second-language acquisition. This would then constitute a platform from which curriculum could be opened and a comparative and international dimension developed for all students.

Ambivalence in Transformation

After 18 months of the Aarhus project, it is clear to us that there is ambivalence to exchanging the culturally homogeneous society for a multicultural society. This is expressed in our survey and interview data at various levels. When we asked about school leadership, school profile, development projects, and teachers' attitudes and qualifications, we realized how difficult it would be to face the new cultural complexity, because it would challenge the traditional national understanding of the role of schools. To analyze how transformation is conceived in a local educational system, we suggest a perspective of wider educational changes taking place in late modernity. This perspective is illustrated in Figure 3.

Figure 3 is a preliminary analytic framework that we have developed to question familiar concepts that interact with a new social complexity characterized by ethnic diversity. The horizontal line depicts a transformation from the culturally homogeneous to the multicultural society; that is, a movement away from a time when the nation state was seen as the target of development supported by the identity policy expressed in a nationally based curriculum. Through this, all citizens were assumed to have the same linguistic, historical, and cultural background and to be linked in a common loyalty to state and nation as overlapping entities.

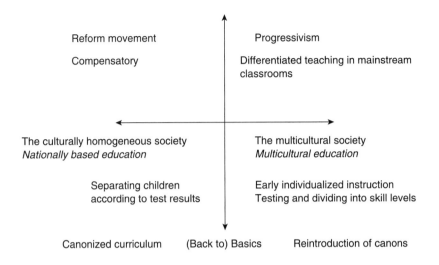

Student and development oriented position

Reform movement   Progressivism

Compensatory   Differentiated teaching in mainstream
                                 classrooms

The culturally homogeneous society   The multicultural society
Nationally based education   *Multicultural education*

Separating children   Early individualized instruction
according to test results   Testing and dividing into skill levels

Canonized curriculum   (Back to) Basics   Reintroduction of canons

Subject-based and functionally oriented position

Figure 3.   Transformation of Education in Denmark

Along the vertical line is a continuum between two traditional positions in the history of education (seen as positions in dialogue with each other and not as contradictions). According to one position, schooling involves all aspects of children's personal, intellectual, and skills development. This is a predominantly student-centered position or a whole-person approach. The other position focuses on children's learning of skills and subject knowledge in the framework and progression given in curriculum. In this concept, good schools achieve high educational outcomes for all children according to their individual capabilities.

When the two dimensions are combined, four sections appear in which major educational approaches are marked in italics and key words are placed from recent Danish educational thinking. Historically, the starting point was a subject-based school that tested and streamed students and that was met with criticism from the reform movement, which claimed that curriculum and schools in general did not adequately reflect children's individual and social background.

When the reform movement was challenged by progressivism, a student-centered approach was introduced with a focus on children's development seen as a broad, holistic category. The teaching of subject knowledge was then changed from being tied to relatively delimited units, each with its distinct core characteristics based on scientific disciplines. This was meant to take place through engagement in learning objectives that were thematically based and that dealt with real-life issues. Furthermore, the development of social competence and dialogic and communicative skills was emphasized through a new balance between individual tasks and group assignments and through the use of various media: writing, oral presentation, collage, audiotape and music, photography, film, videotape, drama, and so forth.

Today a new perspective on learning as an individualized process has gained a foothold while societal pressure grows to promote canonical subject matter (compare to a national curriculum or to "back to the basics"). As the two dimensions meet, new school terminology has appeared: the inclusive school, individualized contracts with parents and students, detailed objectives for all school subjects, stronger leadership with ongoing inspection of all contracts (assessment, evaluation, supervision), giving the individual responsibility, and teacher as facilitator rather than instructor. At the same time, awareness is growing that despite the resources expended, no convincing change is being seen in the reproduction of social and gender patterns in schools (Hansen, 1995). In equity terms, the outcome of schooling seen through international assessments like PISA is disturbingly low, especially for students with an ethnic-minority background. This might lead to reconsideration of practices in the schooling of minority students.

A MULTICULTURAL EDUCATIONAL POLICY FOR THE FUTURE

We believe that the first 18 months of the school development project of multicultural education in Aarhus has been useful in raising important issues about both the teaching of minority students in Danish schools and the development of schools in general. The transformation of society into multiculturalism has exposed not only a new kind of marginalization (based on a naturalized national curriculum) but also invited a reconstruction of well-known educational positions.

The Danish situation is characterized by systematic underachievement of bilingual students, lack of focus on the role of instruction in general, emphasis on children's family background and on social issues in the classroom, and by insufficient training for those who teach minority students. Together these factors support the OECD (2004) criticism of widespread complacency and lack of ambition on the one hand and a socially sensitive school on the other hand. The problem is, as the report stresses, that this kind of school is not strong enough to break the social pattern for underprivileged children. On the contrary, it tends to reproduce inequality in education.

In this report, the OECD (2004) examiners criticized Danish schools for providing "an insufficient support of bilingual children" (p. 123), and they recommended "an intensified effort" (pp. 145–146). In principle, this may be achieved through improved remedial measures or through the development of multicultural education but with different outcomes. At a consensus conference in Norway in 1996 organized by the Norwegian research council, linguists and sociologists met with policymakers to agree on the agenda for further development of schooling for minority students. At this conference, three models for improving the school situation for minority students were compared (Hyltenstam, Brox, Engen, & Hvenekilde, 1996). One model aimed at active bilingualism at school-leaving age as part of a social policy of pluralistic integration (and thus based on the multicultural position in Figure 1). Another aimed at a shift of languages in minority students (from minority to majority language) in which school is considered part of a long-term assimilation process (and thus a weak version of the monocultural position). Finally, a model of low achievement was proposed in which schooling is seen as a tool for early language shift (and thus a strong version of the monocultural position). The normative term *model of low achievement* was used in the report, and this model was said to be most frequently used for teaching minority students in Norwegian schools. It is recommended that the Norwegian school choose Model 1 or 2 because both combine language and subject-matter teaching.

A similar conclusion was reached in a Swedish evaluation of the role of the school for minority students in which a holistic approach is recommended. "The multilingual child gains most from language development and school achievement when both mother tongue and second language are being used in the learning process and this takes place in a supportive environment socioculturally" (Axelsson, Lennartson-Hokkanen, & Sellgren, 2002, p. 218, our translation). The main idea is that languages, school achievement in subject areas, and learning environment be combined.

Finally, Collier and Thomas' (2001) extensive study of ethnic-minority students in U.S. schools offers evidence that bringing in children's linguistic, cultural, and social background as active resources to their learning process is necessary to improve their school achievement. They conclude that quality teaching based not only on students' mother tongue but also on content and organizational issues plays a more important role in the outcome of children's schooling than socioeconomic background. Their main thesis is that languages, school achievement in subject matter, and learning environment must be linked to quality teaching if the situation for minority students is to be improved.

It is notable that all three studies argue in favor of more ambitious academic goals for minority students in public schools without abandoning the student-centered approach of progressive education. In Danish schools, the child's perspective is also widely recognized. However, in the case of minority students, this perspective and its natural link to multicultural education are being stifled by the dominance of the culturally homogeneous position.

REFERENCES

Axelsson, M., Lennartson-Hokkanen, I., & Sellgren, M. (2002). *Den röda tråden. Utvärdering av Stockholms stads storstadssatsningmålområde språkutveckling och skolresultat.* Rinkeby, Stockholm, Sweden: Språkforskningsinstitut.

Banks, J. A. (1997). *Educating Citizens in a Multicultural Society.* Albany, NY: Teachers College Press.

Batelaan, P., & Coomans, F. (Eds.). (1999). *The International Basis for Intercultural Education, Including Anti-Racist and Human Rights Education. a Selection of Articles from Relevant Documents.* International Association for Intercultural Education, UNESCO and Council of Europe. Retrieved June 6, 2006 from http://www.ibe.unesco.org/International/Publications/FreePublications/FreePublicationsPdf/batelaan.

Bourdieu, P., & Wacquant, L. (1996). *Refleksiv sociologi.* Copenhagen, Denmark: Reitzel.

Brisk, M. E. (1998). *Bilingual Education. From Compensatory Schooling to Quality Schooling.* Mahwah, NJ: Lawrence Erlbaum Associates, Inc.

Collier, V., & Thomas, W. (2001). *A National Study of School Effectiveness for Language Minority Students' Long-Term Academic Achievement.* Retrieved June 6, 2006 from http://repositories.cdlib.org/crede/finalrpts/11final

Egelund, N. (2003). *Tosprogede og dansksprogede – forskelle mellem faglige og sociale færdigheder for de 15–16 årige unge.* Copenhagen, Denmark: Pædagogiske Universitets Forlag.

Gimbel, J., Holmen, A., & Jørgensen, J. N. (2000). *Det bedste Københavns Kommune har foretaget sig hidtil. Beskrivelse og evaluering af sproggruppeforsøg i skoledistrikterne 6 og 12 i Københavns Kommunes Skolevæsen 1996–99.* Københavnerstudier i tosprogethed 31. Copenbagen, Denmark: Lærerhøjskole.

Hansen, E. J. (1995). *En generation blev voksen.* Copenhagen, Denmark: Socialforskningsinstituttet.

Holmen, A. (2002). *Betydningen af sprog, tosprogethed og sprogligt bårne kulturformer for integrationsprocesserne.* AMID Working Papers No. 23. Retrieved June 6, 2006 from www.amid.auc.dk

Horst, C. (2003). Retten til modersmålet. In C. Horst (Ed.), *Interkulturel pædagogik. Flere sprog – problem eller resource?* (pp. 53–84). Vejle, Denmark: Kroghs Forlag.

Hyltenstam, K. (2001). *Modersmåls baserede utbildnings system, Kunskapskapital och ekcinisk till våut.* In C. Horst (Ed.), *Interkulturel Pødugejik.* Kroghs Farlag.

Hyltenstam, K., Brox, O., Engen, T. O., & Hvenekilde, A. (Eds.). (1996). *Tilpasset språkopplæring for minoritetselever.* Rapport fra konsensuskonferanse. Oslo, Norway: Norges Forskningsråd.

Klafki, W. (2000). The significance of the classical theories of Bildung for a contemporary concept of Allgemeinbildung. In I. Westby, S. Hopmann, & K. Riquarts (Eds.), *Teaching as Reflective Practice: The German Didaktik Tradition.* Mahwah, NJ: Lawrence Erlbaum Associates, Inc.

Kristjansdottir, B. (2004). Dansk som andetsprog i kejserens nye klæder. In L. Ekberg & G. Haakansson (Eds.), *NORDAND 6. Proceedings fra 6. konference om Nordens sprog som andetsprog* (pp. 115–129). Lund, Sweden: Lunds Universitet.

Law About the Danish Folk School. (1995).Section 4a, l.2.

Læssøe, J., & Baungaard Rasmussen, L. (1989). *Brugerorienterede forskningsmetoder.* Lyngby, Denmark: Institut for Samfundsfag. Danmarks Tekniske Højskole.

Mathiesen, A. (2002). *Sociologiske Feltanalyser.* Research Paper No. 8/02. Roskilde, Denmark: Department of Social Sciences, Roskilde Universitetscenter.

Ministry of Education. (2004). *Statistics on Bilingual Pupils in the Folk School, School Year 2003/04.* Copenhagen, Denmark: Author. Retrieved from www.uvm.dk/statistik/tosprogedeigrundskolenhtm

Ministry of the Interior. (1998). *Foreigners '97.* Copenhagen, Denmark: Statens Information.

Miramontes, O., Nadeau, A., & Commins, N. L. (1997). *Restructuring Schools for Linguistic Diversity.* Albany, NY: Teachers College Press.

Organization for Economic Cooperation and Development (OECD). (2002). *Education at a Glance.* Paris. Retrieved April 23, 2006, from http://www.oecd.org/linklist/0,2678,en_2649_34515_2735794_1_1_1_37455,00.html

Organization for Economic Cooperation and Development (OECD). (2004). *OECD rapport om grundskolen i Danmark.* Uddannelsesstyrelsens temahæfteserie nr. 5. Copenhagen, Denmark: Undervisningsministeriet.

Øzerk, K. (2003). *Sampedagogikk.* Oslo, Norway: Oplandske Bokforlag.

Parekh, B. (2000). *Rethinking Multiculturalism–Cultural Diversity and Political Theory.* Basingstoke, UK: Palgrave.

Reason, P. (1994): *Participation in Human Inquiry.* Newbury Park, CA: Sage.

Sammons, P., Thomas, S., & Mortimore, P. (1997). *Forging Links. Effective Schools and Effective Departments.* London: Chapmann.

School Authorities of Aarhus. (2002). Multicultural Education, Project Design. Retrieved April 4, 2006, from www.aaks.dk

Acculturation and Educational Achievement of Children With an Immigrant Background in German Primary Schools

Leonie Herwartz-Emden, Dieter Küffner, Julia Landgraf
University of Augsburg, Germany

This longitudinal study, Socialization and Acculturation in Environments of Children with an Immigrant Background—School and Family (SOKKE), studied primary school immigrant children in a city in southern Germany. Whereas scholars in various disciplines have focused on the educational situation of immigrant children in general, this study focuses specifically on how migrant children cope with acculturation processes and develop an academic achievement orientation. Because children with an immigrant background are underrepresented in German secondary schools (Herwartz-Emden, 2002; Hunger & Thränhardt, 2001; Krohne, Meier, & Tillmann, 2004), we wished to investigate why this should be so. We designed a framework to represent the acculturation processes, taking into consideration the influences of family and school. We also defined a measure for acculturation school achievement as represented by knowledge of the German language at the time of school enrollment; self-concept and self-esteem; and academic grades in mathematics, reading, and spelling. In addition, we investigated

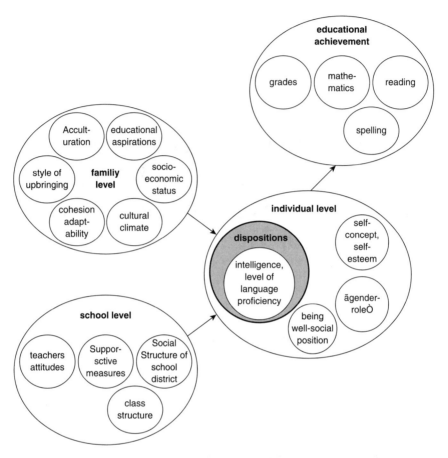

Figure 1.   *Framework of the Research Project Socialization and Acculturation in Environments of Children with an Immigrant Background—School and Family (SOKKE)*

gender role and well-being with respect to social position to expand the frame of interpretation (Fig. 1).

METHODS

To validate the instrument, a pilot study was conducted in a region of southern Germany that had a high proportion of resettled persons (Herwartz-Emden, Küffner, & Schneider, 2004). The survey looked at class structure and followed with preliminary testing and validation of central instruments for the area-specific

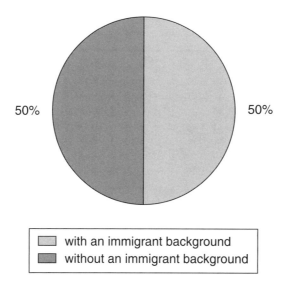

50%   50%

☐ with an immigrant background
■ without an immigrant background

Figure 2. *Immigrants' Backgrounds*

self-concept and self-esteem of students with an immigrant background (Herwartz-Emden et al., 2004).

During the 2003–2004 school year, we surveyed all class supervisors in 29 of 30 primary schools in the selected city. A child on the class list was considered as having an immigrant background based on the following parameters: citizenship, place of birth, religion, language spoken in the family, country of origin of both parents (or resettlement background), participation in supplementary lessons in a mother tongue, placement in transition classes, year of immigration, and knowledge of German. In general, a child would be considered as having an immigrant background if he or she was an immigrant or if either parents or grandparents had immigrated. The parameters mentioned earlier were used in case of uncertainty.

This study confirmed our assumption that by applying these criteria, many more schoolchildren of the total population were found to have an immigrant background than if only ethnicity or nationality were considered (Herwartz-Emden et al., 2004). The characteristics of 5,238 students from 242 classes were used in our analyses, a questionnaire return rate of approximately two thirds of the whole population (Fig. 2&3).

Linguistic Facility in the Primary Language Spoken in the Home

The questionnaire revealed that 47% (1,235 of 2,618) of students with an immigrant background live in Turkish-speaking family settings. Of this number, 16%

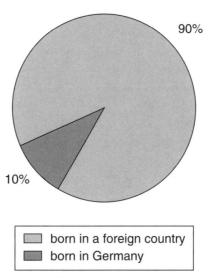

Figure 3. *Immigrants' Places of Birth*

(202) stated that German is their second language. In 18% of the population of children with an immigrant background, German was found to be the primary language spoken in families. In 7% of the population, Russian is spoken in the home; in half of those homes, German is spoken as well. In addition to Turkish, 72 nationalities were represented in the population of immigrant children, and more than 100 languages or combinations of languages were spoken in the home and community. The result is striking; multilingualism is the norm in the lives of many of the children. Apart from the main language of the 72 nationalities surveyed, more than 100 other languages or combinations of languages were added to our data.

On a 5-point rating scale, teachers were asked to evaluate the German-language proficiency of children with an immigrant background. An empirical finding was that the dominant family language had a substantial influence on a child's knowledge of German. This is shown in Figure 4. German language proficiency was estimated highest in the group of children who gave German as their family's dominant language: 68.4% were evaluated as good or very good. The poorest German proficiency was found among the children whose families primarily spoke a native language: only 26% were judged good or very good. A combination of a native language with German ranked in the middle: 51.1% of this group were considered good or very good. The other extreme shows how a family environment where the host country's language is not spoken may negatively affect language acquisition. In this group, only 6.4% of the students were assessed as

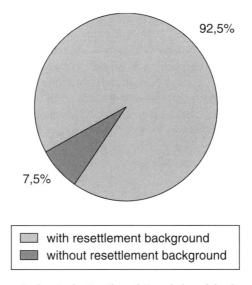

Figure 4. *Language Spoken in the Family and Knowledge of the German Language.*

being very good, and 11% were assessed as having very weak and 27.3% as having weak language skills. The teacher's evaluation is not a valid measure in terms of scientific test theory, because it is assumed that teachers use varying norms as criteria. Nonetheless, a teacher's assessment is significant enough to be acknowledged. On the one hand, the Berlin research project BeLesen (Schneewind & Merkens, 2004) showed that teachers' evaluations were close to results from standardized language tests. On the other hand, the academic success of children depends on the perception and judgment of evaluating teachers. In other words, the evaluation of language skills is probably a determining factor for the final grade or textual report in German, which is a pivotal criterion for future academic endeavors.

On the basis of this structure of the primary school population in the city we examined, it becomes clear in which dimensions heterogeneity manifests itself in today's schools. Delineating groups according to ethical or national criteria is not sufficient, because it is often difficult to make an obvious classification of all children with respect to their specific family background, and no unmistakable cultural orientation is derived from this procedure. Hence, cultural heterogeneity exists not only between native-born schoolchildren and those with an immigrant background but also, to a large extent, among children with an immigrant background. Because the teachers we surveyed probably depended on the information supplied by their students, their statements should be regarded with caution.

Nevertheless, the linguistic heterogeneity is striking; today multilingualism is the norm for many schoolchildren.

At the time of our inquiry, interculturality stood out as a characteristic dimension of the primary school population of the city, which indicates the general situation in Germany's school system. In the light of these data, it does not make sense to assume a uniform problematic basis for children with an immigrant background. When pedagogical interventions are planned, an accurate analysis of the entrance requirements for each locality, school, and school class is needed.

Rating the knowledge of German in children with an immigration background in the context of the class structure elevation supports another thesis for second-language acquisition. It appears that an open attitude to the second language as found in the group language of origin and German as dominant language (versus sole dominance of the language of origin) has a positive effect on the linguistic ability of children. We assume that emotional and motivational aspects play a part, as well as the greater amount of language input and better linguistic performance.

Performance of Acculturation

Compared with nonimmigrant students, children and adolescents with an immigrant background face specific supplementary learning in various areas, as well as the standard age-specific developmental tasks. Thus, the performance of acculturation refers to those learning requirements that include not only learning the language of the host country but also becoming acquainted with new knowledge domains and integrating new values, norms, symbols, and behavior patterns in the acquired value system.

Performance of acculturation can be interpreted as synthesis performances, which in turn can be seen as the foundation for the successful development of a hybrid or bicultural identity. Rather than referring only to broadening one's competences to align oneself with the host country, the performance of acculturation designates a metacompetence, which also allows the individual to assimilate cultural differences productively. In addition to the usual requirements compulsory for entry to primary school, the performance of acculturation needs to be taken into account. Deficits in attaining competences of acculturation have an adverse effect on school achievement or on achievement in specific subjects and vice versa. This interrelation is complex and is explained as follows as we clarify the development of self-concept and self-esteem.

Self-concept represents the sum of cognitive representations of one's own personality or self. Self-concept may be differentiated into a cognitive and a judgmental part—the judgmental part as self-referring cognitions with a strong judgmental component. These cognitions regard evaluations of one's own person, which are based on factual, social, or interpersonal comparative processes. These in turn take place in specific contexts that determine the selective self-attentiveness (Mummendey, 1987; Schauder, 1996; Städtler, 2003). The self-concept in this version reflects self-referring cognitions, contains context-specific self-knowledge, and exerts a regulative function on behavior. In the concept of self-esteem, however, judgments about one's own abilities or characteristics as a person are researched.

Assuming a close positive connection between acculturation and self-concept or self-esteem, the domain-specific self-concept and self-esteem are central constructs of our research and will be evaluated in each school year of our research to distinguish temporal changes and to examine their underlying causes (Herwartz-Emden et al., 2004). The objective of collecting data on self-concept and the integrated aspect of self-esteem is based on results from research on academic achievement that emphasize the significance of self-concept for academic achievement (Helmke, 1992). At the same time, it is the theoretical foundation for the assumption that self-concept (self-esteem) affects school success in the role of a mediator, which means that changes in this area also should be found in school performance. Referring to the theory of social mirroring, the presumed effects should first manifest themselves in the more sensitive area of self-esteem. From there the effects should successively affect the more robust self-concept. If self-concept grasps mental representations of oneself, and the descriptive component of self-esteem grasps the valuation of oneself and the resulting feeling of well-being, we can assume that children differentiate themselves in this central dimension of self-development because of various circumstances and specifically because of the factor of immigrant background versus nonimmigrant background.

Self-concept and self-esteem must be considered as complementary constructs that arise in connection with the self-environment differentiation process. They are social constructs acquired through interactions with those with whom the child relates most closely. In the primary school years, the development of these concepts is brought out decisively because the child's social orbit is no longer confined to the family. It broadens to include peers, and social comparisons become relevant (Bronfenbrenner, 1981). Differentiation of self-concept follows: self-concept about abilities is especially differentiated into several dimensions (Helmke & Schrader, 1998). It must be verified that the self-assessment of one's own abilities is high on entering school but diminishes during primary school (Fend & Stöckli, 1996). A determining setback is seen in Grade 1 when the self-assessment of one's abilities increasingly aligns itself with the teacher's evaluation of performance. Studies have found evidence that it is the teacher's task to enable alternative forms of competence to be achieved beyond social comparison, for example, to enable enhancement of self-concept by providing individual feedback (Lüdtke, Köller, Artelt, Stanat, & Baumert, 2002).

Factors That Influence the Development of Self-Concept and Self-Esteem in Children With an Immigrant Background

Language makes possible or simplifies the transmission of all factual content, rules of behavior, and, not least, the internalization of norms and values. Deficits in the second language, that is, in the official school language (as for many children with an immigrant background), impair learning processes and may lead to diminished self-esteem and well-being.

A child's entry into primary school marks the beginning of a long process that eventually leads away from the area of family influence. School offers children a social world of their own that eventually makes them independent of the norms and rules of the parents. Leaving the family environment behind and entering new surroundings and encountering different educational styles and orientations is a continual challenge during every child's development. For children with an immigrant background, entry into preschool, or at the latest entry into primary school, coincides with their immersion in the host country's language and culture and requires assimilative work connected to established pedagogical goals. Children with an immigrant background must make a specific bridging act when they leave the security of their family. The family provides room for social and ethnic identification and the opportunity to overcome differential experiences and discrimination and as such is an irreplaceable resource for the development of identity. This process does not necessarily create conflict, but it may engender friction. Failure to fulfill these requirements may have decisive consequences for a child's self-esteem and development of performance. According to of Portes and Rumbaut's (2001) theory of segmented assimilation, the most promising prognosis for upward-pointing assimilation for children with a bicultural background is for those whose family environments that are embedded in a functioning community, assimilate discrimination based on ethnicity, iron out the negative influences of urban social settings, and impart positive educational aspirations.

Continuing with this idea, one may presuppose that children have positive self-esteem if they grow up in secure parental relationships and if their peer groups are accepting and empathetic. In the main area of peer acceptance, potential ruptures can be found for children with an immigrant background. Whether in or outside school, negative social mirroring is experienced by this group of children as soon as they are not adequately respected in the social environment or when they experience lack of acceptance or direct discrimination because of, for example, their looks, their behavior, or their mother tongue. Because language can be learned only in a network of relationships, the poor quality of such a network caused by negative social mirroring may explain the children's lack of proficiency in their host country's language. This in turn leads to setbacks in the respective dimension of self-concept.

Furthermore, it can be assumed that deficits arise in school for children with an immigrant background when they actively use their skills and abilities. Experience of one's own competence contributes to knowing which tasks are relevant to self-esteem from which positive feelings arise. Lack of competence in various fields of action may arise because the cultural norms learned by children with an immigrant background do not correspond to the cultural requirements of the host country, and those requirements may have been inadequately transmitted.

These processes vary between boys and girls: The sources and domains relevant for self-esteem are not the same for both sexes or have varying degrees of importance. Reflective and defining people who model gender-specific expectations and social valuations to both sexes have a part in a child's achievement of self-esteem. Individual orientation and societal models of masculinity and femininity can influence the experiences of socialization of children. In primary school, girls and boys are approached differently, not only in physical education classes but also in a host of other school situations where gender constitutes an organizational characteristic. This leads to structurally and institutionally different starting points for the developmental processes of boys and girls, to different "cultural locations" (Hagemann-White, 1992). In a relatively new study, the portrayal of differential courses of self-esteem—until adulthood—shows that gender-specific differences exist in relation to the level of continuity of self-esteem. Whereas men are stable to a high degree, women are more likely to be stable at a low or average level, which indicates a more problematic starting point for women (Sandmeier, 2005). Presumably in primary school, girls develop self-esteem on a completely different level than boys, and this development interacts with the immigrant background. Ormrod (2005) summarizes the U.S. research in his thesis that boys show a generally higher self-esteem than girls toward the end of their primary school years. Ormrod traces these differences to the tendency of boys to overestimate, and the tendency of girls to underestimate, their abilities and possibilities.

Another relevant hypothesis is the assumption that culture-specific influences affect self-concept in diagonal relation to the gender-specific influence. In terms of self-concept, children with an immigrant background are better able to incorporate discontinuities in their academic performance ("interdependent self," Markus & Kitayama, 1991) than is the case for native-born students ("independent self"). The interdependent self is anchored in dominant contexts such as the family or the community and does not necessarily balance such inconsistencies with a universal or independent self. Development of the self is seen as culture specific, as can be said of the self-concept that is its cognitive representation. The group of children with an immigrant background is heterogeneous. The most diverse societal contexts enter into the picture, as well as various generations with various experiences of migration. Hence, a uniform process of identity development cannot be postulated, although it can be assumed that collective orientations leave their mark on individuals or subgroups.

Differentiation between independent self and interdependent self, as used in cognitive psychology to describe the development of the self is based on the dichotomous classification of societies into individualistic and collectivistic or group-orientated. This is done without simplifying the complexity of the relations between the individual and society, in contrast to earlier studies in intercultural psychology (Hofstedte, 1984). Kühnen and Hannover (2003) believe that the cultural context affects the genesis of the self substantially. According to their thesis, the self-knowledge of people from collectivistic (group-oriented) societies is anchored in the realm of experience, that is, in their family or other networks. Therefore, it depends on the context. The self is not an entity as postulated in individualistic societies. It results as much from the experience of one's own competences (knowledge and abilities) as from the collective expectations that are engendered in a network of social relations. This circumstance resolves putative contradictions, because, depending on the context, different, even logically inconsistent, experience of the self is possible. Conversely, the independent self acts autonomously and independently of the context, which allows for greater capacity of action but also causes greater vulnerability for disorders. The independent self does not receive support because it is not rooted in a context. In addition to the theory of social mirroring, the culture-specific development of the self is an important frame of reference for interpreting the development of self-concept. So far, it has hardly been applied to children in research on acculturation.

To promote a positive development of self-esteem, responsiveness and requirements are to be brought into balance. Establishing this prerequisite for each individual in every learning situation is not always guaranteed in heterogeneous primary school classes. One may presume that children with an immigrant background are especially challenged, for example, when acquiring written (second) language competence, that expectations may weigh too heavily on them, and that without adequate feedback on their performance they as a group will suffer from the social norm of reference, namely, school grades. An individual norm of reference in judging their performance would be preferable.

Children with an immigrant background must perform acculturative tasks that surpass the developmental tasks of native-born children. They not only have to learn a second language but also must develop competences that enable them to balance, or rather to integrate, different culturally and linguistically heterogeneous contexts. Meanwhile, these children have to catch up to educational standards and make friends in their peer group. If this is not satisfactorily achieved, deficits in acculturation and setbacks in educational achievement can be expected.

EMPIRICAL RESULTS OF THE PILOT STUDY

First Step: The Process of Intercultural Validation

In addition to the survey on class structure, we worked on the intercultural validation of central instruments, which had not yet produced sufficient results in similar studies. We visited 15 primary school classes (Grades 2 and 3, N = 323) in a city in southern Germany from January to March 2004, where we collected data on self-concept and self-esteem using the self-concept scales for younger and older children of Asendorpf and van Akan (1993a) and the list of statements about self-esteem for children and adolescents (ALS) of Schauder (1996). Our main criterion was defined as immigrant background, which was further combined with gender.

A danger in creating artifacts based on cultural effects arises when research instruments, in our case standardized tests, are used without careful consideration with children of different cultural origin. Therefore, we first had to find out if instruments oriented toward western European or Anglo-American contexts were valid for children from "ethnic families" (Woehrer, 1989). First, intercultural validation can be divided into the etic and emic perspectives, as in intercultural psychology (Berry, 1969, 1986). The etic level describes a universal, intercultural dimension; the emic level describes the culture-specific dimension (Gümen & Herwartz-Emden, 1993). Self-concept and self-esteem should be constructs on the etic level as much as possible for measurement to make sense in a culturally heterogenic school population. To ensure this the reliability of items for students with an immigrant background and for the native-born had to be determined and compared. We did not wish systematic differences between the subgroups to arise.

The essential result of the pretest was that the instruments used were suitable in intercultural contexts. The examination of internal consistency led to this conclusion (see Tables 1–3). The instruments on self-concept were tested in Grades 2 and 3 (see Tables 1 and 2), whereas the instruments on self-esteem were tested only on Grade 28 (see Table 3). Substantial differences between children with and without an immigrant background were not noticeable or were not related to the criterion of immigrant background. Furthermore, the values of internal consistency of the instruments used to measure self-concept are comparable to the results of the Munich LOGIK-study (Asendorpf & van Aken, 1993b). The same applies to the list of statements about self-esteem (Schauder, 1996).

Discussion

Because of the small sample (N = 323) of the pretests, interpretations must be made with caution. However, at least some tendencies are recognizable that correspond to the approach of our research and that we can expect to be replicated in future study.

Group Differences. According to our theoretical assumptions, we should find differences between children with and without an immigrant background and between girls and boys in relation to self-concept and self-esteem. The results of the *t* tests for mean values of cognitive competence relating to the self-concept of Grade 2 students provide exemplary evidence (see Table 4). Girls with an immigrant background answer systematically differently ($p \ll .05$) than girls without

TABLE 1
Mean Values, Standard Deviations, and Internal Consistency of the
Five Self-Concept Scales for Students in Grade 3

Scale	Children With an Immigrant Background				Children Without an Immigrant background			
	N	M	SD	α	N	M	SD	α
Cognitive competence	39	2.97	.64	.73*	39	2.85	.65	.77*
Peer acceptance	39	3.21	.60	.55*	39	2.93	.68	.72*
Performance in sports	39	3.35	.60	.69*	39	3.23	.51	.61*
Appearance	39	3.62	.51	.69*	39	3.44	.73	.85*
Self-esteem	39	3.50	.49	.55*	39	3.36	.55	.72*

Note. Scaling from 1 to 4. An asterisk indicates significance.

TABLE 2
Mean Values, Standard Deviations, and Internal Consistency of the
Four Self-Concept Scales for Students in Grade 2

Skala	Children With an Immigrant Background				Children Without an Immigrant background			
	N	M	SD	α	N	M	SD	α
Cognitive competence	36	3.39	.48	.74*	36	3.10	.48	.61*
Peer acceptance	36	2.91	.60	.70*	36	2.77	.72	.82*
Performance in sports	36	3.49	.48	.66*	36	3.44	.45	.60*
Appearance of mother	39	2.80	.52	.52*	36	2.76	.49	.43*

Note. Scaling from 1 to 4. An asterisk indicates significance.

an immigrant background. The same applies to girls without an immigrant background compared with boys with an immigrant background. Controlling exclusively for immigrant background also indicates a significant difference ($t(70) = 2.573$, $p = .012$) between children with and children without an immigrant background. We concluded that this example could be interpreted as evidence of the existence of systematic group differences.

A comparable result was found in the pretest of self-esteem (ALS) of Grade 2 students. On the school scale, which is closely connected to the cognitive competence scale on content (see Table 4), there is also a significant difference ($t(102) = -2.359$, $p \ll .05$) between children with and children without an immigrant background.

TABLE 3

Mean Values, Standard Deviations, and Internal Consistency of the Scales Measuring
Self-Esteem of Students in Grade 2

Scale	Children With an Immigrant Background				Children Without an Immigrant background			
	N	M	SD	α	N	M	SD	α
Self-esteem School	52	.59	.52	.67*	52	.83	.53	.76*
Self-esteem Leisure time	52	.68	.56	.72*	52	.85	.53	.74*
Self-esteem Family	52	.96	.58	.72*	52	.97	.58	.77*

Note. Scaling from −2 to +2. An asterisk indicates significance.

TABLE 4

T-Tests Scale Cognitive Competence, PSCA-D for Students in Grade 2

	Girls With an Immigrant Background	Girls Without an Immigrant Background	Boys With an Immigrant Background	Boys Without an Immigrant Background
Girls with an Immigrant background (N = 21)	–	*T(41)=2.419, p = 0,02*	T(34) = 0.048, p = 0.962	T(33) = 1.031, p = 0.310
Girls without an Immigrant background (N = 22)	–	–	*T(35) = −2.177, p = 0.036*	T(34) = −1.380, p = 0.177
Boys with an Immigrant background (N = 15)	–	–	–	T(27) = 0.963, p = 0.344
Boys without an Immigrant background (N = 14)	–	–	–	–

Level of significance: $p < 0{,}05$. Italicized values are significant.

Self-Concept and Self-Esteem.   A comparison of the results of the self-concept (PSCA-D) and the self-esteem (ALS) of Grade 2 children shows that children with an immigrant background have higher mean values in all scales of the self-concept than children without an immigrant background (see Table 2). Conversely, the results of the school and leisure time scales of the self-esteem show a contrary trend (see Table 3). Only in the family domain do both subgroups reach similar mean values.

We expected that in consideration of the factors of influence mentioned earlier, children with an immigrant background would have a lower self-concept than those without an immigrant background. A possible explanation for this surprising result may be our assumption that the self-concept of children with an interdependent cultural background is constructed differently. Among these children the self, which is particularly based on the social relations in the family, appears not to be burdened with negative influences of the host country so that children with an immigrant background overestimate rather than underestimate themselves. By the self-esteem scales that refer to the extra-family areas, children with an immigrant background reach lower mean values. Here the children are in direct contact with the host country, that is, context-dependent factors such as, for example, inability to cope with the school language or negative social mirroring, and must perform momentous bridging acts in the acculturation process. To identify this context is a particular goal of our future research.

DISCUSSION AND CONCLUSIONS

To interpret the results of our pilot study, the following observations should be considered. For the main study, the analyses show that girls and boys evaluate themselves differently in terms of self-concept and self-esteem regardless of immigrant or other background. However, we have to assume an interaction between immigrant background and gender. An important finding is that children with an immigrant background have a higher self-concept but lower self-esteem (except on the family scale). This finding leads us to conclude that immigrant background mainly influences affective self-perception. This in turn may contribute to the low level of school performance of children with an immigrant background even if they start with the same prerequisites as others. Compared with the other subgroups, girls without an immigrant background show high self-esteem in the area of school, which appears to confirm this assumption. Furthermore, their school performance is generally better than that of boys.

Generally speaking, it is noted that the differences between girls with and without an immigrant background, especially in Grade 1 are more pronounced than those between boys with and without an immigrant background. This confirms the premise of our research according to which the process of acculturation is gender specific. To what extent differing developmental processes and their respective effects are responsible is still open to further investigation. However, differentiation in the self-concept of all students occurs during the primary school years. Students in Grade 3 have a more negative view of themselves, especially in the cognitive area, than students in Grade 2.

A complex challenge in Germany's elementary schools is the heterogeneity with the classrooms. Teachers and students face not only differences in ethnic origin and culture, but also differences in nationality, language abilities, level of acculturation, and socioeconomic background. In consideration of this and of the increasing number of children with an immigrant background in the German educational system, a main goal should be to provide adequate training to prepare elementary-level teachers for these challenges. Teachers need diagnostic competence to identify language problems, as well as global competence to foster children's language abilities.

This study found that a family's language is especially influential on the school performance of children with an immigrant background. According to teachers' rankings, children whose family language is German have the best results in their subgroup. The consequence of this should be more intensive advancement of children's knowledge of the language of instruction. Support services should made be available to students before and after enrollment to better their chances for optimum school performance.

REFERENCES

Asendorpf, J. B., & van Aken, M. A. G. (1993a). *SPPC-D. Self-Perception Profile for Children.* Berlin, Germany: Humboldt-Universität, Institut für Psychologie.

Asendorpf, J. B., & van Aken, M. A. G. (1993b). Deutsche Versionen der Selbstkonzeptskalen von Harter. *Zeitschrift für Entwicklungspsychologie und Pädagogische Psychologie, 25*(1), 64–86.

Baumert, J., & Schümer, G. (2001). Familiäre Lebensverhältnisse, Bildungsbeteiligung und Kompetenzerwerb. In J. Baumert, E. Klieme, M. Neubrand, M. Prenzel, U. Schiefele, W. Schneider, P. Stanat, K.-J. Tillmann, & M. Weiss (Eds.), PISA 2000. *Basiskompetenzen von Schülerinnen und Schülern im internationalen Vergleich* (pp. 323–407). Opladen, Germany: Leske + Budrich.

Berry, J. W. (1969). On cross-cultural comparability. *International Journal of Psychology, 4,* 119–128.

Berry, J. W. (1986). Introduction to methodology. In H. C. Triandis (Ed.), *Handbook of Cross-Cultural Psychology* (pp. 1–28). Boston: Allyn & Bacon

Bronfenbrenner, U. (1981). *Die Ökologie der menschlichen Entwicklung.* Stuttgart, Germany: Klett Cotta.

Diefenbach, H. (2004): Ethnische Segmentation im deutschen Bildungssystem Eine Zustandsbeschreibung und einige Erklärungen für den Zustand. In Forschungsinstitut Arbeit, Bildung, Partizipation e.V. (FIAB) an der Ruhr-Universität Bochum (Eds.), Bildung als Bürgerrecht oder Bildung als Ware, Band 21/22 des Jahrbuchs Arbeit, Bildung, Kultur (pp. 225–255). Recklinghausen, Germany: FIAB.

Fend, H., & Stöckli, G. (1996). Der Einfluss des Bildungssystems auf die Humanentwicklung: Entwicklungspsychologie der Schulzeit. In F. E. Weinert (Ed.), *Enzyklopädie der Psychologie, Vol. 3, Psychologie des Unterrichts und der Schule* (pp. 1–35). Goettingen, Germany: Hogrefe.

Gümen, S., & Herwartz-Emden, L. (1993). L.: Zur Problematik der Validität im interkulturellen Vergleich. In C. Tarnai (Ed.), *Beiträge zur empirischen pädagogischen Forschung* (pp. 67–79). Münster, New York: Waxmann.

Hagemann-White, C. (1992). Berufsfindung und Lebensperspektive in der weiblichen Adoleszenz. In K. Flaake & V. King (Eds.), *Weibliche Adoleszenz. Zur Sozialisation junger Frauen* (pp. 64–83). Frankfurt, Germany: Thieme.

Helmke, A. (1992). Selbstvertrauen und schulische Leistungen. Göttingen: Hogrefe.

Helmke, A., & Schrader, F.-W. (1998). Determinanten der Schulleistung. In D. H. Rost (Ed.), *Handwörterbuch Pädagogische Psychologie* (pp. 60–67). Weinheim, Germany: Psychologie Verlags Union.

Herwartz-Emden, L., Küffner, D., & Schneider, S. (2004). *Sozialisation und Akkulturation in Erfahrungsräumen von Kindern mit_Schule und Familie.* Unpublished manuscript, Arbeitsbericht an die Deutsche Forschungsgemeinschaft.

Herwartz-Emden, L. & Westphal, M. (2002): Integration junger Aussiedler. Entwicklungsbedingungen und Akkulturationsprozesse. In: Jochen Oltmer (Hrsg.): Migrationsforschung und interkulturelle Studien. Osnabrück: Rasch Verlag, S. 229–259

Hofstede, G. (1984). *Culture's Consequences. International Differences in Work-Related Values.* Beverly Hills, CA: Sage.

Hunger, U. & Thränhardt, D. (2001): Vom "katholischen Arbeitermädchen vom Lande" zum "italienischen Gastarbeiterjungen aus dem Bayrischen Wald". Zu den neuen Disparitäten im deutschen Bildungssystem. In: Bade, Klaus (Hrsg.): Integration und Illegalität in Deutschland. Bad Iburg, S. 51–61.

Knapp-Potthoff, A., & Knapp, K. (1982). *Fremdsprachenlernen und Lehren.* Stuttgart, Germany: Kohlhammer.

Kristen, C. (2002). Hauptschule, Realschule oder gymnasium? Ethnische unterschiede am ersten bildungsübergang. *Kölner Zeitschrift für Soziologie und Sozialpsychologie, 54*(3), 534–552.

Kristen, C., & Granato, N. (2004). Bildungsinvestitionen in Migrantenfamilien. In K. J. Bade & M. Bommes (Eds.), Migration—Integration—Bildung: Grundfragen und Problembereiche. *IMIS-Beiträge, 23,* 123–141.

Krohne, J. A., Meier, U. & Tillmann, K.-J. (2004): Sitzenbleiben, Geschlecht und Migration. Klassenwiederholungen im Spiegel der PISA-Daten. In: Zeitschrift für Pädagogik, 50. Jahrgang, Heft 3, S. 373–391.

Kühnen, U., & Hannover, B. (2003). Kultur, selbstkonzept und kognition. *Zeitschrift für Psychologie, 211*(4), 212–224.

Lüdtke, O., Köller, O., Artelt, C., Stanat, P., & Baumert, J. (2002). Eine überprüfung von modellen zur genese akademischer selbstkonzepte: Ergebnisse aus der PISA-Studie. *Zeitschrift für Pädagogische Psychologie, 16*(3/4), 151–164.

Markus, H. R., & Kitayama, S. (1991). Culture and the self: Implications for cognition, emotion, and motivation. *Psychological Review, 98*(2) 224–243.

Mummendey, H.-D. (1987). Selbstkonzept. In D. Frey & S. Greif (Eds.), *Sozialpsychologie. Ein Handbuch in Schlüsselbegriffen* (pp. 281–285). München, Germny: Psychologie Verlags Union.

Ormrod, J. E. (2005). *Educational Psychology: Developing Learners.* Upper Saddle River, NJ: Merrill/Prentice Hall.

Portes, A., & Rumbaut, R. G. (2001). *Legacies. The Story of the Immigrant Second Generation.* Berkeley, CA: University of California Press.

Roebers, C. M. (1997). *Migrantenkinder im vereinigten Deutschland. Eine Längsschnittstudie zur differentiellen Effekten von Persönlichkeitsmerkmalen auf den Akkulturationsprozeß von Schülern.* Münster, Germany: Waxmann.

Sandmeier, A. (2005). Selbstwertentwicklung vom jugendalter ins frühe erwachsenenalter eine geschlechtsspezifische analyse. *Zeitschrift für Soziologie der Erziehung und Sozialisation, 25*(1), 52–66.

Schauder, T. (1996). *Die Aussagen-Liste zum Selbstwertgefühl für Kinder und Jugendliche.* Göttingen, Germany: Beltz.

Schneewind, J., & Merkens, H. (2004). Schriftspracherwerb bei Kindern mit Migrationshintergrund. Erste Ergebnisse einer Längsschnittstudie. In H. Merkens & F. Schmidt (Eds.), *Berichte aus der Arbeit des Arbeitsbereichs Empirische Erziehungswissenschaften der Freien Universität Berlin* (Nr. 42, p. 6). Previously unpublished work report.

Schwippert, K., Bos, W., & Lankes, E.-M. (2003). Heterogenität und Chancengleichheit am Ende der vierten Jahrgangsstufe im internationalen Vergleich. In W. Bos, E.-M. Lankes, M. Prenzel, K. Schwippert, G. Walther, & R. Valtin (Eds.), *Erste Ergebnisse aus IGLU. Schülerleistungen am Ende der vierten Jahrgangsstufe im internationalen Vergleich* (pp. 265–302). Münster, Germany: Waxmann.

Städtler, T. (2003). *Lexikon der Psychologie.* Stuttgart, Germany: Kröner.

Wode, H. (2002). *Psycholinguistik. Eine Einführung in die Lehr-und Lernbarkeit von Sprachen. Theorien —— Methoden —— Ergebnisse.* Ismaning, Germany: Hueber Verlag.

Woehrer, C. E. (1989). Ethnic families in the circumplex model: Integrating nuclear with extended family systems. In D. H. Olson, C. S. Russel, & D. H. Sprenkle (Eds.), *Circumplex Model. Systemic Assessment and Treatment of Families* (pp. 138–161). New York & London: Haworth Press.

Chapter 4

Inclusion in Schools in Latin America and the Caribbean: The Case of Children of Haitian Descent in the Dominican Republic

Rosa Blanco
Yuki Takemoto
Regional Office for Education in Latin America and the Caribbean/
United Nations Educational, Scientific and Cultural Organization (UNESCO)
Santiago, Chile

THE NEED FOR INCLUSIVE EDUCATION IN LATIN AMERICA

Latin America is said to be the most unequal region in the world. Persistent poverty and inequality in the distribution of wealth have prevented the development of societies with greater integration. Inequality of educational opportunities based on the socioeconomic level of students is one of the most serious characteristics of the region, so it could be concluded that education in general has not been able to break the vicious circle of poverty and social inequality (Blanco, 2005).

Poverty is one of the clearest manifestations of inequality, and it has not diminished substantially despite efforts by all governments in the region. According to studies conducted by the Economic Commission for Latin America and the

Caribbean (ECLAC, 2002–2003), the process of eradicating poverty has been effectively at a standstill since 1997. Between 1999 and 2002, poverty was reduced by a mere 0.4%, from 43.8% to 43.4%. Meanwhile, extreme poverty rose by 0.3%, reaching 18% of the population of the region.

All countries in the region are implementing some kind of educational reform that aims to achieve universal primary education and to improve the quality and equality of education. However, serious inequalities remain in the educational context. This means that greater efforts need to be made for education to fulfill one of its fundamental functions, that is, to contribute to reducing inequalities between students on the basis of their origins so that societies can become more just, equitable, and democratic. For this reason, the rights of immigrants and other displaced populations are an important issue that must be addressed.

Most Latin American countries have adopted the *Declaration of Education for All* into their policies and laws. This document reaffirms the goals of education for all as laid out by the World Conference on Education for All (Jomtien, Thailand, 1990) and other international conferences. In April 2000, participants from 164 countries gathered in Dakar, Senegal, and adopted the *Dakar Framework for Action, Education for All.* This framework commits governments to achieving quality basic education for all by 2015 or earlier. Meanwhile, in reality a number of factors exclude and discriminate in various ways against many students. Despite the considerable advances made in access to primary education, universal education is still not available. In addition, the distribution and quality of education being offered are inconsistent. Approximately 3% of school-aged children in Latin America and the Caribbean were excluded from the education system in 1998, although the numbers vary considerably between countries. Furthermore, data indicate that the collective groups most excluded from the system are precisely those that need education to overcome situations of disadvantage or vulnerability. These are children in isolated rural zones or in extreme poverty, indigenous children, displaced children, and children with disabilities (United Nations Educational, Scientific and Cultural Organization [UNESCO], 2002).

A factor that could contribute to overcoming the vicious circle of poverty is more years of education, because it increases access to the labor market and has a positive influence on the education of the next generation. Despite a reduction in the percentage of absolute illiteracy, 26 million people are illiterate, of whom 56% are women (UNESCO, 2004). Many people between the ages of 15 and 24 have not completed primary education, representing more than 30% in some countries. This means that a considerable portion of the population in the region does not possess the basic abilities necessary to gain access to society and hold productive occupations.

During the 1990s, most of the countries in the region developed strategies and programs of "positive discrimination" that promote access to education and reten-tion of children at risk. However, there are still a great number of students who, for various reasons, find themselves in situations of inequality and face obstacles in gaining access to learning and participation in the education system. Although Latin America does not have the highest figures worldwide for refugees, children have been displaced for economic reasons or as a result of political unrest or armed conflict (Valencia, 2000).

Inequalities based on socioeconomic origins are most notable, especially considering that poverty is associated with other types of inequalities such as living in a rural area, belonging to an indigenous population, being an immigrant, or being displaced in one's own country because of political or economic instability. According to data produced by ECLAC (2002–2003), people from households with scarce resources complete on average 8 or fewer years of education and in most cases become manual laborers. Those from households with greater resources on average complete 12 or more years of education and become professionals, technicians, or executives.

Inequalities based on geographical location are also of serious concern. The highest rate of repetition and dropouts are found in rural areas. The regional average of persons between 15 and 24 years of age who have at least 10 years of education is 50% in urban areas, whereas for rural areas the figure is around 20%. Generally speaking, many rural schools do not enforce compulsory education, and access to school tends to be difficult (UNESCO, 2002).

Children and young people of indigenous origin or of African descent are more likely to face situations of inequality. These populations often live in rural or isolated areas where the incidence of poverty is higher and therefore are more vulnerable. In countries where segregated data exist, indexes of repetition, dropout, and illiteracy are greater among people of indigenous origin. In recent years, some advances in intercultural and bilingual education have been made, but these remain far from adequate.

Children whose educational needs are associated with some kind of disability are a group that faces considerable exclusion and inequality. In many countries, no reliable statistics are available. Where they are available, they reveal that a high percentage of these students receive no kind of education, especially in cases of severe disabilities. Although the tendency in the region is to promote integration of students with disabilities into regular schools, most are in centers of special education—another reason they face considerable discrimination.

In terms of the gender of children, there is no significant difference in terms of access to early and basic education. However, there is a difference in retention. In Latin American countries, dropout and retention rates for girls in rural areas and for those of indigenous origin are greater. Conversely, in Caribbean countries and in some Latin American countries, boys are more likely to drop out of school and achieve lower academic levels than are girls (UNESCO, 2004). Finally, inequality between public and private schools is increasing in some countries, especially in the poorer countries in the region, as a consequence of increasing privatization. This change is widening the gap between rich and poor and is reproducing the stratification and fragmentation of these societies. Immigrants and displaced populations are often the most vulnerable sector of the population and have limited access to economic, educational, and health services and resources.

INCLUSION VERSUS INTEGRATION
IN THE REGIONAL CONTEXT

The movement toward greater *inclusion* has been gaining strength in recent years, as governments have attempted to redress high incidences of exclusion, discrimination, and educational inequalities that exist in most education systems worldwide. As mentioned earlier, despite varying policies and programs that promote equity, the education system has not managed to reduce inequalities or the gap between rich and poor. This is why greater efforts need to be made to transform the education system into a driving force toward achieving greater social equity (Blanco, 2005).

In many countries, there is confusion about the concept of inclusion or inclusive education, because the term is being used to refer to integration into regular schools of children with disabilities or other special educational needs. In other words, the movement toward inclusion and that of integration are believed to be the same, when in fact they are based on two distinct visions and focuses. As a result, policies of inclusion are misunderstood as being part of special education. This confusion limits the possibilities for conducting a comprehensive analysis that would consider the totality of exclusion and discrimination in the education system to formulate integral policies of inclusion.

First, it is important to point out that *inclusion* has a broader focus than *integration.* Integration has to do with people with disabilities or other special educational needs. The integration movement emerged to put into action the right of such people to be educated in regular schools like any other citizen. The inclusion movement, however, aspires to put into action the right to quality education for all. It recognizes that a great number of children worldwide, in addition to those with disabilities, do not have access to education, or they receive education of lesser quality or suffer from various types of discrimination. In other words, inclusion is about access, participation, and achievement of all students, with special emphasis on those who are at greater risk of being excluded or marginalized for various reasons. From this perspective, inclusive education is a policy matter for ministries of education, not simply for divisions of special education.

Second, the focuses of attention are different from each other. The integration movement focuses on transforming special education, not on changing the culture and practice of regular schools so that they become capable of meeting the needs of a diverse student population and eliminate the various kinds of discrimination that exist in schools. The paradox is that many schools integrate children with disabilities, but expel or discriminate against other students. These schools cannot be called inclusive.

Generally speaking, the education system has remained unaltered under the integration movement. It has limited opportunities for learning and participation not only for students with special educational needs but also for other students. In many cases, systems have transferred the model of attention employed by special schools into regular schools. More attention is given to students with special needs (e.g., individualized programs, differentiated strategies, and materials) rather than changing the factors that limit participation and learning in the educational context.

This demonstrates that maintaining a focus on individual difficulties in learning, paying attention only to individual variables (e.g., competence, family situation, social origin), leaves out the considerable influence that the environment has on a person's development and learning. The curriculum, teaching strategies, management of schools, expectations of teachers, and personal relationships are some factors that could facilitate, or hamper, learning and participation.

However, the primary focus of the inclusion movement is about transforming the culture—the organization and educational practices of regular schools—to respond to the diversity of educational needs of all students, which are based on their social and cultural origins and personal characteristics such as competence, interest, and motivation. As opposed to what happens in integration, the teaching is adapted to the needs of children and not the other way around. Attention given to children with special educational needs is framed in the context of the diversity of needs that exist in the whole student population. In other words, it takes into consideration that all children, not only those with disabilities, have varying educational capacities and needs.

In the inclusion movement, the problem is not the child but rather the school or the system. This movement attempts to identify and eliminate or minimize the obstacles that limit learning and participation for all students. It attempts to identify the obstacles put in the way by persons, policies, education systems, and schools.

THE SIGNIFICANCE OF INCLUSION IN EDUCATION

The right to education not only means having access to education but also implies that it be high-quality education and that students can participate and learn as much as possible. Inclusive education aspires to put into action high-quality education for all, which forms part of the foundations of a just and egalitarian society. The right to participation and nondiscrimination for immigrant and displaced children implies that they be educated in schools in their respective communities regardless of their social, cultural, or racial origins or other personal characteristics.

Furthermore, the goal of education is not limited to the socialization or assimilation of people into the culture; it is to enable each individual to retain and develop his or her cultural identity.

Having regular schools with an inclusive orientation is the most effective means of combating discriminatory attitudes. Such schools create welcoming communities and build an inclusive society where education for all can be achieved. Moreover, they provide an effective education to the majority of children and improve the efficiency, and ultimately the cost-effectiveness, of the entire education system (UNESCO, 1994). Equality means securing equal opportunities not only in access to education but also in terms of the number of years of education, quality of education, educational process, what students learn, and access to information technology and communication to reduce the digital divide.

Schools plays a fundamental role in preventing any kind of difference from turning into an educational inequality and eventually into social inequalities. Today the school is not the only space that provides access to knowledge—it is still the only place that can ensure equal distribution of knowledge. Meanwhile, education alone cannot compensate for social inequalities and eliminate the many forms of discrimination that currently exist in our societies.

In the following section, we examine the potential and challenges of implementing the inclusive education model through a project that attempts to realize this model in a concrete setting.

A CASE STUDY: HAITIAN AND DOMINICO-HAITIAN CHILDREN IN THE DOMINICAN REPUBLIC

Since October 2004, OREALC/UNESCO Santiago has been implementing a project titled "Children Affected by Armed Conflict in Haiti: Assuring Their Right to Education, Nondiscrimination, and Participation in the Dominican Republic" under the rubric of the *Program for the Education of Children in Need* run by UNESCO. It is a 2-year project being implemented in the field with the cooperation of the Dominican Republic Ministry of Education (Divisions of Special Education, Basic Education, Directions of Technical and Administrative Affairs of the Office of International Cooperation of the Ministry) and a local nongovernmental organization, the Fundación Tonucci: Educando para la diversidad (Tonucci Foundation: Educating for Diversity).

Background

Haiti has been undergoing a political as well as a socioeconomic crisis in recent years. An outbreak of violence led to the departure of President Aristide in February 2004, and scores of Haitians sought refuge in neighboring countries

(United Nations High Commissioner for Refugees [UNHCR], 2004).[1] This new wave of refugees was in addition to the already significant presence of Haitian immigrants in the Dominican Republic, which, including those of Haitian descent born in country, is estimated at more than half a million (Human Rights Watch, 2002). In addition, Haitians daily cross the road that divides the two countries ("The International Road") to attend schools in the Dominican Republic (World Food Programme, 2000). During the past decade, the Dominican Republic government has deported hundreds of thousands to Haiti, including some born in the Dominican Republic. Haiti is the poorest country in the Western Hemisphere, and 80% of the population lives below the absolute poverty threshold of US$150 per year. Although the Dominican Republic is considered a middle-income country, because of unequal distribution of income, more than 50% of the population lives below the poverty line. The western part of the country, including the border area with Haiti, is among the most economically deprived areas, with high rates of unemployment, illiteracy, shortage of food, and malnutrition. This project was conceived in March 2004 during the sociopolitical chaos that surrounded Aristide's departure.

Description of the Project

The aim of this project has been to complement efforts already being made by various international and national organizations by focusing on Haitian children in the Dominican Republic whose basics needs are not being met, especially their access to quality education. Discrimination against Haitians in the Dominican Republic is a serious issue, which in many cases deprives Haitian children of access to formal and advanced education. Many Haitians do not possess the official documents required to receive public services, including education, but Haitian children, regardless of their legal status, must be given the opportunity to receive quality education.

Although this project was originally planned to focus strongly on children of Haitian descent based on the initial assessment described earlier, it became clear that myriad factors present in the communities called for a more comprehensive approach. In other words, this project has become a demonstrative case of the need for an inclusive approach as described here.

In terms of socioeconomic factors, the border area with Haiti is among the most economically deprived areas of the Dominican Republic. The schools are generally ill equipped, with poor infrastructure and limited teaching materials.

---

[1]It is reported that more than 250 Haitians sought medical attention in neighboring countries, including pregnant women, many who suffer from AIDS and those with gunshot and stab wound (CBC World News, March 11, 2004). According to the UNHCR, 105 Haitian refugees arrived in Jamaica, 30 in Cuba, and more than 300 in the Dominican Republic as of 29 February 2004. (UNHCR, 2004).

There is a shortage of teaching staff, and staff members often have limited abilities and little knowledge about issues such as diversity and inclusion in schools. Government policies toward Haitian immigrants and refugees over the years have reinforced the already embedded prejudices against this population in the respective communities. In terms of educational needs, those of children with disabilities in every school are currently not being met. Sanitary conditions are poor in all schools. Persons are living with HIV/AIDS in some of the communities, and yet children as well as teachers and community members know little about the epidemic, even about preventing transmission. Many children have difficult family situations, which are closely related to the socioeconomic level of the parents or caregivers and their level of education. The schools and communities face an array of difficulties because of their geographic location, such as limited access to information and to services in general (Fundación Tonucci, 2005).

Objectives of the Project

Based on the preliminary observations presented above, this project was reconceptualized to achieve the following objectives:

- To secure the right to education for all children, including Haitian children, in the Dominican Republic
- To promote changes in the schools that would allow all children, including Haitian children and children with physical and mental disabilities, to participate fully in the educational process and to be integrated into the local community
- To raise awareness among teachers and members of the local community about the importance of inclusion in the educational context To this end, the infrastructure of the schools would be upgraded, and educational and recreational materials would be supplied.

Project Site

This project operates near the border between the Dominican Republic and Haiti, which is an impoverished area with a high concentration of Haitian immigrants and people of Haitian descent. Six public schools were identified in two regions based on their needs, as well as their willingness to participate actively in the project. All the schools are attended by many groups of students each day in the morning and in the afternoon, and some are open in the evening for adult classes. Many teachers are in charge of multiple sessions per day.

The educational system of the Dominican Republic consists of the following levels: initial (*nivel inicial*), basic (*nivel básico*), middle (*nivel medio*), and higher (*superior*). Initial or early education is offered to students up to the age of 6, and the last year is compulsory. Basic education consists of 8 years for students aged 6–14, with two cycles of 4 years (Grades 1–4 and 5–8), and constitutes the minimum level of compulsory education. Middle education consists of 4 years, with two cycles of 2 years. All students go through the same first cycle, and three options are offered for the second cycle, namely, general, technical/professional, and arts. Higher education is offered after completion of middle education (Secretaría de Estado de Educación y Cultura, Republica Domincana, 1999).

The schools selected for this project share some basic characteristics and needs. All are located near the border with Haiti, and a considerable portion of the student body comes from Haiti or is Dominican born of Haitian descent. Many children, including those born in the Dominican Republic, do not possess official identity papers, which are not required for students up to Grade 8. Official papers are needed to take the national examination that is required to advance beyond Grade 8. The cost of obtaining these papers is considerable, which makes it extremely difficult for children of limited means to continue their education. Furthermore, many Haitian children adopt names that sound Dominican, which renders it virtually impossible to obtain an official count of Haitian children.

Most students in Grade 2 and some in Grade 3 cannot read or write. Students are generally not interested in school activities, and there is a problem with violence in the schools. Classes are generally conducted in a traditional manner, with rigid, authoritarian teaching styles. Teaching methods involve little participation and tend to be homogenizing. Prejudice is evident among teachers against children of Haitian descent, even though they talk about the importance of equality as an educational value. Contact between the local communities and the schools is limited, and participation by family members in school activities is not common.

Region of Neyba

School 1 is a small unitary and multigrade school with 69 students between Grades 1 and 4. Grades 1 and 2 students attend classes in the morning. The school is equipped with 24 chairs and two blackboards in poor condition. Few official textbooks (issued by the Ministry of Education) are available, and the school has no library. The school building needs complete renovation.

School 2 has 246 students between initial-early education and Grade 4, with four teachers and a principal. There are two classrooms, and a blackboard under a tree outside serves as an additional classroom. Two new classrooms are needed. Of the 130 chairs, 30 are in good condition. Textbooks are in short supply, and there is no additional educational material.

School 3 is a large school with 853 students of initial-early education and basic education; 550 attend morning classes. The school building has recently been rebuilt with funds from the German Development Bank (KfW). There are 19 teachers and a principal. The school is equipped with new furniture, but lacks furniture suitable for younger children.

Region of San Juan de la Maguana

School 1 has 229 students between initial-early education and Grade 6, of which 127 attend morning classes only. There are four classrooms, including a room that is divided by cardboard, and all are in poor condition. The washrooms and kitchen are extremely run down, with floors and windows virtually nonexistent. There are six teachers and a principal. The number of official textbooks is inadequate, and there is little additional teaching material.

School 2 has 130 students between initial-early education and Grade 4, and 71 students attend afternoon classes. There are four teachers and one director. The school building was recently renovated, but the furniture is in poor condition. There are not enough official textbooks or additional teaching material. The school needs an office and a library.

School 3 has 257 students between initial-early education and Grade 7. It has four classrooms in good condition, but the kitchen and washroom are in poor condition. There are not enough official texts or additional material. Land is available for a sports field, but the school has no equipment.

Outcome and Reflections

The project has been implemented in phases that involve a variety of activities. Once the six schools were selected with individual needs assessments, a technical support person was assigned to each school. This person organized support teams for each school, consisting of technical officers of the school district, the school principal, teachers, members of parents' associations, parents, and other community members. Before implementation of programs, organizational meetings were held with members of the technical teams to conduct preliminary diagnoses of the schools. Based on a survey of inclusive schools in various countries, a guidebook was prepared for use by technical teams, especially in conducting the qualitative phases of the diagnoses. This stage involved many visits by members of the Ministry of Education and the Tonucci Foundation and meetings with directors, teachers, community organizations, and parents and caregivers. Additional meetings were held with international organizations to collect practical information and coordinate activities.[2]

---

[2]International organizations consulted for this project include the KfW Entwicklungsbank (KfW Development Bank), UNICEF, UNAIDS (Joint United Nations Programme on HIV/AIDS), Plan International, and United Nations Development Programme.

Based on the results of these initial diagnoses, programs have been implemented on a regular basis in each of the six participating schools. Activities include regular meetings with teachers and parents where concerns or pending issues are discussed with members of the technical team, who act as moderators. Several workshops have been organized where a detailed presentation of the project was given, and participants became familiar with the basic concept of "attention to diversity and development of inclusive schools." As part of the project, improvements are being made to the infrastructure of the schools, depending on their particular needs. Teaching materials such as textbooks and equipment for recreational activities also have been purchased and distributed to the schools. Recreational activities are being organized not only for the children but also for all members of each community. Through the meetings and capacity-building sessions described here, a wide range of community members participated, and the following observations were noted:

- Increased communication between schools and communities
- Strengthening of parents' associations and friends of the schools
- Integration of communication organizations into educational activities, with greater presence of neighborhood associations, mothers' groups, development-related associations in the community, and religious groups

Based on considerable worry about the level of illiteracy among the adult population of the various communities, literacy programs were redesigned with the aid of technical advisors in the region to accommodate parents and other adults in the community. In one school, a strong interest was expressed by parents that resulted in the development of capacity-building activities that specifically targeted women, the rural population, and farmers. In addition, worry was expressed about the integration of Haitians into their respective communities. Every community expressed willingness to integrate children of Haitian descent into the schools; however, subtle remarks and insinuations are commonly heard that indicate resistance or resentment. For example, regardless of their immigration status, they are referred to as "*Haitian children*," as distinct from other Dominican children. Some parents of children of Haitian descent have been present in the meetings, but many do not actively participate in the conversation. It was noted that a special effort should be made to understand what special needs might exist.

During the implementation of the project, some difficulties required that some of the initial plans be modified. Changes in the school district system resulted in reorganization of technical teams and additional informational meetings with the new officials in charge of the school. After the initial selection of schools, resistance became evident among the teachers in one of the schools in San Juan de la Maguana. The principal would be absent from the technical meetings, and there was little cooperation from the teachers. Given the importance of their active participation in attaining the objectives of the project, we decided to replace this school with another one. However, in a consultative meeting to communicate this decision to parents and other community members, there was unanimous support for continuing the project in the school, and participants promised to involve the whole community to provide the necessary support. Given the obvious needs of the children and the enthusiasm expressed by parents and community members, it was finally decided that the school would remain in the project.

All six schools are located in the border area with Haiti, and many are difficult to reach. For the project, this has posed difficulties in terms of added cost in implementing activities, monitoring, and making improvements to the infrastructure of schools. However, this also points to the difficult conditions for the schools, the students, and the communities.

In addition, the project has not yet been able to address an important aspect of the psychosocial needs of children of Haitian descent, namely, their cultural and linguistic heritage. Although the project has placed a strong emphasis on disseminating information on inclusive education and promoting institutional and behavioral changes, going beyond the integration model has not been easy.

CONCLUSION

The degree of inequality in Latin America and the Caribbean is a serious issue— inequality not only in terms of income but also in terms of educational opportunities. One could argue that access to quality education and the achievement of adequate levels of learning depend on the country where a child is born, where he or she lives, and the socioeconomic and cultural level of his or her origins. Children with disabilities who come from conditions of poverty, live in rural areas, or are of indigenous or African descent suffer more from exclusion and discrimination in education. In short, education has not achieved equality of educational opportunities, nor has it been an adequate instrument toward achieving greater social mobility (Blanco & Curato, 2004).

As we argue in this chapter, the problem is not because of the lack of trying. On the contrary, many projects and programs in the region have been sponsored by the Ministry of Education and international organizations that aim to achieve greater equality in and through education. The problem can be analyzed as being twofold. One part is fragmentation among various programs and projects accompanied by lack of consistency or coordination; the other is the absence of policies that integrate both equality and quality in and through education.

Projects and programs often focus on a particular population or a particular issue, not fully taking into account the complexity of the situation that is producing or reinforcing inequalities in a given community. This often results in increased discrimination against the particular group and further social exclusion of that group or sometimes of another group. In short, projects and programs that focus too narrowly on certain forms of social exclusion cannot transform the conditions that produce or reproduce similar inequalities.

Similarly, fragmentation between equality and quality in the educational context prevents transformation of the conditions that produce inequalities and lack of quality. As stated in UNESCO's (2005) EFA global monitoring report entitled *Education for All: The Quality Imperative,*

> Whether a particular education system is of high or low quality can be judged only in terms of the extent to which its objectives are being met. Quality must also be judged in the mirror of equity. An Education system in which there is gender inequality or discrimination against particular groups on ethical or cultural grounds is not a high-quality system. A shift towards equity represents, in itself, an improvement in the quality of education. (p. 17)

Most needed in the region are integral policies that aim to modify or transform systems that produce, reproduce, and reinforce various kinds of inequalities. The project focusing on children of Haitian descent in the Dominican Republic and the communities in which they live represents an example of concrete efforts being made to achieve equality and quality of education through an inclusive approach. Although the objective was a strong focus on children of Haitian descent, the aims and implementation of the project have become much broader. It now aims to promote inclusion not only of children of Haitian descent but also of children with disabilities, and it recognizes the reality of the concerned communities that are generally underprivileged economically and socially. Meanwhile, the fact that the project has not yet been able to address the issue of the cultural and linguistic heritage of children of Haitian descent points to a reality that also must be acknowledged. Resources are limited, and so are the capacities of the professionals who design and implement these projects. Furthermore, promoting new ideas and practices in schools and communities, especially when this forces fundamental change, often meets strong resistance. The value of inclusive education may appear clear on paper, but implementing the idea is never simple. Nevertheless, to make quality education for all a reality, the endeavor consists of these small steps, taken one at a time.

REFERENCES

Blanco, G. R. (2005). Educación de calidad para todos empieza en la primera infancia. Consideraciones para el desarrollo de políticas públicas (Quality education for all begins in early childhood). *Revista Enfoques Educacionales, 7*(1), 11–33.

Blanco G. R., & Curato, S. (2004). Desigualdades educativas en América Latina: Todos somos responsables. (Inequality in education in Latin America: We are all responsible). In J. E. García-Huidobro (Ed.), *Escuelas de Calidad en Condiciones de Pobreza* (*Quality Schools in Conditions of Poverty*). Santiago, Chile: Universidad Alberto Hurtado.

Burman, T. (Ed. in Chief) (2004, March 11). Newsworld [Television broadcast]. Toronto, ON, Canada: CBC.

Economic Commission for Latin America and the Caribbean (ECLAC). (2002–2003). *Panorama Social de América Latina* (Social Panorama of Latin America). Santiago, Chile: Author.

Fundación Tonucci. (2005). *Project Progress Report.* Dominican Republic.

Human Rights Watch. (2002). "Illegal people": Haitians and Dominico Haitians in the Dominican Republic. Retrieved April 24, 2005 from http://www.hrw.org/reports/2002/domrep/

Secretaría de Estado de Eduación y Cultura, República Dominicana. (1999). *Ley de Educación No. 66 '97: Edición Especial Para Padres, Madres, Tutores y Amigos de la Escuela.* (Law on Education No. 66 '97: Special Edition for Fathers, Mothers, Tutors and Friends of the School). Santo Domingo, Dominican Republic: Author.

United Nations Educational, Scientific and Cultural Organization (UNESCO). (1994). *The Salamanca Statement and Framework for Action on Special Needs Education* (Developed at the World Conference on Special Needs Education: Access and Quality, in Salamanca, Spain, 1994). Geneva, Switzerland: Author.

UNESCO Regional Office for Education in Latin America and the Caribbean and Ministerio de Educatión deChile. (2002). *Regional Report: Educational Panorama of the Americas Summit of the Americas.* Santiago, Chili: Author.

UNESCO Regional office for Education in Latin America and the Caribbean. (2004). *Education for All in Latin America and the Caribbean: A Goal Within Our Reach. Regional Monitoring Report on Education for All 2003.* Santiago, Chili: Author.

UNESCO. (2005). *EFA Global Monitoring Report 2005, Education for All: The Quality Imperative.* Paris: Author.

United Nations High Commissioner for Refugees (UNHCR). UNHCR Urges International Support for Haitians and Right of Asylum. Press Release. 26 February 2004. Geneva: Author.

Valencia, A. (2000). *Personas Desplazadas, Refugiados y Personas Que Solicitan Asilo: Practicas Y Politicas Nacionales, Discriminacion Racial en le Pais De Acogica* (*Displaced Persons, Refugees, Asylum Seekers: Practices and National Policies, Racial Discrimination in the Host Country*). Santiago de Chile: Regional Seminar of Experts for Latin America and the Caribbean on Economic, Social and Legal Measures Against Racism, With Special Reference to Groups at Risk.

World Food Programme (WFP). (2000). *Project Summary: School Feeding Programme with Community Participation in Socially and Economically Depressed Areas.* Dominican Republic 5276.01. Washington, DC: U.S. Department of Agriculture.

Chapter 5

Nutritional Challenges Among Immigrant Children and Youth in Norway

Bernadette Kumar
Institute of General Practice and Community Medicine, Norway
Margareta Wandel
Institute of Basic Medical Sciences, University of Oslo, Norway

Urbanization and globalization that result in demographic lifestyle and dietary changes present challenges to public health. The nutritional and epidemiological transitions that follow these developments significantly affect the health of populations. Migration accelerates some of these processes, and migrant studies offer us the opportunity of observing the role of environmental change on various ethnic groups.

Immigration from developing countries is a fairly new phenomenon in Norway, having its origins in the late 1960s. The numbers and ethnicity of the immigrants to Norway have varied over the years. However, the immigrant population as a whole has grown steadily and is now an integral part of Norwegian society. In addition to the first-generation immigrants, a cadre of children of immigrants has been born and brought up in Norway. The immigrant population now makes up 7.3% of the population, and 50% have their origins in developing countries. Norway's capital Oslo has the highest proportion of immigrants (17%), and of these, 40% originate from the Indian subcontinent; origins of other large groups include Vietnam, Iraq, Somalia, Iran, and Turkey (Lie, 2002). These groups warrant special attention. In addition to their genetic variations, obvious cultural and traditional differences affect risk factors that cannot be addressed if they are not identified. The effect of migration on food and nutrition is twofold: migrants adopting and adapting new food patterns, and the host population being exposed to and accepting ethnic foods.

Food is not just a composite of nutrients, and people do not form eating habits based on nutritional composition. Eating habits are based on ethnic origins, culture, and religion, as well as availability, household economy, and individual preferences. Although the basic need for food to alleviate hunger is common to all human beings, the ways and means of meeting this requirement vary tremendously. Foods chosen, meal composition, ways of preparation and eating, the number of meals per day, the time of eating, and size of portions are an integrated part of a coherent cultural pattern in which traditions, customs, and practice each play a part. Food habits are part of a dynamic process called gastrodynamics (Rao, 1996), referring to dynamic changes in dietary styles and eating behavior.

The immigrant's lifestyle includes traditional dietary beliefs and practices, as food is an integral part of a cultural identity. Ethnicity determines how groups choose, consume, and make use of available foods, thus distinguishing them from other groups. Therefore, it is important to map the food habits of immigrants. To collect information from these groups, it is necessary to understand their food habits and how these differ from those of the host population. Constraints to data collection include language and communication barriers, as well as lack of understanding of the underlying context and role of food in their lives. Lessons learned from our studies (Kumar, Wandel, & Holmboe-Otteson, 2003) provide us with valuable insights into how to approach these groups as well as how to interpret the information collected. Our data show that immigrants in Norway face the double burden of nutritional problems linked both to inadequacy and to excess. Although there is no shortage of food, nutritional deficiency diseases such as vitamin D deficiency and iron deficiency anemia are seen in women and children. Conversely, obesity and diabetes are on the rise, particularly among some immigrant groups.

Most immigrants are subject to continual change of their dietary environment. Selection of food is strongly influenced by the various food values: in other words, what the foods mean to them. This is reflected in attitudes toward the use of various food items where preferences are deeply embedded in tradition. Both the traditional and the host culture may influence immigrants' food selection and how they make up their meals. Sometimes this combination may have negative consequences for the health of both adults and children. An example among Pakistanis in Norway is the reduced use of cooked vegetables and lentils following migration, whereas the consumption of animal products, sugars, processed grains, and oil has increased (Dhirad, Kumar, & Holmboe-Otttesen, 2003). For women from the Indian subcontinent, better nutrition may mean a greater intake of fat and sugar as these foods are perceived as nourishing (Dawes, Kumar, & Middlethon, 2005). In developing countries, being overweight (healthy/well fed) is often perceived as advantageous as the opposite of being underweight (unhealthy/malnourished). Because these attitudes conflict with those of the host population, children of immigrants born and brought up in Norway find themselves at a crossroads between the majority (host) and minority (immigrant) cultures. Ethnic adolescents, therefore, may land in double jeopardy with persisting unhealthy habits from their minority cultures and acquiring unhealthy habits from the majority. This is well illustrated in the case of boys from the Indian subcontinent who consume large amounts of both full-fat milk and sugary soft drinks (Kumar, 2004).

Although the consequences of these dietary changes need to be further examined and are by no means conclusive, it is fair to say that these dietary changes are concomitant with the burgeoning diabetes and obesity epidemics among immigrants. This warrants the need to develop appropriate strategies for the prevention of diet-related chronic diseases among this vulnerable group. So far, immigrants have been given Norwegian dietary guidelines, which encourage them to decide and which are difficult for them to follow. Recognition of obvious cultural differences in food selection, habits, and patterns is a prerequisite for nutrition education. In addition, public health education cannot be successful without taking into account the context or life situation of these people. Therefore, we (Kumar/SHD, 2001) developed a brochure especially designed for Pakistani immigrants based on their life situation and their foods; so far, this has been received positively in Norway both by Norwegians and Pakistanis.

Attempts to change food habits to improve nutritional status may be thwarted by failure to understand cultural needs. Because immigrants are now part of the demographics, it is important to stress strategies for health education, promotion, and prevention, because these might be both crucial and successful in delaying or preventing the onset of chronic disease in adult life. We elaborate here on some of the main nutritional challenges facing children and youth in Norway.

NUTRITIONAL CHALLENGES AMONG PRESCHOOLERS

Iron Deficiency

Infants and young children are at especially high risk for developing iron deficiency because of high requirements corresponding to rapid growth (Hercberg, Papoz, Galin, Guery, Farnier, & Rossignol, 1987). The health implications of poor iron status in early childhood have acquired renewed attention among nutritional scientists. Iron deficiency may impede mental and motor development of the child

(Krieger, Claussen, & Scott, 1999; Walter, 1994). Results from several studies indicate that the damage may be irreversible (Alvin, Eden, Mohammad, & Mir, 1997; Beard, 2001; Lozoff, Wolf, & Jimenez, 1996). However, there is no general agreement about the long-term implications of early iron deficiency on mental development (Grantham-McGregor & Ani, 2001; Major, 1994; Politt, 2000).

Iron deficiency anemia is the most common nutritional deficiency among preschool children older than 6 months of age in both industrialized and developing countries (Cook, 1994). It is also the most common nutritional deficiency among immigrant children in Norway. Many children hospitalized in Oslo with severe iron deficiency anemia come from immigrant families (Brunvand & Sander, 1993). A higher prevalence of children with anemia (Solem, 1982) and iron deficiency (Arsky 1996; Wandel, Fagerli, Olsen, Borch-Iohnsen, & Ek, 1996) has been found among nonhospitalized 1-year-olds from Turkey and Pakistan living in Norway. However, differences between Norwegian and immigrant-origin children were no longer significant among 2 and 4 years olds (Antonsen, 2000; Fagerli et al., 1996), and this can be attributed to an increase in the prevalence of iron deficiency among ethnic Norwegian children. A study in Oslo of 2 and 4 year olds from Somalia showed slightly higher rates of iron deficiency compared with those of immigrants in the previous study (Madar, 1997).

Many types of foods contribute substantially to iron intake such as meat, fish, vegetables, and cereals, especially whole-grain products. Because absorption of iron from meat and fish is better than that from plant foods, these are particularly important sources. Cow's milk is a poor source of iron, both because the iron content in milk is low and because it is poorly absorbed. Breast milk, despite its low iron content, is a better source of iron because it is absorbed better than cow's milk. In addition, vitamin C (found in fruits, juices, and vegetables) is known to enhance iron absorption, whereas phytate (found in bread and other cereals) is known to inhibit absorption.

Several hypotheses have been formulated to explain the higher propensity for iron deficiency in immigrant children (Brunvand & Brunvatne, 2001; Brunvand & Sander, 1993; Solem, 1982). These include differences in feeding patterns between immigrant and native families such as longer or shorter periods of breast-feeding, early introduction and excessive use of cow's milk, and the consumption of solid weaning foods with low iron content. It is also possible that poor iron status among immigrant women during pregnancy contributes to these differences. Some data suggest that iron status during the first year of life is affected by iron stored in the body at birth (Fearweather-Tait, 1992).

Vitamin D Deficiency

Rickets is a disease in children caused by vitamin D deficiency. It leads to abnormal bone development with typical deformations in zones of rapid growth, reduced growth in length and height, and convulsions. If a mother has vitamin D deficiency (called osteomalacia in adults), her children will start their lives with poor vitamin D status because of marginal vitamin D stores at birth as well as low vitamin D content in the breast milk. Small children grow quickly and need to build up their bones.

Vitamin D is formed in the skin during exposure to ultraviolet (UV) light. All factors that can prevent the UV light from penetrating the outer skin layer also prevent the formation of vitamin D in the skin. These may be clothing, sunscreen lotion containing a UV-filter, and skin pigmentation (Holick, 1994). Furthermore, in Norway, UV light during the winter months (October to March) does not have the required intensity for the formation of vitamin D in the skin (Brustad, 2004). The dietary contribution of vitamin D is from few foods such as fatty fish, fish liver oil, and egg yolks. In addition, in Norway margarine, butter, formula milk, and a type of partly skimmed milk are enriched with Vitamin D.

Rickets was almost eradicated in Norway in the 1950s and 1960s, but has reappeared among children of immigrants from developing countries. Almost all children treated for rickets in Oslo hospitals are from families who originated in developing countries such as Pakistan, Morocco, Turkey, Bosnia, and the Philippines (Brunvand & Nordshus, 1996).

The higher prevalence of rickets among children of immigrants from developing countries may be attributed to one or more of the following factors: low vitamin D stores at birth, insufficient vitamin D from breast milk, a diet containing few good sources of vitamin D, insufficient exposure to UV light, heavy skin pigmentation, or if they wear too much clothing when outdoors.

FOOD HABITS AMONG IMMIGRANT
MOTHERS AND PRESCHOOLERS

Our Norwegian studies document that although breast-feeding patterns vary a great deal among immigrant groups, some women breast-feed less and introduce formula earlier than is common both in their country of origin and in Norway (Table 1).

Breast-feeding and weaning traditions as well as the adoption of more Westernized habits after migration are important factors in understanding what leads to malnutrition in immigrant children and adults. The official dietary recommendation for infants in Norway is to feed babies only breast milk for the first 6 months and thereafter gradually introduce complementary foods that are rich in vitamin D and iron and that may enhance iron absorption (National Nutrition Council, 2001).

Norwegian children are breast-fed longer than is reported from other industrialized countries (Lande et al., 2003). Many immigrant mothers come from

TABLE 1
Norwegian Dietary Studies Among Immigrant Children

Reference	Study objectives	Results
Arsky (1996)	To study differences in diet and iron status among Norwegian, Pakistani, and other immigrant's children in Oslo. 1-year old children.	No significant difference in length of breast-feeding between the various groups of children. The immigrant children had fewer meals ($p < 0.005$) and more in-between eating ($p < 0.005$), fewer vegetables, meat/fish, and wholemeal bread, and more rice, biscuits, and cookies compared with the Norwegian children ($p < 0.02$).
Wandel et al. (1996)	To find out if there are differences in iron status between Norwegian, Turkish, and other immigrant children, and if there are differences in weaning practices, which may have implications for iron status of the children. 1-year old children	The Turkish children were breast-fed for a shorter time than the Norwegian children ($p = 0.02$) and introduced to formula ($p = 0.05$) and cow's milk (0.01) at an earlier age. At age 1 the Norwegian children had a higher frequency of intake of wholemeal bread and meat/fish ($p < 0.001$), whereas the Turkish children had a higher intake of refined bread, rice, vegetables, sweets, biscuits, and chips (< 0.05). Exclusive breast-feeding and the intake of liver paste were positively related to iron status.
Fagerli, et al. (1996)	To estimate differences in diet and iron status between Norwegian, Pakistani, and other immigrant children at 2 years of age.	The immigrant children ate less wholemeal bread, liver paté, other meat, and more rice, beans, citrus fruits, and tea than the Norwegian children at 2 years of age. No significant differences in iron status between the different groups of children.
Madar (1997)	To contribute to more knowledge about iron status and important factors among 2-4-year-old children from Somalia	The Somali children had adequate energy intake, but the intake of iron and vitamin D was low, 88% of the children had lower iron intake than what is recommended. Positive correlation between vitamin C intake ($p = 0.04$) and negative correlation between fat intake ($p < 0.04$) and iron status.
Antonsen (2000)	To compare changes in diet and iron status at 4 years of age among Norwegian, Turkish and other immigrant children.	All the immigrant children scored higher on foods contributing with sugar and lower on foods contributing with iron compared to the Norwegians ($p < 0.03$). The Turkish children scored higher on vitamin C rich foods ($p < 0.01$). All the children improved iron status from 2 to 4 years and there were no significant differences between the groups.

countries where children traditionally are breast-fed even longer than what is common practice in Norway. However, in some developing countries, the duration of breast-feeding has been reduced, especially for those living in urban areas. A study of mothers who had immigrated to Norway from Turkey showed that they were breast-feeding for a shorter time (median time of exclusive breast-feeding was 1.5 months for the Turkish and 3.5 months for the Norwegian mothers) and introduced formula or cow's milk for their infants earlier than Norwegian mothers (Wandel et al., 1996). They also stopped feeding the iron- and vitamin D-enriched formula when their children were at a younger age than did the Norwegian mothers. Such reduced duration of breast-feeding was not found in another study that compared Pakistani and Norwegian mothers (Arsky, 1996). Thus, immigrant groups may adapt in varying ways to urbanized life in Norway.

Because the mothers' vitamin D status during pregnancy and breast-feeding is important to the vitamin D status of infants, we discuss some studies that describe the diet and vitamin D blood levels among pregnant and nonpregnant immigrant women in Norway. A study of pregnant Pakistani women in Oslo found that they consumed substantially less fish (median 15 g a day) than their Norwegian counterparts (median 56 g a day, $p < .001$), whereas butter, margarine, and egg consumption was not significantly different (Henriksen, 1995). The Pakistani women's median blood serum levels of 25-hydroxy vitamin D (which is the best indicator for vitamin D status) was less than half the recommended level, whereas the Norwegian women had median levels just above the recommended level. A study of adult women from five countries confirmed the low serum levels of 25-hydroxy vitamin D among those from Pakistan (Holvik, Meyer, Haug, & Brunvand, 2005). Those from Turkey, Sri Lanka, Iran, and Vietnam had somewhat higher values, but still substantially below the recommended level. The intake of cod liver oil and fatty fish were powerful predictors of vitamin D status. Length of education and obesity were also predictors of vitamin D status among these women. Thus, it is likely that the mothers from these countries had such low vitamin D status that it affected the vitamin D status of their children.

Pregnant Pakistani and Norwegian women also were studied with regard to iron status. The Pakistani women had significantly lower iron stores as measured by serum ferritin (mean 7 µg/l) compared with the Norwegian women (mean 25 µg/l), whereas no significant differences were found for hemoglobin (Brunvand, Henriksen, Larsson, & Sandberg, 1995). Fewer Pakistani than Norwegian women had received iron supplementation during pregnancy, and no differences were found in the dietary iron intake or the intake of organic fiber, tea, ascorbic acid, meat, or cereals. However, the dietary intake of phytate (which may inhibit iron absorption) from bread and chapati was significantly higher among the Pakistani women. Thus, iron deficiency appears to be far more common among pregnant Pakistani women in Norway than among pregnant Norwegian women, and the main reason may be a combination of a higher parity and a less common use of iron supplementation and a higher content of phytate in the Pakistani diet. Iron deficiency in pregnancy may be an important contributor to infants' low iron stores at birth and iron deficiency among immigrant children.

A critical period may arise when the child is weaned from the breast. A study of 1-year-old children of immigrants (mostly from Turkey) and Norwegian children showed that the Norwegian children had a higher intake of foods that are good sources of vitamin D or iron such as meat, fish, liver paste, and whole-grain bread, whereas the immigrant children had a higher intake of rice, fruit, vegetables, sweets, biscuits, and chips, which are either poor sources of iron or contain iron that is less absorbable (Wandel et al., 1996, see Table 1). Some of these foods also contribute substantially to the intake of sugar and fat. Both the immigrant and the Norwegian children received almost 50% of their iron from iron-fortified infant cereal, and there was no difference between the two groups. It was also found that the duration of exclusive breast-feeding and the intake of liver paste were significantly and positively associated with iron stores (ferritin values), whereas weight gain and the intake of vegetables were inversely related to iron stores. At 2 years of age, the Norwegian children had a higher intake of soft drinks, whole-grain bread, and various iron-rich bread spreads than the immigrant children, who had a higher intake of orange juice and citrus fruits (which may enhance iron absorption) than the Norwegian children (Fagerli et al., 1996).

A study of the same children's diet at 4 years of age showed only a few differences between the children of immigrants and Norwegian children (Antonsen, 2000). Norwegian children ate more iron-rich bread spreads such as whey cheese and liver paste, whereas the immigrant children ate more yogurt and drank more juice. The immigrant children from Turkey obtained a higher score on three indexes consisting of foods rich in sugar, fat, and vitamin C and lower on one index consisting of foods that contribute to iron intake. The other immigrant children scored higher on foods rich in sugar and lower on foods rich in iron. The study of 2- and 4-year-olds from Somalia showed that the percentage of energy from fat exceeded recommendations (National Nutrition Council, 2005), and the intake of sugar was well below recommendations for both age groups (Madar, 1997). However, the intake of iron was only approximately half of that recommended, and the intake of vitamin D only 20% of recommended amounts (for 2 year olds) and 40% (for 4 year olds).

Taken together, these studies indicate that although shortage of food is not a problem for immigrant families, children of immigrants may have nutritional problems that need attention. Children of preschool age consumed more biscuits and cookies, sweets, and chips than did Norwegian children. Immigrant children develop a preference for Western foods in kindergarten and school and often choose foods both for snacks and lunch that override parental preferences. Unfortunately, these Western food preferences are often for foods high in sugar and low in fiber, vitamins, and minerals. The children's nutritional problems are related to the mother's nutritional status with regard to iron and vitamin D, as well as to the content of these nutrients in the diet of the child during weaning. The problem appears to be more aggravated for infants and very young children. However, attention also should be paid to the other preschool children.

NUTRITIONAL CHALLENGES AND FOOD HABITS IN SCHOOLCHILDREN AND ADOLESCENTS

Few studies in Norway have described the nutritional status and eating habits of schoolchildren from immigrant families. A study of 9- and 15-year-old children in Oslo included both ethnic Norwegians and immigrants from both developed and developing countries (Natland Sannan, 2003). In this analysis, the population was divided into Caucasians (originating from Northern and Western Europe except Turkey, North America, and Oceania) and non-Caucasians (from Eastern Europe, Asia, Africa, South and Central America, and Turkey). No significant differences were noted in anthropometrical indexes (height, weight, body mass index [BMI]) between the Caucasian and non-Caucasian children except for the 15-year-old girls: the Caucasian girls were significantly taller (median 168 cm) than the non-Caucasian girls (median 166 cm).

There was no significant difference in the total daily energy intake. However, the non-Caucasian children had a higher intake of foods for which the National Nutrition Council (2005) recommends reduced consumption such as whole milk, table fats, chocolate, and snacks, and they skipped breakfast more often than the Caucasians. However, there was no difference between the groups with regard to the percentage of calories from fat, saturated fat, and sugar. The percentage was higher than that recommended for both ethnic groups and age groups. All the groups had a high intake of sweetened soft drinks, and their consumption of vegetables was far below recommendations. The intake of iron and vitamin D from the diet in both ethnic groups was lower than recommended.

In a large population-based study (2000–2001) of adolescents (15–16 year olds) from all Oslo schools, ethnic differences in BMI also were observed in the immigrant groups. Of the 9.4% who were overweight (above the 85th percentile), the highest proportion originated from Western countries, whereas the highest proportion of adolescents who were underweight (below the 24th percentile) originated from the Indian subcontinent. Interestingly, these differences in BMI were not associated with socioeconomic factors or physical activity. However, significant associations of BMI were found with ethnicity and dietary habits including dieting. An ethnic dichotomy of overweight and underweight is evident, with the Western, Eastern European, and Middle Eastern/North African groups being more likely to be overweight, whereas those from the Indian subcontinent, sub-Saharan Africa, and East Asia more likely to be underweight. However, the overall proportion of overweight adolescents was not as high as might have been expected, especially compared with adolescents in the United States and European countries. Our study shows that the proportion of overweight adolescents from the Indian subcontinent compared with adults (first-generation immigrants) is very low (Kumar, Meyer, Wandel, Dalen, & Holmboe-Ottesen, 2005). Further comparisons with studies from the Indian subcontinent show that the results are not dissimilar from those from urban areas in terms of overweight, but they are lower in terms of underweight, especially in rural areas.

Because adolescents are at a developmental stage in a life cycle of continually changing body size and shape, longitudinal data would have been extremely valuable. This is also a phase when cultural factors play an important role, and ethnic identity, particularly for immigrants, is important in making choices.

Differences in health outcomes of various ethnic groups have received growing attention over the past two decades. Ethnic groups are maintained through culture and socialization, but it is difficult to classify and define them, as this would assume social homogeneity. Differences in socioeconomic status among ethnic groups of adolescents are apparent in our study, where most from non-Western countries belonged to the lower classes. Notwithstanding these limitations, the data indicate an unusually high proportion of uneducated mothers among the ethnic minorities. Most immigrants live in the eastern, more disadvantaged part of Oslo, known and described as the East–West divide. This is in accordance with the contention that people from ethnic minorities are concentrated in particular geographic locations that are likely to be more deprived. Interestingly, our analysis revealed that most immigrants, regardless of social class, live in the eastern part of the city, and this may be attributable to their being more comfortable among their own ethnic group as well as economic factors.

In addition to socioeconomic differences, lifestyle factors varied with ethnicity. Consistent with their food traditions, the Mediterranean group of adolescents consumed more fruits and vegetables. Conversely, the Indian subcontinent group's low consumption of fruits and vegetables deviates from their traditional diet, which is abundant in vegetables and fruits, suggesting postmigration changes. In addition, gender differences showed that boys consumed more soft drinks (58%) and full-fat milk (65.6%) daily than girls (41% and 34%). Snacking is popular, with 49% consuming chocolates or candy and 33% consuming salty snacks daily. The association of skipping breakfast with higher BMI may be because of consuming high-calorie snack foods later in the day or practicing dieting. The inverse relationship with chocolate and candy and full-fat milk consumption and BMI also observed in other studies indicates complex underlying behavioral processes. We found that those who were overweight were more likely to go on diets. Moreover, dieting is a widespread teenage phenomenon that may be independent of weight, particularly in the case of girls. Despite ethnic variations, eating and drinking habits associated with adolescent behavior such as snacking, skipping meals, and dieting are similar to those found in other studies in Europe, and in this regard, ethnic minorities are much like their European peers.

THE ROLE OF CHILDREN IN DIETARY CHANGES

Our recent in-depth study among Pakistani women in Oslo confirmed that dietary changes might be attributable to length of stay in Norway (Dhirad et al., in press). Table 1 shows the most salient postmigratory changes, with a reduced consumption of cooked vegetables, lentils, and chapati (whole-wheat unleavened bread) and an increased consumption of soft drinks and animal and diary products. Interestingly, although total fat consumption may not have changed, the type of fat has changed from ghee (clarified butter) to oil.

Results from a study on women's reports of changes in food habits after migration showed that children greatly influenced the choice of foods for snacks and for family meals (Mellin-Olsen & Wandel 2005). Many of the immigrant women only came into direct contact with the Norwegian food culture in hospitals. Their children, on the other hand, were more familiar with Norwegian cuisine from being exposed to it in kindergarten and school and through their Norwegian peers. Many of these immigrant mothers, because they are not familiar with either the Norwegian culture or language, must rely on their children to gain both access to and knowledge of this culture. Therefore, they are quick to respond to their children's requests, believing that the children know better, and are uncritical of their choices. This is a frequent reason for changes in eating habits following migration. Thus, some traditional dishes such as those made with beans, lentils, and vegetables may be discarded from the menu, because the children will not eat them. Some women make special dishes for their children, typically containing potatoes, fish, or chicken. Others try to find something that the whole family will eat. The following story from a study of Pakistani women in Oslo (Kumar, 2001) exemplifies the role that children may play in the dietary changes of the family.

Salmana and her 4 children left their village in Pakistan in the late seventies and followed her husband to Norway. When asked about food preferences she responded by quoting that the adults preferred traditional Pakistani dishes whereas the children preferred Norwegian food. When asked why they did so, she responded that they were rather contemptuous of the simple dal (lentils) and vegetables (sabzi) as foods to be consumed in the village whereas they preferred the modern Norwegian food (these being pizza, French fries, fish fingers, sweet buns, biscuits and cakes). In many ways, she inclined to agree with their choice but for other reasons. When she arrived in Norway, the variety of vegetables was rather limited, fairly expensive and since she was used to fresh farm produce she felt that the lack of the sun in cold north had interfered with the ripening process and the vegetables were tasteless. Moreover, meat and dairy products were cheap and though she had rarely consumed meat on a daily basis before this had become a part of the lifestyle in Norway. When asked about the traditional dishes she, while recounting, realized that there were changes that she had never reflected upon herself. A curry with mincemeat would consist of half a kilo of mincemeat and nearly 3 times that amount of vegetables in Pakistan whereas the ratios were reversed in Norway indicating changes in both food availability and price. Even though she disapproves of the children's liking for Western foods, she nonetheless goes along with it as it means they eat at home rather than taking to the street food. She prefers this way of doing it, since home preparations are safer and more reliable. In addition, her own resistance to change has also been influenced by the fact that Western food is quick and easy to prepare compared to traditional Pakistani curries and chapati. (p. 000)

This story shows that changes in food habits are tied to practical, everyday life situations where children play an important role. Children also may act as sources of nutrition information that they receive in school or through habits they have picked up in school and visiting friends and neighbors. Often immigrants are not conscious of these changes in food habits (Kumar, 2001).

THE TASK AHEAD: IMPLICATIONS FOR HEALTH POLICY AND NUTRITION EDUCATION

Multicultural societies are here to stay, and they bring with them a new set of public health challenges. Because immigrants are now part of the demographics, determining their health priorities becomes important, and this in turn has implications for health policy, planning, and allocation of resources. It is evident that unfavorable dietary changes and physical inactivity are factors that contribute to the obesity and diabetes epidemics. Minorities must be considered when strategies for health education, promotion, and prevention are being developed in the evolving multiethnic societies of Europe. Children and youth warrant special attention, because changes among them may be crucial in delaying or preventing the onset of chronic disease in adult life.

The change from traditional to more Westernized or Norwegian food habits may have various nutritional consequences in immigrant groups and in various age groups. Many immigrant groups in Norway come from countries where the traditional diet in rural areas is low in fat, sugar, and meat and includes generous amounts of beans, lentils, and greens. Some also include generous amounts of vegetables and fruits. Migration to urban areas in Western countries is often accompanied by an increase in fat, sugar, and meat intake, which together with reduced physical activity may predispose to overweight and lifestyle diseases such as diabetes and coronary disease.

Immigration to Norway also entails less sun exposure, especially during the winter months, and the consequent reduction in outdoor activities also may contribute to this. Those who come from inland areas where fish is not a substantial part of the traditional diet and who do not take cod liver oil (or other fish oils) run the risk insufficient vitamin D in the diet to compensate for less sun exposure. In food preparation, most immigrants use vegetable oils that are not fortified with vitamin D (Råberg, 2005), and it has been shown that the diets of both children and adults are low in vitamin D (Holvik et al., 2005). Thus, a change toward the Norwegian diet that includes fatty fish and supplementation with cod liver oil in the winter months would be beneficial for both children and adults if they could accept this.

It is important that nutrition educators point out the negative aspects of changing to a more Westernized diet, as well more positive aspects (e.g., a change in dietary habits may bring nutritional benefits). It is also important to find culturally acceptable ways to suggest nutritional improvements. Besides determining the content, and tailor made to suit the method of transmission should be relevant to the requirements of these groups. There is a need to increase understanding of the cultural attributes of health-related behaviors. Health education needs to be emphasized, with a focus on nutrition and physical activity. Unhealthy lifestyle choices, especially those that affect the development of eating habits and physical activity in adolescence, need to be further examined. Studies of the underlying processes involved in making these choices are required to gain a better understanding. Finally, the genes only "load the gun," but the environment "pulls the trigger," and we owe it to our future generations to provide them with a better environment that encourages sound nutritional practices.

REFERENCES

Alvin, N., Eden, M. D., Mohammad, A, & Mir, M. D. (1997). Iron deficiency in 1- to 3-year-old children. A paediatric failure? *Archives of Pediatric and Adolescent Medicine, 151,* 986–988.

Antonsen, R. (2000). *Jernstatus, Kostutvikling og Kosthold Med Særlig vekt på Jerninntak Blant Friske Fireåringer (Iron Status, Dietary Changes and Diet With Special Focus on Iron Intake, Among Healthy 4-Year Olds).* Unpublished master's thesis, Institute for Nutrition Research, University of Oslo, Norway.

Arsky, G. H. (1996). *Kosthold, Kostutvikling Og Jernstatus Blant Friske Ettåringer (Dietary Habits, Dietary Changes and Iron Status Among Healthy 1-Year Old Infants).* Unpublished master's thesis, Institute for Nutrition Research, University of Oslo, Norway.

Beard, J. L. (2001). Iron biology in immune function, muscle metabolism and neuronal functioning. *Journal of Nutrition, 131,* 568S–580S.

Brunvand, L., & Brunvatne, R. (2001). Helseproblemer blant innvandrerbarn i Norge (Health problems among immigrant children). *Tidsskrift for den Norske Lægeforening, 121*(6), 715–718.

Brunvand, L, Henriksen, C, Larsson, M., & Sandberg, A.-S. (1995). Iron deficiency among pregnant Pakistanis in Norway and the content of phytic acid in their diet. *Acta Obstetricia et Gynecologica Scandinavica, 74,* 520–525.

Brunvand, L., & Nordshus, T. (1996). Alimentær rakitt. (Alimentary rickets). *Nordisk Medicin, 111*(7), 219–221.

Brunvand, L., & Sander, J. (1993). Jernmangelanemi hos innvandrerbarn fra utviklingsland (Iron deficiency anaemia among immigrant children from development countries). *Tidskrift for Norsk Lægeforening, 113,* 1719–1720.

Brustad, M. (2004). *Vitamin D Security in Northern Norway in Relation to Marine Food Traditions.* Unpublished doctoral dissertation, ISM skriftserie nr 71, University of Tromsø, Norway.

Cook, J. D. (1994). Iron deficiency anaemia. *Bailliere's Clinical Haematology, 7,* 787–804.

Dawes, T., Kumar, B. N., & Middelthon, A. O. (in press). A qualitative study of perceptions of dietary fat intake in Pakistani women aged 42 to 70 years in Oslo. *Abstract Book, 5th Asian Diabetes Conference.*

Dhirad, A., Kumar, B. N., & Holmboe-Ottesen, G. (in press). Lifestyle and health among Pakistani women in Oslo, Norway. *Abstract Book, 5th Asian Diabetes Conference.*

Fagerli, R., Wandel, M., Olsen, P. T., Ek, J., Thorstensen, K., Brekke, O.-L., & Borch-Iohnsen, B. (1996). Iron status and diet at two years of age: A longitudinal study of healthy Norwegian and immigrant children. *Scandinavian Journal of Nutrition, 40:* 58–63.

Fairweather-Tait, S. J. (1992). Iron deficiency in infancy; easy to prevent—Or is it? *European Journal of Clinical Nutrition, 46,* 9–14.

Grantham-McGregor, S., & Ani, C. (2001). A review of studies on the effect of iron deficiency on cognitive development in children. *Journal of Nutrition, 131,* 649S–668S.

Henriksen, C. (1995). Diet and vitamin D status among pregnant Pakistani women in Oslo. *European Journal of Clinical Nutrition, 49,* 211–218.

Hercberg, S., Papoz, L., Galin, P., Guery, M. F., Farnier, M. A., & Rossignol, C. (1987). Iron status and dietary pattern in young children. *Nutrition Reports International, 35,* 307–315.

Holick, M. F. (1994). Vitamin D. In M. Shils, J. A. Olson, & M. Shike (Eds.), *Modern Nutrition in Health and Disease* (8th ed., pp. 308–325). Malvern, UK: Lea & Febiger.

Holvik, K., Meyer, H. E., Haug, E., & Brunvand, L. (2005). Prevalence and predictors of vitamin D deficiency in five immigrant groups living in Oslo, Norway: The Oslo Immigrant Health Study. *European Journal of Clinical Nutrition, 59,* 57–63.

Krieger, E. H., Claussen, A. H., & Scott, K. G. (1999). Early childhood anemia and mild or moderate mental retardation. *American Journal of Clinical Nutrition, 69,* 115–119.

Kumar, B. N. (2001). *Nutrition and Health of Immigrants from South Asia.* Oslo, Norway.

Kumar, B. N. (2004). Food in a Multicultural Nordic perspective. *Abstract Book, 8th Nordic Nutrition Conference, 2004.* Tønsberg, Norway: Norwegian Nutrition Society.

Kumar, B. N., Meyer, H. E., Wandel, M., Dalen, I., & Holmboe-Ottesen, G. (2005). Ethnic differences in obesity among immigrants from developing countries, in Oslo, Norway. *International Journal of Obesity-Related Metabolic Disorders, __,* 000–000.

Kumar, B. N., Wandel, M., & Holmboe-Ottesen, G. (2003). Factors influencing healthy eating habits among ethnic minorities in Oslo, Norway. *Annals of Nutrition and Metabolism, 47,* 400–401.

Lande, B., Andersen, L. F., Bærug, A., Trygg, K. U., Lund-Larsen, K., Veierød, M. B., & Bjørnebo, G.-E. (2003). Infant feeding practices and associated factors in the first six months of life: The Norwegian Infant Nutrition Survey. *Acta Pædiatrica, 92,* 152–161.

Lie, B. (2002). *Innvandring og innvandrere 2002.* Oslo, Norway: Statistisk sentralbyrå.

Lozoff, B., Wolf, A. W., & Jimenez, E. (1996). Iron-deficiency anemia and infant development: Effects of extended oral iron therapy. *Journal of Pediatrics, 129,* 382–389.

Madar, A. (1997). *Kosthold og Jernstatus hos Somaliske Barn, 2–4 år i Osloregionen (Diet and Iron Status Among Somalian Children, 2–4 Years of Age in the Oslo Region).* Unpublished master's thesis, Institute for Nutrition Research, University of Oslo, Norway.

Major, P. (1995–1996). Jernmangelanemi og spedbarns psykomotoriske utvikling (Iron deficiency anemia and psychomotor development in infants). *Tidsskrift for den norske lægeforeningen, 114,* 1995–1996.

Mellin-Olsen, T. & Wandel, M. (2005). Changes in food habits among Pakistani immigrant women in Oslo, Norway. *Ethnicity and Health, 10*(4): 311–339.

National Nutrition Council. (2001). *Anbefalinger for Spedbarnsernæring (Recommendations for Infant Nutrition)*. Oslo, Norway: Statens råd for Ernæring og Fysisk Aktivitet. (www.sef.no).

National Nutrition Council. (2005). *NORSKE anbefalinger for Ernæring og Fysisk Aktivitet (Norwegian Recommendations for Nutrition and Physical Activity)*. Oslo, Norway: Norwegian Social and Health Directorate (www.sef.no).

Natland Sannan, S. T. (2003). *Etniske Forskjeller i Kostvaner Blant 9-åringer og 15-åringer i Oslo (Ethnic Differences in Dietary Habits Among 9-Year Olds and 15-Year Olds in Oslo)*. Unpublished master's thesis, Institute for Nutrition Research, University of Oslo, Norway.

Politt, E. (2000). Developmental sequel from early nutritional deficiencies: Conclusive and probability judgements. *Journal of Nutrition, 130,* 350S–353S.

Råberg, M. (2005). *Kostholdsendringer Blant Voksne Innvandrere i Oslo i Relasjon til Integrering i Det Norske Samfunnet (Dietary Changes Among Adult Immigrants in the Oslo Region in Relation to Integration into the Norwegian Society)*. Unpublished master's thesis, Department of Nutrition, University of Oslo, Norway.

Rao, M. S. A (1986) Conservatism and Change in Food Habits Among the Migrants in India: A Study in Gastrodynamics. In R. S. Khare and M. S. A Rao (Eds.), *Food, Society and Culture: Aspects in South Asian Food Systems* (pp. 121–140). Durham, NC: Carolina Academic Press.

Solem, I. H. (1982). *Barnemat, Kultur og Samfunn. En Undersøkelse av Amming og Småbarns Kosthold og Helse Blant Innvandrere i Oslo (Children's Food, Culture and Society. A Study of Breast-Feeding and Children's Diet and Health Among Immigrants in Oslo)*. Unpublished master's thesis, Institute for Nutrition Research, University of Oslo, Norway.

Walter, T. (1994). Effect of iron-deficiency anaemia on cognitive skills in infancy and childhood. *Baillieres Clinical Haematology, 7,* 815–827.

Wandel, M., Fagerli, R., Olsen, P. T., Borch-Iohnsen, B., & Ek, J. (1996). Iron status and weaning practices among Norwegian and immigrant infants. *Nutrition Research, 16,* 251–265.

Introduction to Part II

They Are Here: Newcomers in the Schools

All over the world, teachers are encountering children different from themselves in race, ethnicity, culture, language, and socioeconomic status. Although some teachers have grown up surrounded by diversity, others lack experience with a heterogeneous society. Many preservice teachers have not themselves attended schools with people of another race or lived in cross-cultural neighborhoods, and their understanding of racially diverse students may be vague (Ford, 1996; Milner, 2003; Milner & Woolfolk Hoy, 2003). As a result, some teachers may rely on stereotypical concepts of racially diverse students that in turn may cause them consciously or unconsciously to think of their racially diverse students through deficit models (Milner; Milner & Woolfolk Hoy). Few teachers are themselves from diverse backgrounds. For example, in the United States, despite an increasingly diverse student population, the teaching force continues to be predominantly European-American, middle-class, and female, with only 10% coming from ethnic minorities (Taylor & Sobel, 2003; Ward & Ward, 2003).

The complex act of teaching requires that teachers understand individual differences in their students as well as the sociocultural context in which they have been raised and socialized (Barrere & Kramer, 1997). Children and youth in immigrant families are the fastest-growing component of the child and youth population in the countries described in part II: Israel, the United States, and Greece. It is expected that the trend for expansion of the population of children and youth in these countries will be through immigrants and births to immigrants and their descendants (Hernandez, 2004; Kasimis & Kassimi, 2004; Organization for Economic Cooperation and Development [OECD], 2005). The studies in part II explore a number of challenges faced by the immigrant and refugee children and their families when they first encounter the school system in the host country. Also described are the challenges faced by teachers in understanding and supporting the complex needs of these children. As the three chapters demonstrate, teachers often have multiple concerns about the students in their classes, including their wide range of academic abilities and some with special learning and behavioral needs. Reaching out to the newly arrived child, particularly when there are language and cultural barriers, adds to what may already be a demanding situation for the classroom teacher.

The study in chapter 3 in part I does not distinguish among immigrant students based on their time of arrival in the host country or the degree to which a family may continue to see itself as an immigrant family after arrival. However, chapter 6 in this part describes only newly arrived children and families and considers the *immediate* adjustment needs of children who enroll in a school system shortly after arrival. Regardless of how researchers define the immigrant student, teachers must teach students from racially, culturally, linguistically, and religiously diverse groups, as well as newly arrived students. This task however, is neither simple nor easy. Chapter 6 shows the limitations of advanced teacher training in addressing the needs of newly arrived students in the class and the need for teacher assistance when the situation arises.

Immigrants have historically tended to cluster in particular destinations, and countries around the world have communities that bear witness to past waves of migration from China, Greece, Italy, and the Nordic nations. Israel and Greece were two of many countries to receive a massive flow of immigrants from the former Soviet Union (FSU) beginning in the late 1980s as a result of radical changes in the Russian political system and its emigration policy (Shamai, Ilatov, Psalti, & Deliyanni, 2002). Chapter 7 reports on the return of Jewish Russian and Ethiopian immigrants to Israel. The authors describe the various levels of social and economic integration of these two groups into Israeli society and the views of fathers on the socialization of their children after immigration both at home and in school. The authors state that despite these two immigrant populations developing ties in their own cultural groups, they experience different levels of social and economic integration into the Israeli system, with the Russian immigrants becoming more highly integrated and the Ethiopian immigrants generally remaining segregated. A theoretical framework of an "*adaptive adult*" is considered in investigating the connection between the cultural ideologies of the child's socializing agents and his or her performance in school. It is suggested that the image of the adaptive adult helps educators understand the cultural basis of immigrant parents' expectations. When teachers recognize cultural differences and understand the cultural lag and cultural logic, they are more likely to avoid the sense of frustration they may otherwise experience in the light of what might otherwise be considered parents' personalities or objections to the host culture's educational approach. Thus, awareness of the differences that exist between cultures helps bridge the gaps by reducing incidences of misjudgment, stereotyping, and misunderstanding.

Shamai et al. (2002) reported that FSU immigrants have influenced how Israeli society treats its minorities, allowing more space to ethnic groups than before because of the cultural negotiation process initiated by the immigrants. Conversely, FSU immigrants into Greece may be more interested in assimilation, which is in keeping with Greek societal views, and many of the immigrants appear to prefer to downplay the differences between themselves and the Greek host society.

The central theme in the Israeli national ethos of reunification of the Jewish nation is reflected in a proactive endeavor to attract Jewish immigration to Israel. However, in Greece, as in many countries, immigrants are kept in the back of people's minds and excluded from the social milieu or even overtly excluded from population statistics as if they did not exist (Fakiolas, 2003). The Greek government has been forced to adopt a regularization procedure under often-contradictory pressures (Kasimis & Kassimi, 2004). From one side, in an environment of growing xenophobia, the public demanded registration of immigrants. From another side, human rights and labor organizations sought more humanitarian and less exploitative treatment. Chapter 8 describes how children of immigrants in northern Greece start preschool and the implications for schools in easing the initial transition of young children into a group setting. The adjustment of the entire immigrant family bears consideration by the schools. Concerns about parents' involvement with their children's education become more intense where there are language and cultural barriers between the newly arrived families and the school personnel. Hernandez (2004) pointed out that immigrant parents may be unfamiliar or uncomfortable with participating in the schooling of their children, and many may have lower levels of education than average parents in the host country. Parents participating in the studies in this chapter echo these points, together with other problems that create barriers between home and school.

A common issue explored in the chapters in part II is language and its role in acculturation and school success. Research indicates that nearly all language-minority children and adolescents are language brokers for their parents and other family members (Tse, 1995). Children from diverse language backgrounds as young as 8 or 9 years old perform difficult and demanding linguistic and communication tasks normally done by adults, both related and unrelated to school activities. Brokering itself exposes the children to more language and helps them acquire better language skills. For immigrants and refugees, the brokering process typically begins soon after arrival in the host country. Studies in the United States also suggest that brokering helps students maintain native language skills as well as develop skills in English. English-language skills achieved through brokering are not always reflected in academic achievement, however, suggesting that school settings do not always provide an accurate picture of students' competence. Alternative assessment methods are usually needed to measure the skills of newly immigrated students.

REFERENCES

Barrere, L., & Kramer, L. (1997). From monologues to skills dialogues: Teaching the process of crafting culturally competent early childhood environments. In P. J. Winton, J. A. McCullum, & C. Catlett (Eds.), *Reforming Personnel Preparation in Early Intervention* (pp. 217–251). Baltimore, MD: Paul H. Brookes.

Fakiolas, R. (2003). Regularising undocumented immigrants in Greece: Procedures and effects. *Journal of Ethnic and Migration Studies, 29,* 535–561.

Ford, D. Y. (1996). *Reversing Underachievement Among Gifted Black Students: Promising Practices and Programs.* New York: Teachers College Press.

Hernandez, D. (2004). Children and Youth in Immigrant Families: Demographic, social, and educational issues. In J. A. Banks & C. A. McG. Banks, *Handbook of Research on Multicultural Education* (pp. 404–419). San Francisco: Jossey-Bass.

Kasimis, C., & Kassimi, C. (2004). *Greece: A History of Migration.* Washington, DC: Migration Policy Institute. Retrieved November 8, 2004, from http://www.migrationinformation.org/Profiles/display.cfm?id=228

Milner, H. R. (2003). Reflection, racial competence, and critical pedagogy: How do we prepare pre-service teachers to pose tough questions? *Race, Ethnicity and Education, 6,* 193–208.

Milner, H. R., & Woolfolk Hoy, A. (2003). A case study of an African American teachers' self-efficacy, stereotype threat, and persistence. *Teaching and Teacher Education, 19,* 263–276.

Organization for Economic Cooperation and Development (OECD). (2005). *Trends in International Migration: Annual Report, SOPEMI, 2004 Edition.* Retrieved August 19, 2005, from http://www.databeuro.com/acatalog/sopemi_2004_TOC.pdf

Shamai, S., Ilatov, Z., Psalti, A., & Deliyanni, K. (2002). Acculturation of Soviet immigrant parents in Israel and Greece. *International Journal of Sociology of the Family, 30*(1), 21–49.

Taylor, S. V., & Sobel, D. M. (2003). Missing in action: Research on the accountability of multicultural, inclusive teacher education. *Essays in Education, 2*(2), 1–23.

Tse, L. (1995). *When students translate for parents: Effects of language brokering.* San Diego, CA: California Association for Bilingual Education. (ERIC Document Retrieval Service No. ED402733).

Ward, M. J., & Ward, C. J. (2003). Promoting cross-cultural competence in pre-service teachers through second language use. *Education, 123,* 532–536.

Chapter 6

Teachers', Children's, and Parents' Perspectives on Newly Arrived Children's Adjustment to Elementary School

Leah D. Adams
Eastern Michigan University, USA

Krista M. Shambleau
Michigan State University, USA

The increased mobility of families around the world influences schools and challenges educators. Children in immigrant families are the fastest growing segment of the child population in the United States, with one of every five children in the United States living in a household where one or both parents are foreign born. (Hernandez, 2004). During the 1990s, more than 14 million immigrants entered the United States, exceeding the flow in any decade in the nation's history. Entry of another 14 million immigrants is expected between 2000 and 2010 (Fix & Passel, 2003). Friedlander (1991) wrote that the wave of immigration in the latter decades of the 20th century had such a profound effect on the society that it could almost be regarded as the equivalent of a demographic revolution. This impact is perhaps most obvious in the schools.

While the ethnic profile of newly arrived children (NAC) is diverse, the effect of the rapidly changing demographics in communities means that educators across the land face a similar agenda of challenge and opportunity incorporating the new arrivals into the schools. (Northwest Regional Educational Laboratory [NWREL], 2001). NAC enroll with various degrees of preparation and educational competencies, and most present significant challenges to the educational setting. Some of the needs include developing English language skills and understanding academic concepts that are required to function effectively in US schools. In addition, some NAC have inadequate or missing academic preparation, which complicates their placement within age-appropriate classrooms.

Children may have missed critical years of classroom experience, often cannot read or write in their own language, and have not mastered the basics of either rote learning or the use of higher-level cognitive strategies (Suárez-Orozco & Suárez-Orozco, 2001). Others have needs that go beyond academic concerns, such as difficulties at home or personal traumas, which need attention along with their education (NWREL, 2001).

School is the defined environment where the child comes in continuous, first-hand contact with other cultures through the multiple interactions within that context (Sam & Oppedal, 2002). At school, immigrant children are immediately and vigorously challenged with the new culture. Even if the people within the school context represent a variety of cultures, their activities within the school setting are determined by a superimposed group culture of the majority. Success in the new culture means establishing successful peer relations, learning the language, and doing well in school (Kirova & Wu, 2002). The school context includes numerous interactions with teachers and other children that may or may not support the function of adaptation in cognitive and social development.

In American society, it is generally expected for school-age children to achieve in school (academic competence); to get along with other children and develop friendships (social competence); and to follow rules of behavior in the home, school, and community (conduct) (Masten & Powell, 2003). Early intervention in the education of immigrant children has been reported as being critical to later well-being. (Beiser, Dion, Gotowiec, Hyman, & Vu, 1995; Hyman, Vu & Beiser, 2000). The implication is for educators to have the knowledge and skills that allow them to support children with immigrant backgrounds through their transition and adjustment in both the cognitive and social domains.

The purpose of this study was to investigate a variety of elementary school classroom strategies that support the transition and adjustment of NAC. The study was based on the assumptions that the number of immigrant students is a significant factor in the schools, the diversity of cultures in the classroom affects the teaching–learning process (Yale Center in Child Development and Social Policy, 2003), and the school is a primary resource for the adjustment of NAC and their families (Suárez-Orozco & Suárez-Orozco, 2001).

METHOD AND PROCEDURES

Sample

Administrators from four school districts in a Midwestern urban/suburban area identified the schools in their districts with the highest percentage of newly immigrated students. A total of nine schools in the four districts were selected and 112 elementary teachers in those schools were surveyed about teaching strategies they use in the classroom. The teachers were invited to participate in a more extensive follow up interview, and 25 (22%) chose to be interviewed.

A summary of demographic information for the teacher sample used for this study is presented in Table 1. The sample was a multiethnic group with considerable teaching experience (mean 12.8 years, SD = 9.3). The majority (83%) reported having previous experience teaching NAC with an average of 6 years of experience (SD = 5.5). They had an average of 24.41 students in their classrooms (SD = 5.8), including an average of two NAC (SD = 2.2) at the time of the survey. Table 2 summarizes the number of NAC by region that the teachers had experience with in their classrooms. The demographics for the 25 teachers who volunteered to be interviewed were almost identical to those for the total teacher sample in terms of grades taught and race or ethnicity. The teachers who were interviewed had an average of 14 years teaching experience (SD = 9).

In addition, 10 parents who had arrived in the United States within the past 3 years were interviewed along with 11 of their children. The families had been in the United States for an average of 2 years at the time of the interview. Table 3 displays genders and native countries of the parents and children.

Procedures and Measures

The project investigator attended a staff meeting at each school where permission had been granted to collect data. Teachers were made aware that participation was voluntary and that all responses would remain anonymous. The survey forms contained both closed and open-ended questions and focused on teaching strategies that teachers have used or would use for NAC. After completed surveys were submitted, teachers were invited to volunteer to discuss their strategies and experiences in greater detail in an individual interview.

Parent and child participants were identified by community agencies, groups, and people outside of the schools who had contact with newly arrived families. The parents and children were assured anonymity. They were interviewed at the location of their choice. An interpreter was used for 30% (*n* = 3) of the parent interviews and 18% (*n* = 2) of the child interviews.

The parent interview questions asked about the family's transnational migration, family support system, English proficiency, and perspectives on their

TABLE 1
Survey Teacher Ethnicity and Grade Levels

Characteristic	Number	Percent
Ethnicity		
African American	7	6%
Arab American	14	13%
Asian Pacific Islander	2	2%
Caucasian	84	77%
Native American	1	1%
Bi-Racial	1	1%
Current Grade Levels		
Kindergarten	11	10%
1st grade	21	19%
2nd grade	20	18%
3rd grade	17	15%
4th grade	22	19%
5th grade	21	19%

TABLE 2
Newly Arrived Children by Region

Region	Number	Percent
Africa		
Eastern Africa	3	2%
The Americas		
Caribbean	4	2%
Central America	28	17%
South America	3	2%
Asia		
Eastern Asia	43	26%
South-central Asia	10	6%
Western Asia	54	32%
Europe		
Eastern Europe	1	1%
Southern Europe	16	10%
Western Europe	4	2%

TABLE 3
Parent and Child Demographics

Characteristic	Number	Percent
Parent Gender		
Male	1	10%
Female	9	90%
Parent Country		
Pakistan	1	10%
India	1	10%
Turkey	1	10%
China	1	10%
Columbia	1	10%
Yemen	1	10%
Lebanon	2	20%
Mexico	2	20%
Child Gender		
Male	7	64%
Female	4	36%
Child Country		
Pakistan	1	9%
India	1	9%
Turkey	1	9%
China	1	9%
Columbia	2	18%
Yemen	1	9%
Lebanon	1	9%
Mexico	3	27%

children's school experiences. The child interview questions asked children about their transnational migration, school experiences, and social relationships at school. Some of the same questions were asked of both parents and children.

Analysis

The method of data collection allowed the project investigators to analyze school experiences from multiple perspectives within the confines of qualitative analysis. Qualitative data analysis was used to find patterns of congruence and incongruence among teachers, children, and parents in terms of their understandings and misunderstandings of each other. Analysis of teacher, child, and parent interview responses entailed systematically grouping and summarizing the answers. Qualitative inquiry was used to understand the school context of NAC and to reflect on the strategies that parents and teachers use to support children's transition and adjustment.

Teacher surveys responses were coded for 36 descriptors, which were grouped into five categories: (a) teaching strategies, (b) social support strategies, (c) language related issues, (d) cultural diversity, and (e) factors external to the classroom or school (family and community). To initially test reliability and understanding of the coding scheme, the investigators applied the coding system to randomly selected samples, engaging in lengthy discussions regarding the coding of each item. Revisions were made to the coding system until it was possible to reach a interrater reliability greater than 80% on independent coding. A Cohen's κ was calculated at _ = .87, well above the .70 considered satisfactory for that interrater reliability analysis.

Response frequencies were calculated for each of the open-ended questions on the survey. Further, frequencies were calculated to compare those teachers who reported that they had previous experiences teaching NAC (n = 93) with those who reported that they did not have prior experience (n = 19). Finally, independent t tests were calculated to determine whether there were significant differences among the use of social and cognitive strategies between these two groups of teachers. The teacher interviews provided some additional depth and insight to the survey responses.

RESULTS

Teacher Surveys and Interviews

The first two open-ended questions on the survey focused on teaching strategies employed for the social-emotional domain and for the cognitive domain. Experienced teachers were asked to share strategies that they had used with NAC. Those without experience teaching newly arrived students were asked to write the strategies they thought they would use. The frequencies of coded responses shown in Table 4 are the total number of survey responses coded for each category and may represent as many as three statements from an individual teacher.

Strategies for Providing Social Emotional Support for NAC

Teachers prioritized making children feel at home in their classrooms ($f = 138$). One teacher said, "In my opinion, the most important step is to make the child feel welcome. I consider my classroom to be an extension of the family or community. We build that relationship from the first day of school." The surveyed teachers offered several strategies to make NAC feel at home by providing emotional support and

TABLE 4
Social, Emotional, and Cognitive Support Strategies

Strategy Type	Social/Emotional f	Cognitive f
Teaching strategies	65	238
Social support strategies	138	35
Language	66	69
Cultural diversity	27	2
External support	21	13

showing a caring attitude ($f = 38$), such as smiling frequently, staying near the newcomer so the teacher's proximity can be reassuring, and touching or hugging the child, if appropriate to the child's culture. One teacher said in an interview that she was fortunate that she always had at least 24 h notice before a NAC was placed in her class. She could tell the class that a new classmate was joining them and give them the child's name and home nation. She always prepared a name card for the child's desk and discussed with the class what they could do to make the newcomer feel welcome.

Using appropriate teaching strategies was cited as a way to help child feel at home in the classroom ($f = 65$). The most frequent responses were to pair the NAC with another student ($f = 60$), often referred to as a "buddy," and to put the NAC in a small group of students for class work ($f = 23$). Some teachers suggested having work buddies, a lunch buddy, a playground buddy, and so forth to show the new child different rooms throughout the school and to help the child become more comfortable in the school environment. This enables the NAC to form multiple connections with other students and avoids giving any one child extensive responsibility for the newcomer.

Strategies used to address language barriers ($f = 66$) often included locating a student, a sibling in the school, another teacher, or someone from outside the school ($f = 51$) who could communicate with the newcomer and explain the classroom routines and procedures. One teacher told how the school secretary located a Polish-speaking high school student who came into the classroom to help a Polish-speaking NAC for the day.

The need to reach out to families was reflected in every survey and interview question. A frequent response was to invite the child or family to tell the class about the home culture. The teachers said that helping the others in the classroom develop an appreciation for the new child's culture is a high priority. A kindergarten teacher said she gave some of her own money to a family so they could come and prepare a typical meal from their home nation for the class. She found it was a turning point for the new child in terms of feeling more confident and secure in school.

Strategies for Supporting the Cognitive Development of NAC

Teachers reported a range of strategies for how they help NAC learn. Assisting with language acquisition was cited frequently ($f = 69$), as it was for social-emotional domain (see earlier). Using visuals ($f = 46$); adjusting standards ($f = 39$); and using appropriate teaching materials such as manipulative materials, materials at an appropriate ability level, and, when possible, materials in the child's native language were frequent responses ($f = 31$). Strategies such as demonstrating, using gestures, and repeating instructions further addressed the language challenges.

Experienced teachers' responses confirmed their resourcefulness and flexibility. Music was often suggested as a way to reach NAC, such as teaching the entire class a song or chant in the native language of the student. Others suggested the use of songs and stories with repetitive English words, offering the new student a way to learn and remember some words. Many teachers suggested labeling items around the room with English words to help teach vocabulary. One teacher, with a clear eye on the benefits for the entire class, suggested having some students make bilingual signs in the newcomer's language as well as English, giving the class a vocabulary lesson in an unfamiliar language. Teachers pointed out that having the entire class attempt to learn the child's language often helps the students realize the linguistic challenge for the newcomer. A kindergarten teacher suggested that a bilingual adult could come in and read an already familiar story to the class in the newcomer's language. Technology was useful to teachers with NAC through the use of free Internet language translation programs and the use of computer games to teach basic concepts to the newcomer.

Using a wide variety of teaching approaches ($f = 46$) and assessing NAC in an appropriate way ($f = 24$) were strategies cited. Teachers reported having NAC write in their native languages or illustrate their answers. Sometimes the teachers used oral rather than written assessment for NAC. One teacher said that appropriate assessment included reading the test questions from an overhead transparency, adding that "students (NAC) have communicated to me that they are able to focus more on the actual question rather than struggling to read the question and (trying to) grasp what the question is."

Some teachers ($f = 33$) found assistance from school district support personnel, such as English as a Second Language specialists and bilingual adults, was useful. However, the duration and intensity of the support was considered inadequate. Also identified was the benefit of support groups within the schools consisting of social workers, principals, teachers, and parents to brainstorm ideas and strategies to meet the many challenges that they were experiencing with teaching NAC. Language barriers ($f = 59$) and the lack of sufficient time for giving individualized attention to the NAC ($f = 37$) were cited as impeding their success in teaching NAC.

TABLE 5
Experiences Helpful in Working With Newly Arrived Children (NAC)

Experience	f
Personal Experience[a]	102
Teaching experience	87
Personal experience (outside)	40
Personal experience (multicultural)	56
Formal Education[b]	83
Classes before certification	55
In-service classes	75
Graduate classes	36

[a] Refers to personal experience either related to teachers' own teaching experience, experience outside of the school setting, or within a multicultural setting.
[b] Refers to formal education either related to teachers' classes taken before certification, in-service training, or graduate level classes.

TABLE 6
Influence on Strategies

	Number of Respondents Mentioning item as a "Higher Influence"
Higher Influences	f
Child's response	104
Personal experience	100
Class size	96
Class composition	94
Time constraints	92
Support from school	90
Availability of information on child	79
Parent interest	71
Training	55
School policies	44

Note. "Higher Influence" was indicated as the two highest points on a 4-point scale.

Perceived Helpfulness of Experience and Training

On the survey, the teachers were asked to indicate how well prepared they felt. Twenty-two teachers reported that they felt "well prepared," 66 teachers reported "somewhat prepared," and 24 reported "not at all prepared." In addition, the teachers were asked to rate the helpfulness of experiences for teaching NAC (Table 5) and to rate the level of influence on their teaching strategies from a variety of sources (Table 6).

TABLE 7
T-tests for Experienced and Not Experienced Teachers

Strategy Type	df	t	p
Social/Emotional			
Connecting with family	109	−1.2	.24
Cooperative learning	109	2.5*	.02
Cognitive			
Multiple teaching approaches	109	2.0*	.05
Standard adjustments	109	2.7*	.01
Visuals	109	−1.4	.17

*p<.05.

Teachers ranked their own personal experience more highly than formal education completed before teaching. In-service training (formal or informal training while on the job) was also ranked high and was considered more helpful than preservice training, indicating that professional development based on need is most valuable. The strategies that experienced teachers use are significantly different than those that nonexperienced teachers said they would use in three areas. Experienced teachers use more cooperative learning strategies ($t = 2.5$, $p = .02$), use more multiple teaching approaches ($t = 2.0$, $p = .05$), and adjust the standards more often ($t = 2.7$, $p = .01$), compared with what the nonexperienced teachers' projections of the strategies they would use (Table 7).

Teachers' Advice for New Teachers With NAC in the Classroom

The final open-ended survey question was "If you could pass on two pointers to a teacher who has never worked with NAC, what would you choose to tell them?" The advice offered ranged from lowering standards to "stick to your curriculum and expectations." The range reflects the diversity of experiences in the teacher sample as well as the NAC they had taught. Some teachers had multiple experiences with non-English speaking children who had little or no prior schooling. Others had experiences with NAC of successful, well-educated parents, who had acceptable English fluency on entering the classroom.

The largest number of pointers coded social-emotional support ($f = 119$), included 46 responses advising the new teacher to be patient, because the child *will* succeed in the class. In addition, they advised how to prepare both the classroom and the other students for the new arrival. Other frequent responses were tips on teaching techniques ($f = 58$) and how to deal with language barriers ($f = 27$). The suggestions included having NAC engage in nonlanguage activities where they can be successful and to offer them nonacademic options such as sports, games, and art activities to boost their confidence and further peer interactions.

Audio recordings of English books and computerized lessons were other strategies found to be successful in teaching non-English speaking children when no bilingual assistance was available.

Parent and Child Interviews

The parent and child interviews varied greatly in format because of the individual situations, cultural differences, and communication challenges. Some participants had only moderate fluency in English, and some needed to use an interpreter. An effort was made to keep each interview relaxed and informal. Although the interviews followed a list of prepared questions, the questions were sometimes altered or skipped, and sometimes the subjects provided the direction for the interview. Therefore, many of the interview narratives were idiosyncratic. A selected portion of the data that relates to the teacher results is summarized here. All names have been changed to preserve anonymity of the participants.

The parents' and the children's responses are congruent with the teacher findings that identified language as the biggest initial barrier for NAC entering school in the United States. One mother from Mexico had friends who had moved to another city in the United States and were able to enroll their children in bilingual schools. She had naVvely assumed that her child would be able to speak Spanish at school anywhere in the United States. She was shocked to learn that no other children in his classroom spoke Spanish, nor did their mothers or the school personnel.

Although the parents and children were uniformly concerned about the language barrier, they did not necessarily put forth intense effort to learn English and 4 of the 10 families spoke little or no English at home. Parents wanted children to learn English at school, and indeed, the children learned English from interaction with friends, help from the teacher, from special bilingual teachers, or other school support personnel. In addition, they learned from watching television, if English-language television was watched in the home.

The parents expressed satisfaction with American schools. One Pakistani parent said, "I came to America, I want them to learn American schooling." They commented on how much their children enjoyed school, that there were more choices and materials available, and that teachers and other school personnel were friendly and competent. Four parents mentioned how much more homework was required in the home nation but that students here "seem to know more," "were smarter," or "were clever" seemingly sensing the value of the development of thinking skills and motivation for learning. Both parents and children found that adjustment to school was satisfactory once friendships had been formed and the child had learned some English, if lacking fluency at the time of enrollment. Shyness and aggressiveness where mentioned by both parents and children. Three parents felt that their child's shyness had slowed the child's adjustment to the new school, whereas three other parents admitted that their sons had behavior problems at the beginning. The same three boys also "confessed" to being a disruptive force in the classroom when interviewed about the beginning days of school, but they did not express remorse. Joe, 9 years old from Columbia, brushed it off with "I didn't know how to talk to the other kids and I couldn't understand the teacher." When the interviewer asked if he still gets in trouble, he said he is better and his mother "is happier now because she doesn't get so many phone calls and notes." These comments were congruent with some teacher comments about the difficulty of keeping the non-English speaking NAC engaged in positive behaviors in the classroom. NAC also may be victims of bullying, as one boy reported and as mentioned by two teachers as something they had to watch out for and prevent.

What Parents and Children Would Say to Teachers

Each parent and child was asked what they would like to say to a teacher. The parents' responses revealed their uncertainties about how their family would adjust to U.S. schools and specifically how children would be able to achieve in the unfamiliar school environment. One Chinese parent recommended "It's good if teachers … talk about what's different here and specifically and what problems families may have." The language gap and the differences in school systems creates anxiety for parents who are accustomed to having each child in the class ranked according to their performance or who have come from nations where there is a strict national curriculum and each school level is clearly defined. A Yemeni father said he wanted the teacher to explain the school level of performance for his son, a request that would not be easy for a teacher struggling to assess the NAC's precise skills and depth of knowledge. A Lebanese mother wanted clear feedback about problems, because she felt her son "is smart" but is not doing well.

When a teacher has children from several nations in the classroom, it may be unrealistic to expect the teacher to learn to speak the native tongue of the NAC. A Pakistani mother suggested the teacher might simply ask a parent "what four words from your language are important to know?"

Three of the parents specifically mentioned that the teachers need to show patience with the child, and two said they would thank the teacher for all that they were doing. The children also spoke to the need for patience and the fact the teachers are helpful: "I can be good when you give me time to catch on." "Explain things, teach me, take care of me." Raj (India) would explain to another boy coming to school in the United States that, "the teacher won't get mad if you don't know the answer … she would just correct him."

DISCUSSION

Teachers bring varying cultural experiences to the classroom, challenging them to recognize the influence of their own culture on the teaching strategies they choose to use with NAC. Cooperative learning, individualization, integrated curriculum, family involvement, authentic assessment, and active learning are a few of the strategies that the teachers in this study reported as successful for working with NAC. A high number of responses for the social emotional realm were mutually related to cognitive development, demonstrating teachers' sense of interrelationships between a student's level of comfort, motivation, and learning.

Learning how to learn is a critical proficiency that teachers want their students to possess. This requires that teachers seek insight into children's abilities, motivations, and cultural knowledge; look for meanings and connections to what and how they are teaching; and make decisions about appropriate teaching strategies. The teachers in this study show wisdom in trying to match the assignments and teaching approaches to the students' level and experience. Meyer (2000) suggested that students without the background knowledge to complete assignments or learn new concepts in addition to language difficulties may experience a heavy cognitive load. The experienced teachers in this study were perceptive of that heavy cognitive load and were flexible in finding ways to help NAC succeed in the classroom.

For immigrant children, social isolation and loneliness appear to be common experiences regardless of their racial, ethnic, and linguistic backgrounds (Kirova & Wu, 2002). The need to belong is a fundamental human motivation (Baumeister & Leary, 1995). If immigrant children's struggle to belong is unsuccessful, its impact on their emotional and cognitive patterns will be negative. Helping a newcomer feel comfortable in the school environment is fundamental.

The teachers used a myriad of approaches to help NAC feel a part of the classroom community, including pairing NAC with a "buddy" in the classroom. Clayton (2003) suggested that a buddy needs to be someone who really wants the responsibility. She also stated that it is best to indicate the pairing is short term in case the buddy finds the responsibility to be a burden or the relationship does not take hold (2001, p. 43.) Her suggestions are already a part of what many of the teachers reported that they do. In keeping with their claim that teaching experience is what best enhances their performance in the classroom, it is quite possible their experience taught them that assigning multiple buddies on a short-term basis worked better than asking one student to help an NAC.

Essential to these developmentally appropriate strategies, however, is building on the strengths and experiences that children bring to the classroom. With NAC, understanding what their previous experiences have been and knowing their ability levels is challenging. A strong connection between children's home experiences and the school environment is essential to the success of children from diverse cultures (Yale Center, 2003).

Children are required to behave in culturally appropriate ways to fit in with their peers, but they also have to show respect for their parents' values to achieve their parents' support and approval (Hynie, 1996). Igoa (1995) emphasized the inclusion of parents in the education and acculturation process. The teachers in this study recognized the cultural gap and the need to reach out to parents and the parents wish for close communication with the school. When teachers and families do not share a spoken language there is a barrier to communication, even though it is desired by all parties. It is not surprising that some teachers expressed disappointment that more parents were not working harder to learn English and did not speak it in the home. Their concern that the parents sometimes lacked the insight on how difficult it was for the child to grasp the curriculum content and to prepare for the state mandated testing program without a proficiency in English was well founded. Research studies show that when there is little or no English spoken in the home, it is less likely the child will do well in school (Children Now, 2004).

Manning and Baruth (2004) suggested that individual and cultural differences can provide an effective framework for teaching and learning experiences and can enrich and contribute to individual teaching and learning situations. The elementary teachers in this study were cognizant of the individuality of the students. While they understood the impact of cultural differences, most responses related to getting to know the individual child and there was a noticeable absence of responses related to any cultural stereotypes. The teachers' responses showed a desire to help the NAC become an integral part of the class and to learn to the best of his or her ability.

Teachers have varying degrees of preparation in supporting NAC and their families. Takanishi (2004) reported that surveys of teachers at the prekindergarten and K–12 educational levels indicated that teachers do not feel that they are adequately trained to work with children and families diverse cultural and linguistic backgrounds. "To work well with immigrant children, educators must understand immigrant, cultural, and ethnic diversity in communities in the United States, examine and clarify their own racial and ethnic attitudes, and develop appropriate pedagogical knowledge and skills" (Rong & Preissle, 1998, p. x.). The teachers in this study felt, on an average, moderately well prepared. However, the difference in responses between experienced and inexperienced teachers supports the role of training, particularly when the teacher has NAC in the classroom.

Parents want teachers to be patient with their children, which is congruent with the teachers' advice to other teachers and to families. However, being patient can be incongruent with the teachers' need for children to become adjusted socially and learn English so that they can progress more rapidly to grade-level academic achievement. It also can be incongruent with the parents' wish for their children to catch up with the other students. There are no easy or simple answers for teachers or families when it comes to school success for NAC.

IMPLICATIONS FOR PRACTICE

NAC in the classroom have distinctive needs that must be understood and addressed by teachers to support their learning. All children have their own learning challenges, but some NAC who may not have had previous schooling or who had interrupted schooling may have had fewer or less refined skills than their peers. These new arrivals may have lower literacy skills, lack of curriculum knowledge, lack of formal learning skills, and possible emotional and behavioral problems caused by stress and trauma. Teachers must be concerned about building on what strengths children do posses through formative assessment and thoughtful planning.

Connecting with NAC and their families, while considering their distinctive needs and the multifaceted issues that may be present (e.g., embarrassment about language and literacy skills, unfamiliarity with school regulations and routines), calls for teachers, schools, and districts to respond with understanding. Consideration for the parents' transition to the United States and into the school context is also necessary. Starting school can be traumatic for any child because of the uncertainties of the new situation and the process of facing up to the new level of independence from home. It is often stressful for parents also because of the introduction of new authorities and persons of influence in the child's life. When the additional factors of cultural differences and tenuous ties with the new place of residence are present, we can expect that school enrollment for the newly arrived immigrant child is not easy.

The implications that can be drawn from this study include the following:

1. Teachers, parents, and children all suggested that time and patience was required for children's social adjustment and academic success during the school transition.
2. Families and schools must work together, even with challenging language barriers and cultural differences. The busy elementary school teacher, with curriculum goals to be met and a classroom of students with a multiple needs and learning styles, needs support. Other school personnel, the family, the teacher, and those who can assist with language translation, if needed, must form a coalition of stakeholders who care about the child's success in school.
3. Mentoring, in-service training and, to a more limited extent, preservice education, will increase the likelihood teachers will use effective strategies for offering social emotional support and will use the most salient teaching strategies to reach the newly arrived child.
4. Support for the classroom teacher from other school personnel and provision of appropriate classroom instruction materials will enable the teacher to more effectively work with the newly arrived child and the newly arrived family.
5. NAC and families as well as experienced teachers have insight and many suggestions for how to help NAC adjust to U.S. elementary schools. Their voices must be heard, and their ideas must be considered.
6. Being an immigrant family is not easy. Being a newly arrived student is not easy. Being the teacher of a newly arrived child presents multiple challenges. However, families, children, and teachers agree that the time and effort required for a successful transition results in benefits for all, and schools and communities are enriched by the integration of the newcomers.

REFERENCES

Baumeister, R. F., & Leary, M. R. (1995). The need to belong: Desire for interpersonal attachments as a fundamental human motivation. *Psychological Bulletin, 117,* 497–529.

Beiser, M., Dion, R., Gotowiec, A., Hyman, I., & Vu, N. (1995). Immigrant and refugee children in Canada. *Canadian Journal of Psychiatry, 40*(2), 67–72.

Children Now. (2004). *California Report Card 2004: Focus on Children in Immigrant Families.* Oakland, CA: Author. Retrieved August 17, 2004 from http://publications.childrennow.org/publications/invest/reportcard_2004.cfm

Clayton, J. (2003). *One Classroom, Many Worlds: Teaching and Learning in the Cross-Cultural Classroom.* Portsmouth, NH: Heinemann.

Fix, M. & Passel, J. (2003, January). U.S. Immigration—Trends and Implications for Schools. Paper presented at the National Association for Bilingual Education NCLB Implementation Institute, New Orleans, LA.

Friedlander, M. (1991, Fall). The newcomer program: Helping immigrant students succeed in U.S. schools. *NCELA Program Information Guide Series,* Number 8. Retrieved April 23, 2006, from www.ncela.gwu.edu/pubs/pigs/pig8.htm

Hernandez, D. (2004). Children and Youth in Immigrant Families: Demographic, social, and educational issues. In Banks, J. A. & Banks C. A. McG. (Eds.), *Handbook of Research on Multicultural Education* (pp. 404–419). San Francisco: Jossey-Bass.

Hyman, I., Vu, N., & Beiser, M. (2000). Post-migration stresses among Southeast Asian refugees youth in Canada: A research note. *Journal of Comparative Family Studies, 31*(2), 281–293.

Igoa, C. (1995) *The Inner World of the Immigrant Child.* New York: St. Martin's Press.

Kirova, A. & Wu, J. (2002). Peer Acceptance, Learning English as a Second Language, and Identity Formation in Children of Recent Chinese Immigrants. In M. Wyness & A. Richardson (Eds.). *Exploring Cultural Perspectives, Integration and Globalization* (pp. 171–190.). Edmonton, ON: ICRN Press.

Manning, M. L., & Baruth, L. (2004.) *Multicultural Education of Children and Adolescents.* Boston: Pearson/Allyn & Bacon.

Masten, A., & Powell, J. (2003). A resilience framework for research, policy, and practice. In Luthar, S. (Ed.) *Resilience and Vulnerability: Adaptation in the Context of Childhood Adversities* (pp. 000–000). New York: Cambridge University Press.

Northwest Regional Educational Laboratory (NWREL). (1998). *Improving Education for Immigrant Students: A Resource Guide for K-12 Educators in the Northwest and Alaska.* Denver: Author.

Rong, X. L., & Preissle, J. (1998). *Educating Immigrant Students: What We Need to Know to Meet the Challenges.* Thousand Oaks, CA: Corwin Press.

Sam, D. L., & Oppedal, B. (2002). Acculturation as a developmental pathway. In W. J. Lonner, D. L. Dinnel, S. A. Hayes, & D. N. Sattler (Eds.), *Online Readings in Psychology and Culture* (Unit 8, Chapter 6). Bellingham, Washington: Center for Cross-Cultural Research, Western Washington University.

Suárez-Orozco, C. & Suárez-Orozco. M. (2001). *Children of Immigration.* Cambridge, MA: Harvard University Press.

Takanishi, R. (2004) Leveling the playing field: Supporting immigrant children from birth to eight. *The Future of Children: Children of Immigrant Families, 14*(2), 61–79.

Yale Center in Child Development and Social Policy. (2003). *Portraits of Four Schools: Meeting the Needs of Immigrant Students and Their Families.* New Haven, CT: Author.

Chapter 7

The Role of Home and School in the Socialization of Immigrant Children in Israel: Fathers' Views

Dorit Roer-Strier
The Hebrew University of Jerusalem, Israel

Roni Strier
Haifa University, Israel

Schooling is at the heart of how we can help immigrant children succeed in a host culture without losing their own (Suárez-Orozco & Suárez-Orozco, 2001b). Current discussions of immigrant children's education around the globe reflect public concern about the extent of immigration and its meaning for a national culture. Language proficiency is regarded in many countries as the vehicle for the integration of immigrant children, a necessary part of belonging, of being a citizen. However, "Equating language acquisition with acculturation is a constrained view of nationalism. This limited view of culture that misses the great depth of what culture is in terms of values, worldviews, and social practices" (p. 40).

According to Suárez-Orozco and Suárez-Orosco (2001a), the role of the school is to accommodate, even embrace, the immigrants' expressive values (e.g., their worldview and patterns of interpersonal relationships) while teaching the instrumental skills necessary for them to succeed in the host culture (e.g., communication and technical skills and behaviors). In this chapter, we suggest that a

103

parental image of an "Adaptive Adult" (Roer-Strier, 2000) can be used as a conceptual framework to investigate "expressive values" (Suárez-Orozco & Suárez-Orozco, 2001a) in two ethnic groups: Russian and Ethiopian fathers. Such an investigation can help educators and other professionals to familiarize themselves with these images and to understand some of the differences that may exist between their own images and those held by the parents, which in turn may influence their own practices.

The cultural ideologies and expressive values "are reflected by the image of the 'Adaptive Adult' in a given culture" (Roer-Strier & Rosenthal, 2003). The *Adaptive Adult* metaphor organizes childrearing ideologies and values on the basis of a wide cultural context that is influenced by its physical aspects (e.g., climate, geographic location), social aspects (e.g., political regime, family system, values, laws), and cultural aspects (e.g., religion, tradition). The basic assumption is that a given culture develops its childrearing and education practices over a long period with two purposes: (a) to ensure children's survival to adulthood and (b) to ensure that children acquire the competences essential for fulfilling their adult cultural tasks (Ogbu, 1981).

THE ADAPTIVE ADULT IMAGE

Parents may not be totally aware of the Adaptive Adult image that influences their own ideas and practices. They may also find it difficult to answer direct questions about this image. However, the image of the Adaptive Adult clearly emerges in their answers to questions about developmental expectation. Answers to questions such as "How do you envisage your child as a successful adult?" "What traits would you like your child to have when he grows up?" (Buki, Ma, Strom, & Strom, 2003; Frankel & Roer-Bornstein, 1982; Hess & Azuma, 1991; Ninio, 1988; Pomerleau, Malcuit, & Sabataier, 1991) clearly unfold the image. The Adaptive Adult metaphor also may be deduced from an analysis of childrearing customs and ceremonies, songs, and proverbs, especially in traditional societies. The "cultural logic" is the reason socializing agents in a particular culture choose to reinforce a specific trait in their children and regard it as adaptive. For example, traits such as independence, autonomy, assertiveness, and self-sufficiency are adaptive to Western technological and industrial societies and are reflected in Israeli teachers' images of the Adaptive Adult (Roer-Strier, 2000), whereas interdependence, respect for elders, good manners, and solidarity may be reinforced by cultures that are more community-oriented (Roer-Strier & Rosenthal, 2003).

When parents emigrate, they do not leave this image behind. Parents tend to preserve the Adaptive Adult image in times of cultural transition. Studies of immigrant families suggest that parental social cognition, childrearing ideologies, expectations, norms, rules, and beliefs tend to preserve meaningful elements of their original cultures (Frankel & Roer-Bornstein, 1982; Greenfield & Cocking, 1994; Honig, 1989; Roer-Strier & Rosenthal, 2003). Parents' preservation of their Adaptive Adult image aimed at preserving cultural cohesion produces what Goldman (1993) called a "cultural lag"—a transient period during which immigrant parents hold onto the home culture traditions, sometimes resulting in clashes with the educational system of the host culture.

It is, therefore, important to identify this image and assess its adaptability in cultures undergoing transition (e.g., following immigration) in situations where the cultural norms of home and school differ or in families where parents come from two separate cultures. The immigrant child often faces different, sometimes conflicting, images of Adaptive Adult: cultural and social values held by parents on one hand and by the host country's educators on the other hand.

In many cases, neither the immigrant parents nor the educators of the host culture are familiar with or even aware of the Adaptive Adult image held by the other party. Therefore, they cannot appreciate the intrinsic cultural logic and inherent advantages of that other image. For example, the image of the Israeli Adaptive Adult held by many teachers in Israel promotes values, norms, and expectations aimed at creating an independent, autonomous, assertive person. Conversely, Adaptive Adult images held by Ethiopian immigrants to Israel stress respect for authority and self-control in expressing emotions (Roer-Strier, 1996). Conflicting images of the Adaptive Adult are often the source of cultural misunderstanding. For example, Israeli teachers often misinterpret the politeness of Ethiopian children who avoid eye contact as their lacking an opinion or as being dishonest (Ben Ezer, 1992). Several studies describe such misunderstandings leading to conflicts in the triangular meeting of the parents–child–education system of the new culture (Delgado-Gaitan, 2001; Dolev-Gindelman, 1989; Menuchin-Isickson, 1989; Ramirez, 2003; Rosen, 1989). It was suggested that these conflicts had long-term detrimental effects on family functioning (Cohen & Yitzhak, 1989; Dolev-Gindelman, 1989; Weisner et al., 2001), on the success of the child's integration into the education system (Hazan, 1987; Horowitz, 1984, 1986, 1989, 2005; Liebkind, Jasinskaja-Lahti, & Solheim, 2004; Lopez, 2001; Orr, Mana, & Mana, 2003), and on the development of immigrant children's self-identity (Gitelman, 1982; Gottesberg, 1988; Kahane, 1986; Kim, 2002).

RECENT WAVES OF IMMIGRATION TO ISRAEL

Israeli society has been galvanized by a continual influx of immigrants from Jewish communities throughout the world. This migratory character embodies a central theme in the Israeli national ethos of the reunification of the Jewish nation. This ethos is reflected in a proactive endeavor to attract Jewish immigration (Leshem, 2003). Almost 40% of the current Jewish population was born abroad.

In its 54 years of independence, Israel has absorbed more than 50% of its population through immigration. Immigration to Israel came in waves, or migratory movements, from common demographic origins. Two current waves are from the former Soviet Union and Ethiopia.

IMMIGRANTS FROM THE FORMER SOVIET
UNION AND FROM ETHIOPIA: BACKGROUND

In this chapter, the term *Russian fathers* is used for immigrants from the former Soviet Union. The largest wave of Russian immigration began in 1989 and brought 1 million immigrants to Israel who currently represent more than one fifth of the total population. Most Russian immigrants are professionals, highly educated, and secular, and they have formed small nuclear families. Studies report high levels of psychological stress related to issues of employment and social adjustment (Baider, Ever-Hadani, & DeNour, 1996). However, this immigrant population maintained a sense of accomplishment in achieving the goal of migration and a high degree of satisfaction with the new situation (Al-Haj & Leshem, 2000). Russian immigrants to Israel also were found to have a basic trust in their families but a deep distrust of Israeli institutions and services (Leshem, 2001).

Ethiopian immigration to Israel formed two waves that arrived in the 1980s and 1990s, together consisting of approximately 80,000 people. The motivations for this migration are structurally similar to the parallel migration from the former Soviet Union, namely, acute economic distress, an unstable political climate, and a concomitant wish to live in a Jewish society. The traditional, mostly rural, and religious Ethiopian Jewish families with relatively little formal education or professional training faced dramatic transformations on immigration to Israel. Exposed to both overt and covert manifestations of discrimination such as public questioning of the legitimacy of their Judaism, remarks related to color, and concentration of communities in underdeveloped areas of Israel in "absorption centers," the Ethiopian community experienced deep feelings of exclusion (Ben Ezer, 1992; Itzhaky & Levy, 2002; Offer, 2004; Ojanuga, 1994). This situation has been adversely affected by the paternalistic way this community is approached by the organizations and bureaucracies responsible for immigrants' integration (Dolev-Gindelman, 1989; Leshem, 2003). The traumatic vicissitudes of immigration, the culture shock of a drastically different society, and a disturbing sense of discrimination engendered in the community painful feelings of hopelessness and despair (Ben-David & Ben-Ari, 1997; Ben-Eliezer, 2004). In this context, the Ethiopian community experienced high levels of distress that resulted in a high suicide rate (Friedmann & Santamaria, 1990) and an intense identity crisis (Weil, 1995; Zegeye, 2004).

Although these two migrant populations develop social ties within their own cultural groups, they experience different levels of social and economic integration into the Israeli system, the Russian immigrants being more highly integrated and the Ethiopian immigrants generally being more segregated (Bar-Yosef, 2001; Ben-David & Biderman, 1997; Benita & Noam, 1995; Lazin, 1997). Despite extensive research by Israeli scholars on both cultural groups, studies have rarely addressed or documented the perceptions of immigrant fathers and the meaning they attribute to their role and to paternal involvement during the period of cultural transition.

METHODOLOGY

Greenfield and Cocking (1994) called for a methodological paradigm for studying minority and immigrant families based on methods of data collection that aim to study participants' perceptions and attributions of meaning to the studied phenomena. Following this model, focus group and in-depth interviews were chosen as the primary source of data collection for this study. The Israeli portion of the Canadian–Israeli study presented in this chapter was funded by the Israeli Ministry of Science. The main purpose of the study was to develop an understanding of fathers' experiences, to enhance and promote programs that support fathers and fathering, and to ensure that the specific needs of immigrants or refugees are met by both specialized and mainstream welfare and educational services for children and families. The objectives of the project were to identify and understand the unique barriers to paternal engagement and participation that may arise as a result of the immigrant or refugee experience in an international cross-cultural context. The study also aimed to develop a series of training manuals and workshops for practitioners (e.g., teachers, social workers, and program directors) that would provide guidelines and strategies for developing and implementing culturally appropriate programs to support immigrant or refugee fathers.

Participants and Data Collection

Purposeful sampling and snowballing were used (Patton, 1990; Stainback & Stainback, 1988) to obtain diverse perspectives on fathering. All the participants were fathers of preschool and elementary school children and had arrived in Israel within the previous 7 years; the average time in Israel was 3 years. The average age of the fathers was 34, with both younger (in their early 20s) and older fathers represented. We attempted to include both employed and unemployed men. Most of the fathers in the Russian group were employed, whereas 50% of the Ethiopian fathers were unemployed. These rates are in accordance with the national unemployment rates for both immigrant groups.

Focus groups were used as a preliminary step to identify fathering issues for further exploration in individual interviews. We draw on the results based on interviews with 15 Russian-born fathers and 15 Ethiopian-born fathers. Interviews were conducted in the men's native languages to guard against barriers to participants' self-expression. The interviews, conducted in the interviewees' homes, were completed in one to two meetings and were 2 to 4 h long.

Data Analysis

The analysis consisted of identifying key themes that emerged from the data. Coding sheets were developed in the interview transcripts to enter quotations made by the fathers on each theme. After relevant sections of the interviews were entered on coding sheets; each of the authors and the research coordinator independently rated the frequencies (Creswell, 1998). The team compared ratings and reached consensus on differences. Attention was given to metaphors (Bogdan & Biklen, 1992), proverbs, and common images frequently used by participants (Huberman & Miles, 1994).

COMMON THEMES

Without exception, when responding to the question about values and beliefs that parents would like to inculcate in their children, the participants told of beliefs about honesty, integrity, and respect for others. Respect for families, with a particular emphasis on respecting adults and elders, was found in both cultural groups, but most consistently in the Ethiopian group. In both groups, fathers expressed a desire for their children to grow up educated, financially secure, and with positive family relations.

Images of Fathers and Expectations of an
Adaptive Adult for the Ethiopian Fathers

In Ethiopia, the father's role in the socialization of children is essential. As one of the Ethiopian fathers said, "According to our culture, the father is the one responsible for the family. He has the honor. He is responsible for forming the child's personality. In Ethiopia fathers are very respected." Indeed, the word *father* evokes in Ethiopia a sense of honor and distance as one interviewee stated dramatically: "Only in Sudan (on the way to Israel) I had the courage to look up and see my father's face."

For most of the fathers interviewed, expectations for their children as adults were similar to those held in Ethiopia. One father said, "I expect my son to be honest, to respect his elders, to preserve the Jewish religion and the Ethiopian tradition." Another father noted, "I want my sons to have good families to be able to provide for the children, to help their relatives and community members, to be strong, to be able to endure life's struggles." Yet some included in their image a new element of the host culture, the importance of formal education for future success:

> I expect my child to be educated to know right and wrong. I want him to preserve the religion. In Ethiopia a child could be a successful farmer, but here in Israel you have push your kids to get education to go to high school or university.

Conflicts Between Adaptive Adult Images and Fathers' Roles of Ethiopian Fathers and Those of the Host Culture

For fathers in Ethiopia, one of the main goals in socializing Adaptive Adults was that sons contributed to the family and worked with their fathers. Because educating children to be good providers and workers was the father's role, rural children were rarely sent to school. Those who did attend school stayed with relatives in cities or walked long distances (Ben Ezer, 1992). Parents were not involved in school activities. In Israel, conversely, education is a principal element in the socialization of an Adaptive Adult. Education is compulsory, and parents are expected to take an active part in monitoring children's homework assignments and participating in parents' activities. Ethiopian parents who did not attend parents' meetings at school were sometimes regarded by teachers as neglecting their paternal role.

One father noted the conflicting expectations: "In Ethiopia the school was completely responsible for your child's education, In Israel you are seen as responsible for your child's education." Another father reported:

> In my son's school parents come to school all the time. They speak to teachers freely. I did not know about that at the beginning since I never went. I did not speak Hebrew well; for me the teacher is the one who has to know how to teach my son and make him learn, not me telling the teacher how to do her work. The school social worker came one day. She was angry. The teacher told her I am not coming to school and not helping my child with homework. She said I was neglecting my child.

Another father lamented,

> My son reads and speaks Hebrew. He has social contacts. If he gets confused I don't have the wisdom to guide him. The teacher invites the father, calls the boy and tells him to translate. The child takes advantage of the father's inability to write or read and translate other things, does not bring letters from the school. This causes much disrespect for the father. He loses his power.

Whereas the Ethiopian image of Adaptive Adult emphasizes respect for elders, the Israeli image involves assertiveness and equality. Israeli teachers encourage children to speak up, verbalize their ideas and feelings, and maintain eye contact. Fathers in Ethiopia, however, encouraged their children to refrain from speaking in front of adults and to lower their eyes when speaking to them.

An Ethiopian father noted,

> I went to school and was shocked with the Israeli children's behavior. They were so disrespectful. They talked back to teachers, looked them in the eye as if the teachers were children and not elders. I am afraid to send my kids to this school.

Attitudes Toward Intervention Programs

Not all changes associated with immigration were reported as negative. Ethiopian fathers regarded favorably some changes with regard to their fathering practices. Given the importance of scholastic achievement for upward social mobility in Israel, these fathers reported that they had learned to care a great deal about their children's progress in school and had become involved in this area. Some had decided to invest in helping and monitoring their children's performance in school. Others had taken a more active role in child care and household chores. A young father who participated in an early childhood program called Haetgar in which parents are encouraged to take active part in promoting their children's cognitive development explained,

> Now I spend the afternoons with my children, I sit with them, I buy booklets in math and reading to supplement what they do at school. They are so happy to do this with me. They feel there is someone they can count on and that can help them. It gives them courage and strength and happiness. To be a father in Israel you need to be a genius with lots of good will.

Most of the Ethiopian fathers reported that they were willing to participate in intervention programs, particularly those related to school: "When the school invites me I usually come. There are children who do not have parents to protect them at school, to encourage them." One father would participate only with the prerequisite that programs must take into account the values and traditions of the Ethiopian community and try to build a bridge between the host culture and that of their country of origin. One father commented, "You need to consult the community when planning programs. You cannot continue based on our culture. You need variations of both cultures."

Images of Fathers and Expectations of an Adaptive Adult for Russian Fathers

Participants' reports depicted a multifaceted father figure in families emigrating from the former Soviet Union. Most of these fathers described themselves as having had a critical role in the family and a well-recognized status: "Fathers in Russia had an a priori status." According to many Russian fathers, they were perceived as the primary breadwinners in their country of origin: "Gender equality was on paper only. In real life men earned more than women and his salary was the main source of income." Nearly half the Russian participants reported that fathers in their culture served as moral educators, authority figures, a source of wisdom, and contributors to the cognitive and intellectual development of their children. "In Russia the father's role was to educate to collectivism and excellence … My father did not simply do crossword puzzles with me: We were engaging in mathematical dilemmas."

The Russian father also was portrayed as distant and busy by some of the participants, who stated that the Russian father was more involved in the world of work than in the family sphere. Congruent with the view of Russian fathers as busy and distant, some participants defined them as emotionally detached.

> I wanted my father to spend more time with me; I dreamed that he would play with me. One day I tried to argue with him and he told me, "Do not speak back to me, I am not your friend." Is it so bad that a father is also a friend?

One third of the Russian fathers indicated that setting limits was a part of their role: "I am what you may call a tough father, I set limits. However the same limits I set for myself. It is like the Chinese wall, it limits but it also protects."

When the men were asked about their image of an Adaptive Adult, the values of independence, intelligence, hard work, and achievement orientation surfaced. As one father said, "As an adult, I want my children to be successful in their profession, to study hard, to be polite, know how to behave." Another said, "I want my children to be responsible, to know how to achieve things, to be intelligent."

Some fathers said they had the same expectations that their own fathers had. "Like my father I want my children to be 'cultured' to like literature to have respect for their culture. I want them to do well in school to get high degrees and to provide for their families."

Conflicts Between Adaptive Adult Images and the Father Roles of Russian Fathers and Those of the Host Culture

A major element of the Adaptive Adult image for Russian parents was to be educated and "cultured." Although most sent their children to public Hebrew-speaking schools, Russian fathers regarded the concept cultured differently than did the Israeli educators and mentioned their role in contributing to their children's education and in preserving cultural continuity.

> I want my children to be cultured. I want them to read books in Russian. Now I read to them and sing Russian songs. We see videos in Russian. I consciously do it for

them to preserve my culture of origin. It is important for me to educate them using the same books I was raised on.

Israeli educators, however, did not necessarily see the importance of preserving the Russian language and heritage as a part of the Israeli Adaptive Adult or as a part of formal education. One of the fathers had the following story.

> My daughter came crying from school. She wrote a book report on a book she read in Russian. The teacher told her that this book will not be a part of the final exams and thus she needs to read more books of Israeli writers instead. This teacher also asked her not to speak Russian in school with the other Russian children.

Although the Russian fathers saw independence as a part of the characteristics of the Adaptive Adult, many referred to instrumental independence (doing things by oneself) and not to psychological independence (deciding what to do oneself) embedded in the Israeli image of Adaptive Adult.
One father noted,

> In Israel, teachers encourage children to make their own decision. This is too much. My 6-year-old daughter came one day from school and told me the teacher felt she should not continue with her piano lessons, if my daughter decided not to play or switch to another musical instrument. This is unheard of in Russia. I was 23 and my parents still decided what I was going to study.

However, we also encountered fathers who said they were taking into consideration Israeli society when thinking about what would be adaptive to their children in the future.

> When I think about my children growing up in Israel, it is different from what I would say if you asked the same question in Russia. Here they need to be more independent because they go to the army at 18. They need to make life-and-death decision on their own. We cannot decide for them like my parents did in Russia. They cannot be too polite because people will push them around. They need to know how to "grow elbows."

Much of the Russian fathers' discussion of the effect of immigration focused on role changes that were regarded as positive. Some appeared to be renegotiating their roles in this new cultural climate:

> Immigration to Israel has affected me positively. I am sure that had I lived in another country I would have reacted differently. My encounter with a different culture helped me review my theories about life. I had my ideas on child socialization, but when they tell me differently here I am willing to consider it, to negotiate, to be more attentive to the views of other people.

Accordingly, immigration may represent an opportunity for the immigrant to reinvent himself as a man and as a father:

> In Russia everything is dictated, while in Israel children are given the freedom of choice; grow up, do whatever you want as long as you are a good person. The same freedom of choice is given to fathers.... You have the freedom in your personal growth, in your profession, and in your role as a father.

Attitudes Toward Intervention Programs

Most of the Russian fathers who valued education appeared at the same time to be critical of the Israeli education system: "The truth is that my faith in the educational system is limited. Teachers do not seem to have a high level of professionalism. Unfortunately there are not many talented people in the education system." Only one father mentioned schools as a source of possible support. In turn, most of the fathers from the former Soviet Union indicated that they mainly sought help from medical professionals and experts. One father said,

> Almost everything has a medical cause, so the first thing I would do is to go to a physician. For example, when a child cries at night. Then I will go wherever he sends me. Unlike psychologists, doctors give a clear diagnosis and a clear treatment plan.

Although nearly half the Russian fathers preserved the cultural norm of asking for help from friends and family, most had never participated in any intervention program, saying that the primary reason for this was that they were not invited. Some did express willingness to take part in programs (a) that provided information on child development and guidance, (b) that included experts, (c) that were adapted to fathers' work hours, (d) that enabled meetings with other fathers, (e) that allowed intimacy and closeness with children, and (f) that supported empowering images of fatherhood.

Comparison Between Ethiopian and Russian Fathers' Views

The findings show that the participants of this study shared elements of the Adaptive Adult image such as honesty, integrity, and respect for others. Respect for families, with a particular emphasis on respecting elders, was found in both cultural groups, but most consistently in the Ethiopian group. In both groups, fathers expressed a desire for their children to grow up educated, financially secure, and with positive family relations.

Although both groups saw education as a means to future success, Russian fathers more than the Ethiopian fathers were highly critical of the Israeli education system. Similarly, although both Ethiopian and Russian fathers expressed a strong desire for their children to preserve the culture and traditions of their countries of origin, the Ethiopian fathers' traditions were related to both religion and Jewish cultural heritage, whereas the Russian fathers emphasized secular elements of Russian culture such as literature, poetry, language, music, and so forth. Although fathers from both cultures were interested in intervention programs to support fathers and children, all had reservations about what they perceived as the paternalistic attitudes of intervention programs and their coordinators. In contrast to Ethiopian fathers who reported that they would turn to the education system for guidance, most of the Russian fathers seemed to prefer the guidance of other professionals such as physicians and specialists.

DISCUSSION

When observing parental images of Adaptive Adult in their cultural context, cultural logic seems to unfold. For example, the valuing of community relations and preservation of tradition expressed by the Ethiopian fathers interviewed in this study can be seen as highly adaptive to the Ethiopian context in which Jewish tradition was preserved for many generations in relative isolation from Western influences. Maintaining family and community cohesion and valuing human relationships and mutual help and support are seen as particularly adaptive for Ethiopian Jews who resided in rural areas far apart from one another.

Our findings in part support the notion of Goldman (1993) that childrearing ideologies that are related to the image of the Adaptive Adult tend to preserve elements from the host culture (e.g., preservation of culture, respect for elders), thus demonstrating cultural lag. However, we can observe many interrelated and interacting factors that make up the cultural and personal image of an Adaptive Adult and influence stability and change in this image (Roer-Strier, 1996, 2001). Some of our interviewees specifically described how they integrated elements from the host culture that they believed would be crucial for their children's success in the host society (e.g., education according to the Ethiopian interviewees; assertiveness and making decisions according to the Russian interviewees).

Although some parents managed to integrate the home and host culture and to give up some of the values they now regarded as maladaptive in the host culture (e.g., politeness), others could benefit from interventions aimed at comparing images of Adaptive Adult held by home and host culture, acknowledge conflicts in this image, and discuss how to overcome them.

The main merit of the proposed image of Adaptive Adult lies in its potential contribution as a tool for understanding the immigrant family's situation and for identifying children who might be at a higher risk for difficulties in the future. Many educators may not be aware of the images and expectations held by the parents of the immigrant children they teach.

In a survey of Israeli educators that we conducted in 1998 (Roer-Strier, 2000), 200 Israeli kindergarten and elementary schoolteachers who work with immigrant families were asked their opinion about the effect of the parental image of Adaptive Adult on their work. Eighty-five percent of the teachers were annoyed that the image was preserved and regarded it as undermining the teacher's authority or as disrespect. Some teachers described parents' behavior as uncooperative and destructive, challenging the basic important role assigned to the teacher by the Israeli community in socializing the child. However, 15% regarded as acceptable the right of parents to preserve elements of their image in a democratic society.

The duality between expectations of fast acculturation and cultural pluralism also was evident when teacher were asked what was their major role in working with immigrant children. Eighty percent considered "helping immigrant children to assimilate" as their principal role and as the country's duty, expecting immigrant children to "become" Israelis within 3 to 12 months. Only 18% of the teachers were familiar with the cultural background and values of the immigrant parents and had accurate knowledge of what the parents expected of the Israeli educational system.

Using the Metaphor of the Adaptive Adult in Working With Home and School

Familiarity with various metaphors of Adaptive Adult may lead to the identification of similarities between some aspects of the metaphors. Such similarities could be then expanded and emphasized in the educational curriculum. It is proposed that educators, parents, and children learn to appreciate various metaphors of the Adaptive Adult as well as the childrearing values and customs of their respective cultures. Values and behavior are better understood when the cultural context of the home country is explained. The term *cultural logic* was found to be useful in training sessions with educators, psychologists, and social workers who wished to learn more about socializing children in other cultures. Through our work in cross-cultural training of teachers, we have found that this framework offers educators an opportunity to become more aware of their expectations of immigrant children, which are based on their own image of Adaptive Adult and their own cultural approach to the socialization of immigrants. Being aware of the differences that exist between the two cultures helps bridge these gaps by reducing incidences of misjudgment, stereotyping, and misunderstanding. Educators in training regarded the study of parental expectations and their cultural logic as enhancing their empathy toward immigrant parents. This understanding of cultural differences occurred with immigrant parents as well. After sessions in which images of the Adaptive Adult were discussed, immigrant parents noted that they had revised their evaluation of teachers' behavior (Roer-Strier, 2001). Parents reported becoming aware of the logic behind educational goals and thus more accepting of educational practices that initially seemed strange and inappropriate.

Implications for Children's School Success

The lack of congruence between home and school does not necessarily carry risk for immigrant children or hinder their school performance. In many cases where the home had a different image of Adaptive Adult from school and held different norms and values, children were found to perform well in both systems. However, the ground for this success seems to be related to the trust the parents had in the education system, the respect with which educators treated immigrant parents, home–school collaboration, and lack of conflict between home and school. In these situations, children did not have to choose between home and school (Hess & Azuma, 1991). Pluralistic educational systems, in which parents are reassured they can hold onto cultural customs and cultural characteristics, enable immigrant parents to feel more at ease and to regain confidence in their role. At the same time, encouraging immigrant families to familiarize themselves and to be more open to understanding the values of their new country will reduce their need to protect their children from the "bad" influences of the new educators and consequently reduce the probability of open conflicts and rigid coping styles.

In societies that accept pluralism, a school consultant working with immigrant parents may raise the family's awareness of the option of agreeing to *disagree* with the extrafamilial system. This approach will help reduce stress and confusion as well as convey to the family the respect of the consultant and the school for their cultural background.

Our data also suggest that fathers' voices may shed new light on implementing interventions for immigrant fathers. In many Western countries, interventions geared toward immigrants in the educational system are usually directed at children (e.g., language acquisition programs) and mothers (e.g., reproductive health literacy); few are directed at immigrant fathers. Most of the fathers expressed a desire or need to participate in programs related to their children. The Israeli immigrant fathers interviewed in our study were rarely invited to participate in community or school-based or any other type of intervention. Fathers expressed hope that programs would be less paternalistic and a desire for interventions to be designed with input from program participants and with programs using participants' cultural terminology and cultural preferences.

If teachers recognize the cultural differences and understand the cultural lag and cultural logic, they may avoid the sense of frustration that arises as a result of what may otherwise be perceived as parents' personalities or objections to the host culture's educational approach. Understanding the child's position at the crossroads between home and school, each with his or her own expectations and image of Adaptive Adult, may contribute to the design both of educational programs for immigrant children and special training programs for teachers who educate children from other cultures.

REFERENCES

Al-Haj, M., & Leshem, L. (2000). *Immigrants from the Former Soviet Union in Israel: Ten Years Later: A Research Report.* Haifa, Israel: University of Haifa, Center for Multiculturalism and Educational Research.

Baider, L., Ever-Hadani, P., & DeNour, A. (1996). Crossing new bridges: The process of adaptation and psychological distress of Russian immigrants in Israel. *Psychiatry, 59*(2), 175–183.

Bar-Yosef, R. W. (2001). Children of two cultures: Immigrant children from Ethiopia in Israel. *Journal of Comparative Family Studies, 32*(2), 231–246.

Ben-David, A., & Ben-Ari, A. T. (1997). The experience of being different: Black Jews in Israel. *Journal of Black Studies, 27*(4), 510–527.

Ben-David, A., & Biderman, P. (1997). East meets west: A view from Soviet student newcomers to Israeli society. *International Journal of Group Tensions, 27*(2), 99–108.

Ben-Eliezer, U. (2004). Becoming a Black Jew: Cultural racism and anti-racism in contemporary Israel. *Social Identities, 10*(2), 245–266.

Ben Ezer, G. (1992). "Yegan Mevrat." *Migration and absorption of Ethiopian Jews in Israel* [in Hebrew]. Jerusalem, Israel: Reuven Mass.

Benita, E., & Noam, G. (1995). The absorption of Ethiopian immigrants: Selected findings from local surveys. *Israeli Social Science Research, 10*(2), 81–96.

Bogdan, R. C., & Biklen, S. K. (1992). *Qualitative Research for Education: an Introduction to Theory and Methods.* Boston, MA: Allyn & Bacon.

Buki, L. P., Ma, T. C., Strom, R. D., & Strom, S. K. (2003). Chinese immigrant mothers of adolescents: Self-perceptions of acculturation effects on parenting. *Cultural Diversity and Ethnic Minority Psychology, 9*(2), 127–140.

Cohen, R., & Yitzhak, R. (1989). Bridging the old and the new: Constructing the parents' role for Ethiopian immigrants. In R. Tokatli (Ed.), *Lifelong learning in Israel values and practices* (pp. 143–149). Jerusalem, Israel: Ministry of Education.

Creswell, J. W. (1998). *Qualitative Inquiry and Research Design: Choosing Among Five Traditions.* Thousand Oaks, CA: Sage.

Delgado-Gaitan, C. (2001). *The Power of Community: Mobilizing for Family and Schooling.* Lanham, MD: Rowman & Littlefield.

Dolev-Gindelman, Z. (1989). *Ethiopian Jews in Israel: Family Images, Multi-Dimensional Context* [in Hebrew]. Jerusalem, Israel: NCJW Research Institute for Innovation in Education, Hebrew University.

Frankel, D. G., & Roer-Bornstein, D. (1982). Traditional and modern contributions to changing infant-rearing ideologies of two ethnic communities. *Monographs of the Society for Research in Child Development, 47*(4) (No. 196), 1–51.

Friedmann, D., & Santamaria, U. (1990). Identity and change: The example of the Falashas, between assimilation in Ethiopia and integration in Israel. *Dialectical Anthropology, 15*(1), 56–73.

Gitelman, Z. (1982). *Becoming Israeli.* New York: Praeger.

Goldman, L. (1993). Misconceptions of culture and perversions of multiculturalism. *Interchange, 24,* 397–408.

Gottesberg, M. (1988). *Cultural Transition: the Case of Immigrant Youth.* Jerusalem, Israel: Magnes Press.

Greenfield, P. M., & Cocking, R. (1994). *Cross Cultural Roots of Minority Child Development.* Hillsdale, NJ: Lawrence Erlbaum Associates, Inc.

Hazan, H. (1987). *Educators and Environment Effecting the Education of Ethiopian Students* [in Hebrew]. Jerusalem, Israel: Ministry for Immigrants Absorption.

Hess, D. R., & Azuma, H. (1991). Cultural support for schooling: Contrasts between Japan and the United States. *Educational Researcher, 30*(9), 2–8.

Honig, A. S. (1989). Cross cultural aspects of parenting normal and at risk children. *Early Child Development, 50,* 1–204.

Horowitz, R. T. (1984). Patterns of cultural transition: Soviet and American children in new environments. *Journal of Cross-Cultural Psychology, 15,* 399–416.

Horowitz, R. T. (1986). *Between Two Worlds: Children from the Soviet Union in Israel.* Lanham: MD: University Press of America.

Horowitz, R. T. (1989). *The Soviet Man in an Open Society.* Lanham, MD: University Press of America.

Horowitz, R. T. (2005). Integration of immigrants from the former Soviet Union. *Israel Affairs, 11*(1), 117–136.

Huberman, A. M., & Miles, M. B. (1994). Data management and analysis methods. In N. K. Denzin & Y. S. Lincoln (Eds.). *The Evaluation Handbook* (pp. 428–444). Thousand Oaks, CA: Sage.

Itzhaky, H., & Levy, D. (2002). Source contributions of self-esteem and gender to the adaptation of immigrant youth from Ethiopia: Differences between two mass immigrations. *Journal of Social Work Research and Evaluation, 3*(1), 33–46.

Kahane, R. (1986). Informal agencies of socialization and the integration of immigrant youth into society: An example from Israel. *International Migration Review, 20,* 210–239.

Kim, E. (2002). The relationship between parental involvement and children's educational achievement in the Korean immigrant family. *Journal of Comparative Family Studies, 33*(4), 529–540.

Lazin, F. A. (1997). The housing policies for Ethiopian immigrants in Israel: Spatial segregation, economic feasibility and political acceptability. *Nationalism and Ethnic Politics, 3*(4), 39–68.

Leshem, E. (2001). Immigration from the former Soviet Union and the secular/religious fissure in the Israeli society. In M. Lissak & L. Leshem. (Eds.), *From Russia to Israel: Identity and Culture in Transition* (pp. 124–148) [in Hebrew]. Tel-Aviv, Israel: Hakibbutz Hameuchad.

Leshem, E. (2003). Israel as a multi-cultural state at the turn of the century. In E. Leshem & D. Roer-Strier (Eds.), *Cultural Diversity: A Challenge to Human Services* [in Hebrew]. Jerusalem, Israel: Magnes Press.

Liebkind, K., Jasinskaja-Lahti, I., & Solheim, E. (2004). Cultural identity, perceived discrimination, and parental support as determinants of immigrants' school adjustments: Vietnamese youth in Finland. *Journal of Adolescent Research, 19*(6), 635–656.

Lopez, G. R. (2001). The value of hard work: Lessons on parents' involvement from a migrant household. *Harvard Educational Review, 71,* 416–437.

Menuchin-Isickson, S. (1989). Anthropological description of the encounter between the Ethiopian and the Israeli cultures [in Hebrew]. *Alim,* 15–21.

Ninio, A. (1988). The effects of cultural background, sex, and parenthood on beliefs about the timetable of cognitive development in infancy. *Merrill Palmer Quarterly, 34,* 369–388.

Offer, S. (2004). The socio-economic integration of the Ethiopian community in Israel. *International Migration, 42*(3), 29–55.

Ogbu, J. U. (1981). Origins of human competence: A cultural ecological perspective. *Child Development, 52,* 413–429.

Ojanuga, D. N. (1994). Absorption of Ethiopian Jews: A study of multiculturalism in Israel. *Jewish Social Work Forum, 30,* 86–97.

Orr, E., Mana, A., & Mana, Y. (2003). Immigrant identity of Israeli adolescents from Ethiopia and the former USSR: Culture-specific principles of organization. *European Journal of Social Psychology, 33*(1), 71–92.

Patton, M. (1990). *Qualitative Evaluation and Research Methods.* Newbury Park, CA: Sage.

Pomerleau, A., Malcuit, G., & Sabatier, C. (1991). Child-rearing practices and parental beliefs in three cultural groups of Montreal: Quebecois, Vietnamese, Haitian. In M. H. Bornstein (Ed.), *Cultural Approaches to Parenting* (pp. 45–67). Hillsdale, NJ: Lawrence Erlbaum Associates, Inc.

Ramirez, A. Y. (2003). Dismay and disappointment: Parental involvement of Latino parents. *Urban Review, 35*(2), 93–110.

Roer-Strier, D. (1996). Coping strategies of immigrant parents: Directions for family therapy. *Family Process, 35,* 363–376.

Roer-Strier, D. (2000). Socializing immigrant children: Coping with cultural differences at school and at home. In *New Vistas in Education and Society Series: Special Issue on Education, Multiculturalism, Identity and Language Development* (pp. 115–142). The NCJW Institute for Innovation in Education, Hebrew University of Jerusalem. Jerusalem, Israel: Magnes Press.

Roer-Strier, D. (2001), Reducing risk for children in changing cultural contexts: Recommendations for training and intervention. *Child Abuse and Neglect, 25,* 231–248.

Roer-Strier, D., & Rosenthal, M. K. (2003). Goals for human development: Images of an "Adaptive Adult" in multicultural societies. In E. Leshem & D. Roer-Strier (Eds.), *Cultural diversity: A challenge to human services* (pp. 000–000). Jerusalem, Israel: Magnes Press.

Rosen, H. (1989). Ethiopian culture and behavior: keeping teachers in touch [in Hebrew]. *Youth Aliya Bulletin,* 1–20.

Stainback, S., & Stainback, W. (1988). Educating students with severe disabilities in regular classes. *Teaching Exceptional Children, 21,* 16–19.

Suárez-Orozco, M., & Suárez-Orosco, C. (2001a). *Children of Immigration.* Cambridge, MA: Harvard University Press.

Suárez-Orozco, M., & Suárez-Orozco, C. (2001b). Immigrant children and the American project. *Education Week, 20*(27), 40–56.

Weil, S. (1995). Collective designations and collective identity among Ethiopian Jews. *Israeli Social Science Research, 10*(2), 25–40.

Weisner, T., Ryan, G. W., Reese, L., Kroesen, K, Bernheimer, & Gallimore, L. R. (2001). Behavior sampling and ethnography: Complementary methods for understanding home-school connections among Latino immigrant families. *Field Methods, 13,* 20–46.

Zegeye, A. (2004). The Beta Israel: Return to the source? *Africa Insight, 34*(1), 69–75.

Chapter 8

A Challenge of Transnational Migration: Young Children Start School

Eva L. Vidali
Technological Educational Institute of Thessaloniki, Greece

Leah D. Adams
Eastern Michigan University, USA

Before 1980, the educational system in Greece reflected the national, cultural, and linguistic homogeneity of the nation. The convergence between nationally oriented education and local community control was generally accepted in the Greek monocultural social context. In recent decades, however, economic and cultural globalization has permanently altered the homogeneity of the Greek educational system and society.

During the last 10 years, Greece has faced three major changes, which have affected the educational system and created new conditions in the school context and new challenges for all participants in the educational process. First, there has been a major influx of immigrants. Greece, historically a labor-exporting country, began receiving each year hundreds of thousands of foreign immigrant workers with their families. In proportion to its population among the countries of the European Union, Greece has, in the past decade, accepted the largest number of immigrants. Approximately 1 million legal and illegal immigrants constitute approximately 9% of the overall population of the country (Lakasas, 2003).

121

The immigrant population represents more than 150 nations, but the largest group (75%) is from the Balkans. Nearly half (48.1%) of the Balkan immigrants have a low educational background, and only 17.2% have higher education (Katsikas & Politou, 2005). The immigrant population is on a whole younger than the native Greek population: 16.7% are aged 14 or younger, approximately 80% are 15–64 years old, and only 3.5% are older than 65. By contrast, among the native-born population, 17% are older than 65. Many of the immigrants from the United States, Canada, and Australia are older than 65 years because they are primarily pensioner returnees of Greek origin. Newly arrived Albanians, who are mainly married couples raising families, are the youngest population group (Kasimis & Kassimi, 2004). Children of immigrants face both educational and social challenges and have a direct effect on the composition of student populations in the schools (Psalti & Deliyanni-Kouimtzi, 2001).

The second major change is the large numbers of Greek emigrants who have returned to Greece in recent years and who have often found repatriation difficult. They may lack sufficient financial resources and find social adaptation difficult, and psychological and personal problems make resettlement in Greek society all the more difficult (Kotsionis, 1995; Psalti & Deliyanni-Kouimtzi, 2001).

Repatriation is a return to a motherland that could offer parents a new life and a better job. Their children must adapt to a new social, cultural, and educational setting. Furthermore, the returnees and their children are often unable to communicate in Greek, which affects not only the parents' careers but also their children's progress in school. A case study of young students of Pontic-Greek origin from the former Soviet Union carried out by Veikou (2004) highlighted the struggle of returnee students to develop their identity and position in Greek society. They described themselves as "Greek by ancestry, Pontic by origin and Russian by birth," which makes them a minority in the school system.

The third major change is that native Greeks, who are used to living in a highly homogeneous country with common language, religion, tradition, and culture, have, in a short time, found themselves negotiating between maintaining their cultural identity and adapting to the continual social change that surrounds them. Galati (2004) stated that immigration in Greece can be described as an impetuous torrent, continually in flood and creating growing pressure in an unprepared society. The reality of cultural diversity in their everyday life has forced the native population to adopt new behavioral patterns and attitudes toward a multicultural society. The immense change in such a brief period has affected both newcomers and native-born people (Vidali & Giangounidis, 2003).

BACKGROUND AND AIMS OF THE STUDY

Ethnographic studies have analyzed important issues about the transition from child to student and the child's new role (Bourdieu, 1990; Pollard & Filer, 1996;

Willes, 1983). However, little research has examined essential aspects of the adaptation of young children of immigrant parents into early childhood settings in the Greek context.

This research was inspired by university students who were practice teaching in culturally diverse early childhood settings. The students noticed that although many early childhood settings were friendly places for all, there were underlying salient problems related to teachers' attitudes and to children's behaviors and adaptation processes in the group setting. By exploring the issue further through available research, we realized that although both theory and research on learning and instruction in early childhood education have advanced in recent years, the educational needs of the young immigrant child barely have been studied. Questions arose as to how early childhood educators understood the many complex issues related to immigrant children's first experiences in schooling, which may begin at 3 or 4 years of age. In the Greek context, we found that most relevant research has tended to examine the problems of immigrant children in primary or secondary education, and minimal attention has been paid to preschool factors that may have important effects on development and educational success.

The main hypothesis of this study was that the role of preprimary education is instrumental in facilitating the adjustment process of immigrant students to Greek schools. Questions such as whether such children are prepared for the new environment, how they feel about school, and what factors may play a significant role in their adjustment needed to be answered for educators to understand how immigrant children adjust to school.

Researchers agree that a child's first experience of school is an important passage in life and has profound influences for his or her identity (Woods, Boyle, & Hubbard, 1999). The starting point for our research was the question of how immigrant children, as well as their parents, experienced this passage and what variables might affect their feelings, experiences, and adjustment to the new environment. We believed that by exploring how children understand and interpret the new environment, as well as how they communicate feelings to their parents, would further our understanding of the issues of transitional migration and intercultural education.

The theoretical framework used in this study was based on the ecological approach (Bronfenbrenner, 1979; Knoff, 1986; Nuttall Romero, & Kalesnik, 1992). Bronfenbrenner's ecological model of development explains the enabling variables that influence the developmental process of a human being. His approach places the educator, the diverse learner, and the parents in an ecological model that allows for a broad understanding of many issues that affect them. Bronfenbrenner locates the preschool setting or the microsystem (where the educator and the native-born children constitute the new environment for the child) in the mesosystem (including the network of settings such as family, neighborhood, and the like). This in turn is located in the macrosystem (the broad sociocultural, economic, and political context of the particular country). This is included in the exosystem (the global network) and identifies the importance of the various links that develop among these systems during the child's development.

In his theory, Bronfenbrenner (1979) stressed the importance of supportive links between the microsystems and the variables that affect a child's initial transition to a new setting. He argued, "Upon entering a new setting, the person's development is enhanced to the extent that valid information, advice and experience relevant to one setting are made available, on a continuing basis to the other" (p. 217). Children who experience a connection and continuity between school and family settings have advantages, because there is an optimum developmental context of "information-advice and experience" (Brooker, 2002). When this context is missing and there are no natural ties between home and school, children may experience difficulties that in most cases are easily noticeable from the start.

The challenge of globalization expands these links into new dimensions where knowledge of language, others' culture, and communication codes is required more frequently in the microsystem than before. Education gradually but steadily tends increasingly to integrate the concepts of intercultural education. We wished to learn more about how young children from immigrant families and their parents develop the necessary supportive links with the first schooling experience in preschool.

The purpose of this research was to explore the feelings, experiences, and needs that underlie adjustment to the school environment by looking at immigrant children's feelings about being new and how they form friendships. We also wished to ask what advice they had for other (immigrant) children and parents in their role in their child's adjustment and to find out how parents communicated with their child and what advice they had for other (immigrant) parents.

METHOD

The research was conducted in the area of Thessaloniki, the second largest city in Greece. The sample consisted of 88 immigrant families with preschool children who attended local authority early childhood programs. The families came from eight countries of origin, the largest number being from Albania (52.3%), followed by Georgia (13.6%), Russia (11.4%), and Armenia (6.8%). There were 2.3% each from Abzcahzia, Germany, Turkey, and Czechia.

Interviews With the Children

A structured interview protocol was designed to investigate children's feelings about their new environment and how friendships were formed. The interviewers were university students who had been trained in the collection of interview data and took place in the preschool classroom or outdoors using an informal conversational style.

Interviews With the Parents

A structured interview protocol was designed to measure parents' perceptions of their level of involvement in their child's adjustment process to preschool. A pilot study was conducted with 12 parents and their children to determine the best interview procedures. The results of the pilot study led us to conclude that the parents would speak freely only with their child's teacher, so we asked the teachers to conduct the interviews in the preschool classroom using an informal conversational style. The teachers spoke in Greek, the language of the school; in many cases older children served as translators.

It became evident to the teachers during the interviews that most of the parents were under stress and were hesitant to respond because of their newly immigrated status. The teachers sensed that in some instances this might have related to low self-esteem or self-consciousness because of their financial circumstances or possibly to their overall level of comfort in the new host country. In such instances, the teachers took time in the interview to encourage the parents and to make them more comfortable by offering friendship and support. We analyzed the qualitative materials using content-analysis methods and the quantitative using chi-square.

RESULTS

Children's Interviews

The children's interview protocol was designed to investigate feelings about being new, the formation of friendships, and the advice children would give to others who were moving to a new country. The 54 boys and 34 girls were between 4 and 7 years of age.

In response to the questions *Do you want to say anything about your first day to school?* and *What did you do?*, 37.2% of the children showed a positive attitude toward the experience, 27.9% showed a negative attitude, and 34.9% were neutral. Positive attitudes included answers from children who were active and participated in activities (*I was playing, I was drawing, I heard a story*). Negative attitudes included answers such as *I was crying all the time, I couldn't understand,* and *I didn't know where to go.* Responses such as *I was sitting* or *I was waiting* were considered neutral and may have reflected that they felt they were behaving as expected in the setting or were possibly following parental instructions about how to behave in school.

All the children said that they remembered the first day of preschool, who went to school with them, where they sat, and who first greeted him or her. For 68.2% of the children, one or both parents accompanied them on the first day, and 27.3% said that another family member had accompanied them. Only 4.5% said they had gone to school alone on the first day. We made no attempt to check with the parents for the accuracy of the children's responses.

Assuming that their memories of the first day at school were accurate, more than half (53.5%) of these immigrant children sat in the middle of the room. Approximately one fifth (20.9%) said that they had sat at the first table, and the rest (25.6%) remembered sitting somewhere in the back of the room. The teacher was the first to greet them according to 75.6%, 22% said that someone else had greeted them, and 2.4% could not remember being greeted.

The interviews were conducted 5 months into the school year so that we could investigate the children's feelings about school after some time had passed, although the time lapse may have affected the accuracy of their memories about the beginning of the school year. Interviewers reported that the children answered quickly, willingly, and with apparent sincerity and did not give the impression of having memory gaps. When asked if they liked school, 76.3% of the children said *Yes*, 5.3% said *No*, and 18.4% said they did not know. This was in marked contrast to the 27.9% negative and 34.9% neutral responses about the first day of school, which may indicate that the adaptation process had been somewhat successful for these children. We were unable to identify whether the children with the more negative or neutral attitudes were those who were still unable to communicate readily in the classroom because of language barriers.

Friendships are of high importance in children's adaptation processes, and 95.5% said that they had friends in school, which indicates that the preschool environment created opportunities for making friends. However, the neighborhood plays a larger role in determining friendships, and 45.2% said that they were friends with another child because he or she lived in the same neighborhood. Having a friend in the classroom was next at 38.1%, and 16.7% of friendships were forged because the children were from the same country and spoke the same language.

Because many immigrant families live in clusters, the neighborhood may have some similarities with the home culture that they miss. It is noteworthy that 77.7% of the children said that what they most missed about their home country was their grandmother. The adaptation process is complex, and the emotional gap in the family system may affect the speed of adaptation and level of satisfaction with the new environment. Children's advice to other children who were moving to a new place reflects the importance of friendships and play, the single highest number of answers (25%) relating to play with other children. However, when the answers about behavior patterns are added together, it can be seen that the children were well aware of their parents' and the preschool's expectations about what is or is not considered acceptable behavior and of the importance of classroom rules (Table 1.)

Parents' Interviews

Of the 70 mothers and 18 fathers interviewed, 34.1% had been in Greece more than 6 years, 27.3% for 3 to 6 years, and 38.6% for fewer than 3 years. Most of the parents could speak Greek but could not write it.

TABLE 1
Acceptable and Unacceptable Behavior

Play with other children	25%
Be a good boy	24%
Listen to your teacher	13.5%
Be quiet	11%
Don't complain	9%
Don't fight (with children)	6.5%
Don't hit the children	4.5%
Don't be ashamed	4.5%
Don't cry	2%

Parents' perceptions of variables that positively or negatively affect their child's adaptation also may influence the child's attitude. Parents most valued the neighborhood in facilitating their child's adjustment, with 34.9% saying that it was the most positive influence. The school was selected by 30.2% and friendships by 11.6%, indicating parents' lower appreciation of the role of peer friendships. The parents' answers about what had facilitated adjustment show similarities to the children's responses about why their friendships developed, with living in the same neighborhood given as the most influential variable. At the same time, nearly half (47.7%) of the parents placed high importance on friendships when asked how they knew when their child had adapted to the new host environment, saying that it was when the child made friends. An equal number (47.7%) said that it was when he or she adapted to being in school.

Only 52.3% of the parents believed that their child liked school or felt comfortable during the first week; 40.9% said that their child felt bad, and 6.8% believed that their child was indifferent. By contrast, their responses about the school at the time of the interview (5 months into the school year) were markedly positive, with 86.4% saying that their child loved school and only 13.6% giving a negative response.

Responses to what the parents believed had hampered their child's adaptation to the new country show that parents' personal emotional concerns may have been a factor. One interpretation could be that they believed that they were missing out on spending time with their child and felt somewhat responsible, as the highest number of responses related to their absence from the child (Table 2).

Parents reported relatively little communication with their children about the move before migrating to the new country. When asked what they had said to the child before the move, nearly 50% said they had said nothing, and more than half said that they had started to prepare the child only a few days before the move (Tables 3 and 4). Half the parents said that the child had not asked about the (coming) move, whereas the other half said the child had asked.

TABLE 2
What Hampered Adaptation

Loneliness during parents' work time	34.9%
Not speaking (Greek) language	29.5%
Fear of the unknown	11.4%
The absence of help from the school	6.8%

TABLE 3
How Parents Prepared the Child for the Move

Nothing	47.6%
That you are going to a place with a better job and more income	23.8%
That you are going to a new place where he will make many friends	19%
Something else	9.5%

When asked for details about what they might have discussed with the child before the move, the responses from 54% of the parents fell into the category of *a new life with different language and people.* Only 38.1% said that they had discussed school with the child; 61.9% said they had not. In response to a question about whether the child now felt better about the move than when they had first arrived, 65.9% said *Yes*, 4.5% said *No*, and 29.5% believed that their child's attitude toward the move was unchanged.

Parents were asked if they were to migrate to another country, if they would do something different to prepare the child based on their experience with this move. About one third (34.1%) said that they would do something different, but 65.9% said they would not. Of those who said they would do something different, 93.3% said that they would provide more emotional support. The remainder (6.7%) said they would do more (Greek) language preparation.

Advice to Other Parents

Asked what advice they would give to other parents preparing to migrate to another country, the comments were as follows:

- The mother should learn first the new language and then teach it to her child, thus helping him or her to communicate better.
- I would tell them a lot of things about this country.
- I would tell them to talk more with [their] children.

TABLE 4

Pre-Immigration Preparation for the Child

A few days before	52.8%
Six months earlier	30.6%
A year earlier	17.7%

- I would tell them to show understanding to the difficulties of his child and to provide emotional support for the child.
- I would tell them to discuss more with his child before leaving and to prepare her child for the experience.
- I would tell them to show to her child how much she loves (the child).
- I would tell them to decide to leave while the child is young.
- I would tell them to discuss more about the way of living (in the new country).
- I would tell them to have patience and to help the child with adjustment.

DISCUSSION

The importance of the early years in child development gives early education a vital role to make certain that children develop as successfully as possible. For most young children, entering preschool is their first exposure to a group experience. Teachers and the school environment play a vital role in the development of positive or negative attitudes toward learning, the self-identity of the children, and the development of social skills. Starting school is a major transition in the life of a child, and children approach school with diverse individual experiences, attitudes, and expectations (Fabian, 2002). A successful start in preschool can have long-term benefits for future learning. Studies have highlighted the importance of children's experiences of transition to a preschool environment and the potentially detrimental effects if it is not a positive experience (Barrett, 1986).

Uncertainties about being in preschool may be matched by the parents' own feelings about having the child enrolled in preschool, especially when there are cultural and language differences between home and school. Ethnographic studies show that children from minority groups experience more difficulties than majority-group children because of a number of frustrations, including the language and the educational establishment (Gregory & Biarnes, 1994; Woods et al., 1999).

If the reported memories are correct for the young immigrant children in this study, most had positive feelings during their first day in the preschool, mainly because they were engaged in play or felt that they were not causing a disturbance in the classroom. The role of the teacher is also important and supportive during the first days in the school environment. Although no formal data were collected from the teachers, they told us that behavior problems of the immigrant children at the beginning of the school year (e.g., crying. displaying other signs of unhappiness, or noncompliance with rules) were not perceived as any worse than those of native-born children.

The neighborhood and the school are two important environments where children from immigrant families come to terms with various experiences as they develop their sense of self. Both environments play a role in establishing emotional security. Feelings about being new are associated with the kind of interactions young children have with significant adults and other children (Kirova-Petrova, 2000). Interactive contexts appear to be highly significant and are related to the formation of friendships as substantiated by the interview results. Both parents and their children pay particular attention to interpersonal relations in their neighborhood, and the need for peer interaction to develop positive peer relationships needs to be a concern for parents and teachers. The nature of interactions of young children from immigrant families with others in the neighborhood can either support or negate their interactions in school. If the neighborhood does not support development of the host country's language (Greek) and acculturation and social relationships beyond the immediate neighbors, it may be more difficult for the child to adapt to the culture of the school (Paleologou, 2004). This study highlights the need for further investigation of ties not only between school and home but also with neighborhood.

During the research project, it became evident to both of us and to the teachers that most of the immigrant parents functioned with a sense of low self-efficacy, because they demonstrated higher rates of depression, negative affect, and greater perceptions of their child's difficulties. Certainly, immigration is a stressful life transition, because unfamiliarity with the new country, difficulties in securing satisfactory employment, and the cultural adjustments all affect feelings of self-efficacy. Parents perceived their role as disappointingly low in their responses about their children's adaptation. Our findings showed minimum preparation for children at home, and it appears that the parents had high expectations that the school would take care of most aspects of the children's adaptation process. In reality, school–home connections were minimal because of language differences and teachers' limited time for making more contact with the children's families outside school. There was little or no opportunity for parents to find out about how to enhance their children's readiness for school and to contribute to their smooth transition.

Communication skills and collaboration between teachers and parents of newcomer children is a matter of great importance. Theories about school–home relations such as those of Bernstein (1990), Bronfenbrenner (1979), and Epstein and Dauber (1991), recognize the essential links between both microsystems for the subsequent development of the child.

In Greek early childhood settings, language problems are the main factor that gives rise to inadequate communication between teachers and children and parents from minority groups. Inability to communicate with the child and the family can in turn affect the level of professionals' effective teaching. Professionals who are confident about the efficacy of their teaching instruction and pedagogical discourse usually have good relations and collaborate successfully with minority parents (Giangounidis & Vidali, 2004).

Most of the teachers who served as interviewers took this as an opportunity to develop closer relationships with parents. It was the first time they had had the chance to discuss such important issues with them. One teacher said, "I never thought that this family had such [unfortunate] experiences." We hope that the parents found it equally useful and that the interviews served as a key to better communication and further collaboration between parents and school personnel.

Statistical analysis using chi-square for the pairing of some of the questions—such as what the child remembered about the first day of school and how the child responded to how he or she felt about school—revealed few significant differences. No differences were found based on the gender or age of the children and their responses to interview questions. Response patterns from the data indicate a possible relationship between children's reporting of how they felt about school, who had greeted them on the first day, and whether they felt positive about school 5 months later ($p \gg .01$). Similar links were determined between how children felt about the first day, where they sat, and whether they formed friendships with classmates. This, of course, does not imply that a teacher's greeting on the first day of school makes a difference in the child's overall school adjustment and comfort in the classroom. However, it does suggest that if a child has made good adjustment to school, he or she is more likely to view the beginning as positive and would have been comfortable in the school setting from the beginning. In other words, the child who makes a good start is more likely to feel positive about the school experience in general. Welcoming the child, helping the child to feel comfortable anywhere in the room, and helping the child to form friendships are all important.

The limited extent to which parents reported that they had prepared their child for the move was a disappointing finding. In addition, there was a significant difference between what parents said and what children reported about how he or she felt about the first week of school. Parents were more likely to report that the child was fine at school, whereas the child was more likely to say that he or she was not happy ($p \gg .01$). Whether this difference emerged because of poor communication between parent and child, parents' reluctance to tell the teacher that the child had not been completely happy at the beginning of school, or the children's inaccurate memory is impossible to determine. Regardless of the reason, the difference suggests that it might be worthwhile investigating whether parents' perceptions of a child's adjustment to preschool are accurate and whether additional communication is needed between parents and the school. Children may not share feelings at home because they are reluctant to speak or lack opportunities to share feelings with their parents or because of cultural behavior patterns of adult–child interaction. In any case, the school personnel could alert parents to the need to offer emotional support if this appears warranted. It also points to the need for the school, with or without assistance from the home, to provide as much support as possible to assist the child in the transition to school. Consideration of how children are welcomed to the group setting, seating arrangements in the classroom, and formation of friendships in school are all in the realm of what good teachers do to create a high-quality preschool environment.

Because our data are qualitative, the question of the reliability of a child's memory, even when the time has been only 5 months, and the hesitancy of some of the immigrant parents to express their feelings openly, mean that few conclusions can be confidently drawn. It is more appropriate to suggest potential directions for further research to seek answers to the questions raised.

IMPLICATIONS

The continually increasing number of immigrant families is forcing teachers to deal with many factors that affect classroom dynamics and school–parent relationships. In Greece, a nation where it is estimated that school enrollment is decreasing by 3%–4% annually, the recent waves of immigrants have brought an approximate 50% increase in minority students (Hatziprokopiou, 2003). Teachers must face their own personal reluctance toward working with families and ensure that the immigrant children are made welcome in the classroom, modeling acceptance of all children (Dimakos & Tasiopoulou, 2003). Language can be a challenge for any child beginning school, especially when the teachers use unfamiliar words and expressions. The problem is exacerbated when the language of the school is different from the language of the home: The child may become socially isolated in the classroom (Fabian, 2002). Teachers and other school personnel need to support the child in learning the language of the classroom and to provide extra services as available and appropriate.

Immigrant parents have many stressors on their lives, and the data from this study open a tiny window of insight into their lives. Although firm conclusions cannot be drawn from these data for several reasons, there is evidence that some immigrant children enter preschool with minimal preparation from the home environment for such a major transition. The integration of migrants into a host country is a dynamic process and one through which the new arrivals must build their lives in the new setting. As one of the most significant experiences for children, school must work cohesively with the community to welcome immigrant children and their parents (Hatziprokopiou, 2003).

Starting school is a time of psychological and social change not only for the child but also for the family (Fabian, 2002). The interviews with children and parents reported in this study showed that there is room for improvement in preparing children for the school experience and providing support for them until they reach a level of adaptation to the school setting. The results suggest that further study is needed about how newly immigrated families can become more aware of their role in helping the child make the transition to school, including how to use neighborhood social contacts mentioned by many of the parents to gain such knowledge.

The results also clearly show a need to educate and support teachers in their efforts to incorporate immigrant children smoothly into the classroom.

REFERENCES

Barrett G. (1986). *Starting School: An Evaluation of the Experience.* London: Assistant Masters and Mistresses Association.

Bernstein B. (1990). *Class, Codes and Control. Volume IV: The Structuring of Pedagogic Discourse.* London: Routledge.

Bourdieu, P. (1990). *The logic of practice.* Cambridge, UK: Polity Press.

Bronfenbrenner, U. (1979). *The Ecology of Human Development.* Cambridge, MA: Harvard University Press.

Brooker, L. (2002). *Starting School.* Milton Keynes, UK: Open University Press

Dimakos, I., & Tasiopoulou, K. (2003). Attitudes towards migrants: What do Greek students think about their immigrant classmates? *Intercultural Education, 14,* 307–316.

Epstein J., & Dauber, S. (1991). School programs and teacher practices of parent involvement in inner-city elementary and middle schools. *Elementary School Journal, 91,* 289–303.

Fabian, H. (2002). *Children Starting School: A Guide to Successful Transitions and Transfers for Teachers and Assistants.* London: David Fulton.

Galati P. (2004, November 21). The profile of immigrants in Greece. *Kathemerine,* p. 30.

Giangounidis, P., & Vidali, L. E. (2004). Language differences in preschool education: Views of early childhood teachers. In Kuriakido Brothers (Eds.), *Proceedings of 4th Pan-Hellenic conference of Pedagogical Society* (pp. 535–545). Alexandroupolis, Greece: Kuroalodp Brothers.

Gregory E., & Biarnes, J. (1994). Tony and Jean-Francois: Looking for sense in the strangeness at home and at school. In H. Dombey & M. M. Spencer (Eds.), *First steps together* (pp. 17–29). Stoke-on-Trent, UK: Trentham.

Hatziprokopiou, P. (2003). Albanian immigrants in Thessaloniki, Greece: Process of economic and social incorporation. *Journal of Ethnic and Migration Studies, 29,* 1033–1057.

Kasimis, C., & Kassimi, C. (2004). *Greece: A History of Migration.* Washington, DC: Migration Policy Institute. Retrieved November 8, 2004, from http://www.migrationinformation.org/Profiles/display.cfm?id=228

Katsikas, C., & Politou, E. (2005). *Repatriates and Immigrants in the Greek School. Outside the Classroom the Different?* Athens, Greece: Gutenberg.

Kirova-Petrova, A. (2000). Researching young children's lived experiences of loneliness: Pedagogical implications for language minority students. *Alberta Journal of Educational Research, 46,* 99–116.

Knoff, H. (1986). *The Assessment of Child and Adolescent Personality.* New York: Guilford.

Kotsionis, P. (1995). The historical-cultural identity and the educational tradition of repatriate Pontic Greeks as a prerequisite for their children's adaptation. *Ta Ekpedeftika, 39–40,* 33–45.

Lakasas, A. (2003, November 6). Institute for the Greek Diaspora Education and Intercultural Studies (IPODE) October 2003. *Kathimerini,* p. 3.

Nuttall, E. V., Romero, I., & Kalesnik, J. (1992). *Assessing and Screening Preschoolers. Psychological and Educational Dimensions.* Needham Heights, MA: Allyn & Bacon.

Paleologou, N. (2004). Intercultural education and practice in Greece: Need for bilingual intercultural programmes. *Intercultural Education, 15*(3), 317–329.

Pollard, A., & Filer A. (1996). *The Social World of Children's Learning: Case Studies of Pupils from Four to Seven.* London: Cassell.

Psalti, A., & Deliyanni-Kouimtzi, V. (2001). The education of students from the former Soviet Union and Albania in the context of the cultural-ecological approach. In V. Deliyanni-Kouimtzi & A. Psalti (Eds.), *Scientific Annals of the School of Philosophy* (vol. 4, pp. 287–316). Thessaloniki, Greece: Art of Text.

Veikou, C. (2004). Cultural differences in Greek education: A negotiation of identities. In N. Terzis (Ed.), *Intercultural Education in the Balkan Countries* (pp. 107–114). Thessaloniki, Greece: Kyriakidis Brothers.

Vidali, L. E., & Giangounidis, P. (2003). Multicultural perspectives in early childhood education: A study on early childhood teachers' views and their problems in Greece. In N. Terzis (Ed.), *Intercultural Education in the Balkan Countries* (pp. 221–237). Thessaloniki, Greece: Kyriakidis Brothers.

Willes, M. (1983). *Children into Pupils.* London: Routledge & Kegan Paul.

Woods, P., Boyle, M., & Hubbard, N. (1999). *Multicultural Children in the Early Years.* Clevedon, UK: Multilingual Matters.

Introduction to Part III

Views and Voices of Immigrant Children

Although the development and experiences of today's immigrant children cannot be understood apart from family roles, they cannot be reduced to the class backgrounds of their parents. The factors involved in shaping the changing lives of immigrant children are very complex. For example, the incoming resources include family socioeconomic status, parental literacy, and education, as well as children's previous physical and psychological health, previous school experiences, proficiency in the language of instruction, and legal immigrant status. The host culture variables include occupational opportunities for immigrants in their local settings, structural barriers to immigrants, neighborhood safety and ethnic relations, and quality of available schooling (Trueba & Bartolome, 2000). In part III, the authors explore immigrant children's experiences of schooling in their new host countries as they describe them. Children's hope and worries, likes and dislikes, and strategies for forging peers relationships are explored. Research about immigrant children's school experiences, however limited, points to the multiple problems these children face in learning a new language, in coping with the disruption of family life and poverty, and adjusting to a new culture that often conflicts with their own cultural values (Duran & Weffer, 1992; Gonzalez-Ramos & Sanchez-Nester, 2001; Suárez-Orozco & Suárez-Orozco, 2001). The authors of chapter 9 demonstrate the importance of listening to children's voices in gaining a better understanding of children's experiences of immigration from mainland China to Hong Kong. Although these children were not racially different from the majority peers, they experienced segregation, prejudice, and marginalization based on their accents and dialects. Adapting to a new school and social environment while leaving friends behind and learning new languages of instruction (i.e., Putonghua and English) were identified by the children as their main difficulties. Chapter 9 suggests that schools in general and teachers in particular have an important positive role in children's social adjustment. In addition, the study's results demonstrated that peers too have an important role in immigrant children's adjustment to the school culture. Adjustment to the mainstream peer culture as part of the overall acculturation process, however, involves an active application of strategies for initiating and maintaining peer relationships (Kirova-Petrova & Wu, 2002). The fact that immigrant children in the study were able to provide specific advices to new immigrant children coming from the mainland suggested that they are active agents in this process.

Asking immigrant children to give advice to a newcomer in a school inspired the development of a visual story—fotonovela about the rejected attempts of a new girl in a school to join an on-going game on the basketball court (chapter 10). The study presented in this chapter explored the role of understanding or misunderstanding of nonverbal behaviors in the process of establishing interpersonal relationships among children from diverse cultural and linguistic backgrounds. Cultural misunderstandings can result in prejudice and discrimination, and newly immigrated children, already struggling with an unfamiliar language and confusing cultural changes, must also work to overcome the impact of negative attitudes (McBrien, 2005). The method developed by the authors allows for going beyond social learning through observations (Bandura, 1977) as a sufficient means for newcomers to navigate their school social environment.

Learning to understand the observed behaviors presents a distinct set of challenges for newcomers who wish to engage in and maintain peer relationships in multicultural and multilingual school contexts. Although nonverbal translation has been recognized as a remedy for potential intercultural misunderstanding (Hanna, 1984), teaching children nonverbal communication has been largely neglected because of "the pre-eminent status of the word in technologically advanced societies" (p. 400). Unlike Feldman et al. (1991), who suggested formal training for improving the accuracy of decoding for students in Grades 5 and 6, the authors of chapter 10 suggest that developing and sharing visual narratives in the form of fotonovelas that depict life in school can promote understanding of peer interaction between children from varying cultural and linguistic backgrounds.

Peer interactions also have a great impact on children's sense of who they are as they negotiate their identities between home and school cultures. Many aspects of our "selves" contribute to our understanding of who we are: race, gender, class, occupation, age, language and culture, among others (Kanno, 2003). Identity refers to our sense of who we are and our relationship to the world. However, with regard to immigrants' identities, Norton Peirce (1995) conceptualized individual identity as "diverse, contradictory, and dynamic; multiple rather than unitary, decentered rather than centered" (p. 15). Norton (2000) stated that social identities are born out of the interaction between the learner and the learning context. In the case of young children, learning context produces certain identities for the learners that they have little power to resist (Toohey, 2000).

Learning does not happen only in the classroom; learning context goes beyond the school and the home to include not only the larger community but also the reality created by the mass media in the globalized world. Chapter 11 explores (a) how the popular television shows provide "space" for children of all cultures to have shared experiences and to communicate and build social relationships with other children and (b) how the content of the programs and the conversations about them allow children to develop their own identities. Even when language fluency was not present, acting out a scene from a television program allowed access and acceptance into a peer group.

According to Cushner et al. (2003), the media and the school curriculum may be similar in the eyes of the immigrant student: blurring information with entertainment, chaotic, inconsistent, and laden with conflicting messages. However, the author of chapter 11 points out that people use media to maintain past connections and to build new social relations and sense of place in the process of migration. Media assists them to develop new skills to live different places and identities and to learn to be multidomestic. Globalized media allows children to view the same programs in different languages and in different places as they move around in search of a place that they can call home. On the one hand, this provides a sense of continuity in children's lives. On the other hand, television played a significant role building autobiographical memories and histories. Through the use of media, children were active agents in the creation of their new lives rather than passive victims.

Immigrant children's sense of agency in making their new countries their homes and feeling at home in the host country's language are discussed in chapter 12. The author argues that the experience of immigration invites children to ask, "In what relation do I live to the language I speak?" The opportunity that immigration opens for asking this question is of the utmost importance in awakening children's awareness of their relation to language, both the language of home and the home of language. This investigation showed that for young children the creative and active relation-making processes are not limited to language. Rather it is young children's ability to engage with the world both nonlinguistically and linguistically, as in play, that allows them not only to live between languages but also to develop their relation to the language of home and the home of language. Thus chapter 12 challenges the traditional assumptions about immigrant children as lacking agency, competence, and knowledge by opening up considerable pedagogical possibilities as it emphasis young immigrant children's capacity to perceive and construct new relatedness through what is dissimilar rather than to deduct from what is known.

By providing rich first-hand accounts of immigrant children's experiences of immigration, all four chapters in this part allow the reader to gain deeper understanding of the role of informal learning experiences in which immigrant children exercise their agency, competence, and knowledge and to construct their relationships to the cultures they live in and build bridges between them.

REFERENCES

Bandura, A. (1977). *Social Learning Theory.* New York: Holt, Rinhart & Winston.

Corson, D. (1998). *Changing Education for Diversity.* Buckingham, UK: Open University Press.

Cushner, K., McClelland, A. & Safford, P. L. (Eds.). (2003). *Human Diversity in Education: An Integrative Approach* (4th ed.). Boston: McGraw-Hill.

Duran, B. J., & Weffer, R. E. (1992). Immigrant aspirations, high school process & academic outcomes. *American Educational Research Journal, 29,* 163–181.

Feldman, R. S., Philippot, P., & Custrini, R. J. (1991). Social competence and nonverbal behavior. In R. Feldman & B. Rime (Eds.), *Fundamentals of Nonverbal Behavior* (pp. 329–350). Cambridge, UK: Cambridge University Press.

Gonzalez-Ramos, G., & Sanches-Nester, M. (2001). Responding to Immigrant Children's Mental Health Needs in the Schools: Project Mi Tierra/My Country. *Children and Schools, 23*(1), 49–63.

Hanna, J. L. (1984). Black/white non-verbal differences, dance and dissonance: Implications for desegregation. In A. Wolfgang (Ed.), *Nonverbal Behavior: Perspectives, Applications, Intercultural Insights* (pp. 373–409). Toronto, ON: C. J. Hogrefe.

Kanno, Y. (2003). *Negotiating Bilingual and Bicultural Identities: Japanese Returnees Betwixt Two Worlds.* Mahwah, NJ: Lawrence Erlbaum Associates.

Kirova-Petrova, A. (2000). Researching Young Children's Lived Experiences of Loneliness: Pedagogical Implications for Language Minority Students. *Alberta Journal of Educational Research, XLVI*(2), 99–116.

Kirova-Petrova, A., & Wu, J. (2002). Peer Acceptance, Learning English as a Second Language, and Identity Formation in Children of Recent Chinese Immigrants. In A. Richardson, M. Wyness & A. Halvorsen (Eds.), *Exploring Cultural Perspectives, Integration and Globalization* (pp. 171–190). Edmonton, AB: ICRN Press.

McBrien, J. L. (2005). Educational needs and barriers for refugee students in the United States: A review of the literature. *Review of Educational Research, 75*(3), 329–364.

Norton, B. (2000) *Identity and Language Learning: Gender, Ethnicity and Educational Change.* Harlow, England: Pearson Education.

Norton Peirce, B. (1995). Social identity, investment, and language learning. *TESOL Quarterly, 29*(1), 9–29.

Suárez-Orozco, C., & Suárez-Orozco, M. M. (2001). *Children of Immigrants.* Cambridge, MA: Harvard University Press.

Toohey, K. (2000). *Learning English in School.* Clevedon, UK: Multilingual Matters.

Trueba, E. T., & Bartolome, L. I. (Eds.) (2000). *Immigrant Voices: In Search of Educational Equity.* Boston: Rowman & Littlefield Publishers Inc.

Chapter 9

Listening to Children: Voices of Newly Arrived Immigrants From the Chinese Mainland to Hong Kong

Nirmala Rao and Mantak Yuen
University of Hong Kong

Hong Kong, a former British colony, has a unique situation with regard to school-aged immigrants. Before 1997, children from 6 to 14 years could not legally immigrate from mainland China. Only after Hong Kong's reunification with the Chinese mainland in 1997 could dependent children of a Hong Kong resident and a mainland Chinese spouse be permitted entry into Hong Kong. Therefore, the educational and psychological needs of immigrant children are a relatively recent concern. Table 1 shows the number of children from mainland China admitted to primary schools between 1998 and 2003. The number peaked in 1998 at 17,988, and now more than 6,000 school-aged immigrants from mainland China attend primary schools in Hong Kong every academic year (Hong Kong Government, 2004). The need to provide appropriate educational support for young immigrants has presented challenges both to the government and to nongovernmental organizations.

The term *new arrivals* is used in all government documents to refer to people who have immigrated from mainland China and lived in Hong Kong for less than 1 year. Youth younger than 20 years of age are considered *new arrival children*

TABLE 1
Number of Children From the Chinese Mainland Admitted Into Primary Schools in
Hong Kong and Repetition Rate (1998–2003)

Year	No. of NAC admitted to Primary Schools	Number % of children Who Had to Repeat a Grade
1998	17,988	n.a.
1999	17,518	10,379 (59.2)
2000	11,630	7,302 (62.8)
2001	8,775	4,276 (48.7)
2002	6,549	2,781 (42.5)
2003	6,989	2,881 (41.2)

Source. Hong Kong government (2004, p. 20), Appendix

(NAC). These children perhaps have different experiences from those of their counterparts in other parts of the world because of their proximity to their place of origin before immigration and because of their ethnicity. For example, some school-aged children continue to reside in mainland China and commute to Hong Kong every day to attend school. Ethnically, the new immigrants are indistinguishable from those in the host territory. Indeed, Hong Kong itself is a land of immigrants; most originate from southern China.

CHALLENGES FOR IMMIGRANTS FROM THE CHINESE MAINLAND

Surveys conducted by the government and independent research teams indicate that immigrants from the Chinese mainland face a number of challenges (Chan, Ip, & Yuen, 1996; Chan, Yuen, Lau, Wu, & Ip, 2003). These include (a) securing age-appropriate school placements; (b) adjusting to a new educational system and curriculum; (c) adapting to a new school and social environment; (d) confronting segregation, prejudice, and marginalization; and (e) adjusting to changes in family ecologies (Rao & Yuen, 2001). Each of these challenges is discussed in greater depth in the following sections.

Securing Age-Appropriate School Placements

Of the 6,989 students admitted into primary schools between 2002 and 2003, 71.6% were admitted to the lower primary grades (Primary 1 to 3). A relatively large proportion of these students (41.2%) had to repeat the same grade or a lower grade already completed in mainland China. In fact, among students admitted into Primary 4 to Primary 6, 4.7% had attended secondary school in mainland China before immigrating to Hong Kong. Not surprisingly, many of these children (54.4%) were overaged or in a class that was not commensurate with their chronological age (Hong Kong Government, 2004).

Some of the children admitted into primary schools in Hong Kong between 2002 and 2003 attended either kindergarten in Hong Kong or an induction program for NAC. Apart from these, 73.4% of the remaining 4,379 children were enrolled in schools within 3 months of arrival in Hong Kong. Approximately 600 students were not enrolled in schools for more than 6 months after immigrating to Hong Kong. Some returned to the mainland and continued schooling there while waiting for admission to Hong Kong schools.

Adjusting to a New Educational System

There are differences between the educational systems of Hong Kong and mainland China. One major difference lies in the language of instruction. Putonghua, the spoken form of standard modern Chinese, is used in schools in the Mainland, whereas Cantonese is spoken in Hong Kong classrooms. The written script also differs. Simplified Chinese characters are used in mainland China, whereas traditional characters are used in Hong Kong. English is taught as a subject beginning in kindergarten in Hong Kong, but this is typically not the case in mainland China. Hence, many students have problems related to the language of instruction and learning English.

Adapting to a New School and Social Environment

In addition to coping with a different school curriculum and different pedagogies, immigrant children must adjust to a new social milieu in schools. Leaving friends behind and having to make new ones can cause children to experience loneliness and feelings of isolation. These feelings can affect their school adjustment and achievement (Chan et al., 2003).

Segregation, Prejudice, and Marginalization

Despite their ethnic similarity to Hong Kong Chinese, newly arrived immigrants from the mainland are identifiable by their accents and dialects. There have been numerous reports of discrimination by the majority population (Rao & Yuen, 2001).

Adjusting to Changes in Family Ecologies

Immigrant children may be separated from their mothers and younger siblings, because their mothers may not yet have received the right of abode in Hong Kong and so must remain in mainland China. Chan and colleagues (1996) found that 19% of the mothers of NAC in the Sham Shui Po district were still living in mainland China.

Research suggests that schools that adopt a holistic approach to meeting the developmental needs of immigrant children are more effective in reaching them and their families than schools that provide academic instruction without other support. Schools that provide structured opportunities for children to interact socially, overcome their loneliness, develop close friendships, and deal with academic challenges (Bhavnagri, 2001) promote the adjustment of newly arrived children and enable them to reach their full potential.

There is little research on immigrant children's feelings of loneliness and isolation in school (Kirova, 2001; Rubin & Bhavnagri, 2001). This is disturbing because children's thoughts affect their perceptions of everyday experiences in school. It has been argued that "only when educators understand how immigrant children's experiences affect their quality of life and learning at school can they take pedagogically sensitive actions to help the children develop higher self-esteem and become successful members of the school community" (Kirova, 2001, p. 250).

In this chapter, we present the results of an empirical study that had the following objectives: (a) to gain an understanding of the social and academic challenges that children who have immigrated from the Chinese mainland to Hong Kong experience in their school setting and (b) to make recommendations on how schools can better meet the social and academic needs of these children.

METHODOLOGY

In our qualitative study, we conducted semistructured interviews to gain an understanding of immigrant children's perceptions of their experiences. Information about demographic variables was obtained from both children and their parents.

Participants

We selected three schools known to have admitted many NAC from mainland China. These schools were located in each of Hong Kong's three main regions: Hong Kong Island, Kowloon, and the New Territories. We approached the principals of these schools, informed them of the objectives of our study, and asked them to allow us to write to parents requesting permission for their children to be interviewed. All three principals agreed, and 37 primary schoolchildren enrolled in these three schools were interviewed in individual sessions.

We interviewed 21, 9, and 7 students in schools Y, H, and F respectively. The sample included 21 girls and 16 boys ranging in age from 9 to 14 years. Twenty-two children were enrolled in Primary 3 or 4, and 15 were enrolled in Primary

5 or 6. Guidance teachers in the three schools helped to identify children who had lived in Hong Kong for fewer than 2 years, and then we contacted the parents to obtain permission to interview their children.

Most of these students had come from Guangdong province (92% of the mothers and 87% of the fathers were from Guangdong). This is significant, because 55% of the children reported using Cantonese in their places of origin, and 65% reported using Cantonese in their home in Hong Kong.

Mothers ranged in age from 30 to 46 years, and fathers ranged from 30 to 74 years. Of the mothers, 30% had completed only primary education, whereas 57% had finished junior secondary and 10% had completed senior secondary school. Among the fathers, 5% had no education; 30%, 41%, and 19% had completed primary, junior secondary, and senior secondary education, respectively. Approximately 25% of the participants were only children, and 51% had one to two siblings.

Data Collection Methods

An interview protocol that consisted of questions about school issues (17 questions), family issues (9 questions), neighborhood issues (5 questions), and feelings about Hong Kong (8 questions) was developed in English and translated into Chinese. A backtranslation procedure was used to ensure the accuracy of the translation (see appendix I). Standard demographic information was collected from students and parents. Some information, for example, when the child started attending school, was verified by checking school records.

Procedure

Three female graduate students in a faculty of education in a university in Hong Kong were trained to administer the interview. All were fluent in English and Cantonese, and two also spoke Putonghua. They practiced interviewing and coding transcripts with children not included in the study until they achieved an interrater reliability of 95%.

The three graduate students interviewed the children in their schools in individual sessions. The interviews, which took place in November 2003, were conducted in Cantonese, but children were asked if they preferred to speak Putonghua. All interview sessions were tape-recorded and transcribed by the interviewers. Interrater reliability for the transcription of the data was determined by asking one of the graduate students to listen to an interview conducted by a colleague. Interrater reliability was approximately 95%.

We repeatedly read the interview transcripts and identified ideas and themes in the answers related to our research objectives, that is, to determine the main academic and social challenges faces by NAC.

RESULTS AND DISCUSSION

School Issues

Seventeen of the 37 children said that they were apprehensive on the first day of school but were well adjusted by the time of the interview. A typical response was, "I felt nervous and scared on the first day because of the unfamiliar environment, but I am not nervous or scared any more." The following is an atypical response:

> It is still very difficult to get used to the school life here. Sometimes I feel like crying. Especially when I ask them for help, they all say they do not know. The teacher does not know that I am unhappy and the teacher cannot help me with my studies.

A consistent picture emerged of the school and the attitudes of the principal, staff, and students toward NAC in school Y. When asked about what they liked about school Y, 10 of the 21 respondents said that they liked the principal, teachers, and classmates because they were very welcoming of NAC. The principal and teachers made extra efforts to talk to the NAC and understand their needs and provided some children with extra academic tutoring after school. Six of the children mentioned that they liked the extracurricular activities provided by the school, and four said that they liked the physical environment.

Six of the seven children from the school F mentioned that they liked the better facilities, equipment (e.g., computers), and teaching in this school; two also reported liking the teachers and classmates. Among those in school H, five of the nine children mentioned that they liked the better facilities, teaching, and school environment; three said that they liked their teachers or classmates. A common response was, "I like the school because the school has lot of computers and audiovisual equipment such as overhead projectors and TV sets. The equipment is outdated and old in my previous school in the Chinese mainland."

It is clear that teachers' actions have an important effect on the feelings of immigrant children. The principal and teachers in school Y made a concerted effort to welcome NAC and support them. In this school, approximately half the children particularly mentioned their fondness for the principal and teachers. Only 2 of 7 in school F and 3 of 9 in school H mentioned this. In the other schools, 5 of 21 children mentioned that they liked the school facilities and physical environment the best. Public schools in Hong Kong have better facilities than their counterparts in the China mainland, and the three schools in Hong Kong are comparable in terms of resources for learning. Responses suggested that children of this age appreciate psychological support for learning. In the school where children perceived this the most, it was noted as the characteristic they most liked about the school. This suggests that schools catering to NAC should place as much emphasis on psychological support as on support for academic learning.

Interestingly, 7 of the 21 children in the sample specifically stated that they liked the fact that there were no bullies in the school, which leads one to wonder about the extent of bullying in schools in mainland China.

Hopes and Worries

Children were asked to articulate their hopes and worries and were overwhelmingly concerned about academic achievement and performance in examinations. Thirty of the 36 children interviewed hoped that they would have better academic achievement, and 23 were worried about their academic performance. Students were particularly concerned with their performance in English-language examinations: 13 hoped they could do better in English, and 12 of the 36 mentioned that they were worried about their standard of English or performance in the English school examinations. Typical responses included "I hope to get the best academic results in the class and get the first rank in class" (boy in Primary 3); "I wish to be smarter. I particularly want to do better in English" (girl in Primary 4); "I hope I can do better in all subjects, particularly in English and other general subjects" (girl in Primary 5).

We need to interpret these findings in the Hong Kong context. Immigrants from the mainland have not had the same exposure to English as have primary school students in Hong Kong schools. Hence, their English proficiency is likely to be lower than that of their nonimmigrant counterparts. Although all primary schools in Hong Kong use Chinese as the language of instruction, only 114 secondary schools in Hong Kong are allowed to use English as the language of instruction. These are Band 1 schools for children with high academic ability. Academic achievement is highly valued in Chinese societies, and education is regarded as the path to success and financial gain. Parents of immigrants may consider education as the path to upward social mobility, and children are aware of this. University places in Hong Kong are still limited to approximately 18% of the school-leaving age group, and all parents want their children to be admitted to Band 1 schools, because they believe that this will improve their children's chances of attaining a place in university.

Two children were concerned with their immigration status and worried about being able to stay in Hong Kong. Another was concerned that his mother was not allowed to return to Hong Kong. Three children who were living with one parent hoped that they could again live with both parents. Examples of children's responses were "I hope I can stay in Hong Kong from now on" (girl in Primary 3); and "I wish my mum could migrate to Hong Kong from mainland so that she could be with me" (girl in Primary 4).

Family and Neighborhood Issues

Most of the children lived in intact nuclear or extended families. Six lived with their mothers and siblings in Hong Kong while the father worked in mainland

China and visited them in Hong Kong. Two lived with their fathers in Hong Kong, because their mothers did not have the right of abode in Hong Kong. Four lived in the Chinese mainland and commuted to Hong Kong (approximately 4 h every day) to attend school. This was probably because of the higher cost of living in Hong Kong and because parents believed that children who were educated in Hong Kong would have better prospects later in life. In general, children were not well integrated into their neighborhoods and typically played only with siblings. Although 10 children mentioned community centers, they were not aware of the social services available to new immigrants.

Ten of the 37 children were positive about living in Hong Kong, and some were still becoming adjusted. They were aware of the opportunities that being educated in Hong Kong would provide. Many said they liked the parks and the Hong Kong environment generally. Responses to questions about their feelings about living in Hong Kong included "I feel good about the move to Hong Kong because there are lots of things to do in Hong Kong such as going to the playgrounds" (boy in Primary 3); "I feel good about the move to Hong Kong because there are lots of places to play in Hong Kong. Sometimes my mum will take me to the parks or swimming pools" (girl in Primary 3); and "The place is cleaner than my hometown. The social order is better. People here queue up for buses" (girl in Primary 3).

Others who came from rural areas in China missed their larger living quarters. When asked what they missed the most about living in the mainland, most said that they missed their grandparents, cousins, friends, or pets. For example, a girl in Primary 4 said, "I miss my grandpa because he is very good. I can go back to visit my homeland once a few months."

Eight of the 37 children had not yet returned to the mainland, some still lived there, and the rest visited the mainland monthly or during holidays. The proximity of their place of origin to Hong Kong enabled frequent visits, which is something that may not be possible for immigrants in other countries.

Likes and Dislikes

We asked the children to articulate what they liked and disliked about Hong Kong, and their responses reflected their developmental level and their particular situation. Children who were not living with both parents before immigration were happy to be in an intact nuclear family. Five commented that they liked the parks and the better-developed economy in Hong Kong. Six disliked living in smaller apartments, and three said they disliked the air pollution.

When asked what advice they would give new immigrants from China to help them adjust to Hong Kong, they said that they would tell them to learn English and Cantonese, to take the initiative in making friends, and to deal with problems and display civic behavior. Examples of their advice include the following:

- Learn English and traditional Chinese characters well before arriving in Hong Kong. (Boy in Primary 3)
- Read the newspaper and watch TV to learn the local language. (Boy in Primary 4)
- Make friends by wandering around the school during recess time. The other children will come and play with you naturally and voluntarily. (Girl in Primary 3)
- Volunteer to help others and make friends. (Boy in Primary 3)
- Turn to classmates and teachers when you meet with difficulty in your study. (Girl in Primary 5)
- Be relaxed and do not worry too much. Talk more to others and ignore what others think about you. (Girl in Primary 4)
- Follow the school rules … do not fight with the others. Do not be scared and be relaxed. (Boy in Primary 4)
- Don't run around in the street for the traffic is very busy and dangerous. (Boy in Primary 6).

CONCLUSIONS

The voices of young immigrants suggest that they have generally adjusted well to living in Hong Kong. This is consistent with other studies using quantitative methods (Chan et al., 2003; Cheung & Hui, 2003). Our study has enabled a more in-depth understanding of how children experience the acculturation process (Schmitz, 2003). At first, children were apprehensive about moving to Hong Kong and studying there, but most said that they are happy now. The findings also reveal individual differences among children. Clearly some were not happy, and certain factors such as not living with both parents caused distress. Our interviews also suggested that school staff may play a crucial role in the adjustment process. Children in one school particularly appreciated the role played by the principal and teachers. Responses to interview questions suggested that children missed their extended families and friends in the mainland and that they were not generally well integrated into their neighborhoods.

Children's responses to interview questions reflected the value placed by Chinese parents on academic achievement. Immigrants from mainland China clearly share a strong cultural connection with Hong Kong Chinese people. However, there are still subcultural variations and distinctions between the two groups and children must adjust to a new educational system. Rubin and Bhavnagri (2001) argued that it is important for educators to have an insider's perspective to enable them to devise the most effective strategies for supporting these children. Indeed, in a survey of 1,680 newly arrived children from the Chinese mainland, Chan (2002) found that feeling lonely was the best predictor of acculturation of these young immigrants.

In a follow-up study on the effects of a school-based group guidance program, children from the Chinese mainland reported that the program had taught them valuable social skills (Chan, Yuen, & Lau, 2003).

Our findings suggest that teachers have an important role in children's social adjustment. Schools should develop and implement appropriate policies to meet the needs of immigrants. Specifically, they should continue to provide educational support services to deal with immigrants' social needs and concerns about their academic performance.

ACKNOWLEDGMENTS

This project was partly funded by the Sik Sik Yuen Education Research Fund. We thank Eve Chen, Ellen Zhang, Marine Yeung, and Candace Zhang for their help with the data collection and analyses and Leah Adams for suggestions for interview items.

REFERENCES

Bhavnagri, N. P. (2001). The global village: Migration and education. *Childhood Education, 77*(5), 256–259.

Chan, M. C., Ip, K.-Y., & Yuen, M. (1996). *Adaptation and Needs of Young New Arrivals from Mainland China in the Sham Shui Po District.* Hong Kong: 3A Printing.

Chan, R. M.-C. (2002). Acculturation of young new arrivals from Mainland China to Hong Kong. *Dissertation Abstracts International, 63*(1-B), 584.

Chan, R. M.-C., Yuen, M., Lau, P. S.-Y., Wu, S.-W., & Ip, K.-Y. (2003). *Acculturation of Young Arrivals from the Mainland.* Hong Kong: Hong Kong Baptist University Center for Educational Development.

Chan, S., Yuen, M., & Lau, P. (2003). The effects of a group guidance programme on the self-esteem of newly arrived children from Chinese Mainland to Hong Kong. *Asia Pacific Journal of Education, 23*(2), 171–182.

Cheung, H. Y., & Hui, S. K. F. (2003). Mainland immigrant and Hong Kong local students' psychological sense of school membership. *Asia Pacific Education Review, 4*(1), 67–74.

Hong Kong Government. (2004). *Survey on Children From the Mainland Newly Admitted to Schools October 2002 to September 2003.* Hong Kong: Author, Statistics Section, Education and Manpower Bureau.

Kirova, A. (2001). Loneliness in immigrant children: Implications for classroom practice. *Childhood Education, 77*(5), 260–267.

Rao, N., & Yuen, M. (2001). Accommodations for assimilation: Supporting newly arrived children from the Chinese Mainland in Hong Kong. *Childhood Education, 77*(5), 313–318.

Rubin, L., & Bhavnagri, N. P. (2001). Voices of recent Chaldean adolescent immigrants. *Childhood Education, 77*(5), 308–312.

Schmitz, P. G. (2003). Psychological factors of immigration and emigration: An introduction. In L. Loeb Adler & U. P. Gielen (Eds.), *Migration: Immigration and Emigration in International Perspective* (pp. 23–50) London: Praeger.

APPENDIX I

School Issues

When did you start attending this school?
Was this the first school you attended in Hong Kong?
Did you attend any special programs in the People's Republic of China or in Hong Kong for children who will be coming to schools in Hong Kong before you started school?
How long did you have to wait before you were admitted to school?
Tell me what you dislike about this school.
Tell me what you like about this school.
Do you find the studies difficult?
What is your most favorite/least favorite subject?
Tell me about your first day of school. What did you do? How did you feel?
How do you feel about school now? Why?
If I were to ask your mother/father how you feel about school, what do you think he/she would tell me?
Was it easy for you to make friends here? Why or Why not?
Who are your friends now?
Find out about social group—does he or she mix with only immigrant children?
What has been helpful to your adjustment in this school in Hong Kong?
Tell us about your worries in the past three months
Tell us about your hopes for the coming year.

Family Issues

Where were you born?
Which city/province in China does your family originally come from?
How often did you come to Hong Kong before you moved?
When did you get your papers to move to Hong Kong?
Is your mother in Hong Kong? Is your whole family in Hong Kong? How many brothers and sisters do you have? What are their ages? Do they attend school in Hong Kong?
What about grandparents? Extended family?
How often do you go to the mainland for holidays?
Do you think you will stay in Hong Kong for a long time?
Who helps you with your homework at home? English homework?

Neighborhood Issues

How many people are in the household? Name and relationship to target child.

Who plays with you in the household? In the neighborhood? Where do you go for leisure time?

Are there many people from the mainland in your district?

Community centre/support?

Feelings About Hong Kong

Have you heard the word immigrant? What does immigrant mean?

What is something good about moving here? Can you tell me something else that is good (about the move)?

What is something that is not so good about moving here?

Can you tell me something else that is not so good (about the move)?

What do you miss the most from (homeland)?

What else do you miss?

If another boy/girl were going to move to a new country, what advice would you give him/her?

What would you tell them about making friends?

Chapter 10

Immigrant Children's Understandings of Nonverbal Peer Interactions Through the Development of Visual Narratives

Anna Kirova and Michael Emme
University of Alberta, Canada

Data from the 2001 Census show that the foreign-born population of Canada is at its highest level in 70 years (Statistics Canada, 2003a). The Conference Board of Canada projected that by 2025 immigration will account for all population growth in the country. Because of greater diversity of ancestry and countries of origins among immigrant families, the number of visible minorities has tripled since 1981. In the large city in western Canada where our study took place, the most common 10 source countries were Philippines, India, China, Hong Kong, Vietnam, Poland, United Kingdom, United States, Bosnia or Herzegovina, and Lebanon. According to the 2001 Census, 17% of the 1.8 million immigrants who arrived in Canada during the 1990s were children aged 5 and 16 years. Currently in urban centers, nearly one of every five children has immigrated within the past 10 years (Statistics Canada, 2003b).

Immigrant children and youth are diverse in their educational backgrounds. Immigrant children with an English as a second language (ESL) background are often at risk in terms of literacy, academic achievement, and dropout. In Alberta,

151

the province in which the study took place, high school ESL students have over-all noncompletion rates between 61% and 74% compared with 30% for all Alberta high school students (Alberta Learning, 2001; Derwing, DeCorby, Ichikawa, & Jamieson, 1999; Watt & Roessingh, 1994). These numbers indicate that although many success stories illustrate the high levels of adaptability and integration of immigrant children into Canadian society, a significant number struggle to adjust to the Canadian school system.

Peer relationships have been found to be a predictor of more general school adjustment (Pelligrini & Blatchford, 2000; Pelligrini, Kentaro, Blatchford, & Baines, 2002). School peers are prime contributors to positive and negative expe-riences in school (Deegan, 1996), and they play a key role in the process of cul-tural reproduction (James, Jenks, & Prout, 1998). Positive social interactions with school peers contribute to the development of a strong sense of belonging among immigrant children (van Ngo, 2004). However, interactions with school peers are not without problems (Deegan, 1996). In earlier research (Kirova-Petrova, 2000), Kirova (2001) showed that social isolation and loneliness are common experi-ences among immigrant children, regardless of their racial, ethnic, or linguistic backgrounds. Children reported that because they were unable to be accepted as members of their peer group, they experienced the loneliness of being excluded, unwanted, and disliked. Other studies (Osterman, 2001) also showed that being excluded or ignored leads to intense feelings of anxiety, depression, grief, envy, and loneliness.

The problems associated with loneliness and isolation acquire even greater significance when viewed from the hypothesis that the need to belong is a funda-mental human motivation (Baumeister & Leary, 1995). Immigrant children's inability to satisfy this need may result in personal difficulties such as negative feelings about oneself and others. The relationship between oneself and others affects children's capacity for integration into the school culture (Winicott, 1971). Among the barriers faced by immigrant children in gaining the acceptance of their peers are unfamiliarity with Canadian patterns of oral, written, and nonverbal communication and social rules; differences in communication styles; and misinterpretation of cultural behaviors (van Ngo, 2004). A study of recent Chinese immigrants in elementary school (Kirova-Petrova & Wu, 2002), for example, suggested the possibility that miscommunication during their integra-tion into the school culture might be caused largely by their misinterpretation of the nonverbal cues of their classmates. Peer conflicts were about misunderstand-ings on the part of both the newcomers and their peers from the majority (non-Chinese) culture. In most reported cases, these misunderstandings occurred at a nonverbal level, and in all instances, the non-Chinese peers' behaviors were per-ceived by the newcomers as overt rejection and evoked either an aggressive response or hurt feelings, sadness, isolation, and loneliness.

Because nonverbal behavior (NVB) is the product of a continuing process of socialization in a given culture (Archer, 1997; Kendon, 1984; Pearce & Cronen,

1980; Watzlawick, Beavin, & Jackson, 1967), an immigrant or any newcomer to the culture decodes a nonverbal message according to his or her cultural heritage. This interpretation is usually not what the encoder means and is sometimes the opposite of what is meant (Archer, 1997; Schneller, 1985, 1988). The difficulty is heightened by the fact that most of the gestures that appear similar, differ greatly in their emblematic meaning (Efron, 1941; Ekman, 1983; Heslin & Patterson, 1982; Leach, 1972; von Raffler-Engel, 1980). This leads to false decoding (Poyatos, 1984, 1999) that produces miscommunication and misunderstanding (Mehrabian, 1971; Mehrabian & Weiner, 1967).

Although NVB plays a central role in the process of establishing interpersonal relationships (Feldman, Philippot, & Custrini, 1991), its importance has been overlooked in studies of young immigrant children, especially their understandings of their own and their peers' nonverbal communication in the context of their everyday interactions in school. The primary concern of the study reported in this chapter, therefore, was to help newly arrived immigrant children to examine the nonverbal strategies they used to gain access to majority-culture peers. Typically, research on immigrant children (Class, Stead, Arshad, & Norris, 2001; Kirova, 2001; Kirova-Petrova, 2000; Osterman, 2001) has been based on interviews with children. As a result, little is known about the actual NVBs used both to initiate interactions with peers and to cope with rejection or conflict. As studies have shown, cultural differences at a nonverbal level are implicit and exist at a deeper, more subtle level than people can describe (Archer, 1997; Hall, 1976, 1984). Thus for the purposes of this study, an innovative, arts-based research methodology was developed to allow immigrant children to explore their own and their peers' nonverbal strategies in their relationships. The main research question was: Could visual experiences, such as producing visual narratives in the form of fotonovelas, help immigrant children understand their own and their peers' NVBs? In this chapter, we use the Spanish spelling of the word fotonovela rather than the Anglicized version of the term photo novella (Emme & Kirova, 2005). Because it is our hope that our methodology is culturally sensitive, it is essential that we acknowledge the well documented origins of fotonovela in the popular literatures of Mexico and Italy (Curiel, 2001; Reed, 1998). To the best of our knowledge the much shorter 10-15-year history of the anglicized term has not been documented but we have concerns that this English term has the colonizing effect of distancing the service work it describes from the meaningful complexities of its cultural origins.

METHODOLOGY

In this study, we used an arts-based methodology with still photography as the primary visual data-collection method. Both the children and the researchers took photographs as members of a photo club organized and maintained for 18 months by the research team. Photography in general has been defined as a valuable participatory technique for eliciting children's opinions (Ells, 2001). The visual methodology used in this study, however, was unique in that the still photographs were not only used as a basis for discussion but also were manipulated and arranged in a narrative format as a fotonovela. As a storytelling form, the fotonovela can combine the familiar framing devices, sequencing, and text balloons of the comic book with posed or candid photographs of participants in place of pen-and-ink sketches. The fotonovela was a form of popular literature in Mexico, Italy, France, Portugal, and Quebec in the 1960s and 1970s. This blending of a highly entertaining and approachable narrative structure with the *naturalness or realism* of photography (Emme, 1989; Emme & Kirova, 2005) suited the melo-dramatic content of its popular form (Reed, 1998).

Current literature on the fotonovela as a research tool is found in the fields of health care and nursing. For example, Berman, Ford-Gilboe, Moutrey, and Cekic (2001) used the fotonovela as a research method in encouraging Bosnian refugee children to represent their memories and their first experiences in Canada. In this and other studies (Wang & Burris, 1994) the fotonovela is seen as a leveling, and even liberating, medium in a context where varying literacies create inequities and representational disparity. However, to our knowledge we were the first to use the fotonovela approach in educational research with both immigrant and nonim-migrant children. In this chapter, we used the process of creating one such fotonovela, "*Getting into Basketball*," to illustrate the methodology and to ana-lyze the content of the fotonovela to gain insights into children's understanding of nonverbal behaviors in peer interactions.

In addition to using still photography, we used elements of performative research in developing the fotonovelas. Acting scenes to be photographed as tableaus was one such element. As another form of arts-based research, perfor-mative research provided deeper insights into participants' lives. Originating from anthropology and communication and performance studies, "performance is regarded as both a legitimate and ethical way of representing ethnographic under-standing" (Conrad, 2004, p. 9). According to Conrad, performing allows partici-pants to depict and examine their real-life performances, thus "providing insight into their lived experiences and their cultural world" (p. 10).

From the point of view of the main research objective, namely, helping children explore their own and their peers' nonverbal behaviors in peer interac-tion, developing the fotonovelas had two distinct purposes. First, the children who created the visual narrative explored their own and their peers' bodily ways of communicating feelings in peer interactions. In creating the fotonovelas, the children had to act out the situation they wished to represent and show the feel-ings that the situation engendered in the participants. Through informal conver-sations about the relationship between one's feelings and one's expression of these emotions, the children became aware of how nonverbal messages were sent and received. Second, once developed, the fotonovela served as a visual medium for communicating the feelings of the characters in the scene to other children who had not taken part in its creation. *"Getting into Basketball"* was shown to children in Grades 4 and 5 who had not taken part in developing the visual narrative, and they were invited to respond to the story as they perceived and made sense of it.

Other data-gathering methods used were semistructured and unstructured individual and group interviews conducted with the children on an ongoing basis. These focused on children's experiences of schooling in Canada and took place during the lunch hour as part of the photo club. All but two children were fluent in spoken English and so could be interviewed in English; a bilingual research assistant interviewed the two Mandarin-speaking children in their native tongue. Consent forms for parents and children were translated into seven languages and sent home. Although all children who wished to participate in the photo club became members and participated more or less regularly in its activities, data were gathered only from the children whose parents consented to their participation in the study.

THE SETTING, THE PARTICIPANTS, AND THE RESEARCHERS

This study took place at Greenview, an innercity elementary–junior high school in a large city in western Canada. The school had a free lunch program because of the large number of low-income students enrolled. Visible minorities were a high percentage of the students. Some of the main demographics were Aboriginal, Chinese, Vietnamese, Korean, Arab, East Indian, and African. Many were first-generation immigrants and were classified as ESL students. More than seven languages were spoken among the 204 children in the school. Over the course of the study, which began in February 2004, the research team worked with 28 children from Grades 4, 5, and 6 who expressed interest in participating in the lunch-hour photo club. Over the course of the study, various children worked on a number of topics for example, lunchtime, the life of the playground, and me pretending. Three children, two from Grade 5 and one from Grade 4 were involved in developing the fotonovela described in this chapter. Of these, one was a nonimmigrant Caucasian, one was a recent immigrant from China, and one was from Vietnam.

The research team involved in the development of this particular fotonovela was made up of two education professors and two graduate students. The major strength of the research team was its diversity of professional and cultural backgrounds and personalities. During the study, team members engaged in various dialogues that were seen as a primary feature of the research method. These yielded a rich fertilization of ideas, changing roles, and shifting leadership positions, all of which allowed for growth not only in the participating children but also in each member of the research team (Emme, Kirova, Kamau, & Kosanovich, in press).

DEVELOPING THE "GETTING INTO
BASKETBALL" FOTONOVELA

At recess, the school playground provides a rich but underused venue for the study of school-aged children's peer interactions (Boulton & Smith, 1993; Hart, 1993; Pelligrini et al., 2002). Researchers agree that recess is one of the few opportunities for children in the strictly structured school to interact and engage in both games and free play with their peers. However, interactions among peers on the school playground appear only on the surface to be free. A growing body of literature on children's geographies (Holloway & Valentine, 2000) indicates that school playgrounds have become institutionalized spaces where adults attempt to control children and where differences between children have been reinscribed (Aitken, 1994). Researchers of peer interactions (Waters & Sroufe, 1983) suggest that interactions with peers at recess are both motivating and demanding for children. Engaging in games such as basketball, for example, requires a fair level of social and cognitive sophistication (Sutton-Smith, 1975), including knowing the rules of the game and being able to subordinate one's personal views and desires to those rules and to the positions of one's peers (Pelligrini et al., 2002). Research suggests (Kirova-Petrova, 1996) that games with rules may facilitate immigrant children's interactions with peers. Games such as basketball, in which the roles and rules are universally recognized and followed, may provide immigrant children who know and follow these rules a greater chance of acceptance by their peers than in games with loose or childmade rules that are context specific. However, in this study, the major challenge facing immigrant children was not following the rules but getting into the game itself.

Getting into basketball as the topic of the fotonovela emerged from an exploration of a larger topic, *Life on the Playground,* undertaken by the participants in the photo club. After their initial open-ended visual documentation of the playground, the Grade 4 and 5 children generated a checklist of ideas about the various activities of the playground. These were games, playing with equipment, listening, talking, being alone, leading, following, being together, following children's rules, and following grownups' rules. To explore these ideas, the children were sent in pairs to the playground to take documentary photographs of each of the categories on the list. The members of the research team supervised the activity but made no suggestions to the children about which shots to take or what to focus on.

The photographs taken by each pair were then printed, and the photographers were asked to examine them and color code how each photograph represented one or more categories on the checklist.

The topic of getting into basketball arose when one of the research assistants drew two girls into a world of make-believe. She told them of her imaginary niece who was coming to their school from a foreign country with no knowledge of school or city life. She enlisted them to help her to prepare her niece for the experience.

Margaret and Veronica, who were immigrant ESL students themselves, were eager to help the new girl (named Amy). In conversations, the girls began to tell the researcher about some of the unspoken rules of the playground and the etiquette that governed children in play and their outdoor behavior. The most animated discussions were about the basketball area. Here the children followed a strict code of conduct that would need to be explained to a newcomer. The girls gave the following advice to the imaginary new student: "Amy, if someone's shooting, don't go by." "If the ball rolls to you, don't take it." "Ask if you can play." Inspired by the girls' thoughtful engagement in the activity, the researcher suggested that they make a fotonovela of one such playground place and send it to Amy.

The next step was to use a storyboard to divide the story into frames that could be separately acted out and photographed. The children chose the basketball court as the setting for their story and suggested that Amy and a girl from the school should act in a scenario of what to do and what not to do there. The story was about a new girl trying to join in a basketball game and was told effortlessly by Margaret as if she had experienced it herself. Speech bubbles and thought balloons on sticky notes were used to record the dialogue.

The dialogue and the performance of the episode according to the already-developed storyboard required the children to examine the real world of a new child in the school. With the help of the researchers, the girls were led in a creative process of self-exploration that involved entering the world of the new girl. As a result of this process, the two girls were able to imagine and articulate Amy's probable reactions during her first day at school. They recognized that Amy would be interested in playing with everyone and that she would probably not be aggressive. However, they also realized that the friendship of their characters transcended anything else in the school.

When a third girl, Shannon, who wished to join Margaret and Veronica in acting out the story, was asked to take the role of Amy, she decided to portray her character's frustration nonverbally by raising her arms. The researchers were convinced that this gesture was so powerfully eloquent that anyone could fill in her unspoken words. The act of surrender portrayed a rejected child who had no alternative than to step away from the terrible experience.

The series of six photos presented in Figure 1 are a fotonovela that depicts a simple and common playground scenario. Because of the everydayness of the fotonovela, and because the girls' representation and performance of their story was credibly done, it could be shared with everyone in the school.

SHARING THE FOTONOVELA: INSIGHTS GAINED

The fotonovela, "*Getting into Basketball*," was shared with two groups of children for different reasons and at different times. Because two of the girls who

participated in developing the fotonovela were in Grade 5, it was first shared with
the rest of the Grade 5 students during their regular class time: a total of 15
children. The research objective was to observe how the children who had not
participated in the development of the visual narrative would respond. The
fotonovela was presented to the class by the creators, and it included both the title
and the text as originally written by them. The children in the class were immediately drawn to its content. The characters' speech and gestures were readable
and personal for the children in a story about their own playground community.
The part about the new girl's exclusion, disappointment, and loneliness on the
basketball court was well portrayed in the fotonovela. Although the comic was
short, the children revisited the images and dialogue several times and agreed
among themselves that this was "what happens the first recess when you don't
know anyone in the school."

The fotonovela was shown a second time to some Grade 4 students 4 months
later. Based on the first experience of presenting the fotonovela, the research
objective was to learn how children who had not participated in developing the
fotonovela would interpret the scenario based solely on their reading of the
participants' body language. Therefore, this time the black-and-white copies of
the fotonovela given individually to each child in the class were without titles,
speech, or thought balloons. The title was left blank, and separate pages of blank
speech and thought balloons were provided for the children to cut out and place
as they saw fit. The sharing took place during regular class time, and 13 children
were present that day.

The first sharing of the visual narrative gave us a general sense of how readable the visual narrative was for the children; the second experience provided a
detailed understanding of the meanings assigned by the individual children to

each frame. Analysis of these meanings provided some insights into how the children's understanding and interpretation of the nonverbal behavior of their peers varied. The analysis presented in the following section is based on the content of text provided by the individual children for each of the six frames of the fotonovela. Some commonalties and differences also are described.

The most interesting part of the analysis of the text for Frame 1 is that all the children identified the new child. The general intention of the new child—to play with the other two girls—also was generally understood. Of 11 children who ascribed text to this image, 8 ascribed an active role to the new child. It was she who initiated the contact and asked if she could play. The other 3 children had a different view of this. One drew a picture of the new child imagining that 1 of the girls was passing the ball to her; another drew a sad face in a thought balloon; the third had the new child telling the other 2 that she was "open" by saying so orally. Interestingly, the new child's gesture, which the researchers interpreted as surrender to the power of the two peers who did not allow her to get in to the game, was not read as such by the children. The text bubbles indicate that most of the children interpreted the gesture as a request. Examples included "Can I play?" (2 children) and "Pass the ball/Give the ball to me/Can I please have the ball?" (5 children). One child interpreted it as an indication of being open to passes from the other basketball players ("I am open!") and another as an indication of resistance to the peer pressure to leave the basketball court ("You are mean but I am not going away").

The children were consistent in how they interpreted the intentions of the other two characters in the story. None interpreted the verbal exchange among the three characters as positive. According to the texts in this frame, the reply to the new child's request to play was clearly a rejection (e.g., "What are you looking at? You can't play!" "I am never gonna pass it to that freak," "No way, girl! You little wimp," "Don't make me take out my cap gun!"). These few examples demonstrate not only rejection of the new child's plea but also an attempt to hurt her feelings by using insulting language and threats. One child wrote a number of lines about this exchange as follows.

New child: Can I play"
Cindy: No!
New child: How come?
Cindy: Because you are too bad!
New child: I don't remember hurting you.
Cindy: Because you have a bad memory. Yuck!
Mary: Why are you stopping the game?

In this case, it appeared that the new child already had a "bad history" with Cindy and was being punished for something she did not remember doing. The variety in the verbal exchanges suggest that in writing the text to this fotonovela the children were probably drawing on their own experiences as newcomers.

Frame 1

In Frame 2, the children saw the role of the new child as being much less active. Only two of the children had her initiate a verbal exchange. Two of the children thought she was still trying to get the ball by complaining that they never being passed it to her ("You never pass it to me," and "Come on!!"). In both instances, these attempts were rejected ("I am passing it to Cindy," and "NO! Get out of here!"). The text for another fotonovela indicated that the new child was asking if the line "Then take that!!" from one of the girls was a threat ("Are you threatening me?"). The overall tone of the exchange was still negative: the two girls were either engaged in an exchange that excluded the new girl ("I am open. Pass the ball," "I am not passing it to you"), or they made remarks about her like "She is such a crybaby." One child even wrote "Go die!" as a comment from one of the girls to the new child.

Five of the 13 children ascribed no text to Frame 3. Those who did, however, depicted a momentary shift in power. It appeared to them that for a moment the new child had possession of the ball and was trying to keep it. This was evident in the text of several fotonovelas. For example, 1 child wrote that the new girl was thinking to herself, "I got to run. Run!!" Four children wrote that the other girl in the scene was trying to get the ball back from the new child (e.g., "Hey, give me back the ball. That's not yours," "Give me that ball," and "Pass me the ball"). It was interesting that one child interpreted the events in this frame such that the new child not only had possession of the ball but also was not giving it up easily.

Frame 2

Her ability to resist peer pressure and to exercise agency was evident in 1 child's text, which clearly indicated the new girl's determination to keep the upper hand, "You are mean and I am not giving it to you."

One child had a unique perspective of the events depicted in this frame. According to the text of the fotonovela, the new girl attempted to use her momentary advantage to suggest a new game that the 3 of them could play together. She said, "Let's play 'Monkey in the middle.'" The response from the other girl was a clear rejection as expressed in a thought balloon, "We won't let her play!"

Once again, fewer children ascribed text to this Frame 4. However, the seven children who did write for the scene were consistent in their interpretations. They saw it as a loss for the new child (e.g., a thought balloon "She got me, I thought that I could get it") and a victory for the other girl (e.g., "Ha, ha, ha, I got it!" "Ha, ha. I got the ball," "What a baby," and "I told her she can't get my ball!").

The fact that Frame 5 was similar to the first frame made analysis of the meaning of the positions and gestures of the characters assigned by the individual children interesting in relation to the main research question. Once again, the new girl was seen as being an active player. Although her position in relation to the other girls and her gesture were almost identical in the two frames, the interpretation of her role was quite different. Whereas in the first frame the new girl pleaded for acceptance into the game, the text for the fifth frame indicated that she had, to some extent, lost hope that this would happen.

Frame 3

The text indicated some children's desire to explain her action in getting the ball as shown in the previous frame. She sounded almost apologetic in "I just wanted to play" and "I really wanted to play." According to other children, the new child was not sure what had happened and why the other two girls would not let her play (e.g., "What did I do? Even if I did something, she should have told me."). Others indicated her frustration with the situation by drawing her dreaming about her big brother coming to rescue her or by saying, "I am going to cry if you are not going to let me play." Three children interpreted her gesture as indicating her growing sense of agency by resisting the other two girls' comments to her (e.g., "You are rude," and "Stop being greedy") or by openly saying that she had changed her mind and no longer wanted to play (e.g., "You know what, I don't want to play, so buzz off!").

The overall tone of the exchange among all players was negative, reinforcing the two girls' decision not to let the new child play. One of the girls said to the new child, "Be quiet, shrimp!" and the other said, "You'll never play with us. Never, never, never!"

Analysis of the text for Frame 6 suggests that all the children but one interpreted the new child's position and body language to indicate hurt feelings (e.g., "Oh that hurts," "Stop it, that hurts") or that she was crying (e.g., "You made me cry"). Several children also drew crying faces in thought balloons. Only one

Frame 4

speech bubble indicated that the new child forgave the other two for what they had done: "I forgive you." The responses from the other two girls to having made the new child cry or at least having upset her were different in all fotonovelas. These ranged from showing no compassion or regret as in, "Yeah! Go home!" and "Don't make me pull a trigger to your head," to feeling apologetic and accepting her as a partner in the game as in, "I am sorry I never passed the ball to you," "Oh no, sorry," and "Come and play." Two children thought that the other girls were apologizing for making her cry, and only one ended the story with the new girl being accepted as a partner in the game.

SUMMARY AND DISCUSSION

Analysis of the fotonovelas clearly demonstrates that the playground is more than a recreational space. It is a pedagogical space full of "performers" who form, negotiate, and practice inclusive or exclusive interactions. Understanding the nature and meaning of these interactions depends on one's familiarity with the larger cultural context in which they occur and on one's earlier experiences. In the case of immigrant children, earlier experiences of interacting with school peers may not be helpful, as now they must interact with peers from a different

Frame 5

Frame 6

cultural background from their own. The study reported here suggests that the understanding of the intentions and meaning of school peer interactions is not uniform, and it can be a challenge not only for the immigrant children but also for all children in multicultural contexts. The fotonovelas show that ways of expressing and understanding meanings, feelings, and emotions through body language appear to be quite different not only from culture to culture but also from one individual to another. However, we concur in Feldman and colleague's (1991) conclusion that nonverbal behavioral skills are primary aspects of social competence as they affect and control to a large extent exchanges in social interactions.

Our finding suggest that children, regardless of their cultural backgrounds, have varying interpretations of the nature and meaning of interactions among peers, especially if they rely solely on observations rather than language. Thus social learning through observations (Bandura, 1977) may not be sufficient to allow newcomers to navigate their school social environment. Learning to understand the observed behaviors presents a distinct set of challenges for newcomers who wish to engage in and maintain peer relationships in multicultural and multilingual school contexts. Other studies (Hanna, 1984) have suggested that nonverbal translation is a recognized remedy for potential intercultural misunderstanding. However, teaching children nonverbal communication has been largely neglected because of "the pre-eminent status of the word in technologically advanced societies" (p. 400). The method developed and used in this study provides an avenue for children to explore their own and their peers' understandings of the various ways that intentions, desires, feelings, and emotions can be expressed and interpreted. Unlike Feldman et al. (1991), who suggested formal training to improve the accuracy of decoding for students in Grades 5 and 6, we suggest that developing and sharing visual narratives in the form of fotonovelas that depict life in school can promote understanding of peer interaction between children from varying cultural and linguistic backgrounds.

The results of the study indicate advantages in having the students both create fotonovelas and read those created by others. Fotonovelas created *by* children *for* immigrant children can be used as a tool to help them decode body language and meaning. The reader benefits from the use of both photography and words as presented in sequence. This format can offer clues about the cultural workings of the world they have entered. The nuances of body language and social structure can be seen through the photographs and through the accompanying written language. Similarly, a fotonovela format can provide cultural clues to help understand unspoken conventions of language, informal communication, and social roles.

The creation of fotonovelas *by* immigrant students who also are second-language learners offers them an opportunity for expression otherwise inhibited by traditional methods. The visual narrative is quickly produced, and the dialogue is not complicated. The visual literacy of photography can span cultural barriers and help the child to be understood and thus be less isolated. The visual format of the fotonovela appeals to children for whom comics are a part of their personal culture and reading community. As evidenced by the work presented here, which represents only a beginning, the form offers the possibility of "polyvocal" narrative inquiry that can embrace word, gesture, image, time, and space.

REFERENCES

Aitken, S. C. (1994). *Putting Children in Their Place.* Washington, DC: Association of American Geographers.

Alberta Education. (2001). *Removing Barriers to High School Completion—Final Report.* Retrieved Sept. 10, 2004 from www.education.gov.ab.ca

Archer, D. (1997). Unspoken diversity: Cultural differences in gestures. *Qualitative Sociology, 20*(1), 79–105.

Bandura, A. (1977). *Social Learning Theory.* New York: Holt, Rinehart & Winston.

Baumeister, R. F., & Leary, M. R. (1995). The need to belong: Desire for interpersonal attachment as a fundamental human motivation. *Psychological Bulletin, 117,* 497–529.

Berman H., Ford-Gilboe M., Moutrey B., & Cekic S. (2001). Portraits of pain and promise: A photographic study of Bosnian youth. *Canadian Journal of Nursing Research, 32*(4) 21–41.

Boulton, M., & Smith, P. K. (1993). Ethnic, gender partner, and activity preferences in mixed-race children's social competence develop in the context of interacting with their peers in the UK: Playground observations. In C. Hart (Ed.), *Children on Playgrounds* (pp. 210–238). Albany, NY: SUNY Press.

Class, A., Stead, J., Arshad, R., & Norris, C. (2001). School peer relationships of minority children in Scotland. *Child: Care, Health and Development, 27*(2), 133–148.

Conrad, D. (2004). Exploring risky youth experiences: Popular theatre as a participatory, performative research method. *International Journal of Qualitative Methods, 3*(1). Retrieved April 6, 2005, from http://www.ualberta.ca/~iiqm/backissues/3_1/pdf/conrad.pdf

Curiel, F. (2001). *Fotonovela rosa, fotonovela roja.* México: Coordinación de Difusión Cultural, Dirección de Literatura/UNAM.

Deegan, J. (1996). *Children's friendships in culturally diverse classrooms.* London: Falmer.

Derwing, M. T., DeCorby, E., Ichikawa, J., & Jamieson, K. (1999). Some factors that affect the success of ESL high school students. *Canadian Modern Language Review, 55,* 532–547.

Efron, D. (1941). *Gesture, Race and Culture.* The Hague, The Netherlands: Mouton.

Ekman, P. (1983). Three classes of non-verbal behavior. In W. von Raffler-Engel (Ed.), *Aspects of Nonverbal Communication* (pp. 89–102). Lisse, The Netherlands: Swets & Zeitlinger.

Ells, H. (2001). Talking pictures in working school lunches: Investigating food choice with children and adolescents. *British Food Journal, 103,* 374–382.

Emme, M. (1989). The meaning(s) of lens meaning. *Journal of Social Theory and Art Education, 9,* 26–35.

Emme, M., & Kirova, A. (2005). Photoshop semiotics: Research in the age of digital manipulation. *Visual Art Research, 31*(1) 145–153.

Emme, M., Kirova, A., Kamau, O., & Kosanovich, S. (in press). Ensemble research: Immigrant children's exploration of peer relationships through fotonovela. *Alberta Journal of Educational Research.*

Feldman, R. S., Philippot, P., & Custrini, R. J. (1991). Social competence and nonverbal behavior. In R. Feldman & B. Rime (Eds.), *Fundamentals of Nonverbal Behavior* (pp. 329–350). Cambridge, UK: Cambridge University Press.

Hall, E. (1976). *Beyond Culture.* New York: Doubleday.

Hall, J. A. (1984). *Non-Verbal Sex Differences: Communication Accuracy and Expressive Style.* Baltimore, MD: Johns Hopkins University Press.

Hanna, J. L. (1984). Black/white non-verbal differences, dance and dissonance: Implications for desegregation. In A. Wolfgang (Ed.), *Nonverbal Behavior: Perspectives, Applications, Intercultural Insights* (pp. 373–409). Toronto, ON: C. J. Hogrefe.

Hart, C. H. (Ed.) (1993). *Children on Playgrounds: Research Perspectives and Applications.* Albany, NY: SUNY Press.

Heslin, R., & Patterson, M. L. (1982*). Non-Verbal Behavior and Social Psychology.* New York: Plenum.

Holloway, S., & Valentine, G. (2000). Children's geographies and the new social studies of childhood. In S. Holloway & G. Valentine (Eds.), *Children's Geographies: Playing, Living, Learning* (pp. 1–28). London: Routledge.

James, A., Jenks, C., & Prout, A. (1998). *Theorizing childhood.* New York: Teachers College Press.

Kendon, A. (1984). Did gesture have the happiness to escape the curse of the confusion of Babel? In A. Wolfgang (Ed.), *Nonverbal Behavior: Perspectives, Applications, Intercultural Insights* (pp. 75–114). Toronto, ON: C. J. Hogrefe.

Kirova, A. (2001). Loneliness in immigrant children: Implications for classroom practice. *Childhood Education, 77,* 260–268.

Kirova-Petrova, A. (1996). Toward pedagogical understanding of children's feelings of loneliness. *Early Childhood Education, 29*(2), 9–15.

Kirova-Petrova, A. (2000). Researching young children's lived experiences of loneliness: Pedagogical implications for linguistically diverse students. *Alberta Journal of Educational Research, 56,* 99–116.

Kirova-Petrova, A., & Wu, J. (2002). Peer acceptance, learning English as a second language, and identity formation in children of recent Chinese Immigrants. In A. Richardson, M. Wyness, & A. Halvorsen (Eds.), *Exploring Cultural Perspectives, Integration and Globalization* (pp. 171–190). Edmonton, AB: ICRN Press.

Leach, E. (1972). The influence of cultural context on non-verbal communication in man. In R. Hinde (Ed.), *Non-Verbal Communication* (pp. 315–347). Cambridge, UK: Cambridge University Press.

Mehrabian, A. (1971). *Silent Messages.* Belmont, CA: Wadsworth.

Mehrabian, A., & Weiner, M. (1967). Decoding of inconsistent communications. *Journal of Personality and Social Psychology, 6,* 109–114.

Osterman, K. F. (2001). Students' need for belonging in the school community. *Review of Educational Research, 70,* 323–367.

Pearce, W. B., & Cronen, V. E. (1980). *Communication Action and Meaning—the Creation of Social Realities.* New York: Praeger.

Pelligrini, A. D., & Blatchford, P. (2000). *The Child at School: Interactions With Peers and Teachers.* New York: Oxford University Press.

Pelligrini, A. D., Kentaro, K., Blatchford, P., & Baines, E. (2002). A short-term longitudinal study of children's playground games across the first year of school: Implications for social competence and adjustment to school. *American Educational Research Journal, 39,* 991–1015.

Poyatos, F. (1984). Linguistic fluency and verbal-nonverbal cultural fluency. In A. Wolfgang (Ed.), *Nonverbal Behaviour: Perspectives, Applications, Intercultural Insights* (pp. 431–459). Toronto, ON: C. J. Hogrefe.

Poyatos, F. (1999). Non-verbal communication and translation. *University of Toronto Quarterly, 69*(1), 119–120.

Reed, J. L. (1998). The fotonovela. *Camerawork: A Journal of Photographic Arts, 25*(2), 4–5.

Schneller, R. (1985). Heritage and changes in the non-verbal language of Ethiopian newcomers. *Israeli Social Science Research, 3*(1/2), 33–54.

Schneller, R. (1988). The Israeli experience of cross-cultural misunderstanding: Insights and lessons. In F. Poyatos (Ed.), *Cross-Cultural Perspectives in Non-Verbal Communication* (pp. 153–193). Toronto, ON: C. J. Hogrefe.

Statistics Canada. (2003a). *2001 Census Analysis Series—Canada's Ethnocultural Portrait: the Changing Mosaic.* Ottawa, ON: Author. Retrieved July 14, 2004 from http://www12.statcan.ca/english/census01/products/analytic/companion/etoimn/pdf/96F0030XIE2001008.pdf

Statistics Canada. (2003b). *Ethnic Diversity Survey: Portrait of a Multicultural Society.* Retrieved September 30, 2003, from http://www.statcan.ca/english/freepub/89–593-XIE/free.htm

Sutton-Smith, B. (1975). *The Study of Games: An Anthropological Approach.* New York: Teachers College Press.

van Ngo, H. (2004). *Immigrant Children in Focus: a Map of Needs, Strategies and Resources.* Calgary, AB: Coalition for Equal Access to Education.

von Raffler-Engel, W. (Ed.). (1980). *Aspects of Non-Verbal Behavior.* Lisse, The Netherlands: Swets & Zeitlinger.

Wang, C., & Burris, M. A. (1994). Empowerment through photonovella: Portraits of participation. *Health Education Quarterly, 21,* 171–186.

Waters, E., & Sroufe, L. A. (1983). Social competence as a developmental construct. *Developmental Review, 3,* 79–97.

Watt, D., & Roessingh, H. (2001). The dynamics of ESL dropout: Plus ça change ... *Canadian Modern Language Review, 58,* 203–223. Retrieved Nov. 5, 2004 from http://utpjournals.com/product/cmlr/582/582-Watt.html

Watzlawick, P., Beavin, J. H., & Jackson, D. D. (1967). *Pragmatics in Human Communication.* New York: Norton.

Winicott, D. W. (1971). *Playing and Reality.* Harmondsworth, UK: Penguin.

Chapter 11

Talking Television Across Cultures: Negotiating Inclusion and Exclusion

Liesbeth de Block
Institute of Education, University of London, United Kingdom

There is still a tendency in many schools to equate multicultural diversity with the need to keep children's sense of origins alive. The multicultural events that arise from this approach—such as international food evenings, national costume days, or even the celebration of various religious festivals—can often involve immigrant communities in performances of their *difference* rather than promoting real interaction with one another and those from other cultures. This then further *others* them, promoting an essentialist view of culture as unchanging and always impenetrable. The danger is that we do not acknowledge how children themselves prioritize fitting into their current local environments rather than holding an attachment to the past. Connected to this is the need to recognize how the meeting of cultures is a dynamic process of negotiation and change, both for the arriving and the receiving people and communities. This means that we should be focusing on what children already do to facilitate their entry into new places of residence and what resources they use to allow them to communicate and build social relationships with other children. It means that we should become more aware of where the meeting points are, where children have shared experiences, rather than focusing only on the differences and where their lives are separated. We need to learn more about the processes of change and what resources children draw on in negotiating new identities and new belongings.

MEDIA GLOBALIZATION: TELEVISION VIEWING
AND SOCIAL PURPOSE

Television has long been seen as one of the institutions that can create what Anderson (1983) termed "the imagined community," which promotes a sense of national belonging. Globalizing media have changed this, and although there is still a demand for local media (mainly radio and newspapers), in the main media are increasingly globalized (Morley & Robins, 1995). We no longer all watch the same program at the same time, but with satellite and cable, we can select from a range of national, regional, transnational, diasporic, and global broadcasts according to language, religion, culture, and special interests. By using the term *mediascapes* to describe globalizing communications systems, Appadurai (1990) illustrated the cross-flows of imagination and connection that are central to the experience of migration. Migration is no longer unidirectional, nor are the communication flows that accompany migration. Appadurai stressed that we now draw on an array of media in varying ways at varying times and in various social formations. It is the social contexts of viewing, using, and discussing media that are arguably the strongest force in our media choices. In terms of television, we might choose to watch certain programs with friends, others with siblings, still others with each parent or other adults, and still others alone. Children and young people also choose what they watch according to social needs and contexts (Buckingham, 1996; Gillespie, 1995).

For migrant and refugee children, such choices are more diverse (de Block, 2002). Family viewing might revolve around satellite television from their country or region of origin in their own language, or it might equally center on a national soap opera in their new country of residence. It also could include a program they used to watch before migration that was a global product from the United States or Brazil or a Hindi film (CHICAM, 2004). It is now possible for immigrant families to watch only culturally specific broadcasts and to ignore national programming. Where schools and classes are culturally mixed and where children have access to a range of television broadcasts, they might watch quite different programs from their friends in the home country. Despite this, there is usually a core of shared programs that each friendship group will watch, talk about, and use in their negotiations of inclusion, exclusion, and identity. Thus, their viewing will reflect both their local and international interests and connections. It is neither purely nostalgic nor solely concerned with their current location. Rather, it demonstrates the complex mix of past allegiances and memory while also acknowledging that those places of origin have changed and that their present and future are not always tied to their places of origin. It is the details of how media, or in this case television programs in particular, become resources for building and maintaining social relations across and within cultures that I concentrate on here.

METHODOLOGY AND STUDY DESIGN

Study

The discussion in this chapter is based on an ethnographic study involving 18 months of fieldwork, that I carried out as a single researcher with a small group of refugee and migrant children and their friends in a primary school in north London. Children from long-standing local and immigrant communities, as well as children who had recently arrived from many parts of the world, attended the school. More than 30 languages were represented. I used ethnographic design in the study. Based on participant observations, I kept an extensive field diary of observations, drawings, notes of conversations, and thoughts. I conducted semistructured and unstructured interviews with both individuals and groups, sometimes using an interpreter. During the fieldwork, I "hung out" on the playground; spent time with the children in their neighborhoods; and observed in classrooms, lunchrooms, and corridors. As the fieldwork progressed, I moved to making short animations with the children about aspects of their lives and gave them video cameras to use in their neighborhoods. I interviewed the children, teachers and parents several times over the course of the fieldwork and gradually built a picture of the children's varied and full media lives and the role that media played in building social relationships in their new places of residence.

Participants

I focused on two friendship groups. Both groups were mixed in their countries of origins, immigration status, and social class. The first was a group of four 8-year-old girls; the second was a group of four 11-year-old boys.

Girls' Group:

- Rhaxma: Somalia, refugee, living with her mother who was at home with younger children and a stepfather who was studying. Had previously lived in Italy. Muslim.
- Nyota: Democratic Republic of the Congo. Both parents had previously been employed in high-status jobs as asylum seekers; they were now not allowed to protestant.
- Morwen: Born in London of Welsh and Grenadian parents. Father a bus driver.
- Juba: Born in London. Parents from Ghana. Father setting up businesses between the United Kingdom and Ghana. The family aspiring to moving out of central London to a more suburban setting.

Boys' Group.   The following is a description of the boys in the boys' group:

- Samuel: Kenya. Asylum seeker. Recently converted to Jehovah's Witness Church.

- Jima: Ethiopia. Asylum seeker. Here with his father alone.
- Estava and Denis (twins): Portugal. Father in Angola. Had extended family in London. Mother setting up own business and buying a private apartment.

Others.   I also followed several children who were on the edges of these main groups. These included children from Turkey (Kurdish), Kosovo, Palestine, Somalia, Bangladesh, and several children born in London both of White English families and of families who had settled in the United Kingdom one or two generations before.

STUDY FINDINGS AND INSIGHTS

TV Talk as Shared Space

It is in the informal spaces of school life that friendships are made and broken, that language is practiced and learned, that shared histories are built, and that behavior is modeled and patrolled (Epstein & Steinberg, 1997). Talking about what one has seen on television is one of the main topics on the agenda at these times. TV talk can take many forms, but its function is clearly social. Television programs were frequently referred to during the children's games and general chat. These were rarely full descriptions of programs or episodes, but took the form of gestures, phrases, songs, and key words. It became clear that to follow the references and be included in the repartee, the children needed knowledge that required a huge commitment of time and energy on their part.

Although the children were creative in their use of such programs, the possibilities open to them were not infinite. Their social context, their peer and family relations, and the texts themselves all placed boundaries on invention. In fact, these boundaries and the children's developing understanding of them are central to TV talk. TV talk allows the children to use programs both to develop group and individual identities and to negotiate and understand these social contexts and their own place in relation to them.

Learning About Family: A Case of The Simpsons

The Simpsons provided endless story lines to be learned in detail, and it provided word plays and jokes. It was possible to act out the scenes and characters without the need for words. The show related to everyday scenes with which the children were familiar and could use as references and comparisons with their lives. It provided dialogue and possibilities for verbal mimicry. Above all, it was funny and therefore adaptable to a range of purposes and situations.

The Simpsons is about a U.S. nuclear family: father, mother, older son, younger daughter, and baby. They live the good suburban life, and yet this dream is betrayed. Wells (2002) compared the father figure in *The Flintstones* with Homer Simpson. Both are portrayals of white, blue-collar workers. The difference is that although one remains in an establishment that appears to promote social aspiration while at the same time confirming the status quo, the other sets out to be a self-conscious critic of this status quo. Homer parodies Fred Flintstone. He is often distant or out of control; more often than not, he does the wrong thing, but on many occasions, he manages to muddle through and do the right thing. Jozajtis (2002) described Homer as an essentially moral man, a good father with human flaws. He carries much of the emotional charge of the program. Meanwhile, Marge, the mother, is the sensible and more intelligent person who holds the family together and acts as the community's social conscience. However, she too has her failures, as when she develops a gambling habit that threatens to undermine the family as a functioning unit. Bart, the son, is the naughty boy and also often the stupid boy. His focus is his friends and his locality. He is frequently in trouble, but this is usually despite himself. His predominant motivation is to please. When he wears his "genius" T-shirt, the ironic humor is clear. Lisa, conversely, is declared a genius, but is still the annoying little sister. The baby, Maggie, is the foil over whom many family conflicts are enacted. We feel superior, yet at the same time, we sympathize and identify with the family. Despite the cultural specificity, the locations of home, school, and local landmarks such as shops, playground, street, and neighbors (both troublesome and friendly) are familiar to most children in varying forms. These are places of danger and of safety.

Several aspects of the program both frame and facilitate TV talk. First, its subject matter is the everyday life and events of one family, which allows the children to discuss both the faults and successes of this family and their own. In many respects, it is subversive. The show is peopled by stereotypical characters (and behaviors) that can be matched by people in the children's own lives. For example, Samuel recognized the grandfather in one episode who is so deaf one cannot communicate with him and compared him to his own profoundly deaf grandfather who was visiting from Kenya. Jima, who often watched the show with his father, often described himself as Bart and his father in terms of his similarity to Homer.

Jima: A Young Ethiopian Asylum Seeker.   One of the boys, Jima (11), who had come with his father from Ethiopia as an asylum seeker, never mentioned learning the language as the most important factor in making friends when he arrived. He focused on learning how children behaved and particularly what they talked *about.* He said that he became interested in television when he realized to what extent it formed a focus of social relations.

When I asked him why it was important to have a television, his instant reply was that then you had something to talk about with your friends. His priority was clear. Television was not a route to escape, but an important aspect of his social life.

Jima aimed to develop a group of friends, so it was important that his interests and knowledge facilitate this. He developed an interest in wrestling so that he could talk about World Wrestling Federation broadcasts, and his second passion was *The Simpsons* and *South Park*. TV talk about these programs facilitated this sense of group togetherness that he and his friends sought. Second, for Jima in particular, being the expert and being called on to demonstrate this knowledge gave him a status in the group that other activities did not. It gave him access to the group and therefore to friendship and inclusion. He was also adept at using TV references to promote a connection and sense of togetherness. Often, after initiating a topic, he would sit back and let the discussion flow, only intervening either to keep it on track or to take it in a new direction. All these programs allowed him and his friends to gossip and act out. More than other programs, *The Simpsons* allowed a wide range of discussions about family, friendship, and social conventions. Jima and his group adopted certain episodes to cement and symbolize their friendship and to include or exclude other children who wished to join.

Jima's family life was troubled. He lived alone with his father, who was deeply depressed that they were still, several years after their arrival in the United Kingdom, living temporarily from day to day awaiting a final decision on their asylum application, unable to build any permanence into their lives. Just as Jima said that he watched television so that he could make friends, he also said that he learned about family life from shows like *The Fresh Prince of Bel Air* and *The Simpsons*. Bachmair (1990) argued that the subjective experiences and preoccupations that constitute children's personal *themas* and that motivate them individually are acted out and interpreted through their friendships. Television has a symbolic resonance in this interpretative play between the social and the personal. Particular programs carry particular resonance for certain children or friendship groups according to their personal experiences and psychological needs. Certainly, for Jima, his favorite programs and how he drew on them in his personal relations reflected his personal *thema* of family and belonging. He used TV talk to promote his own social inclusion while also using it to protect his privacy and to survive the difficulties in which he and his father found themselves. Television gave him access to experiences that he felt were lacking in his own family life and helped him find solutions to problems or to come to terms with his difficult circumstances.

Creating Continuities.   For many migrant children, programs such as *The Simpsons* became a point of continuity. One mother from Somalia related how her children had watched the program in Somalia, then again in Kenya in a refugee camp, and again once they arrived in the United Kingdom, each time in a different language. She said that it had traveled with them and given them an instant point of contact. Indeed, this contact did not need spoken language. Others spoke of similar experiences with this and other programs. On a weekend away with the upper school, the whole group watched *The Simpsons* in their separate shared rooms. Half way through the program when they were called to dinner, they all emerged from the chalet rooms buzzing with Simpsons talk. In one of the scenes, Homer had shown his buttocks, and many of the children were acting this out. Veton (11), a Kosovan boy who had fairly recently arrived in the United Kingdom as a result of the war and was still finding his place in the class, was the most exaggerated and persistent in his gestures, trying to gain the attention of the group. He succeeded, and they all went to dinner together. So the acting out of a questionable scene allowed Veton to be accepted into the group without the need for language fluency.

The Simpsons combined both a lightness of touch and subversive humor with the raising of serious issues that directly concerned the boys: various family lifestyles, belonging in your neighborhood, negotiating friendships, and learning about social institutions. The boys saw aspects of their lives and their personal options presented in a way that was subversive and funny and therefore possible to talk about. These examples that illustrate some of the ways the children in the study used a particular program could apply to any children, not only to refugees or migrants. However, these children's experiences and uses of media are different in several ways. TV talk can overcome some language barriers, thus becoming an early means of making contact. Global media products facilitate an instant shared space through which children can participate in playground humor, narrative, and character. Significant is the focus and energy that these children invested in acquiring their knowledge and how through talking about *The Simpsons,* they negotiated their differences and learned about one another. This was a safe, shared space where they could be the same, while at the same time acknowledge and negotiate some of their differences.

Creating Playground Games That Build Shared Histories.   It was Opie and Opie's (1959) study that first brought the drama and hidden histories of the school playground to adults' attention. As Blatchford (1998) stated, this was a romantic vision of creative and situated play and games. The other side of Opie and Opie's study are those that focused on bullying and other bad behavior in the playground. What happens in the playground and how children themselves perceive it has taken on more importance as children's freedom of movement becomes more restricted and they have fewer opportunities for social interaction. There is also a growing realization of the importance of this peer social interaction in the development of social skills, cultural transmission (Grugeon, 1993; Sluckin, 1981), and identity formation. Some studies have focused on specific aspects of identity formation, particularly in relation to gender (Thorne, 1993) and sexuality

(Epstein, 1999). Yet there has been remarkably little focus on the role of media in these playground interactions.

Playground games build a shared history, as do shared media memories. Together these can become a powerful bonding force. Often the children referred to programs they had watched when they were younger. This was generally as part of the process of claiming greater maturity than that of younger children, but it also served to reinforce a shared history. In the boys' group, children's (and girls') programs such as *Power Puff Girls, Rug Rats,* and *Teenage Ninja Turtles* were mentioned and ridiculed, although the boys did often watch them. For the girls there was almost hysterical excitement when they remembered watching programs such as *The Tweenies* or *Rosie and Jim.* Similarly, playground games also performed the function of building a group memory on which they could draw in times of tension. Many of the games had been played so often and many of the television stories had been told so many times over long periods that they formed a resource that the children could draw on for security to overcome current arguments.

Rhaxma and Juba: Playing Together. Both in the family and with friends in and out of school, television played a significant role in building autobiographical memories or histories. Television appeared to be able to locate the children in time and place almost as family photos or stories can (Kuhn, 1985; Spence & Holland, 1991). Some of the refugee and migrant children mentioned programs that they had watched before they came to the United Kingdom. Rhaxma still enjoyed watching an Italian program she had watched as a toddler although she no longer understood much Italian. It provided her with a personal historic reference point. She had no photos from that time, but the television program kept the memory alive. Estava and Denis (from the boys' group, aged 11, from Portugal) often talked about what they watched when they visited Portugal, enjoying the fact that these memories felt unique. However, many children were reluctant to mention these " home" programs in school, preferring to keep them as private histories.

The games formed the core of group histories. The children often played them repeatedly over a long period, and the cumulative effect of these shared television-based interactions formed the basis of many friendships. Many games had set forms that were repeated day after day. One was what I called the Titanic game, although the children made no direct reference to the film. The following is Rhaxma's (an 8-year-old girl from Somalia) telling me again what was happening as we watched others in her class playing on the main climbing structure from the other side of the playground.

People are on board.
The ship started to sink.
We are outside in a dark place.

We get trapped.
We can't open the door.
Someone, George, comes and opens the door.
He starts killing people; we want to climb up but get stuck on the tires [the play structure is surrounded by tires].
We fall down sometimes.
We climb up and get stuck on the black things in the water.
George runs after us.
It ends when we all swim to the surface and the helicopter comes.

This was told without hesitation. Although she was not herself playing on this occasion, she identified with the players, using *we* in the description. She had played it often before, and George, acting as the master of ceremonies, played a similar role in several of the games owned by the girls. Several weeks later when I was making a video animation with the group about their playground games, they talked a lot about this game, drawing the climbing frame and the figures and discussing various occasions when they had played and various versions of the game. It was clearly part of their group repertoire. They took varying roles, which they all understood and which often spilled over into other games. Partly because of the continual nature of the games, but also because of their intimacy, certain games were reserved for certain *players*, as with George, and specific locations.

Juba (11) loved witch games both at home and at school, but she was clear that the games she played at home were different and were based on other programs. In an individual interview, she talked about how she and her home friends always watched and played *Hocus Pocus* together. (*Hocus Pocus,* 1993, is a film about three witches from Salem who return on Halloween. The girls' games were based on this film). Each took the part of a particular character from the film. They played games based on this program over a long period, but they demanded the same players. This game was not transferable to school because not all members of this group attended the same school. The games Juba played at school also continued over a long period. She described another witch theme game based on another program and yet another that was based on sisters, but had a heavily school-oriented theme of teachers who needed slaves because they could not do everything themselves. Therefore, her relationships with both groups of friends involved either the close or long-distance sharing of specific TV shows. It depended not only on location but also on the playing of games that evolved over time from these TV series that they all knew intimately. Knowledge of specific episodes was the ticket to entry, and if a child failed this test, he or she risked exclusion.

Depending on their home circumstances, children had more or less access to the programs. Several of the children in the study needed to invest much energy at home in negotiating access to television. Sometimes parents regulated their viewing and banned certain shows such as *South Park,* something the children often found it necessary to hide from their friends. For Rhaxma, the issue was very much related to her being a girl and a Muslim. She was not allowed to watch, and indeed did not wish to watch, scenes with any sexual acts, yet she did wish to be able to talk about them at school. Soap operas were often problematic, as were some music videos, but she watched what she could and became adept at filling in the gaps. Often it was knowledge of the genre rather than of a specific title that allowed children to join in television-related games. The hospital drama was often played in a particular part of the playground where the playground furniture served as operating rooms and beds. Several programs would be combined into one game, everyone drawing on his or her separate knowledge of the form to be included in the action. However, some genres were less acceptable than others. Several of the Bengali children said that they talked about the Hindi films they watched at home only among themselves or with one of the classroom assistants who was also Bengali. This was not only because other children would not have seen the films but also because the form and content would be considered too *other* by the children and they would risk opening themselves to ridicule. It was safer to keep some home viewing private.

Establishing Location and Belonging

Playing media games on the playground helped to build a location where most children could participate. Similarly, the children often used TV talk to make connections in their local neighborhoods outside school. Often when going from place to place together, they would remark on a person or place and immediately cite a television reference about which they could all then laugh, joke, or argue. These incidents served to bring the group together in sometimes-alien environments, particularly when they were outside their immediate locality or when they had not seen one another for a few days and needed to reestablish contact. In this extract, Jima, Samuel, and I were walking from Jima's home to Oxford Street in London's West End. This was Jima's backyard. He took us through the British Museum as a short cut. The two boys had not seen each other for a week or so, as it was holiday time. They rarely saw each other out of school; Samuel's parents disapproved of the amount of freedom that Jima was allowed. Their social backgrounds and family expectations were different. They had spent almost the entire walk thus far talking about what they had watched on television and the relative merits of *The Simpsons* and *South Park.* Samuel was not allowed to watch *South Park,* so after gaining status from pointing out that he had been allowed to watch it (see extract that follows), Jima moved the talk back to *The Simpsons*, a topic that they could share. Jima had mentioned the hot dog stand outside the British Museum, the significance of which I did not understand at first. Clearly Samuel did. They recited a hot dog refrain for several minutes, of which the following is an extract.

Jima:	Hot dogs hot dogs.
Samuel:	Homer is so, he is so funny.
Jima:	He goes to the funeral and the hot dog man comes …
Samuel:	Yeah, "hot dogs hot dogs." And Marge goes, "Why are you following my husband around?" and he goes, "Because he's good value for money." Aha that was so funny. My dad laughed and laughed and laughed when he heard that bit.
Interviewer:	When he heard "good value for money"?
Samuel:	Yeah, 'cause there's this hot dog man and they are going to a funeral and there is this hot dog man.
Jima:	And he always follows.
Samuel:	And he is always following Homer and then Marge goes, "Why are you following my husband?" and he goes, "'Cause he's great value for money'." Cause he always pays for something. There it is Jima [pointing out the hot dog stand]. "Hot Dogs Hot Dogs." Two pounds? A hot dog for two pounds?
Interviewer:	Yeah, we're right by the British Museum you see.

The talk brought them together and created a shared space that they could both enjoy without explanation. They used their environment to trigger other shared memories. The exchange also allowed other, more private topics to be broached. Samuel (line 6) mentioned how his father enjoys the show. It also introduced the question of cost (line 15) and expenses. As asylum seekers, both boys shared the experience of economic hardship, a fact they generally avoided talking about when in the company of their other friends. However, during this afternoon they returned to this topic several times. This exchange also provided Jima with the opportunity to show off his television expertise, to score status points, and to locate himself firmly in his neighborhood.

News Media as a Social Reference.   Although I had not anticipated spending much time talking about the news with the children, it was clearly an important part of their media lives. In all my discussions with the children's parents and guardians, they had said that they considered the news as the most important television program.

Those from other countries gave news as the reason for their decision to have satellite or cable TV. Many wished to watch the news in their own language to gain greater understanding even when their English was fluent. Some children also stressed the importance of the news for their wider family. Estava and Denis talked about their wish to have satellite television for their grandmother, who was living with them. She spoke no English, so they believed that if she could watch Portuguese news programs she would not feel so isolated. Of course, it was not always possible to watch in their own languages as no Somali or Ethiopian channels are available. Many of the Somalis watched either Italian or Arabic channels.

I gained a sense that the national UK TV news was not enough, that there was not enough news from their parts of the world. For example, many watched CNN news, because it was seen to be more international. It was almost as if receiving news from beyond the national borders in which they now lived was a necessary part of their identities as migrants, as non-British. In addition, national and Western news is often seen as presenting a point of view that maintains the current world order (Boyd-Barrett, 1997). In seeking other news channels, these families were also seeking different analyses of news events. This was so during the Gulf War (Gillespie, 1995), it increased during the events of September 11, 2001, and it increased again during the more recent (and current) Afghan and Iraqi wars (Al-Ghabban & Banaji, 2005).

While "connecting" and creating continuities for these families, the news also had other powerful influences, especially on the children. I was struck by how often groups of children would talk to one another about the international news. The school lunchroom was often where major news items were discussed. I was spending much time in the school at the time of the war in Kosovo (1999), and a lot of the news conversation in the lunchroom was about this topic. Veton (11), a Kosovan boy who had recently come into Year 6, was clearly preoccupied at this time and looked tired and pale. He was up late most nights watching CNN news with his father. One lunchtime, a group of his class were sitting together, and one of the girls came and joined them. She cut across all the previous conversation and started talking about the bombing that had begun the previous day. The group rapidly joined in. Veton struggled to participate, but found this difficult because of the general noise in the room and the language. Despite the difficulties he persisted.

All the children were interested. They made connections between what Veton was saying and the reports they had all watched on television. He described talking to his grandparents on the telephone and what they had told his family: many houses in their area had been burned down; they could hear shooting nearby; people had come to their house for shelter. The group conversation moved on, but Veton continued talking to me. He asked me for more details about the shooting down of a helicopter, because he had not understood everything on the news. His interpretation was that the Russians were to blame as only they had supported Milosovec in refusing peace talks. At this point Jima came to the table and immediately joined in the conversation, saying that he had been watching the news and agreed with Veton that the Russians and the Yugoslavs were to blame. He made a connection with what was happening at that time with the new fighting between Eritrea and Ethiopia and with what had happened in the past.

Revived Memories and Personal Connections.   This was all sophisticated, well-informed talk with deeply personal connections and I was aware that this rarely, if ever, happened in the classroom. It must have been important for Veton to be able to talk with peers about what was happening, especially because there appeared to be no forum for him to talk elsewhere outside the home. It also allowed him to find connections with the experiences of other refugee children and to realize that he was not alone. This was the development of a simple and effective public space where new and old identities and relationships were being formed. This relates directly to the arguments made by Buckingham (1996, 2000) about participation, news, and citizenship, but it adds an international dimension.

The news sometimes had direct emotional effects on the children (and on the research). During my fieldwork, two major items of news directly affected the Turkish/Kurdish children. First was the capture of Abdullah Ocalan, the Kurdish leader, in 1999, and second was a major earthquake that followed shortly afterward. On one of my visits to Leyla (11) and Selve's (9) home, the atmosphere was clearly tense. I could not understand why the children kept telling me about men in masks with guns. I assumed it was a film they had been watching, but I could not understand why in that case their mother was so agitated. Only later, when I reached home and heard the news that Ocalan had been captured did I begin to understand.

The capture of Ocalan spurred intense activity in the Kurdish community in London: Leyla and Selve's father was a part of this. They themselves attended several events. Suddenly they felt threatened by the capture, which, although far away, had been so vividly depicted in their living rooms. Ocalan was not captured in Turkey, but in Kenya, so this clearly told them that they were not safe anywhere. The world becomes a small place, and one cannot escape danger. The atmosphere was clearly tense at home, but also in their community. There was a police presence at some of the events they attended and they were suddenly on the outside, unwelcome and unsafe.

Over the next few weeks, this developed for Leyla into a reworking of her memories of Turkey. Previously she had painted life there as a golden age of friendship and freedom, but she now described Turkey to me as a bad and dangerous place. This was confirmed when the earthquake followed so soon after the capture of Ocalan and pictures of destruction were on the screens. She now described it as sad and said that she did not want to return there. She was having a particularly difficult time in school, and this was clearly linked to all these events. She must have felt that she had no home, no secure place. Selve too said that she was crying a lot at school, although she clearly did have friends and was coping better than her sister. Leyla described having nightmares of being chased and captured but she did not go to her mother for comfort but into her sister's bed. She told me that she did not talk to her mother about what was happening. This kind of situation is described by Richman (1998) in her teacher's manual about working with refugee children. It describes how refugee children often do not wish to add to their parents' worries and so keep their own fears to themselves.

In a later interview, both children confirmed that they now did not wish to return to Turkey and that although they had good memories, Turkey was really a bad place. The complications of living with contradictory emotions about their birthplace, to which they still had strong emotional connections even though they no longer lived there, appeared to be brought into sharp focus by news items such as these. Visual images of a place one knows can be more powerful reminders than written or spoken words and rather than creating connections, these can exacerbate feelings of separation, especially in times of crisis when one feels far away and powerless. Dearly held memories come into stark opposition with the media-portrayed realities and must make both those memories and what one has today in one's new life feel insecure. For other children who have moved to the United Kingdom as a result of other types of conflicts, news items can also provoke profound memories, emotions, and tensions.

The main and simple point is that news events reported from and about one's country of origin have direct effects on one's life in the new country. Children who have direct experience of war, trauma, and forced migration are affected by similar events elsewhere, and this will revive memories. Children who experienced migration will often see world events as closely connected to their lives and see themselves not as only part of the local environment, but, in a personal way, part of the global environment. This was not reflected in the everyday life of the formal school, but children needed, and often managed to find, informal spaces where they could share these events.

Direct news events can create feelings of separation and isolation, which can be exacerbated by how refugees and migrants are portrayed by the press of the receiving country. Conversely, TV talk about world events, sports, and the kinds of diasporic TV described in this chapter allow children to develop a working understanding of the interrelationships between the local and the global. These are opportunities to work through the multiple places of belonging and home that are essential to the experience of migration.

DISCUSSION AND IMPLICATIONS

Both Brah (1996) and Srebreny (2000) in different ways stressed that the experience of migration is one of parting, as well as one of new beginnings. Morley (2000) described how people use media to maintain past connections and to build new social relations and a sense of place in the processes of migration and how this helps them to develop the skills they need to live in different places with different identities: how they learn to be multidomestic. In this chapter, I focused on how children from varying backgrounds use and talk about television to build and maintain social interaction and contact across cultures. I stressed how these children are active agents in the creation of their new lives rather than passive victims (de Block, in press). School is one of the few places where children and young people are in continual contact with peers from other cultures and with other beliefs. It is the most important place where young people can learn about each other and about other lives and beliefs. They need to find how to communicate and socialize with one another and to do this, they draw on resources that are readily available to them. Television and increasingly other media (particularly the Internet and mobile telephones) facilitate such communication.

Global (US) media products such as *The Simpsons* may not fit easily into our idea of a suitable vehicle for cross-cultural communication, yet they form an important basis for much creative play and discussion between children in their social interactions. News events may appear to be more traditionally educational, and I described the important role these play in children's lives—both migrant and long settled. Yet they rarely form part of classroom discussions. The informal chats that the children engaged in about the news included revelations about their own lives and knowledge. Yet none of these "activities" is considered to be a part of a multicultural curriculum. Rather than encouraging children to present themselves and their lives through formal demonstrations of their foreignness, such communications allow children to talk about how they are the same as and different from each other from a basis of shared (media and other) experience. These informal pleasures that in schools form part of playground culture have important educational implications for multicultural education.

The challenge underlying the discussion here is perhaps one of place. If we see our schools as still promulgating a national or local identity and education for incoming children simply in terms of a process of induction into the ways of the receiving country, then we fail to see how all children are already moving beyond this. They lead local lives while still maintaining global connections. How they use media and how I described their use of television to form social relations and build new multiple identities challenges how we have historically viewed multiculturalism. Schools are rarely seen as international centers of communication, learning, and cultural exchange. This has been reserved for universities, and even there this concept has been contradictory. Yet there is an increasing need to respond to the global lives of all the children attending our schools and to learn from how they are already negotiating their new status.

REFERENCES

Al-Ghabban, A., & Banaji, S. (in press). "Neutrality comes from inside us": Indian and British-Asian perspectives on television news "After September 11." *Journal of Ethnic and Migration Studies.*

Anderson, B. (1983). *Imagined Communities: Reflections on the Origins and Spread of Nationalism.* London: Verso.

Appadurai, A. (1990). Disjuncture and difference in the global cultural economy. In M. Featherstone (Ed.), *Global Culture: Nationalism, Globalization and Modernity* (pp. 295–311). London: Sage.

Bachmair, B. (1990). Everyday life as the subject of television research. In M. Charlton & B. Bachmair (Eds.), *Communication Research and Broadcasting No. 9.* (pp. 45–59). Munich, Germany: KG Saur.

Blatchford, P. (1998). *Social Life in School: Pupils' Experience of Breaktime and Recess from 7–16 Years.* London: Falmer Press.

de Block, L. (2002). *Television as a Shared Space in the Intercultural Lives of Primary Aged Children.* Unpublished doctoral dissertation, Institute of Education, University of London.

de Block, L. (in press). The place to be? Making media with young refugees. In J. Hart (Ed.), *Years of Conflict: Adolescents, Armed Conflict and Forced Migration.* Oxford, UK: Berghahn Books.

Boyd-Barrett, O. (1997). Global News wholesalers as agents of globalization. In A. Sreberny-Mohammadi, D. Winseck, J. McKenna, & O. Boyd-Barrett (Eds.), *Media in Global Context: a Reader* (pp. 131–144). London: Arnold.

Brah, A. (1996). *Cartographies of Diaspora: Contesting Identities.* London: Routledge.

Buckingham, D. (1996). *Moving Images: Understanding Children's Emotional Responses to Television.* Manchester, UK: Manchester University Press.

Buckingham, D. (2000). *The Making of Citizens: Young People, News and Politics.* London: Routledge.

CHICAM. (2004). *Visions Across Cultures: Migrant Children Using Visual Images to Communicate.* Report to the European Commission. Retrieved April 25, 2006, from http://www.chicam.net/reports/download/visions_across_cultures.pdf

Epstein, D., & Steinberg, D. (1997). Love's labour: Playing it straight on the Oprah Winfrey Show. In D. Epstein, D. Steinberg, & R. Johnson, *Border Patrols: Policing the Boundaries of Heterosexuality* (pp. 32–65). London: Cassell.

Epstein, D. (1999). Sex play: Romantic significations, sexism and silences in the schoolyard. In D. Epstein & J. Sears (Eds.), *A Dangerous Knowing: Sexuality, Pedagogy and Popular Culture* (pp. 25–42). London: Cassell.

Gillespie, M. (1995). *Television, Ethnicity and Cultural Change.* London: Routledge.

Grugeon, E. (1993). Gender implications of playground culture. In P. Woods & M. Hammersley (Eds.), *Gender and Ethnicity in Schools: Ethnographic Accounts* (pp. 11–33). London: Sage.

Jozajtis, K. (2002, February 4). Homer Simpson: The new television evangelist. *The Independent,* p. 4.

Kuhn, A. (1985). *The Power of the Image: Essays on Representation and Sexuality.* London: Routledge.

Morley, D. (2000). *Home Territories: Media, Mobility and Identity.* London: Routledge.

Morley, D., & Robins, K. (1995). *Spaces of Identity: Global Media, Electronic Landscapes and Cultural Boundaries.* London: Routledge.

Opie, I., & Opie, P. (1959). *The Lore and Language of Schoolchildren.* Oxford, UK: Clarendon Press.

Richman, N. (1998). *In the Midst of the Whirlwind: A Manual for Helping Refugee Children.* Stoke on Trent, UK: Trentham Books.

Sluckin, A. (1981). *Growing Up in the Playground: The Social Development of Children.* London: Routledge & Kegan Paul.

Spence, J., & Holland, P. (1991). *Family Snaps: the Meaning of Domestic Photography.* London: Virago.

Sreberny, A. (2000). Media and diasporic consciousness: An exploration among Iranians in London. In S. Cottle (Ed.), *Ethnic Minorities and the Media* (pp. 000–000). Milton Keynes, UK: Open University Press.

Thorne, B. (1993). *Gender Play: Girls and Boys in School.* Milton Keynes, UK: Open University Press.

Wells, P. (2002). "Tell me about your Id, when you was a Kid, Yah!" Animation and Children's Television Culture. In D. Buckingham (Ed.), *Small Screens: Television for Children* (pp. 61–95). Leicester, UK: Leicester University Press.

Chapter 12

Moving Childhoods: Young Children's Lived Experiences of Being Between Languages and Cultures

Anna Kirova
University of Alberta, Canada

For adults, voluntary migration is a conscious decision, a choice they make in the name of a better, brighter, and more secure future. International migration research indicates (e.g., Ackers, 1998) that within the European Union, for example, the majority of moves (67%) were motivated by parental (and mainly paternal) employment consideration. To the extent to which teenage children were permitted to engage in migration decision-making, it was usually within a restricted framework of choices including the choice to remain physically located within the family unit, or the choice of developing some independence outside of the family. As for the younger children, it was assumed they want what their parents want, and even if they express disagreement, they are expected to obey their parents. "In no cases were children permitted any influence on decisions guiding the family as a whole" (Ackers & Stalford, 2004, p. 123). Yet do adults understand what life is like for a child whose entire universe has changed overnight? What is the lived experience of a child when his or her home is replaced by a space to live and when the new language does not serve as a guide to the world? What are the lived experiences of immigrant children in their day-to-day living between languages and cultures?

In this chapter I argue that the experience of immigration invites children to ask, "In what relation do I live to the language I speak?" The opportunity that immigration opens for asking this question is of the utmost importance in awakening children's awareness of their relation to language, both the language of home and the home of language. If language is one way of being in the world for humankind that has an immediate presence in the world, and it is one form of discourse, as Heidegger (1982) suggested, then what is it to learn another language? What is the relation of the new language to the first way of being in the world? Is beginning to feel at home in the new country an essential aspect of feeling at home in a "language-ing" way?

METHODOLOGY

Hermeneutic Phenomenology

The methodological framework for the investigation presented in this chapter was hermeneutic phenomenology as a human science research methodology (van Manen, 1990). This methodology uses questions of meaning to gain understanding of the significance of lived experience. Phenomenology emphasizes lived phenomena precisely as they are lived, because it "affirms the primacy of the life-world as a point of departure for research over scientific explanations of the same phenomena" (Giorgi, Fisher, & Murray, 1975, p. 99). By the life-world, phenomenologists mean "the everyday world as it is lived by all of us prior to explanations and theoretical interpretations of any kind" (p. 99). Life-world, however, is fundamentally intersubjective; it is a social world (Schutz & Lukmann, 1973). Our knowledge of the world and how we understand it is not derived from the world as it is but from daily interactions between people. These interactions are mediated through language (Cattanach, 1997), which is the main means of communication, and phenomenology tries to make this universal means more rigorous by providing adequate contexts for all descriptions (Giorgi et al., 1975).

Human Science as a Dialogue With Children

Because I aimed to understand young children's lived experiences of immigration, my role as a human science researcher was to gain access to the children's everyday world. The best way to enter a person's life-world is to participate in it (van Manen, 1990). My challenge was how to discover the personal meaning of immigration for each of the children. Beekman (1983) suggested that, "As a rule, one discovers this only in an ongoing relationship which allows an expressive dialogue to take place" (p. 40).

Human science requires the researcher to engage in a dialogue with the participants in the research and carefully analyze "the diverse possibilities inherent in the dialogue between adults and children" (Beekman, 1983, p. 37). Such dialogues occur naturally if, as in ethnographic research, the researcher suspends the ontological terms of *child* and *adult* and participates in the child's social world as a child (Mandell, 1988). In phenomenological research, however, such dialogue is more typically enabled through research conversations or informal interviews.

The experiential accounts included in this chapter come from conversations with my son about his childhood as an immigrant child, from the interviews that I conducted with 10 immigrant children about their experiences of loneliness as part of my doctoral study on the phenomenon of childhood loneliness (Kirova-Petrova, 1996), and from interviews with four recent Chinese immigrant children within 6 months from their arrival in Canada (Kirova-Petrova & Wu, 2002). In addition, my videotaped observations over 5 months of a 4-year-old immigrant child provide snapshots the child's daily life in a preschool setting in which English is the only language of instruction and communication (Kirova, 2002).

The phenomenological investigation presented here was guided by the following questions: What is childhood like for a child a who moves from his or her birthplace to a foreign place that he or she must make the home of existence? What happens when a child is forced to learn a language that is not a language of home? What is childhood like for an immigrant child for whom moving between cultures, homes, and languages is a way of life?

BETWEEN HOMES

The Objects in the Home

Children view migration differently and often have a different concept of home that that of their parents (Ackers & Stalford, 2004). The first and most noticeable change in an immigrant child's life is the loss of the familiar world of home. For many, this means losing the familiar objects in the house where the child was born and raised. Why do objects appear to have such power in children's sense of "at-home-ness"? One reason is that the everyday objects in the house and their use become habitual. A child does not question them: They are just there; they are taken for granted. With the move to a completely unfamiliar environment such as in immigration, the relationships between the child and the things at home are altered, and a child loses his or her sense of at-home-ness. Even possessions brought from home may be experienced differently in the new space. This is how Luka, a 10-year-old boy from the former Yugoslavia, recalled his feelings when his family immigrated.

At the beginning when we moved here we rented a house and I didn't like it. Everything was strange … my posters, even my toys were somehow different in my new room. They almost didn't look like mine. I just didn't feel at home, I guess. I knew that the house was not bad, but I missed my old house back home. (Kirova, 2001, p. 262)

Luka's experience of moving homes reveals his desire to reconstruct some aspects of his lost home in the new space. What aspects of home can people make or remake? How does one make a house into a home?

The walls of the house are the boundary of inner and outer space, but we rarely think of a home in terms of the walls of the house. Rather, it is the objects in the home that give us the feeling of at-home-ness. The space of home is in the things themselves. Yet bringing things from home that were familiar and loved did not appear to have had the expected effect on Luka's sense of at-home-ness. What was missing? Heidegger (1964) suggests that the notion of "boundary" as in the walls of the house should not be conceived as "that at which something stops," but as the Greeks recognize, the boundary is that from which something *begins its essential unfolding* (p. 332). It appears that in Luka's experience, however, the boundary was in fact lived as "that at which something stops." For something to begin "its essential unfolding," our bodies need to inhabit the space behind the walls: the space of the home. "The space gradually acquires a *feel* to it that is familiar–we come to know when something has been moved even before we see what has been moved. To know the space in this way is to inhabit it" (Winning, 1991, p. 139). The home we come from is the home we have inhabited, where the space is known through our bodies.

Home is intimately tied up with my sense of self, who I am. A sense of attachment to a particular place is important to the development of self-identity (cf. Searless, 1960; Wenkart, 1961). A house, conversely, which, as in Luka's experience, has not yet become home, does not evoke a sense of belonging. Godkin (1985) suggested that having no sense of belonging to a particular place is a feeling of uprootedness, which "interferes with the integrity of one's identity" (p. 75). Does the new home ever replace the first? If it does, how is an immigrant child's sense of identity embodied in the new home? "Identities are a key means through which people care about and care for what is going on about them" (Holland, Lachicotte, Skinner, & Cain, 1998, p. 5). Thus, it is through the caring for and about things at home that one develops an identity in relation to this home. Taking care of things is included in the original meaning of bauen, which in Heidegger's writing also meant to be or to dwell (1971).

People in the Home

A child's sense of at-home-ness, however, is also connected to the people who share the space at home. These people, usually the child's parents, siblings, and other members of the family, are those who have shown the child what objects at home are and how they are used and cared for. Home is where we can feel together with people. What we see is commonly understood. Through the objects we observe and how they are visible to us, we can be together with others (Van Den Berg, 1955). One's identity includes life experiences and knowledge, which have shaped the way the world is understood. How does one understand the world? How does a child understand that something is? "Only where the word for the thing has been found is the thing a thing. Only thus is it. The word alone gives being to the thing" (Heidegger, 1982, p. 62). Thus Heidegger says, "Something is only where the appropriate and therefore competent word names a thing as being, and so establishes the given being as a being" (p. 63). Home, then, is where language gives being to the things at home.

Whereas for a child everything at home is, as it has been appropriately named, what is the world like outside home where things are nameless or where other people's words are not understood? "Where word breaks off no thing may be" the poet said (George in Heidegger, 1982, p. 60). What is the child's experience of a world where the new language no longer shows the essential being of things? Does the new language ever serve the same purpose as the mother tongue?

BETWEEN LANGUAGES

All immigrants experience not understanding what others say if they do not speak the language of the new country. Yet if the "being of anything that is resides in the word," and as a result, "language is the House of Being," as Heidegger (1982) suggested, then losing one's ability to name things in the new world is more than an inconvenience. DeSaussure argued that words achieve their meaning not just from the things they refer to but from associations created in the mind (quoted in Loomba, 1998). Perhaps it was this lack of associations in the new language that made Roxanne, an 8-year-old Chinese girl who had immigrated 2 months before her first interview, view life as meaningless. She said during her first interview, "I have no friends here. Life has no meaning. I can't understand the teacher. I don't know how to ask for help. I want to go home."

Learning a new language is more than learning another linguistic code. To learn the language, says Paulo Freire (1972), is a mode of "cultural empower-ment" and development of self-identity. Through language, all immigrants, including children, come to understand their new world. The new language can help them to know how best to become what they may become in the new country. However, if Language is the House of Being, then different cultures live in differ-ent houses. Is dialogue *from house to house* possible? How does a child live between these two *houses?*

Being in the Others' House

This is how my son described his experience of learning English in the first few months after our arrival in an English-speaking province in Western Canada:

> It was like I couldn't control what was going to come out of my mouth. It was in my head, I could hear the appropriate sounds but when I opened my mouth, the sounds were very different from the ones I thought they would be. I was really embarrassed and didn't want to talk at all. It was like I couldn't trust myself any-more. I felt so stupid. Sometimes it was very difficult for me to find the word I needed, so I would replace it with another English or Bulgarian word. Nobody seemed to make sense of what I was trying to say so they just ignored me or even worse, laughed at me. It was lonely, you know. (Kirova, 2001, p. 263)

As in the experience of turning a house into a home, the experience of learning to use another language brings feelings of discomfort and lack of belonging. The experiential accounts provided by several other immigrant children reveal how unsettling being "language-ly" in others' houses was for these children. These accounts, however, also reveal the experiences of the children where **language spoke itself as language**

> when we cannot find the right word for something that concerns us, carries us away, oppresses or encourages us. Then we leave unspoken what we have in mind and, without rightly giving it a thought, undergo moments in which language itself has distantly and fleetingly touched us with its essential being. (Heidegger, 1982, p. 59)

Heidegger suggested that an experience we have with language draws our attention to our relation to language so that we may then remember this relation. So we can ask, "In what relation do I live to the language I speak?" In speaking their mother tongue, children, like adults, talk about many topics: a set of facts, an occurrence, a question, a matter of concern. For example, young children's curiosity about the world is expressed in their questions. "What is this?" "How does it work?" "Who made it?" "Where did you get it from?" are questions that we all hear when we are with children. Their purpose is to find out about the things in the world. "Only because in everyday speaking language does not bring itself to language but holds back, are we able simply to go ahead and speak a language, and so to deal with something and negotiate something by speaking" (Heidegger, 1982, p. 59). Thus there is an "essential self-forgetfulness" (Gadamer, 1976, p. 64) to language.

However, as the experiential accounts provided by the children show, this self-forgetfulness does not apply to those who are learning to speak another language, especially when this language is the only language spoken by the others outside of their homes. In fact, immigrant children are conscious not only of what they say, but also how they say it. An 8-year-old child, Roxanne, said this during her third interview, only 4 months after her family came to Canada from China:

> I speak English in school now. [But] sometimes I just ... ah ... I can't ... and I think hard but I can't think it out. Sometimes I can say it, sometimes I can't, and sometimes I dare not ... When I dare not express myself, I just, I just sit there, I just stand ... I just ... stand aside. I wish my English is better.

As a new language learner, Roxanne tried to choose the right word and to think how to say it. Sometimes she was successful; other times she was not. Native speakers, on the other hand, rarely have to concentrate much on what to say. When we are at home in a language, the words seem to choose us. In a self-forgetful mode of thinking and speaking, the interaction is truly conversational or dialogic. The mode for using a new language implies a particular type of **reflective thinking** rather than prereflective living with language. This way of speaking, of choosing the right words, implies a reflective approach to language: an approach that involves suspension from an immediate stance and results in more self-consciousness, "making normal social interaction uncomfortable" (van Manen, 1991, p. 13). Thus the act of speaking the new language becomes thoughtful in that "it requires that one distances oneself from the situation and contemplates the way in which to act before acting" (van Manen, 1991, p. 17). For immigrant children, speaking the new language is a thoughtful and distancing act that requires extracting oneself from the immediacy of the situation. Winning (1991) suggested that in contrast, when one is at home in a language, speaking is a "thought-less" way of being: thoughtless not because it does not require thought, but because the thought is an incorporated *intuneness* with the dialogic situation.

Unlike learning one's native language, learning a new language is a conscious, purposeful activity. This is how Jennifer, a 9-year-old recent Chinese immigrant to Canada, recalled this activity: "So every day I go home and memorize new words. This becomes my homework. I am now working hard to learn new vocabulary." To come to dwell in the language, however, is to come to a different level of experience. Like dwelling in a new space, dwelling in a new language requires more than memorizing the meaning or the position of the words in a sentence to know how use them. Learning a new language does not mean learning a corresponding system of signs for what one already knows. This aspect is only part of the story. Rather, "to learn a language is to increase the extent of what one can learn" (Gadamer, 1989, p. 442). Gadamer showed that language comes into being as language through dialogue and therefore comes to an understanding through conversation:

> Coming to an understanding is not a mere action, a purposeful activity, a setting up of signs through which I transmit my will to others. Coming to an understanding as such, rather, does not need any tools, in the proper sense of the word. It is a life process in which a community of life is lived out. (p. 446)

How does this life process look to an immigrant child? What community of life must he or she live out in the new world for the new language to come to being through genuine dialogue?

Playing Is Being in Between Houses

The world of children's play is shared. It requires and creates a sense of togeth-erness, which does not mean doing things only together or behaving playfully. Rather, the true meaning of play comes to life only if the players intentionally let themselves be absorbed into the spirit of play. In the world of play, the sense of togetherness represents itself not only through the boundaries of shared space but also through the boundaries of shared meanings of objects used in play. These meanings are shared both through language and gesture and thus open possibili-ties for a genuine dialogue between native and non-native speakers.

I observed Bethen, a 4-year-old girl from Turkey, for the first 5 months after her family arrived in Canada. For her learning the new language occurred through play with her English-speaking peers. It was play that allowed her to engage in a dialogue with the world around her. And yet the answer is not this simple unless we understand how play provides such an opportunity for a dialogue between the world of the native speakers and the world of the language learners. How does play help an immigrant child to appropriate the new world?

A child at play does not limit himself or herself to the objects in the world. Play takes the player beyond the immediate setting. "Play happens 'through' the world in which it is observably set" (Holland et al., 1998, p. 236). A child at play responds to the presence and absence of things. Play creates openness where things can be anything. Through play, we see how the things in this world need not have fixed meanings. What in the "open sense-making is a pencil now suddenly is a bridge, a road block, a soldier, or a house" (Langeveld, 1984, p. 216). The complete openness of possibilities in play allows new things to emerge. This openness allows changes and newness to emerge in the play world. The play experience is rich and exciting; it is here and now. The power of openness provides an opening and an invitation to enter life, which allows children to experience the endless evolving ways of seeing and feeling the world around them. "In the moment of creation, children are making and remaking the world in their hopeful, hateful, anguished, joyous, and wondrous images" (Alexander, 1984, p. 478).

How is this related to immigrant children's building of their "language-ly" being in the new world? In the openness of play is *naming*. In play, often a child is looking for something in particular, and when this something is found, a word calls it into being. "To assign the naming word is, after all, what constitutes find-ing," says Heidegger (1982, p. 20). Naming gives rise to an image, creating con-creteness in children's landscapes of images, giving enormous creative possibilities. Yet once something is named, it *is,* and it *is* the same for everyone involved in the naming. Thus, a shared meaning is created. For Heidegger (1982) "The word itself is the relation, by holding everything forth into being, and there upholding it. If the word did not have this bearing, the whole of things, the 'world,'would sink into obscurity" (p. 73).

However, not all making and creating in play requires naming. There is also silence, a pause for observing the others, looking for other children to join, gathering one's thoughts, or pondering ideas. "The silence that precedes and surrounds speech is not void, but a silence with a promise of speech, a silence pregnant with meaning, like a pause in a conversation or a gap between each ring of the telephone" (Spurling, 1977, p. 51). In this silence, all speakers, both native and nonnative, are equally engaged in the "symbolic understanding" of the life world. Perhaps this is why in play the possibility is open for "wandering back and forth between different language realities" where a child may sense that the source of reality is the same from which arise the fundamentally different languages of his or her home and the language of the new home. Thus in play it becomes possible to learn to understand the language of the others.

PEDAGOGICAL CONSIDERATIONS

To consider the pedagogical possibilities for ensuring an "equitable and just treatment" (Soto & Inces, 2002) of immigrant children, we need to ask, "What are the human possibilities—other than equal access to education, information, and political process of a nation—of which they are deprived if their first language no longer opens a region of relatedness for their dwelling?" Furthermore, we need to ask, "What are the new possibilities that are open when the language of home fades away and children are thrown into unfamiliar status of being?"

Lost Possibilities

If language is the house of being, and humans dwell in language Heidegger, (1982), then as the experimental accounts provided by immigrant children show, while learning of the host country, the possibility of dwelling genuinely in this new language is absent. For example, the fact that Jennifer learned English as homework and that for my son and for Roxanne it was difficult to find the words they wished to use in a conversation with the others suggests that the new language was something "out there," something they still needed to grasp. Language was experienced as a skill yet to be acquired. Many of the children I interviewed said that they felt inferior because of their language abilities. Mustafa, a boy from Iran, for example, felt that he had "something less than anyone else" (Kirova, 2002). Feelings of inferiority and fear of being laughed at silenced many children during their initial acquisition of the new language. This is how Mustafa described his experience.

> I just sat on the hill and watched the others but I couldn't even enjoy watching the game they were playing because I didn't know what they were trying to do. I felt like there was a hole in my chest. (Kirova, 2001, p. 264)

Feeling lonely and isolated from the rest of their peers was a common experience among immigrant children (Kirova, 2001). Losing their sense of being at ease in social interactions and the difficulties of finding the "right" word led children to lose the ability to express their own personalities appropriately. They felt like strangers, who, regardless of what they did or said, were not understood. "Nobody understood me and nobody really cared," said Luka. Speaking their own language and speaking another still-unfamiliar language were for immigrant children two modes of existence in the world.

Not being at ease in the new language was experienced as being unable to share jokes with their peers. Sharing humor creates a sense of "we-ness" in any classroom. To share this experience with her classmates, Jenny was willing to do "as the rest of the students do" even without understanding why they did it. This is how she described her participation in shared activities in her second interview.

> Sometimes ... sometimes the whole class is engaged in telling small jokes. Well, not really small jokes but little something to make the others laugh. Then I would perform with them. I don't even know what it is about but I just follow them. I just jump and jump, and jump there and someone falls, and gets picked up, and someone says something, and he laughs really loud ... They asked me to jump. They jumped and asked me to follow. (Kirova-Petrova & Wu, 2002, p. 177)

Being unaware of the language that accompanied the physical portion of the joke, she was just "performing with them." For a joke to be understood, there must be a common meeting ground, which does not exist for an immigrant child. Thus participating only physically in the world of the others did not bring a sense of belonging or satisfaction. When asked, "Is there anything that you are happy about in school?" Val replied, "Happy? I don't have any."

> To think in one language and speak in another is somewhat like trying to make a motel room into a home. When one is thinking in one language but speaking another, it is the spoken language that is in a way being borrowed for a purpose; it is not where one is "living" (Winning, 1991, p. 153).

To think in one language and have to translate this into another language in speech means that a different mode of thinking is activated. In one's own language, thought is accompanied by the unfolding of speech. The way of thinking is different when that thought is not accompanied by an unfolding speech. This can change some new language learners' mode of thinking, which was interpreted by many of the interviewed children as being stupid. Roxanne, for example, recalled her first month at school as follows. "I just listened in class, dumb and foolish." This account also revealed that Roxanne felt that in school silence was seen as a lack of knowledge or even intelligence. "Silence as a lack of something reflects Western ways of thinking and viewing the world" (Viruru, 2001, p. 40).

In a school system that does not honor immigrant children's first languages, these children are always the "receivers of knowledge" (Belenky, Clinchy, Goldberger, & Tarule, 1986), which may lead them to believe that their own way of thinking has little or no value.

Gained Possibilities

Do new possibilities open when the first language fades away and a new one is learned? People become able to speak genuinely and creatively once they "are presented and together with those with whom they speak, in whose neighborhoods they dwell because it is what happens to concern them at the moment" (Heidegger, 1982, p.120); and when they listen to the accompanying opening field of human possibilities. A person cannot remain the same after learning another language: "A person learns a new language and, as we say, gets a new soul ... [he] becomes in that sense a different individual" (Mead, 1934, p. 156). Learning a language involves coming together with people in understanding a new way of looking at things in the world. Words have a propensity to call forth a world.

> As humans we exist in language and we continually weave the linguistic web in which we are embodied. We coordinate our behavior in language, and together in language we bring forth our world. "The world everyone sees, is not the world but a world, which we bring forth with others." (Maturna & Varela, as cited in Capra, 2002, p. 54)

In meeting our own ways of taken-for-granted suppositions about behavior, there is opportunity for change and growth. Heidegger (1982) suggested that the breaking up of what is taken for granted is "the true step back on the way of thinking" (p. 108). Whether or not the new way is adopted or rejected, there is the chance to reflect on our basic way of living. Through such encounters in which one breaks out of unquestioned frameworks and meets the other in face-to-face situations, there is an opportunity to understand the other better. As the experiential accounts indicate, play makes it possible for such encounters in which children become *neighbors*. Furthermore, such encounters help immigrant children to understand themselves better in terms of where and how they come to be as they are and what and how they will be when they are home in the new world. Winning (1991) suggests that this should not be a one-way process. Barber (1989) too points out that there is an opportunity for learning on behalf of the home group:

> A similar self-discovery and the de-absolutization takes place in those who directly relate with the stranger and so insert themselves into a situation analogous to the Stranger's. When the natural attitude's blinders to Otherness fall from our eyes, we can recognize some of our own intentionalities, including relevances, through which

the world is given to us, as never before, as well as recognizing that other intentionalities are possible and that our own are not absolute. (p. 125)

Learning a new language becomes the possibility of re-authoring self (Bakhtin, 1984, 1986). I am conscious of myself and become myself only while revealing myself for another, through another, and with the help of another (Bakhtin, 1984). This possibility is available to children in the openness of play, where a departure from the boundaries of learning the new language as homework, as something that is out there for them to grasp as knowledge located outside themselves becomes possible. Play allows acquisition of the new language to be experienced as dialogic, as a process that is on the border between the self and the other. "The self is a position from which meaning is made, a position that is 'addressed' by and 'answers' others and the world (the physical and cultural environment)" (Holland et al., 1998, p. 173). Thus, it is possible in play to re-author self in a dialogue, as this closes the distance one feels when using the new language. Children's unique ability to engage in activities in which, as in play, meaning is created rather than imposed shows our human capacity to construct new relatedness to the world and to others. As Holland et al. (1998) put it,

Habit or habituation forcefully communicates the bodily aspect of activity and thinking, yet it overlooks our ability to fantasize, to envision other worlds, to create other worlds by recombining elements from those we know. (p. 237)

The investigation of the phenomenon of moving childhoods as experienced in immigration based on Heidegger's notion of language as the house of being helps us to explore the creative and active relation-making processes that immigrant children engage in as they perceive and create new childhoods among scattered and conflicting events and experiences. Furthermore, Heidegger's notion that the breaking up of what is taken for granted is "the true step back on the way of thinking" (1982, p. 108) allows us to explore how language helps immigrant children experience themselves in the two worlds that live in—their home and outside of their home, as well as in-between these worlds. However, this investigation also shows that for young children these processes are not limited to language. Rather it is young children's ability to engage with the world both nonlinguistically and linguistically—as in play—that allows them not only to live between languages but also to develop their relation to the language of home and the home of language. Thus, this approach challenges the traditional assumptions about immigrant children as lacking agency, competence, and knowledge by opening up considerable pedagogical possibilities as it emphasis our human capacity to perceive and construct new relatedness through what is dissimilar rather than to deduct from what is known.

REFERENCES

Ackers, H. L. (1998). *Shifting Spaces: Women, Citizenship and Migration Within the European Union,* Bristol, UK: Policy Press.

Ackers, H. L., Stalford, H. (2004). *A Community for Children? Children, Citizenship and International Migration in the EU.* Hampshire, UK: Ashgate.

Alexander, R. (1984). What are children doing when they create? *Language Arts, 61*(5), 478–479.

Bakhtin, M. (1984). *Problems of Dostoevsky's Poetics* (C. Emerson, Trans.). Minneapolis, MN: University of Minnesota Press.

Bakhtin, M. (1986). *Speech Genres and Other Late Essays* (V. W. McGee, Trans.). Austin, TX: Texas University Press.

Barber, M. (1989). Otherness as attending to the other. In A. Dallery & C. Scott (Eds.), *The Question of the Other: Essays in Contemporary Continental Philosophy* (pp. 119–126). Albany, NY: SUNY Press.

Beekman, T. (1983). Human science as a dialogue with children. *Phenomenology + Pedagogy, 1,* 36–44.

Belenky, M., Clinchy, B., Goldberger, N., & Tarule, J. (1986). *Women's Ways of Knowing: the Development of Self, Voice and Mind.* New York: Basic Books.

Berger, P., & Luckmann, T. (1971). *The Social Construction of Reality.* Harmondsworth, UK: Penguin.

Capra, F. (2002). *The Hidden Connections: Integrating the Biological, Cognitive, and Social Dimensions into a Science of Sustainability.* New York: Doubleday

Cattanach, A. (1997). *Children's Stories in Play Therapy.* London: Kingsley.

Freire, P. (1972). *Pedagogy of the Oppressed.* New York: Herder and Herder.

Gadamer, H. (1976). *Philosophical Hermeneutics.* Berkeley, CA: University of California Press.

Gadamer, H. (1989). *Truth and Method* (2nd ed.). New York: Crossroads.

Giorgi, A., Fisher, C. T., & Murray, E. (1975). An application of phenomenological method in psychology. *Duquesne Studies in Phenomenological Psychology* (Vols. 1, 2). Pittsburgh, PA: Duquesne University Press.

Godkin, M. A. (1985). *Phenomenology and Psychological Research.* Pittsburgh, PA: Dusquesne University Press.

Heidegger, M. (1964). *Basic Writings.* New York: Harper & Row.

Heidegger, M. (1971). *Poetry, Language, Thought.* New York: Harper & Row.

Heidegger, M. (1982). *On the Way to Language.* New York: Harper & Row.

Heidegger, M. (1996). *Being and Time.* New York: SUNY Press.

Holland, D., Lachicotte Jr., W., Skinner, D., & Cain, C. (1998). *Identity and Agency in Cultural Worlds.* Cambridge, MA: Harvard University Press.

Kirova, A. (2001). Loneliness in immigrant children: Implications for classroom practice. *Childhood Education, 77*(5), 260–268.

Kirova, A. (2002, November). *Non-verbal behaviour, coping strategies and peer acceptance in young immigrant children: A case study.* Paper presented at the National Association for the Education of Young Children (NAEYC) Annual Conference, New York.

Kirova-Petrova, A. (1996). *Exploring Children's Loneliness Feelings.* Unpublished doctoral dissertation, University of Alberta, Edmonton, Canada.

Kirova-Petrova, A., & Wu, J. (2002). Peer acceptance, learning English as a second language, and identity formation in children of recent Chinese immigrants. In M. Wyness & A. Richardson (Eds.), *Exploring Cultural Perspectives, Integration and Globalization.* (pp. 171–190). Edmonton, AB: ICRN Press.

Langeveld, M. (1984). How does the child experience the world of things? *Phenomenology + Pedagogy, 2,* 215–223.

Loomba, A. (1998). *Colonialism/Postcolonialism.* London: Routledge.

Mandell, N. (1988). The least-adult role in studying children. *Journal of Contemporary Ethnography, 16,* 433–467.

Mead, G. H. (1934). *Mind, Self and Society.* Chicago: University of Chicago Press.

Merleau-Ponty, M. (1999). *Phenomenology of Perception.* London: Routeledge & Kegan Paul.

Schutz, A., & Lukmann, T. (1973). *The Structure of the Life-World.* (R. Zaner & H. T. Engelhardt, Jr., Trans.). Evanston, IL: Northwestern University Press.

Searless, H. F. (1960). *The Nonhuman Environment.* New York: International University Press.

Soto, L. D., & Inces, R. Q. (2002). Children's linguistic/cultural human rights. In G. Cannella & J. Kincheloe (Eds.) *Kidworld: Childhood Studies, Global Perspectives, and Education* (pp. 181–197). New York: Lang.

Spurling, L. (1977). *Phenomenology and the social world.* London: Routledge and Kegan Paul.

Van den Berg, J. H. (1955). *The phenomenological approach to psychiatry.* Springfield, IL: Thomas.

van Manen, M. (1986). *The Tone of Teaching.* Toronto, ON: Scholastic.

van Manen, M. (1990). *Researching Lived Experiences: Human Science for an Action Sensitive Pedagogy.* London, ON: Althouse Press.

van Manen, M. (1991). *The Tact of Teaching: The Meaning of Pedagogical Thoughtfulness.* London, ON: Althouse Press.

Viruru, R. (2001). Colonized through language: The case of early childhood education. *Contemporary Issues in Early Childhood, 2*(1), 31–46.

Wenkart, A. (1961). Regaining identity through relatedness. *American Journal of Psychoanalysis. 21,* 227–233.

Winning, A. (1991). *The Language of Home and the Home of Language: Pedagogical Considerations for ESL Practice.* Unpublished doctoral dissertation, University of Alberta, Edmonton, Canada.

Introduction to Part IV

Far From Home With Fluctuating Hopes

Whether sought or impelled, migration is fraught with hazard, uncertainty, and distress (Rong & Preissle, 1998). Whatever the situation before the relocation, a new *normal* must be defined for daily life. This is not easy, because the new home no longer looks or feels like home. It can be even more traumatic for both children and adults who find themselves to be a visible minority. People around them may look different from those they were accustomed to. Dress and appearance, hygiene, cooking odors, and behaviors of both children and adults in the new situation are only a few of the new normals that must be faced. The old comfortable face of normal is redefined, and the old one will not return. Families in the home country may have been large, but in the new country, apartment owners may not rent to families with more than a few children, if children are welcome at all.

Solidarity in the immediate community may have been prevalent in the home country but impossible to find in the new one. Even when compatriots live nearby, conflicts may develop between newcomers and those who preceded them. Segal (1993) makes the point that despite the best-intentioned policies, newer immigrants may not be as welcome either by the government or by immigrant communities when resources are limited in the host country.

Australia, Canada, and the United States, three major receiving nations for transnational migrants, are also among the nations that accept quota refugees from places such as refugee camps (Global Commission on International Migration [GCIM], 2005). These refugees often have escaped war and have experienced trauma. Jaycox et al. (2002) interviewed more than 1,000 recently immigrated students in Los Angeles and found many who reported high levels of exposure to violence, both as personal victims and as witnesses. They concluded that there is a need for intervention to address the psychological symptoms that may result from such experiences.

Part IV considers the special challenges for refugee children and includes chapters that create a compelling picture of the hardships frequently experienced by families and children who are involuntary or forced migrants. Forced migration refers to a person or family being coerced to move away from home or the home region. It often connotes violent coercion and is used interchangeably with the terms displacement or forced displacement. If the displaced person has crossed an international border and falls under one of the relevant international legal instruments, he of she is considered a refugee. *Convention refugees* are defined as people who leave their country because of a well-founded belief that they will be persecuted because of their religious beliefs, race, nationality, political opinion, or membership in a given group. *Humanitarian-designated refugees* are defined as people who are personally affected by situations including civil war and armed conflict. *Asylum seekers* is another term used to define people who are compelled to leave their home countries because of external aggression or domination or by events that seriously undermine public order (United Nations High Commissioner for Refugees [UNHCR], 2005).

According to the author of chapter 13, Australia is the only Western country to enforce a policy of mandatory detention of asylum seekers who arrive in the country without documents, irrespective of their age or family situation. Although changes were made to the system in 2002 so that now approximately half the children can attend local schools outside the detention compound, other children are still living and attending school in the detention centers and are isolated from mainstream culture. The author recommends that education be pursued as a protective factor for displaced children and their families.

The other three chapters in part IV focus on the experiences of refugee families and children who struggle to understand and adjust to mainstream education systems in the host countries of the United States and Canada. The apparent physical differences in the educational setting experienced by these two groups of refugee children become less salient when one reads the authors' description of the difficulties that the children face in these settings. Lack of adequate psychological support for the children who have experienced trauma, insufficient funding for learning the new language, inappropriateness of the curriculum, and lack of appropriate curriculum resources are common challenges faced by the refugee children who participated in the studies presented in part IV. In addition to the major adaptation barrier of discrimination, refugee children may have negative memories that stall their adjustment. Refugee children between 3 and 10 years of age on arrival in the new host nation will remember their country, the war, and the long, difficult trip. It may take time, but they will learn English, and their experiences of trauma and change can be dealt with orally. Asher (1984) suggested that for refugee students, school personnel must be particularly careful to be gentle and soft spoken because of the experiences refugee children bring with them and because the children may not be prepared for the directness found in the new culture.

Chapter 14 points to the difficulties faced by school personnel in addressing the needs of refugee children, partly because by law teachers and school districts in the United States are not allowed to ask for immigrant status. This lack of information creates challenges in developing a support system to deal with refugee children's experiences of trauma. Unfortunately, this information is not readily obtainable through parents, who, out of fear of deportation or other legal consequences, may not always wish to tell about their child's experiences. The authors of this chapter provide a number of strategies that schools can use to support the adjustment of refugee children to schools in the United States.

It is not only children who struggle with the inadequacy of education systems. Parents also struggle to help their children meet their hopes and aspirations for education in the host countries. The need for changes in educational policy and practice to meet the unique needs of refugee children and their families is stressed by all authors in part IV. The role of the school in helping parents become advocates for their children is emphasized in chapter 15. The study presented in this chapter indicates that minority parents who are marginalized in society are often powerless to change programs in the schools their children attend and are excluded from the process of making decisions about their children's education. The author suggests that schools need to consider the students' and parents' opinions about the structure of ESL programs and their cultural and linguistic backgrounds.

There are many sources of stress for refugee families undergoing acculturation, and these may include anxiety about family and friends left behind, underemployment and unemployment, cultural conflict, and changing family roles. Chapter 16 presents a study conducted with parents of preschool children from seven refugee communities now living in large city in western Canada, including Afghan, African French-speaking, Cambodian, Eritrean, Kurdish, Somali, and Sudanese parents. Each ethnocultural group offered information about resettlement issues that affect refugee families in the process of adjusting to a new culture. The conflicting values and beliefs that newcomer parents face are revealed through first-person narrative. A strong theme running through parents' comments is a desire to see their children receive a "good" education.

The chapters in part IV do not differentiate between the experiences of male and female refugees in general and refugee children in particular with regard to their adjustment to the host culture. However, it is worth noting the suggestion from Corson (1998) that the least visible groups in pluralist societies are girls from certain immigrant and refugee cultures. They may be doubly marginalized: first as members of different cultures and then as females in those cultures. He also points out that their invisibility in education is increased by their marginal place in research and practice.

Although schools may not be responsible for such interventions, school personnel need to be aware of the possibility of symptoms of posttraumatic stress disorder in refugee children and help the family to find appropriate support services. Migration Watch UK (2003) stated that coordinated assistance of various agencies is important in helping schools manage the successful integration of the large numbers of refuges and children from asylum-seeker families and integrate them successfully into school and community.

The main educational issue identified by the authors in part IV is the lack of policies and programs to address the psychological and educational needs of the children of these migrant families.

REFERENCES

Ascher, C. (1984). The social and psychological adjustment of Southeast Asian refugees. *ERIC/CUE Digest, 21,* 1–4. Accession No. ED252638. New York: ERIC Clearinghouse on Urban Education. Retrieved April 25, 2006, from http://www.ericdigests.org/pre-921/asian.htm

Corson, D. (1998). *Changing Education for Diversity.* Milton Keynes, UK: Open University Press.

Global Commission on International Migration (GCIM). (2005). *Migration at a glance.* Retrieved October 21, 2005, from http://www.gcim.org/attachements/Migration%20at%20a%20glance.pdf

Jaycox, L. H., Stein, B. D., Kataoka, S. I. H., Wong, M., Fink, A., Escudero, P., & Zaragoza, C. (2002). Violence exposure, posttraumatic stress disorder, and depressive symptoms among recent immigrant schoolchildren. *Journal of the American Academy of Child and Adolescent Psychiatry, 41,* 1104–1110.

Migration Watch UK. (2003). *Education: The Impact of Asylum Seekers, 28 February 2003.* Retrieved September 17, 2005, from http://www.migrationwatchuk.co.uk/frameset.asp?menu=publications&page=publications.asp

Rong, X. L., & Preissle, J. (1998). *Educating Immigrant Students: What We Need to Know to Meet the Challenges.* Thousand Oaks, CA: Corwin Press.

Segal, A. (1993). *An Atlas of International Migration.* New Providence, NJ: Hans Zell.

United Nations High Commissioner for Refugees (UNHCR). (2005). *Definitions and Obligations.* Retrieved October 21, 2005, from http://www.unhcr.org.au/basicdef.shtml

Chapter 13

Transnational Displacement of Children: An Australian Perspective

Ann Farrell
Queensland University of Technology, Australia

Transnational displacement of children has become a global phenomenon and includes children of refugees, asylum seekers, and voluntary migrants. The United Nations High Commission for Refugees (UNHCR) estimates that 25 million children are currently uprooted from their homes. Australia claims to be one of the world's leading resettlement nations, having accepted some 130,000 refugees, with 12,000 having arrived in 2001–2002. This chapter examines Australia's policies for the early education and care of displaced children and their families against the backdrop of the *United Nations Convention and Protocol Relating to the Status of Refugees 1951* and Australia's *National Inquiry Into Children in Immigration Detention* (2002). Of importance are children's premigration, migration, and postmigration experiences, their physical and mental health issues, and their treatment according to their status as "authorized" or "unauthorized" arrivals. The displacement of children presents significant challenges for early childhood practitioners working in education and care settings with these children and their families, particularly in the design of programs to promote resilience and to ameliorate the adverse effects of displacement.

BACKGROUND

Australia is a multicultural nation with a diverse cultural, ethnic, linguistic, and religious mix. In the state of Queensland alone, 4 people in 10 are migrants or the children of migrants (Office of Economic and Statistical Research, Queensland Treasury, 2002). The UNHCR (2005), the premier international organization associated with resettlement, estimates that almost half of the world's refugees are younger than 18 years old. This represents a critical challenge for the education and care of young children in the global community.

The global flows of peoples typify the new times of risk-producing, global societies (Beck, 1992; Farrell, 2004; Giddens, 2001).

> While flows of people and goods have take place across history, it is the changed intensity and speed of such flows which present challenges for social relations in the current period ... some flows are perceived and experienced as smooth and benign, and others as turbulent and disruptive. (Christie & Sidhu, 2002, pp. 1–2)

Children are seen as at particular risk (Danby & Farrell, 2004) in the new global order, although none more so than children experiencing transnational displacement.

Early childhood services are often at the frontline of educating and caring for these children and their families. These services have the potential to improve resilience and to ameliorate the negative consequences of displacement by developing a sense of community, social integration, and social engagement. In this chapter, I focus on the important work of early childhood professionals with one group of displaced persons, that is, refugee children in Australia.

REFUGEE CHILDREN

Refugees are defined broadly as people who have fled or been driven from their countries of origin and cannot return for fear of persecution, war, or oppression. Ironically, although the Australian government makes an annual contribution to the UNHCR, Australia ranked 17th of 21 industrialized countries receiving refugees (HREOC, 2003). In recent years, Australia has earned the reputation as the only Western country to enforce a policy of mandatory detention of asylum seekers who arrive without entry documents irrespective of their age or family situation (Mares, Newman, Dudley, & Gale, 2002; Silove, Steel, & Watters, 2000). Amnesty International (2001) indicated that 1,103 children were held in immigration detention centers in Australia in 2000–2001 with no legal limit placed on the duration of their detention. Most unauthorized-arrival children and families detained under Australia's mandatory detention laws have been held in secure immigration detention facilities such as Woomera, Port Hedland, Curtin, and Baxter (Human Rights and Equal Opportunity Commission [HREOC], 2004). These children often arrive in Australia having experienced war, natural disaster, genocide, or poverty and may also have experienced people-smuggling, currently one of the most lucrative global criminal activities (Szwarc, 2001).

Australian Human Rights lawyer Rayner (2001) referred to this new class of "illegitimate" children, whom she argues Australia has treated badly and unethically.

> A child, who, from her dress and appearance, belongs to a despised and feared religion, presents to an Australian immigration official. She has no travel documents or identity papers. She may be with someone who says she is her mother or, perhaps, she arrives on her own. She doesn't speak English. She doesn't say much at all. She seems jumpy. Where she came from has been in upheaval, poor, divided, disturbed. Law and order has broken down: there are arbitrary arrests and detention, possibly torture and/or executions or even war. She has probably seen terrible things … so we lock her up. (p. 1)

This category of child also could be theorized sociologically as the *minority-group child* (James, Jenks, & Prout 1998), denoting an existing set of power relations between adults and children that "deprive[s] some people of freedom in order to give it to others" (Oakley, 1994, p. 32).

Australia's DIMIA indicates that refugees experience more social and general health problems than migrants (McLennan, 1997). Research shows that refugee parents and children have reduced recuperative capabilities, making them less resilient in the face of hardship (Garbarino, Kostelny, & Dubrow, 1991; Schweitzer, Melville, & Steel, 2004) and putting them at increased risk of short- and long-term distress (Beiser, 1988; Chung, Bemak, & Wong, 2000; Silove, Steel, McGorry, & Mohan, 1998; Steel, Silove, Phan, & Bauman, 2002). Such negative effects are particularly severe for unaccompanied children (Comerford, Armour-Hileman, & Waller, 1991; Harding & Looney, 1977; McCallin, 1993).

The conditions under which children are detained also can exacerbate their distress. They can be confined in harsh and isolated conditions with double razor wire and locked gates and subjected to dehumanizing practices such as being assigned a number rather than being called by name. Australian researchers Mares et al. (2002) cited a case in which a 3-year-old was detained.

> The centre where this family have been detained for at least eight months was indeed totally barren, the only small area of grass and shrubs being around the offices, an area not accessible to detainees. The compounds are barren, harsh areas of dust and stones with no shade, surrounded by two fences of razor wire…. a few children were seen standing in the open or hanging on to the fences, moving rubbish bins from one place to another, kicking stones. There was nothing for them to

do ... many of the children, even up to the age of 12 are incontinent day and night, and many mattresses lay outside in the sun against the fences. (p. 93)

Many refugee children show adverse physical and psychological sequelae of their migration-related trauma, from their premigration dislocation to the ongoing stressors of resettlement and acculturation in a new country (Beiser & Hou, 2000; Gorst-Unsworth & Goldenberg, 1998; Miller et al., 2002; Silove et al., 1998; Sinnerbrink Silove, Field, Steel, & Manicavasagar, 1997, see Table 1 for a summary of selected Australian research that demonstrates the effect of migration-related stress on children).

Mares et al. (2002) also cited the case of a couple with a 2-year-old and a 5-month-old baby born in detention. The detained parents reported in an interview, "The toddler doesn't trust us anymore. He can't play, he won't eat, he can't sleep" (p. 912).

Clearly the daily routines and everyday interactions within the family are compromised by detention, and the protective factors that may strengthen these children's ability to cope with displacement are significantly reduced. This picture of family life in detention is consistent with compelling evidence that children of depressed parents are at risk of developing psychological difficulties later in life. In the case of refugees, this relationship is found to be particularly strong in relation to the mother's mental health (Adjukovic & Adjukovic, 1993; Ekblad, 1993; Miller, 1996).

For those who are living with parents, the effect of living in detention may be moderated to some extent, but this depends on the parents' ability to cope (Garbarino et al., 1991). The entire family is affected, because children learn that it is not the parents who are in control, but someone else (Comerford et al., 1991). Conversely, where conditions enable refugees to maintain traditional roles such as a parent going to work, the effects are less severe (Markowitz, 1996; McCallin, 1993).

In summary, the Australian Psychological Society (2004) concluded that detention is a negative socialization experience. It accentuates developmental risk, it threatens the relationship between children and significant caregivers, it limits educational opportunities, it has traumatic effects on child refugees and reduces their potential to recover from trauma, and it exacerbates the effects of other trauma. Given this evidence, it is imperative for early childhood professionals working with these children to seek to provide the protective factors that may increase their resilience and reduce the risk of further harm.

Education of Displaced Children

Despite the adverse sequelae reported in the literature and attested to anecdotally by early childhood professionals, a number of reports (Birman, Trickett, & Vinokurov, 2002; Elbedour, ten Bensel, & Bastian, 1993) agree that education has

TABLE 1
Summary of Australian Research/Reports Into Refugee Children in Australia

Researchers	Year	Research sample & focus	Key findings
McKelvey et al.	2002	519 Vietnamese children and 23 parents living in Western Australia, focused on children's psychiatric disorders; researchers used translators/community leaders in data collection (Diagnostic Interview Schedule for Children [DISC-C])	Prevalence rates of 14%–21% psychiatric disorders in children and adolescents; higher rates among refugee than non-refugee children
Zwi, Herzberg, Dossetor & Field	2003	Case study of distressed 6-year-old boy held in detention	6-year-old was in a state of distress and preoccupied by imprisonment and the violence he had witnessed; child improved when removed from detention with rapid deterioration on return
Davidson et al.	2004	Major review of Australian research literature on refugee children's access to health care	Children found to be at risk of suboptimal health care due to impact of trauma and detention
Sawyer et al.	2000	National mental health survey of 4500 children (4-7 years), adolescents and parents. Parent questionnaire assessed mental health problems (Youth Self-Report & Child Behaviour Checklist); focus on health related quality of life, health-risk behavior and service utilization	Paucity of information on the mental health of children and adolescents living in non-English speaking families

(Continued)

TABLE 1 (Continued)

Researchers	Year	Research sample & focus	Key findings
Sultan & O'Sullivan	2001	Focused on psychological well-being of 10–15 children in a detention center	Children exposed to hunger strikes, self-harm and suicide attempts; wide range of psychological disturbances in children: separation anxiety, nocturnal enuresis, sleep disturbances; children of parents who reached the tertiary depressive stage were vulnerable to developing a range of psychological disorders
Silove	2002	Review of Australian studies examining mental health consequences of contemporary Australian policies for asylum seekers	Research found high rates of trauma, post-traumatic stress disorders (PTSD) and depression in asylum seekers
HREOC: National Inquiry into Children in Immigration Detention	2004	346 submissions from leading individuals and organizations representing education, law, health professions and human services	53 breaches of the *Convention on the Rights of the Child* with regard to children's issues

a mitigating influence in such precarious circumstances. Other mitigating factors include social support, language proficiency, belief systems, and a sense of self-efficacy (Miller et al., 2002). Therefore, education should be pursued as a protective factor for displaced children and their families.

Although a variety of language and literacy programs are available for displaced adults, there appear to be few resources, facilities, and educational programs for their young children. The education programs that are available for displaced children are mainly for those of primary and secondary school age. This means that children under the age of 6 are largely invisible in detention education. Further, the programs that do exist (albeit for older children) have been found to be erratic and to be designed neither to be culturally or linguistically sensitive nor sensitive to individual needs (Christie & Sidhu, 2002; HREOC, 2004; Ozdownski, 2002).

In Australia, the provision of education is the responsibility of state and territory governments, with the Commonwealth funding English as a second language (ESL) programs under the New Arrivals Program. Each state has specialist programs to cater to the educational needs of a cohort of students similar to those in immigration detention. According to Christie and Sidhu (2002), children classified as refugees under the Humanitarian Program are entitled to full federal funding, including funding for ESL teaching, but asylum seekers on temporary protection visas are not. Both classifications of children may have particularly acute needs associated with their second-language learning as well as their migration-related trauma.

Each state has either an ESL curriculum or uses ESL documents as a guide for targeted language teaching for ESL learners in the general curriculum. Students are often taught by specialist-subject teachers who also have ESL qualifications. Some states have a full ESL curriculum; some have documentation that supports ESL learning in mainstream curriculum areas; some use national documents to assist in adapting curriculum for ESL learners (Department of Education, Science and Training, 2006; HREOC, 2005). Also provided are services for trauma counseling, programs that link families and schools (Christie & Sidhu, 2002), and programs to reduce anxiety and engender a sense of safety for children entering mainstream schools (Refugee Resettlement Advisory Council, 2002). Again, these programs target primary and secondary school-aged children, thus leaving younger children largely out of the equation.

Once reliant entirely on internal education (i.e., education in the detention center), by the end of 2002, approximately half of the children in detention were given access to external education (i.e., education in regular schools), with approximately 80% in external schools by mid-2003 (HREOC, 2004). Australia's Human Rights Commissioner Ozdowski (2002) noted that a structured program in a mainstream school with ESL support was a much better learning environment than a detention center, especially when a child had been in detention for a long time.

Attending local schools allows detained children—who otherwise spend 24 hours a day in detention centres—to socialise with Australian children. Given that many detained families are eventually recognised as refugees, it is in Australia's interests to ensure the children get an education that helps them integrate into Australian society as soon as possible. (p. 1)

Although external education may give refugee and migrant children access to language and social networks, this also may accentuate the cultural divide between the center and the school (Christie & Sidhu, 2002).

Children's use of their home language is an important part of their identity construction and capacity to cope with adversity. Yet opportunities for them to learn both in their language of origin and in the language of their new context are severely compromised by detention. Experiencing the loss of his or her first language, culture, and family values can have serious, long-term consequences for children, such as loss of feelings of self-worth, loss of motivation to learn, and breakdown of family relationships (HREOC, 2004). These are key factors that need to be taken into consideration in the early childhood education and care of displaced children, whether in detention or in the general community.

HREOC (2004) noted that education in detention was typically conducted in isolated, harsh, and physically intimidating circumstances despite the existence of performance measures for the assessment of education such as the Immigration Detention Standards (IDS). The IDS require that all detainees have access to education programs and that social and educational programs appropriate to the child's age and abilities be available to all children in detention. In this framework services for children are said to include the following:

- programs for preschool, primary, and secondary school-aged children;
- provision of after-school activities such as sports and arts and crafts;
- entertainment facilities such as videos and computers;
- playgrounds;
- regular excursions; and
- case management of unaccompanied minors and other children with special needs (such as learning difficulties) (Phillips & Lorimer, 2003).

Yet despite this framework, there is skepticism that the services exist. HREOC (2004) challenged whether these children in fact were provided with education of a standard comparable to that provided in the Australian community. HREOC highlighted three key difficulties in providing a full curriculum to children in immigration detention. First, they challenged the appropriateness of a standard Australian curriculum for the special needs of detainee children. Second, they noted that the transitory nature of the detainee population worked against effective education. Third, they cited a severe lack of appropriate curriculum resources.

HREOC (2004) noted that the curriculum taught in detention centers fell far short of that provided in Australian schools for similar children. In particular, no attempts were made to adapt existing state curricula in an ESL framework. In addition, they advocated the key principles that should drive the education of these children until they should be released from detention: flexibility, recognition of the child within the family, sound educational experiences, respect for linguistic and cultural rights, and specially qualified staff suited to work with migrant and refugee children.

It is important to realize that many children who are educated in the Australian community have had similar experiences to those of detainee children. For example, children who arrive in Australia with visas and seek asylum and live in the community on bridging visas, arrive under Australia's Refugee and Humanitarian Program, or are released from detention and live in the community on temporary protection visas all attend Australian schools. So too these children may have culturally and linguistically diverse backgrounds and significant educational, emotional, and social needs (Phillips & Lorimer, 2003). Educational programs for these children also need to be designed to address severe mental health issues that affect their ability and willingness to participate in regular education (Mares et al., 2002). This requires customized programs rather than a one-size-fits-all approach. Although Australia has begun to develop and implement such policies and practices, there is still a considerable way to go to achieve equitable education for young displaced children.

Children's Rights to Early Childhood Education

Australia's policies for the education of displaced children fly in the face of children's rights. The rights of displaced children are articulated in major international conventions such as the Universal Declaration of Human Rights 1948, the Convention and Protocol Relating to the Status of Refugees 1951, and the Convention on the Rights of the Child 1989. "Such provisions advocate that children should not be penalised in relation to education for the views and actions of their parents" (Christie & Sidhu, 2002, p. 5). Moreover, Article 28 of the Convention on the Rights of the Child 1989 (UNCRC) applies equally to all children in Australia whether or not they have been displaced or are in immigration detention, providing education as "compulsory and available free to all." Although the UNCRC sets out the obligation to provide education, it does not establish the quantity, quality, or level of that education in individual states (HREOC, 2004).

Despite the scarcity of early childhood education for these families, some early childhood professionals are leading the way in children's rights by advocating for and working with displaced children and their families. But these may be relatively invisible in regular early childhood services as a result of their small numbers.

Australian academic Waniganayake (2001) commented on the complexities of the
policy context for refugee children in particular.

> It is easy to ignore or forget the particular complexities faced by refugee children in
> policy and planning agendas because, numerically, they are just another minority with
> differing needs, interests and abilities. Australian legislation on children's services, for
> instance, reinforces the minority status of refugees. By assigning refugee children to
> the generic category of children with "special needs" they cannot be distinguished
> easily from children with disabilities or those with poor English language skills. The
> policy focus is on the developmental needs, not on the children's backgrounds (i.e.,
> being a refugee, an immigrant, a displaced person, or an adopted child). (p. 290)

Despite these policy weaknesses, Waniganayake documented three examples of
early childhood professionals working with refugee children: the Rebuilding
Nations Programs, the Safe Haven Play Centres programs, and the Permanent
Resettlement programs. The Rebuilding Nations Program involves early childhood professionals establishing preschool programs in countries from which
children have fled. The account of Australian Andreoni (1998), who worked as
such an educator in Eritrea, challenged Australian early childhood programs to
consider the challenges of working with children who may be all too familiar with
war and weapons of war. The Safe Haven Play Centres is cited as a particular
policy response initiated by the Australian government in 1999 to offer temporary
shelter to displaced Kosovars. The management of these safe havens for children
younger than 5 years of age was the joint responsibility of government agencies
such as the Department of Defence and nongovernmental organizations such as
the Free Kindergarten Association. Notable challenges were faced as the children
played out aspects of war and violence; as children's trust built, staff were able to
help them to explore nonviolent alternatives. The Permanent Resettlement programs identify the difficulties faced by refugees in accessing children's services.
Once in a service, ideally a child is assigned a key worker who works closely with
the child, the family, and the resettlement community to minimize risk and to
build resilience (see also Rutter & Jones, 1998).

Another example of an early childhood organization that seeks to ameliorate
the negative effects of the refugee experience is the Victoria-based Real Rights for
Refugee Children 2004; web resources available at http://home.vicnet.net.at/~
rrrc/news.htm. Established in the early childhood community in 2001 to support
the rights of asylum seekers in Australia and refugees worldwide, it is committed
to working productively with other organizations that provide advocacy, support,
and resources for refugees and asylum seekers. Real Rights for Refugee Children
works to release children from detention, to provide resources to refugee and asy-
lum-seeking children and those working with them, and to advocate for the support of children and their families to recover from trauma. Their advocacy kit,
designed to educate and inform those who work closely with young children, is

distributed to early childhood services throughout Victoria. It provides resources that outline the abuse of refugee children's rights and how services can address these issues in their workplace and community.

Another important advocacy role is played by Australia's premier early childhood body Early Childhood Australia. For the last few years, its national publication *Every Child* has featured key articles on the needs of children in Australian detention in general and in early childhood services in particular. It is committed to promoting children's best interests through community education advocacy.

Every Child notes that "The childhoods of refugee children are characterised by displacement, disease, violence and fear" (Hydon, 2004, p. 14). Hydon of Early Childhood Australia (2004) noted,

> Early childhood practitioners cannot fail to the see the denial of children's rights and take up their role to speak our in their defence … the committee who worked to develop the Early Childhood Australia Code of Ethics (2004) could hardly have imagined a time when the voice of early childhood advocates was so desperately needed. Children continue to be detained in prison-like conditions despite numerous reports, a supposed change in policy and a growing concerned with the community. The voice of concern and the shouts of injustice need to be heard. Not just from those who line the streets and march, but those who know what is right and just for children and can speak with authority about what they know—early childhood educators. The commitment we have to children must be for all children, of not just those enrolled in centres and services, but for those we will never see. (p. 14)

Although there is evidence of advocacy from the early childhood sector and of service-based attempts to address these pressing issues, rigorous, longitudinal research involving these children, families, and communities is also needed to generate meaningful, evidence-based practice that will advance children's life chances beyond settlement. Waniganayake (2001) concurred in the urgent need for research into refugee children's adaptation to life in their new country and the part played by early childhood services in this process.

Future Directions for the Care and Education of Displaced Children

Key challenges have been identified by the Australian Psychological Society (2004) given the inadequacies of current policies and practices for displaced children. Implications for future directions in policy and practice can, therefore, be drawn from their pertinent questions.

- What are the qualifications and training of staff who care for children and their families in Australian detention? What is their knowledge of the issues faced by people who have been subjected to traumatic experiences and are suffering high degrees of anxiety, stress, and uncertainty?

- What provisions have been made for assessment of children's specific learning needs before their attending formal educational programs?
- What provisions have been made for the care of children who are suffering chronic or vicarious trauma as a result of witnessing threatening behavior?
- What critical-incident debriefing procedures are in place for children who have witnessed their parents, other family members, or social acquaintances engaging in acts of self-harm or being harmed? What support is in place for children who themselves have been harmed or have engaged in self-harmful acts while in detention?
- What provisions are in place for parenting programs that provide support for parents of children under extremely difficult psychological and physical circumstances?
- What efforts are being made to provide parents with the opportunity to model traditional family roles for children such as working to earn an income, meal preparation, other household duties, and so forth?
- What opportunities are in place for the assessment of safety issues such as bullying and sexual or physical abuse of children or their mothers in detention centers?
- How are resources distributed to children and families in detention centers?
- What socialization opportunities are available either in detention centers or in the wider community for children to develop skills and independence, engage in social activities, participate in cultural traditions, and communicate and interact with same-age peers and adults from similar ethnic and religious backgrounds?
- What access do children and families have to videos, music, and entertainment from their cultures of origin?
- What provisions are in place to ensure the maintenance of privacy in a manner commensurate with usual cultural practice?
- What is the government's rationale for continuing to implement a policy of mandatory detention of child asylum seekers that is likely to have a pernicious effect on these children's health and well-being?

Although policies about the detention of these children and families may change over time (e.g., a policy shift to have such children placed in the community rather than in detention centers), the challenges associated with their care and education persist.

CONCLUSION

In view of the global phenomenon of transnational displacement and the potential short- and long-term effects of displacement on children and their families, the

Australian community and early childhood educators need to pursue evidence-based policies and practices that may have a positive effect on the health and well-being of these children and families. As global citizens, we have ethical responsibilities to displaced children and their families to work toward democratic communities where people can feel free and capable of participation (Dewey, 1958).

This chapter urges us to exercise our professional and ethical responsibilities as global citizens to work with these children and their families in ways that acknowledge their background, their current circumstances, and their life chances. Early childhood professionals are in a prime position to lead the way in working with and advocating for children and their families who are undergoing a major and often traumatic life transition.

REFERENCES

Adjukovic, M., & Adjukovic, D. (1993). Psychological wellbeing of refugee children. *Child Abuse and Neglect, 17,* 843–854.
Andreoni, H. (1998). Necessity is the mother of invention. Australian and Eritrean early childhood educators sharing skills and experiences. *Australian Journal of Early Childhood 23*(1), 5–9.
Australian Psychological Society. (2004). *Detention of Children of Refugee Families in Australia: The Australian Psychological Society's Position Statement Submitted to the Australian Human Rights and Equal Opportunity Commission's Inquiry Into Children in Immigration Detention.* Retrieved April 3, 2005, from http://www.psychology.org.au/news/media_releases/10.1_58.asp
Beck, U. (1992). *Risk Society: Towards a New Modernity.* London: Sage.
Beiser, M. (1988). Influences of time, ethnicity, and attachment on depression in Southeast Asian refugees. *American Journal of Psychiatry, 145,* 46–51.
Beiser, M., & Hou, F. (2000). Language acquisition, unemployment and depressive disorder among Southeast Asian refugees: A 10-year study. *Social Science and Medicine, 53,* 1321–1334.
Birman, D., Trickett, E. J., Vinokurova, A. (2002). Acculturation and adaptation of Soviet Jewish refugee adolescents: Predictors of adjustment across life domains. *American Journal of Community Psychology, 30*(5)*,* 585–607.
Christie, P., & Sidhu, R. (2002). Responding to globalisation: Refugees and the challenges facing Australian schools. *Mots Pluriels, 21.* Retrieved March 11, 2005, from http://www.arts .uwa.edu.au/MotsPluriels/MP2102pcrs.html
Chung, R. C., Bemak, F., & Wong, S. (2000). Vietnamese refugees' levels of distress, social support and acculturation: Implications for mental health counselling. *Journal of Mental Health Counselling, 22*(2), 150–161.
Comerford, S. A., Armour-Hileman, V. L., & Waller, S. R. (1991). *Defenceless in detention. Vietnamese children living amid increased violence in Hong Kong.* Hong Kong: Refugee Concern Hong Kong.
Danby, S., & Farrell, A. (2004). Accounting for young children's competence in educational research: New perspectives on research ethics. *Australian Educational Researcher, 31*(3), 35–49.
Davidson, N., Skull, S., Burgner, D., Kelly, P., Raman, S., Silove, D., Steel, Z., Vora, R., & Smith, M. (2004). An issue of access: Delivering equitable health care for newly arrived refugee children in Australia. *Journal of Paediatric Child Health, 40,* 569–575.
Department of Education, Science and Training (DEST). (2006). *English as a second language—New arrivals (ESL-NA) programme.* Retrieved March 20, 2006, from http://www.dest.gov.au/sectors/

school_education/programmes_funding/programme_categories/special_needs_disadvantage/english_ as_a_second_language_new_arrivals_programmehome.htm

Department of Immigration and Multicultural and Indigenous Affairs (DIMIA). (2003). *Fact sheets.* Retrieved May 10, 2006, from http://www.immi.gov.au/refugee/migrating refugeehtm

Devereaux, J. (2004). Lessons from behind the wire. *Australian Educator, 41,* 14–17.

Dewey, J. (1958). *Experience and Nature.* New York: Dover.

Early Childhood Australia. (2004). *Code of Ethics.* Canberra, ACT: ECA. Retrieved April 3, 2005, from http://www.earlychildhoodaustralia.org.au/abtus_resources_cofe.htm

Ekblad, S. (1993). Psychosocial adaptation of children while housed in a Swedish refugee camp: Aftermath of the collapse of Yugoslavia. *Stress Medicine, 9,* 159–166.

Elbedour, S., ten Bensel, R., & Bastien, D. T. (1993). Ecological integrated model of children of war: Individual and social psychology. *Child Abuse and Neglect, 17,* 805–819.

Farrell, A. (2004). Child protection policy perspectives and reform of Australian legislation. *Child Abuse Review, 13,* 234–245.

Garbarino, J., Kostelny, K., & Dubrow, N. (1991). What can children tell us about living in danger? *American Psychologist, 46,* 376–383.

Giddens, A. (2001). *Sociology* (4th ed.). Cambridge, UK: Polity Press.

Gorst-Unsworth, C., & Goldenberg, E. (1998). Psychological sequelae of torture and organised violence suffered by refugees from Iraq. *British Journal of Psychiatry, 172,* 90–94.

Harding, R. K., & Looney, J. G. (1977). Problems of Southeast Asian children in a refugee camp. *American Journal of Psychiatry, 134,* 407–411.

Human Rights and Equal Opportunity Commission (HREOC). (1998–9). *Those who've come across the seas: The report of the Commission's Inquiry into the detention of unauthorised arrivals.* Canberra: HREOC.

Human Rights and Equal Opportunity Commission (HREOC). (2002). *National Inquiry Into Children in Immigration Detention.* Retrieved May 23, 2006, from http://www.hreoc.gov.au/human_rights_ detention/19th_Sept.htm

Human Rights and Equal Opportunity Commission (HREOC). (2003). '*Submission to National Inquiry into Children in Immigration Detention from The Australian Psychological Society*' Retrieved 24th May 2006 from http://www.humanrights.gov.au/human_rights/children_detention/ submissions/aus_psch_society.html

Human Rights and Equal Opportunity Commission (HREOC). (2004). *"A Last Resort?" Report of the National Inquiry Into Children in Immigration Detention.* Retrieved March 24, 2005, from http://www.humanrights.gov.au/human_rights/children_detention_report/

Hydon, C. (2004). The erosion of children's rights: A plea to the early childhood sectors. *Every Child, 10*(3), 14.

James, A. Jenks. C., & Prout, A. (1998). *Theorising childhood.* Cambridge, UK: Polity Press.

Mares, S., Newman, L., Dudley, M., & Gale, F. (2002). Seeking refuges, losing hope: Parents and children in immigration detention. *Australasian Psychiatry, 10*(2), 91–96.

Markowitz, F. (1996). Living in limbo: Bosnian Muslim refugees in Israel. *Human Organization, 55,* 127–132.

McCallin, M. (1992). *Living in detention: A review of the psychological wellbeing of Vietnamese children in the Hong Kong detention centres.* Geneva: International Catholic Child Bureau.

McCallin, M. (1993). *The psychosocial wellbeing of Vietnam minors in the Philippines: A comparison with Hong Kong.* Geneva, Switzerland: International Catholic Child Bureau.

McKelvey, R., Sang, D., Baldassar, L., Davies, L., Roberts, L., & Cutler, N. (2002). The prevalence of psychiatric disorders among Vietnamese children and adolescents. *Medical Journal of Australia, 177*(8), 413–417.

McLennan, W. (1997). *Mental health and wellbeing: Profile of adults, Australia.* Canberra Act: Department of Immigration, Multicultural and Indigenous Affairs. Retrieved May 10, 2003, from http://www.abs.gov.au/AUSSTATS/abs@nsf/DetailsPage/4326.01997?OpenDocument

Miller, K. E. (1996). The effects of state terrorism and exile on indigenous Guatemalan refugee children: A mental health assessment and an analysis of children's narratives. *Child Development, 67,* 89–106.

Miller, L., Weine, S., Ramic, A., Brkic, N., Djuric-Bejdic, Z., & Smajkic, A. (2002). The relative contribution of war experiences and exile-related stressors to levels of psychological distress among Bosnian refugees. *Journal of Traumatic Stress, 15,* 377–387.

Oakley, A. (1994). Women and children first and last: Parallels and differences between women's and children's studies. In B. Mayall (Ed.), *Children's Childhoods: Observed and Experienced.* London: Falmer.

Ozdowski, S. (2002). *Education of detained asylum seeker children and young people at state government schools.* Media release. Retrieved March 24, 2005, from http://www.humanrights.gov.au/media_releases/2002/65_02.html

Office of Economic and Statistical Research, Queensland Treasury. (2002). Demographic trends and implications for Queensland. Brisbane, Queensland, Australia: Author.

Phillips, J., & Lorimer, C. (2003). *Children in Detention.* Retrieved March 17, 2005, from http://www.aph.gov.au/library/intguide/SP/Childrendetention.htm

Rayner, M. (2001, October). *Political Pinballs. The Plight of Child Refugees in Australia.* Walter Murdoch Lecture. Canberra, Australia. Retrieved April 3, 2005, from the Real Rights for Refugee Children Web site http://home.vicnet.net.au/~rrrc/news.htm

Refugee Resettlement Advisory Council. (RRAC) (2002). *Strategy for Refugee Young People: An Overview.* Canberra, Australia: Department of Immigration and Multicultural and Indigenous Affairs.

Rutter, J., & Jones, C. (Eds.). (1998). *Refugee Education. Mapping the Field.* London: Trentham Books.

Sawyer, M., Arney, F., Baghurst, P., Kosky, R., Clark, J., Graetz, B., Waites, L., Nurcombe, B., Raphael, B., Patton, G., Prior, G., & Zubrick, S. (2000). *Mental Health of Young People in Australia: Child and Adolescent Component of the National Survey of Mental Health and Well-Being.* Canberra, Australia: Mental Health and Special Programs Branch, Commonwealth Department of Health and Aged Care.

Schweitzer, R., Melville, F., & Steele, Z. (2004). *The Relationship Between Trauma, Family Connectedness and Emotional Wellbeing in Resettled Refugees From the Horn of Africa.* Paper in preparation based upon an Honours Thesis (F. Melville). Queensland University of Technology.

Silove, D. (2002). The asylum debacle in Australia: A challenge for psychiatry. *Australian and New Zealand Journal of Psychiatry, 36*(3), 290–296.

Silove, D., Steel, Z., McGorry, P., & Mohan, P. (1998). Trauma exposure, postmigration stressors and symptoms of anxiety, depression and post traumatic stress in Tamil asylum seekers: Comparison with refugees and immigrants. *Acta Psychiatrica Scandinavica, 97,* 175–181.

Silove, D., Steel, Z., & Watters, C. (2000). Policies of deterrence and the mental health of asylum seekers. *Journal of American Medical Association, 284,* 604–611.

Sinnerbrink, I., Silove, D., Field, A., Steel, Z., & Manicavasagar, V. (1997). Compounding of remigrations trauma and postmigration stress in Asylum Seekers. *Journal of Psychology, 131*(5), 463–470.

Steel, Z., Silove, D., Phan, T., & Bauman, A. (2002). Long-term effect of psychological trauma on the mental health of Vietnamese refugees resettled in Australia: A population based study. *Lancet, 360,* 1056–1062.

Sultan, A., & O'Sullivan, K. (2001). Psychological disturbances in asylum seekers held in long term detention: A participant observer account. *Medical Journal of Australia, 175,* 593–596.

Szwarc, J. (2001). *Faces of racism.* London: Amnesty International.

United Nations Convention and Protocols in Relation to the Status of Refugees (1951). Retrieved April 2, 2005, from http://www.unher.org/cgi-bin/texis/vtx/protect/opendoc.pdf?tbl=PROTECTION&id=3bbbc2aa10

United Nations Convention on the Rights of the Child (1989). Retrieved April 2, 2005, from http://www.ohchr.org/english/law/pdf/crc.pdf

United Nations High Commission for Refugees (UNHCR). (2005). *Statistics. Refugees, Asylum-Seekers and Others of Concern to UNHCR.* Retrieved April 3, 2005, from http://www.unhcr.ch/cgi-bin/texis/vtx/basics/opendoc.htm?tbi=BASICS&page=home&id3b028097c

Universal Declaration of Human Rights 1948. Retrieved April 2, 2004, from http://www.un.org/Overview/rights.html

Waniganayake, M. (2001). From playing with guns to playing with rice: The challenges of working with refugee children. An Australian perspective. *Childhood Education, 77*(5), 289–294.

Zwi, K., Herzberg, B., Dossetor, D., & Field, J. (2003). A child in detention. Dilemmas faced by health professionals. *Medical Journal of Australia, 179*(6), 319–322.

Chapter 14

Exploring the Needs of Refugee Children in Our Schools

Judit Szente
University of Central Florida, USA

James Hoot
State University of New York at Buffalo, USA

Hassan is 11 years old and has been living in New York State for 3 years. He was born in Afghanistan, but when he was only 3, his father was killed in the war. Fearing for their lives, Hassan's mother took him and his brother to Pakistan hoping for help from the United Nations. The help arrived in 5 years, when the family could receive refugee status and fly to the United States. Being a single woman, Hassan's mother had to go through nine rigorous interviews until they were granted the right to go to one of the refugee resettlement cities in the United States. During their first month in Buffalo, NY, 8-year-old Hassan and his brother had to move from school to school because they were unable to receive English as a Second Language services. Eventually a public school was found that could offer the best possible accommodations. Hassan was scared of school at first, but he felt safe when he learned that "teachers don't hit children in school." He said, "I was afraid that schools would have weapons and they could kill us." Three years later, however, he is well adjusted and is eager to become a dentist one day.

This story is just one of the many that describe the lives of refugee families and children. Although each story is unique, the stories share some common elements.

Most refugee families flee their homes because of war or political uprising and have to reduce their belongings to what they can carry with them. Typically, most of their previous experiences are nothing more than "hiding and running for their lives," as one of the refugee parents stated. Further, many parents and children have witnessed friends or family being murdered or know someone who left for water and did not return.

According to Church World Service (CWS) statistics, currently the number of refugees and asylum seekers in the world totals 11.9 million. Each year since 2001, the United States has established an "admission ceiling" of 70,000 refugees. During 2004, the number of actual arrivals was 52,826 (CWS). Between 1997 and 2006 a total of 51,257 refugees were resettled in New York State Office of Temporary and Disability Assistance, 2006. Of these, 8,550 were 18 years old or younger. Once admitted to the United States, the nation "upholds the rights of refugees" and provides refugee families with "food stamps, low income housing, and educational services" (Arlington Diocese Office of Resettlement, 2004, p. 3).

According to Anderson, Hamilton, Moore, Loewen, and Frater-Mathieson (2004), there are currently approximately 6 million refugee children in the world. Some of these children are separated from their families, and their number increases each year. After reaching the United States, refugee children face additional challenges. Hamilton (2004) stated, "One of the major tasks facing the refugee child when arriving in a new country is to adapt to a new school environment." (p. 83). For refugee children to adjust successfully, however, educational systems also need to make adequate adjustments. Anderson et al. (2004) stated,

> Although some countries have experience in accommodating the special needs of refugee children, many educational systems currently do not have special support systems in place to assist schools, refugee families and students in the process of adapting refugees to their new schools. (p. 2)

Although by law teachers and school districts are not allowed to ask for immigration status, principals and teachers usually know which children are sponsored by refugee resettlement agencies.

Rutter (1994) further suggested that schools should make a host of provisions to welcome the new students appropriately. These provisions include making sure that (a) an educational policy (or government refugee policy) is in effect for refugee children; (b) teachers have at least basic knowledge of multicultural and English as a Second Language (ESL) education, as well as the characteristics of refugees; and (c) an overall positive educational framework is established in the school that prepares children "for life in a multi-ethnic democracy" (p. 53).

As the statistics indicate, many refugee children find themselves in our schools. Classroom teachers, however, often do not feel sufficiently prepared to meet the unique needs of these children (Minnesota Department of Children, Families and Learning, 2002). As also indicated earlier, schools systems often are not adequately prepared to accommodate refugee students' needs. More studies need to be conducted in various settings to explore the specific accommodations necessary for schools and refugee children.

PURPOSE OF THE STUDY AND STUDY DESIGN

The purpose of this study was to explore the unique needs of refugee children in Buffalo, NY, schools and to identify practices to support the social–emotional and academic development of these children.

The following research questions guided this study: (a) What issues do our schools face in meeting the unique social–emotional and academic challenges of refugee children?, and (b) How can schools help refugee children be successful? To address the research questions, the study presented in this chapter used qualitative research methodology. Focused interviews allowed the participants (teachers, refugee parents, school counselors, a school administrator, and social service providers) to reflect on their experiences and to provide suggestions for present and future teachers of refugee children.

Study Sample

Twenty-six refugee participants from 11 countries were included in the study. In addition, nine professionals who worked with refugee families and children were included. Table 1 summarizes the demographic characteristics of the participants (N = 35).

Selection of Participants

Refugee families in our study were sponsored by Catholic Charities, one of the 10 agencies approved by the U.S. Department of Health and Human Services to aid in the resettlement of refugees. Because this agency has the most refugee resettlement cases, we contacted Catholic Charities, and their social service providers recommended participants for the interviews.

The main requirement for selecting parents was that they had school-age children (5–8 years old) in the Buffalo Public Schools or in schools in the Buffalo suburbs. The teachers, counselors, and principal were selected based on their experiences working with refugee children.

Data Collection

Researchers conducted focused interviews with all the participants. English was used as the main language of the interviews; however, when needed, interpreters were called in. All the interviews were tape-recorded except in one case in which the

TABLE 1

Demographic Characteristics of the Study Sample

	Age	Sex	Countries Represented	Length of Stay in United States	Residence
Refugee Parents (n = 26)	25–50 years	16 male 10 female	Afghanistan, Iran, Kenya, Somalia, Iraq, Ukraine, Sudan, Ethiopia, Liberia, Ivory Coast, Rwanda	6 months-5 years	Buffalo, NY
Teachers of Refugee children (n = 4)	25–40 years	4 female 2 regular education teacher 2 ESL teacher	USA	Resident	Buffalo, NY
School Principal (n = 1)	45 years	1 male	USA	Resident	Buffalo, NY
Social Service provider (n = 2)	35–50 years	2 female	USA	Resident	Buffalo, NY
Counselor (n = 2)	30–35 years	2 female	USA	Resident	Buffalo, NY

participant did not agree to be recorded. The interviews lasted 1½ h on average, and, when needed, follow-up interviews were conducted with some participants. The interviews took place either in homes, schools, workplaces, or at Catholic Charities.

Parents could choose individual, pair, or focus-group interviews. Four chose individual interviews, two chose pair interviews, and the remainder chose focus groups. Social service providers and the principal were interviewed individually, whereas teachers and counselors were interviewed in teams.

Data Analysis

All tapes were transcribed, and emerging themes were identified. Notes from the unrecorded interview also were included in the analysis. Transcripts were analyzed in relation to the research questions. In some cases, contradictory views were clarified in follow-up interviews and informal discussions. Parents and teachers' views were compared and are presented in the following sections. Counselors', administrators', and social service providers' views are included when appropriate.

RESULTS: A REFUGEE IN A CLASSROOM—ISSUES FOR CONSIDERATION

Research Question 1: What Issues Do Our Schools Face in Meeting the Unique Social-Emotional and Academic Challenges of Refugee Children?

Results of the qualitative analysis in relation to the first research question suggested two major themes in participant responses: (a) lack of background information on children, and (b) (in)appropriate academic assessments. In each theme, several subthemes were identified; they are reported here. Each subtheme was supported by claims and evidence from the interviews.

Lack of Background Information on Children

Basic Biographic Information. The principal, teachers, and social service providers all reported that refugee children seldom arrived in the United States with official birth certificates. Thus no one, often not even the parent or guardian, knew the day and year the child was born according to our calendar. To respond to the plethora of documents needing to be completed by refugee families, "Agencies often give the birth date of January 1st or December 31st to refugee children, and the year of birth is often just a guess," a social worker stated. Further, although the gender of the child can often be identified by names, hairstyle, or physical features, in some cases errors do occur. Consider the following example provided by a teacher.

> One day a child showed up at my classroom. From the name, manner of dress, and very short hair, everybody thought that the child was a boy. In addition, the child's biographical sheet indicated gender as "male." After recess the child was sent to the bathroom with the boys. Upon returning to the classroom, the child looked confused. It turned out that the child was female and she figured out that there had been a mistake when she did not see other girls around her in the bathroom. (Team Teacher Interview, February 18, 2005)

Many parents expressed their inability to provide adequate biographical information about their children, because they themselves had not been educated or learned to read. Therefore, they could not even verify the information in their official paperwork. Parents also indicated that in their native countries, official documentation of birth was not common.

Experiences of Trauma or Horror. In many cases, refugee children have witnessed humanity at its worse. Teachers and social service providers felt that they should be provided with as many details as possible about the trauma or horror the child might have experienced. Consider this comment from a teacher.

> In order to respond more appropriately to these [refugee] children, we should be aware of their prior experiences. Such information is essential when we are trying to establish a safe and nurturing relationship with the child within a school setting.... It would definitely help our work if we knew what these children had experienced before joining us here. (Team Teacher Interview, February 18, 2005)

Teachers believe that such information is invaluable to supporting children's adjustment to both the school and the new country. Parents, conversely (regardless of whether the interviews were conducted individually, in pairs, or in focus group), did not wish to share information about their child's previous experiences. A father, for example, commented,

> I don't want to share anything about our experiences with the teacher. I believe that my child should be treated equally to the other, non-refugee children.... The teacher should try to help my children only if the child starts sharing. (Focus Group Interview with Parents, February 18, 2005)

Another parent added, "Teachers don't need to know why my children left their country and what happened to us. But I expect the teacher to educate my children like she does with the other children." Such differences in views make the work of teachers, social service providers, and counselors a little more difficult. Nevertheless, all nonrefugee participants agreed that parents' views should be respected at all times, and the establishment of trust between home and school was viewed as one of the most important steps in the healing and adjustment process.

Teachers also commented that they observed refugee children responding to their life experiences in numerous ways. One teacher, for example, said, "Some refugee children I had were very quiet and reserved and never acted inappropriately in school. Other children, exhibit aggressive behaviors while some appear lethargic and exhibit symptoms of a major depression."

Another teacher added, "I had a child who was very happy to join the class from the first moment. She frequently burst out in songs and loved playing games with the other children even when everyone else was working."

Although teachers reported varied behaviors of children during the adjustment period, they all agreed that the refugee children were generally respectful toward them and exhibited few behavior problems in class.

Prior Educational Experiences. Teachers often expressed feeling overwhelmed by the experience of teaching refugee children, especially if it appeared that a child had had no previous schooling experience. Consider the following example.

> I had a child, and the paperwork indicated that she was 8 years old. Based on her age, she was sent to my classroom mid-year. I had another 25 children, and soon I noticed that this child had difficulty drawing simple lines and circles. I also noticed that she had difficulty holding a crayon, handling a book, and sitting in her seat. There was no additional help available for me. It was very hard to continue with my class while trying to meet this child's unique needs. (Team Teacher Interview, February 18, 2005)

Regarding previous educational experiences of children, the focus group of refugee parents emphasized that teachers should know the following.

> There are two types of refugee children. Regardless of age, one type has never been to school because of war or poverty. The other type has had at least some schooling but the classrooms they are used to are very different from American classrooms where children have so many choices. (Focus Group Interview with Parents, February 18, 2005).

A parent added that the parents trusted the U.S. teachers' expertise and commitment to educate their children in the best possible way. However, as the teachers frequently commented, they were often alone without adequate help from the school or appropriate agencies. Therefore, teachers found it difficult to differentiate their instruction, especially when there were such major gaps between academic skills and school readiness in the classroom.

(In)appropriate Academic Assessments

Teachers expressed major concerns about academic testing requirements, because most refugee children spoke little or no English. Inability to communicate with the child was a major issue among all the participants. A teacher commented,

> Many times children cannot even be appropriately assessed academically before they can come to our school, because the person providing the assessment is not familiar with the child's native language and there is no one who speaks both English and the child's language who could serve as a mediator. In circumstances like this, I believe that the academic assessment is invalid at best. (Team Teacher Interview, February 18, 2005)

This teacher believed that the prior academic assessments gave a false picture of a child's real skills and knowledge. Furthermore, all participants believed that if children were not speaking adequate English and translators were not available, academic testing posed major concerns. In addition, teachers expressed much concern about being required to submit report card grades for refugee children. One teacher commented,

> While grades for nonverbal classes such as PE, art, and music are relatively easy to be determined, grading becomes more difficult when deciding what grade children have earned in [subjects] like math and social studies, which require English skills.... After a very difficult time, our administration came up with the idea to include a special category in their computerized grading form. For areas where the children could not be appropriately assessed like math, spelling, writing, social studies, reading, science, the category "Unable to evaluate at this time. English language learner beginner" was available. (Team Teacher Interview, February 18, 2005)

Perhaps even more troubling than grading is the concern for state-mandated standardized tests. In this regard, a teacher commented,

> State guidelines do permit translators to be used for such testing. However, since children are instructed in English throughout the year, they are unlikely to be familiar with the technical words in their own language when they are taking the tests. In addition, although dictionaries may also be used during testing, it is difficult to find a dictionary for some of the increasingly rare languages spoken by refugee children. (Team Teacher Interview, February 18, 2005)

As these examples indicate, academic testing and grading present a challenge in assessing refugee children's true knowledge without the existence of a common solid language base to use for communication.

Research Question 2: How Can Schools Help Refugee Children to Be Successful?

Data analysis for Research Question 2 resulted in three major themes: (a) providing refugee children with social–emotional support, (b) providing refugee children with academic support, and (c) establishing meaningful family or home partnerships. Several subthemes were identified within each theme, and these are reported in the following sections. Each subtheme is supported by claims and evidence from the interviews.

Providing Refugee Children With Social–Emotional Support

Counseling Services. To help refugee children work through emotional trauma, counselors from the Life Transitions Center, Inc., of Buffalo, NY, offer group counseling sessions after consent forms are obtained from the caseworkers or the refugee families themselves. In most cases, however, therapy is inhibited by children's inability to communicate in English. One of the counselors shared her experience as follows.

> Since they [refugee children] are not able to speak English and we are not able to speak their languages, it is very difficult to design therapeutic activities for the children. You can't ask even basic questions such as: How do you feel? Do you have nightmares? ... Also, many times we know nothing about their background, we do not even have phone numbers for the families. We generally have only the contact information of their caseworkers, who often do not speak the children's native language either. (Team Counselor Interview, February 18, 2005)

In such cases, counselors tend to engage children in activities that use universal languages such as art and music. Through art, play, and music therapy children start working through their experiences nonverbally. Observing the children and their responses enables counselors to understand the children better and plan for further activities. Counselors also indicated that signs of posttraumatic stress disorder were often present in these children, and they welcomed working with teachers and caseworkers to provide additional mental health services to address this disorder.

Social–Emotional Skills-Building Activities. The two ESL teachers reported occasional behavior problems between fellow refugee children in what they believed was "the children's attempt to try to establish their identity and place within the classroom." Teachers believed that such behaviors resulted from children coming from the same country but from different factions or castes. Further, one teacher suspected problems of gender-role differences or expectations when she noticed that sometimes boys did not wish to stand next to girls from the same culture. Similarly, one teacher found that a child whom she later found out was from a higher caste in her native country refused to communicate with a child from a lower caste.

To aid refugee children's social–emotional adjustment, the two regular classroom teachers recommended some programs for the whole classroom: "Through social skills activities such as suggested by the Responsive Classroom model, a feeling of community and belonging can be established within the class even between refugee and non-refugee children." She continued,

> The Second Step: A Violence Prevention Curriculum by the Committee for Children appears to aid all children in building tolerance toward each other while targeting important skills such as empathy, impulse control, and anger management. In addition, character development programs can be utilized to teach children to be respectful toward others and honor each other and our differences. (Team Teacher Interview, February 18, 2005).

Teachers reported that these programs also resulted in nonrefugee children reinforcing the learning of refugee children and suggested that fellow teachers watch for signs of prejudice or racism and try to incorporate proactive strategies as early as possible.

Providing Refugee Children With Academic Support

Translator or Interpreters: ESL Services.   Classroom teachers believed that the first step in providing refugee children with academic support should be to locate translators and interpreters as soon as possible. One of the teachers commented,

> Translators or interpreters should be located for the children and the teachers right away. These can be volunteers or work study interns (perhaps from local universities) who are able to speak the child's language and who do not cost a lot of money for the schools. (Team Teacher Interview, February 18, 2005)

Teachers further believed that online resources were often inadequate for helping teachers learn about a child's background or native language. To aid future teachers of refugee children, one of the teachers suggested the following.

> Presentations or inservice workshops that address the background of refugee students like their culture, language and traditions are invaluable. Simple words in the child's native language such as *hi, come, good,* or *thank you* can make the child feel safer and more comfortable. (Team Teacher Interview, February 18, 2005).

The counselors also recommended using basic sign language symbols. One of the counselors noted, "Children seem to learn basic sign language for friendship, peace, love, caring very quickly. It is believed that such learning will eventually lead to verbal communication." In addition, providing ESL services as soon as possible and developing some type of communication between the teacher and refugee children and their families were strongly emphasized.

Academic Enrichment Opportunities.   After some type of communication is established, teachers need to find ways to help refugee children with academics. One classroom teacher recommended,

> It is best not to assume anything regarding the child's previous experiences. For example, teachers should not assume that the child has had prior experiences with school materials even if the child is older. Neither should they assume that a refugee child knows how to behave or relate to certain situations. And most importantly, teachers should also not assume that refugee children are not capable of learning just because what they have been through and just because they don't speak English. (Team Teacher Interview, February 18, 2005)

As indicated here, teachers often are unaware of children's prior educational experiences, and such information often is not available. Another teacher recommended the following when working with older refugee children who have had no previous school experiences.

> When we notice that the child is lacking important skills, we use toys and materials that are targeted for younger children. For example, when my third graders learn about leaves and trees, I introduce an activity about leaves and trees to the refugee child utilizing materials designed for lower grade level students. This way, all children are learning about the same concepts, however at various levels. (Team Teacher Interview, February 18, 2005)

Teachers also advised caution when using materials for younger children. One suggested, "It is important to use kindergarten materials with an 8- or 9-year-old in a judicious manner. We need to make sure that we do not insult the refugee child." Fortunately, many publishers of ESL materials have responded to the need for content resources with age-appropriate but easy-to-understand subject matter.

Establishing Meaningful Family or Home Partnerships

Classroom teachers commented that it was often challenging for them to establish contact and productive relationships with families in general. In the case of refugee families, teachers said that they generally knew only the resettlement caseworkers and that it sometimes took as long as a year for them finally to meet the parents or guardians of some refugee children. They also commented that refugee families did not attend parent–teacher conferences, probably because they could not understand what the teacher was saying. One teacher shared the following example.

> I had some refugee parents who came to the meeting and said yes to everything I said or asked. I soon realized that it didn't mean that they agreed with me or understood

everything I said. I believe they said yes out of respect for teachers in their culture. (Team Teacher Interview, February 18, 2005)

Another teacher told of a unique case in a parent–teacher conference with a refugee family.

> During one of the conferences, I had a refugee parent come with another refugee parent. I assumed that she was their translator. I found it interesting that she did not translate anything to the family; however, she kept taking notes and looked like she understood what I was saying. After a while I asked her why she was not translating to the family. She told me that she doesn't speak their language, but she is here to take notes, write them down and take it back to the resettlement agency where there is a person who can then read the report and share it with the family. (Team Teacher Interview, February 18, 2005)

The parents also unanimously expressed their concern about language barriers between home and school. At the same time, all the parents wished to voice their concern and commitment to the education of their children. One parent, for example, stated,

> Even though I can't attend the parent–teacher conferences or go to school because I have to work and attend language classes, I want to give every possible opportunity for my child to be successful, something I never had in my life. (Focus Group Interview with Parents, February 18, 2005)

Another parent added,

> Many times we are not able to understand what is said during the parent–teacher conferences because we don't speak good English.... I think teachers should write down all the communication, even the conference notes, so we could take it home and read it and really understand it. If needed, we can also use some help to interpret the reports. Or if we don't attend the meetings, we would still like to have the reports so we can read how our children are doing at school. (Focus Group Interview with Parents, February 18, 2005).

Parents also viewed home visits as beneficial. One parent told this story.

> My children had to move from school to school until they had ESL services for them. My younger son became very emotional after we had to switch schools the third time, and he cried a lot both at home and at school. His teacher came to visit us one day, and she brought some clothes and toys with her. My son really liked that, and he stopped crying. I really liked it also that the teacher came to visit us. (Pair Parent Interview, January 28, 2005).

As the examples indicate, although refugee parents may not be active in school, they are concerned about the education of their children.

SUMMARY AND DISCUSSION

This study explored the views of 26 refugee parents and 9 nonrefugee educators about the unique needs of refugee children in our schools. Two research questions guided the investigation. The first explored the unique issues faced by the schools in meeting refugee children's needs, and the analysis resulted in two major themes: (a) lack of background information on children, and (b) (in)appropriate academic assessments

The second research question explored how schools could help refugee children be successful. Results indicated three majors themes among the responses of the participants: (a) providing refugee children with social–emotional support, (b) providing refugee children with academic support, and (c) establishing meaningful family or home partnerships.

Lack of Background Information on Children

Rutter (1994) described how most refugee children's schooling experience has been interrupted and indicated that they mostly arrive at the U.S. school after the start of the school year. Our study supports Rutter's work. Therefore, considering lack of previous U.S.-type schooling experience, it would appear productive to develop a "good induction policy." Such a formal policy would include inviting parents to interviews with interpreters who are sensitive to refugee families' prior experiences, which could provide valuable information on their background.

(In)appropriate Academic Assessments

Teachers in our study unanimously expressed major concerns about the validity of assessments when refugee children do not speak adequate English. McBrien (2003) cautioned teachers not to "assume that the students are slow or need special education services because they do not speak fluent English" (p. 78). Leung and Franson (2001), as referenced in Loewen (2004), cautioned that "often second language students are assessed not in relation to their own development and achievements but rather in relation to a monolingual English-speaking norm" (p. 51). These are major issues to consider for all kinds of testing of refugee children. Because each child is unique, the length of time necessary to become proficient in the English language varies. McBrien (2003) suggested that it sometimes takes up to 5 years for a child to become proficient in a second language, so appropriate adjustments in testing appear to be necessary for up to 5 years.

Providing Refugee Children With Social and Emotional Support

As participants in our study said, children show signs of stress in various ways. Some may lose interest or become withdrawn; others may become aggressive or angry. Some may become restless and find it difficult to concentrate on tasks. Some may eat more than usual; some may lose their appetite. Crying spells and nightmares also may be common. However, not all children develop symptoms of trauma (Rutter, 1994). Frater-Mathieson (2004) identified four major symptoms of posttraumatic stress disorder in children based on the work of Cole (1996) and Creamer (2000): *affective indicators* such as pessimism or depression, *physical indicators* such as nightmares and headaches, *cognitive distortions* such as self-blame or suicidal thoughts, and *behavioral indicators* such as withdrawal and repetitive play. Being aware of such symptoms and characteristics is beneficial for classroom teachers and parents as they try to ease children's adjustment into the new country.

Counseling services are frequently used for refugee children. Play or art therapy are considered to be the most appropriate forms of counseling in view of these children's inability to communicate in English. Rutter (1994) suggested including activities such as free play, drama, or music when teachers and parents view these as appropriate. Frater-Mathieson (2004) also suggested "poetry or storytelling in the framework of the child's cultural heritage ... to integrate the past, present and future in a way that restores a sense of identity, meaning continuity and belonging" (p. 33). In addition, Dunn and Adkins (2003) recommended giving the students journals in which they can draw and write whenever they wish. Such activities also are viewed as good means of communication between the teacher and student.

Providing Refugee Children With Academic Support

Establishing productive communication is considered the first major step before beginning academic instruction with refugee students. Teachers in our study used many of Rutter's (1994) strategies with their refugee students such as promoting basic ESL strategies; making sure to pronounce the students names correctly; allowing plenty of listening time during the silent period; introducing simple phrases such as *yes*, *no*, and *thank you*; and designing collaborative activities in which refugee children can work in groups with other students. Rutter (1994) also recommended including visual cues and clues with refugee children such as videos, pictures, and flash cards.

Loewen (2004) cautioned about the need to differentiate between the second-language learning of a typical immigrant and a refugee child. She stated that prior education and traumatic experiences may influence children's learning. In addition, Loewen (2004) stated, "refugees with lower levels of education in general and of second language proficiency in particular are at greater risk for inadequate second language development after resettlement" (p. 36). She recommended peer tutoring and peer learning to help refugee children become familiar with the school.

Establishing Meaningful Family or Home Partnerships

McBrien (2003) states that just because refugee parents are not involved at school does not mean that they are not interested in their children's education. Hamilton (2004) further recommends that schools should develop special programs for refugee parents where they can develop their skills in second-language learning and also familiarize themselves with the new cultural and educational expectations. Hamilton also cautions that in some cultures parents and children are not given such opportunities, so parents may need more time to become comfortable with such activities. Communication channels must be kept open between home and school, even when refugee parents do not seem to be involved in their children's education. Building on these ideas, the ECRE Task Force on Integration (2005) concludes that "Education should be a process during which teacher, student, host society and refugee community can learn from each other. The Knowledge brought by refugees should be used to enhance the diversity of the host society" (p. 5).

CONCLUSIONS AND IMPLICATIONS FOR PRACTICE

Over the course of this study, we had the opportunity to work with outstanding teachers, administrators, and social service providers, who with little or no professional preparation took on the challenge of educating refugee children. These people developed numerous strategies to assist in their efforts to make refugee children successful both socially–emotionally and academically. Based on the results of the study, we provide the following suggestions for professionals working with refugee children in our schools.

Lack of Background Information on Children

Teachers and administrators should advocate for finding ways of obtaining more information about a child's background including gender, age, and prior education; they should not make assumptions about children's backgrounds. Translators who are able to verify biographical information of families (including gender and age if possible) should be used to establish communication between home and school.

(In)appropriate Academic Assessments

It is important that educational policies be in place for refugee children before they arrive in our schools. Teachers should be provided with professional development opportunities to ensure that they are prepared to work successfully with refugee children. Close collaboration with administration and policymakers are essential regarding the reliability and validity of testing and grading.

Providing Refugee Children With Social and Emotional Support

Although counselors and social workers can encourage the use of counseling services, parents should always have the right to refuse such services. The reason for and purpose of the counseling services should be communicated to the parents so that they understand fully why children might be provided with such sessions. If counseling services appear appropriate, children should be provided with experiences through which they can express their feelings and tell their experiences and establish a trusting relationship between home and school. Nonverbal clues using pictures and role-playing appear to be productive with children. In addition, Responsive Classroom or Second Step programs appear to be effective in developing empathy and positive relationships in the classroom.

Providing Refugee Children With Academic Support

Teachers and administrators should reexamine educational materials and ensure that appropriate materials are available for refugee children with various levels of skill and knowledge. Appropriate academic interventions should be in place before the child joins the classroom. Volunteers are essential for both assessment and tutoring purposes, especially if they speak the children's native language. In addition, teachers can familiarize themselves with sign language and basic ESL strategies and provide opportunities for peer tutoring and after-school programs.

Establishing Meaningful Family or Home Partnerships

When a refugee child joins a school, information on school policies, expectations, and parents' rights should be translated into the parents' native language. In addition, parent–teacher relationships can be more effective if teachers tape-record or write reports of students' achievement to be sent home. It should not be assumed that parents are not interested in their children's education if they do not attend school functions. Teachers should be aware of the responsibilities that refugee families have (work and language classes) to maintain their status in the United States. Teachers should offer flexible scheduling to the families when planning functions (including home visits).

REFERENCES

Anderson, A., Hamilton, R., Moore, D., Loewen, S., & Frater-Mathieson, K. (2004). Education of refugee children: Theoretical perspectives and best practice. In R. Hamilton & D. Moore (Eds.), *Educational Interventions for Refugee Children: Theoretical Perspectives and Implementing Best Practice* (pp. 1–11). New York: RoutledgeFalmer.

Arlington Diocese Office of Resettlement. (2004). *Refugee Facts.* Retrieved November 13, 2004, from http://www.arlingtonrefugeeservices.com/new_page_3.htm

Church World Service (CWS). (2006). Statistics on-line. Retrieved May 16, 2005, from http://www.churchworldservice.org/Immigration/stats.html

Cole, E. (1996). Immigrant and refugee children and families: Supporting a new road travelled. In M. G. Luther, E. Cole, & P. Gamlin (Eds.), *Dynamic Assessment for Instruction: From Theory to Application* (pp. 35–42). North York, ON: Captus Press.

Creamer, M. (2000). Post-traumatic stress disorder following violence and aggression. *Aggression and Violent Behaviour, 5,* 431–449.

Dunn, B., & Adkins, M. A. (2003). *The Multicultural Classroom: Teaching Refugee and Immigrant Children.* Retrieved November 27, 2004, from http://www.newhorizons.org/strategies/multicultural/adkins_dunn.htm

ECRE Task Force on Integration. (2005). *Good Practice Guide on the Integration of Refugees in the European Union.* Retrieved December 2, 2005, from http://www.refugeenet.org/pdf/education_guide/pdf

Frater-Mathieson, K. (2004). Refugee trauma, loss and grief: Implications for interventions. In R. Hamilton & D. Moore (Eds.), *Educational Interventions for Refugee Children: Theoretical Perspectives and Implementing Best Practice* (pp. 12–34). New York: RoutledgeFalmer.

Hamilton, R. (2004). Schools, teachers and education of refugee children. In R. Hamilton & D. Moore (Eds.), *Educational Interventions for Refugee Children: Theoretical Perspectives and Implementing Best Practice* (pp. 83–96). New York: RoutledgeFalmer.

Leung, C., & Franson, C. (2001). Mainstreaming: ESL as a diffused curriculum concern. In B. Mohan, C. Leung, & C. Davison (Eds.), *English as a Second Language in the Mainstream: Teaching, Learning and Identity* (pp. 177–198). Harlow, UK: Longman.

Loewen, S. (2004). Second language concerns for refugee children. In R. Hamilton & D. Moore (Eds.), *Educational Interventions for Refugee Children: Theoretical Perspectives and Implementing Best Practice* (pp. 35–52). New York: RoutledgeFalmer.

McBrien, J. L. (2003). A second chance for refugee students. *Educational Leadership, 61*(2), 76–79.

Minnesota Department of Children, Families and Learning. (2002). *Serving Refugee Students: Case Studies of Somali, Bosnian and Liberian Students in Minnesota Schools.* Roseville, MN: Author.

Office of Temporary and Disability Assistance. (2006). *Refugees resettled in New York State by provider area.* Retrieved on May 14, 2006, from: http://www.otda.state.nv.us/otda/bria/radata/Resettlement by Region 97-06.pdf

Rutter, J. (1994). *Refugee Children in the Classroom.* London: Trentham Books.

Chapter 15

Crossing Cultural Borders in the United States: A Case Study of a Sudanese Refugee Family's Experiences With Urban Schooling

Guofang Li
Michigan State University, USA

> Everything you have to struggle for it, and then after that at the end you can succeed. (Anne, mother, May 2004)

Since the early 1990s, the United States has received a wave of African refugees. The most recent estimate suggests that the number of African foreign-born immigrants exceeded 1 million in 2004, and the number continues to grow (Grieco, 2004). Most of these refugees came from Sudan after the 1983 outbreak of civil war between the northern Sunni Muslims and the southern animists and Christians and are the largest of these immigrant groups. Most are from southern Sudan and are Christians. Approximately 20,000 Sudanese refugees have resettled across the country, and the number continues to rise (Migration News, 2005).

Because they come from a war-torn country, it is believed that most Sudanese refugees have experienced many difficulties and challenges with regard to language, culture, employment, and education when they resettle in the United

States (Hayward, 1994). Because they are relative newcomers, little research has examined their resettlement experiences. The few studies concerning Sudanese refugees have focused mostly on trauma to the children (Bolea, Grant, Burgess, & Plasa, 2003), their transnational linkages and ties (Shandy, 2003), and their survival stories (Educational Study Guide, 2005). Few studies have examined Sudanese refugees' adjustment experiences in the United States, especially how they adjust to the educational system.

The purpose of this case study was to examine Sudanese refugee families' values and beliefs about education and their perceptions of and adjustment to urban schooling. Using observations and in-depth interviews, this study reports the findings from one low-income, Sudanese immigrant family, the Torkeri family. The Torkeri family has six children, four of whom are school-aged and attend various schools in an urban community. The guiding questions for this research include the following:

1. What are the Sudanese parents' beliefs and values about their children's education?
2. What are their perceptions of the U.S. urban schools, and what are their children's adjustment experiences with these schools?
3. What are the implications of their perceptions and experiences for advancing urban immigrant children's education?

RESEARCHING THE TORKERI FAMILY

The Torkeri family came originally from a southern city in Sudan called Juba. Before coming to the United States in 1999, they spent 3 years in Egypt. At the time of the study, they had been in Buffalo, NY, for 3 years. The mother, 41-year-old Anne, is multilingual and speaks Bari (her tribal language in Sudan), Arabic (Sudan's national language), and English she learned in school. She was raised in a well-off Christian family in Sudan that valued education highly. She attended a private missionary high school called a Comboni school. As an adult, she studied in Sudan for a bachelor's of arts for which she took courses in education, clinical psychology, and women's studies, but she was not able to finish her internship training. After she immigrated to the United States, she worked on an hourly basis as a family educator in "Even Star" programs organized by the Erie regional education authority. She visited other refugee or immigrant families and taught them English and communication skills. After working for a few months, she was laid off. Since then, she has stayed at home to raise her children.

Anne's husband Tifa is 43 years old. He speaks a regional language, Natuka, and Arabic. He studied law in Egypt in obedience to his father, although he wished to become a physician. He left Egypt to immigrate to the United States before completing his studies. He is currently a welder and often works long hours. He wishes to become an auto-body mechanic in the future if he can. Table 1 shows the family profile.

The six children in the family are Owen (15), Nina (13), Fred (11), Irene (6), Jude (3), and Igma (8 months). Owen attends an inner-city high school; Nina and Fred attend an international school designated for refugee children, School X. Owen and Nina also attended school in Egypt for 2 years before they immigrated to the United States. Both they and Fred attend English as a second Language (ESL) programs in school. Fred has special needs because he has a physical problem with his left arm, which requires him to attend three programs—ESL, physical therapy, and occupational therapy—during school hours. He also must attend summer school because of time missed in these therapy sessions. Irene (6) is enrolled in a Head Start preschool program in a charter school where the students wear uniforms. All the children understand and speak Arabic, but cannot read or write it.

The family of eight (see Table 1) live in an upper-level two-bedroom apartment in a two-storey house in an inner-city neighborhood known for its high crime rate and drug and alcohol problems. Anne, who is almost always home, became our main informant. My assistant and I conducted two in-depth, semi-structured interviews with her in her home in May and October 2004. I also talked informally with her by telephone once I got to know the family. The first interview, conducted in May 2004, was to find out about the family and their beliefs and values about their children's education, as well as their adjustment experiences in U.S. schools. During the second interview, we asked more follow-up questions about the children's school experiences, as well as more specific information about the family's specific literacy practices at home (e.g., their access to printed materials and how they used them). Each interview was approximately 2 hours long and was audiotaped and subsequently transcribed. During the interviews, we observed the children's interactions and recorded descriptions of them in field notes. Casual conversations with the participants outside the interviews also were recorded in field notes.

Data analysis in this study was continual throughout the data-collection period. Content and thematic analyses were used to examine field notes and transcripts whereby themes relating to the research questions were identified and illustrated using verbatim comments from formal and informal interviews (Creswell, 2005). To demonstrate better the "true value of the original multiple realities" (Lincoln & Guba, 1985, p. 296), I use direct quotes from Anne to give voice to the participants. In what follows, the Torkeri family's experiences adjusting to the urban schooling experiences in the United States are presented in detail.

TABLE 1
The Torkeri Family Profile

Name	Age	Occupation	Education	Languages	Others
Anne	41	Housewife, previously family educator	Private high school, undergraduate courses in education (Sudan)	Bari, Arabic, English	Left Juba in 1996 for Egypt; Immigrated to the US in 1999
Tifa	43	Welder	University studies in law in Egypt (not completed)	Natuka, Arabic, English	Wants to become an Auto-body mechanic
Owen	15	Grade 11	Brown High School 12 years' schooling in Egypt (1996–1999)	Arabic, English	Born in Sudan ESL program Interested in computer technology
Nina	13	Grade 9	School X (a multicultural school) 2 years' schooling in Egypt	Arabic, English	Born in Sudan ESL program Interested in arts
Fred	11	Grade 5	School X (a multicultural school)	Arabic, English	Born in Sudan Special education (3 therapy sessions including ESL)
Irene	6	Kindergarten	A charter school	Arabic, English	Born in the US Likes to read and write
Jude	3	NA	NA	Arabic, English	Born in the US
Igma	8 mos.	NA	NA		Born in the US

Note. ESL = English as a Second Language.

ADJUSTMENT TO U.S. SCHOOLING

Like many other immigrant families, the Torkeri family experienced many-layered difficulties in adjusting to life in the United States, including language differences, changes in gender roles and cultural identity, employment, and community socialization patterns (Hayward, 1994). In terms of cultural and linguistic differences in their initial experiences in the United States, for example, the family had to learn English, and the children, especially Owen and Nina who were schooled in Arabic in Egypt for 3 years, had to adjust to English instruction. These linguistic and cultural differences profoundly influenced their schooling experiences in the United States. In the following sections, I describe the family's experiences and interactions with urban schools that the children attend. I first describe the family's expectations of their children and their perceptions of U.S. schools. Then I present the family's experiences of learning about the school system and their interactions with schools in relation to the ESL programs their children attend. Finally, I discuss the implications of their adjustment experiences for the education of minority students in urban settings.

Parental Expectations and Hopes for Their Children

Having traveled a long way from Sudan to Egypt and then to the United States, Anne and Tifa were excited about the new opportunities they had in the United States. Like many other immigrant parents who come to the United States to seek better opportunities for their children, Anne stressed the importance of the chances that her children could have here. She compared what they had in Sudan with what was available for their children in the United States and believed that their children should make good use of the opportunities. She expected them to become responsible and successful citizens in the future. She expressed her hopes for them thus:

> I want them, you know, to finish, they go to college, go to university. If they want to do further study, that's good, because there are chances here. Don't miss the chances since you are here. In my country, there is not a lot of chance[s] like that. For me, when I came here, I was thinking, I said, "Oh, my god. If I came when I was young, I will do so many things." But for me, I consider myself now like a late comer … The most important, I want [for] my kids. Then, after that, I can look for myself.

However, as African refugees she also realized that there was discrimination against Blacks in this society and that her children would have to work even harder to succeed. This realization encouraged the parents to put even more emphasis on the importance of education.

You know, education plays a big role. Although I know that sometimes there is discrimination like here, because there are some places that Black people leave their work and you find just White people, and some places you can find out they are mixed up, multicultural group working at the same place … But still there is a chance. Why do you give up for education? … Like us, we came, we try our best … There are chances that you can do.

Anne and Tifa tried to provide their children with a better learning environment at home. Anne did not ask her children to help with household chores during the academic year, because she wanted them to focus on studying. She asked them to help with the housework only during summer vacations. In Sudanese culture, men do not help with housework. However, she asked her sons to help during the vacation so that they could learn to take responsibilities in this Western country that focuses on equal opportunities for men and women. She believed that it was important for them to adjust to the culture of their new home country.

Anne and Tifa also made many personal sacrifices for their children. Anne wanted to take the many opportunities available for her in the United States and update her own knowledge and skills, but she chose to make her children her priority. For example, she wished to take a 1-h computer class that was offered once a week by the government, but she decided not to because it would affect the study time of her eldest daughter Nina. Her family's financial situation did not allow Anne to send her children to a day care center. If Anne attended a computer class, she would have to ask Nina to take care of her young brother and sisters during her absence. Moreover, all the children returned home at different times, and she wished to be there so that they could talk to her about school or other matters and ask her for help when needed. She believed that being always available to her children would create a better home environment and establish a more trusting relationship between her and her children. She hoped that her personal sacrifice would instill strong motivation in her children to achieve.

It's [taking care of her six children] a full job although without pay. I was telling them, I said you know, although now I feel too exhausted … I said only thing I'll be happy if one day I could see you graduate, you are in good process, you are capable for yourself, you are responsible for yourself. That will be the time that I get my pay.

Perceptions of Differences in School

Because Anne and Tifa valued education highly, they paid close attention to the differences between schools in the United States and Sudan. In their opinion, although U.S. schools had more material resources, they were less rigorous than schools in their native country. Comparing them with her own schooling experiences, Anne believed that the schools her children attended in the United States were "too loose" because there were not enough tests and not much homework, especially on weekends. "Today is Friday and they came [home] without any homework—that means [they] have Friday, Saturday, and Sunday [off]. Sometimes, they don't want to do anything."

Anne and Tifa also found that the subjects taught in U.S. schools were different and believed that U.S. schools lacked adequate instruction in what they called general knowledge, which included mathematics, geography, and history. Anne explained,

> Like when before I came here, I know all about, about like geographical, I know all about like the Great Lakes and … all this stuff. I get it in school. So it's not new [to me] like, River Niagara is the longest and the big river in this country, but others [here] they don't know, even if you ask the American family … I think they don't teach. We call this is like … general knowledge. They don't have general knowledge, you know. And it is very important … I am new in this country and I, and their system is different from ours, and their other subjects that they don't even teach, because like [we] taught history, and geography, and it's not like that [here]. Even sometimes I ask them, and even sometimes I watch the TV like Sesame Street. I wonder sometimes, they ask simple [math] question and [students] couldn't answer, I said, "Oh, my goodness." That means you have a limit [in the content of teaching].

In addition to the curriculum differences, Anne also noticed differences in teaching styles. In language teaching, for example, Anne found that there was not enough reading aloud in class.

> Like if they could allow the kids, I mean with the [reading aloud] styles.… When I was in school, they encourage me like we have a reading at class, turn by turn, everybody must stand up and read loudly with colleagues. But I don't think they do that here.

However, the biggest difference the family experienced was in the ESL program in the schools, which was a totally new concept to them. In the following section, I discuss the family's struggle with the ESL programs.

The Struggle With the ESL Programs

Although Anne and Tifa worried about their children's language adjustment from Arabic to English when they first came to the United States, they found that the ESL programs in the schools designed to help immigrant and refugee children became an obstacle to their children's academic progress. Their two sons Owen and Fred were the most affected by the ESL programs. According to New York State regulations, ESL students are assessed and then pulled out of regular classes for small-group English-language instruction. Anne believed that such programs were detrimental to ESL students like her children. She reasoned,

Most of the time, they got pulled out from the classroom, like if they have history in class, and then they come and pull my kid out and while the others are getting the subjects. So he is going to miss the subject. They pull him out and he will go and get that ESL and when he came back, he will find his colleagues, they got their homework, their lecture was over. And they will not lecture for him anymore, so this is really a big problem.

Anne was particularly worried about Owen, who was in the 11th grade and who needed good grades if he was to go to college. She observed that pulling Owen out of his mainstream classes caused problems in his performance in the content areas of his mainstream classes. His teacher did not help him make up what he missed while attending the ESL classes; however, he was graded in the same way as the regular class students. Sometimes he missed hearing about assignments while he was in the ESL classes, failed to submit them, and, as a result, received lower grades. Anne believed that such a situation was unfair to Owen. She said,

And now he is not taking Spanish, and he is losing the marks for that. That's why sometimes his average is not very high. That's what he is complaining. And he said he wants to attend the Spanish class so that he may get the mark for that. But he don't attend that. He get zero for that, which I think is there is no logic here.

That year she noticed that Owen was not allowed to take geometry, a subject she regarded as a core course.

Even now, now I have a problem with my son. I have to go to school and talk to the teacher about it…. They say that he is not going to take geometry because of ESL. So I worry much. I think, why? Geometry is most important even. He need it. Yeah. He is going to miss that because of ESL. He just miss it…. How comes like that? I'm really mad about that, you know. I talk to him before two days because I got a letter at the mail. And it's saying that he should take at least 39 hours for ESL.

Fred, who was in an international elementary school, also was pulled out of mainstream classes during school hours for ESL, as well as physical therapy and occupational therapy for the physical problem he had with his left arm. Despite missing many mainstream classes, however, he finished in the top three in his class. Anne thought that if he could attend the mainstream classes rather than being pulled out for the ESL class, he would do even better. However, regardless of how well he performed in the content areas, he was still not allowed to drop the ESL class, and he had to attend summer school for his therapy sessions. According to Anne, because a common perception among students is that those who do not do well in their studies must attend the summer program, this might affect how Fred felt about himself and how others saw him. He worried that other students might think he was not doing well in school and would distance themselves from him.

Anne said that hers was not the only family experiencing problems with the ESL programs. Many other refugee and immigrant families voiced similar concerns. Anne and other parents went to the schools to express their concerns, but their voices were not heard, and they were told that this was how the ESL program worked. Anne expressed her frustration:

> We discussed it before at school like at the PTO meeting and all this stuff. But they said it's according to the system, they can't change anything. It depend on the government, because this is not the first time that they are doing this, and this is not their fault. If the government could pay for that because we say, "Why don't they teach the ESL like, they select some days, at the evening instead of pulling the kids out from the class, and then leaving the others going on with the lecture?" But they said, "No," they can't do that. They said, it needs like a special budget for that and all this … They said, "What should we do? It is the system."

Realizing that they had to fight the "system," Anne actively sought ways to work the system. In the following section, I describe Anne's efforts to work the system through her choice of schools for her children.

Working the System Through the Choice of Schools

Anne learned from another Sudanese family that if an ESL teacher writes a letter of recommendation, the student can submit a request to City Hall to be taken off the ESL list. So she asked the ESL teacher in Owen's school for such a letter of recommendation so that she could ask that his ESL classes be waived. However, shortly after she spoke to the teacher, she received Owen's report card, which indicated that he was not doing well in English. This meant that she probably would not receive a strong recommendation letter from the teacher. Anne was not convinced and said that she would petition City Hall without the letter.

Anne's frustration with the ESL programs in the two schools made her realize the importance of the choice of schools for her children. However, she did not know what the differences were between the various kinds of public schools such as *government school* (for refugees), *magnet school,* and *charter school.* To learn more, she attended various workshops provided by the schools and communities. As she describes,

> One day I ask about, I ask one of my friends, and she told me there is a difference between magnet schools [and government schools]. The magnet school, usually you go to the City Hall, and then they do it through lottery. If you fill the paper and then after that, if they pick one of your kids, then if they are siblings, they can go through.

Realizing that she could change her children's schools, Anne applied for Owen to attend a magnet school, but the application was rejected. After two attempts to change her children's schools, Anne learned that Owen, Nina, and Fred, who were not born in the United States, had no choice but to attend schools designated for refugee children. She decided that her younger children, who either grew up or were born in the United States, would not attend those schools although they did have advantages (e.g., she liked the administration style in Owen's high school and the multicultural aspects in Nina and Fred's school). Because Irene had no prior schooling experiences in Sudan or Egypt, Anne was determined to send her to another school.

> I would like to apply for my daughter, but I don't want her to go to School X … because she starts here. That means, she don't have any problem with the language … My idea is I want her either go to the charter school, or either to go to the magnet schools. And they said, magnet school, they will not allow her to go there unless you have to apply at the City Hall also. That's the same obstacles. So, but the charter school, if they got the application, they will send me … so they sent me a letter and I took all the paper they needed, documents that they needed, and now she got the acceptance.

Anne was satisfied with the Head Start program in the charter school that Irene attended. This school gave Irene different reading activities from the rest of the class and a great deal of homework every day. Anne described the differences she saw.

> Today they [Owen, Fred, and Nina] don't have homework. But, although today is Friday, Irene will have homework. Usually there is one that she gets it on Monday or Tuesday. And then, she has to submit it today. And then she will get another homework for next Friday. Like a week she has to do it either with me, or sometimes her sister. And she has to read books in the library and she has to write the names of the books and their writers and all. And she has to turn in. And then they have something called "Open Circle." They always discuss.

Anne was happy with the homework assignments and believed that Irene appeared to be more aware of the importance of reading stories because she read a new book every day and discussed the books in school. Anne sometimes asked Nina to take Irene to the public library to borrow more books. She also was happy that the school taught children "applied technology," which showed a difference between Irene and the other children. For example, often when Irene returned home she would go to the computer to play a math-related game, whereas the other children watched television. Anne attributed the difference in Irene's behavior to the different school program she attended.

> She can write the alphabets very beautiful. That's why I'm very happy about her. Maybe because of the system that they insist the homework every day, every night,

she has to do. And reading too. She has books, she has to read when she came from there from school, because every day she has a new book.

Anne was also happy that she could be in frequent contact with Irene's teachers through writing notes and participating in school field trips, which was an improvement over the difficulty she experienced in communicating with the school personnel in schools attended by Owen, Nina, and Fred. Knowing that there were differences in schools and programs, Anne said that she would continue to struggle for her children, "But you have to struggle for yourself. If you didn't struggle, you are not able to [get ahead] from where you start."

CONCLUSIONS AND IMPLICATIONS

The Torkeri family's experiences with urban schooling suggest that they encountered multiple layers of cultural differences and challenges in their adjustment to urban schools in the United States that went beyond the social and linguistic and included the educational and institutional. Contrary to popular deficit views of refugee families, the Torkeri parents valued education highly and tried as hard as they could by making personal sacrifices to provide their children with a better learning environment. They expected their children to earn a college degree, become successful, and have a better quality of life in the future. They wanted them to take advantage of the opportunities available in the United States to make their dreams come true. However, the family had to overcome multilayered barriers along the way. They encountered a range of cultural differences with the U.S. schools, not only in content but also in the style of instruction. Most significantly, they had to learn how the school system worked and how to work the system.

The parents, being actively involved and gravely concerned, tried their best to learn about the system and work it through their own struggles. They understood that the goal of the ESL programs in public schools was to improve non-English speaking children's English proficiency so that they could attend the English-dominant mainstream classes and do well in academic content areas. However, in the parents' opinion, the structure of the existing ESL programs had the opposite result in that they took the students away from content-area instruction. In Anne's words, "If they miss like this, they will have nothing—[not] even the foundation!" Thus she tried to oppose the ESL programs in the schools by petitioning to have her children's names removed from the ESL list. In addition, she (along with some other parents) repeatedly raised these concerns with the schools. Unfortunately, their concerns were not addressed, and the children's programs of study remained unchanged. This story of one family's fight against the ESL programs in two urban schools demonstrates the unequal power relations between the school authorities and minority parents whose first language is not English.

Minority parents like the Torkeri parents, who are marginalized in society, are often powerless to change the school programs their children attend and are excluded from decision making about their children's education (Fine, 1993; Li, 2006). The barriers to the children's adjustment to school and the failure of the school personnel to listen to their voice suggest that some refugee and immigrant children are "overlooked and underserved" in our school system (Ruiz-de-Velasco & Fix, 2001).

This family's struggle with the school system demonstrates a need to consider the students' and parents' opinions about the structure of ESL programs and their cultural and linguistic backgrounds. The Torkeri family's story shows that a rigidly structured ESL program does not always help nonnative–English-speaking children develop their dominant-language literacy skills; on the contrary, it may negatively affect their performance in the content areas of their mainstream classes, as noted by the parents. Moreover, the segregation occasioned by being pulled out of classes for ESL lessons may affect minority students' construction of social identity. This is shown in Fred's experience that being in an ESL program did not foster his sense of pride, but rather that the separate ESL programs often promoted a sense of distance and separation from the other students (Valdés, 2001). Therefore, it is time for critical reflection on the effectiveness of existing ESL programs and how these can best serve the needs of immigrant minority students. Schools may need to consider parents' suggestions about changing the scheduling of the pull-out classes so that ESL students are not doubly disadvantaged by missing regular content-area instruction.

The parents' active involvement and their strenuous efforts to learn about how the school system works in the United States and to work the system on their own suggest a need for educators to help incoming immigrant parents become better advocates for their children's education (Li, 2003). First, as Li (2006) recommends, it is necessary to help immigrant parents gain critical awareness of how the school system works and to learn to negotiate for their children more access in the system. For example, schools and the community, such as immigration agencies, could offer parents workshops on the differences between the various kinds of schools available and how to choose among the various schools. Second, schools need to establish specific communication channels to address the major concerns and questions of parents, families, and teachers about ESL programs and students' academic progress. In terms of the ESL programs, for example, schools might collaborate with parents to find solutions that best facilitate learners' educational needs. In sum, educators must hear the minority parents' voices and mediate for the students between school and home.

REFERENCES

Bolea, P. T., Grant, G., Jr., Burgess, M., & Plasa, O. (2003). Trauma of children of Sudan: A constructivist exploration. *Child Welfare, 82,* 219–232.

Creswell, J. W. (2005). *Educational Research: Planning, Conducting, and Evaluating Quantitative and Qualitative Research* (2nd ed.). Columbus, OH: Pearson.

Educational Study Guide. (2005). *Lost Boys of Sudan.* Retrieved March 1, 2005, from www.LostBoysFilm.com

Fine, M. (1993). [Ap]parent involvement: Reflections on parents, power, and urban public schools. *Teachers College Record, 94*(4), 682–710.

Greico, E. (2004). *The African Foreign Born in the United States.* Migration Policy Institute. Retrieved March 22, 2005, from www.migrationinformation.org/Usfocus/display.cmf?id=250

Hayward, P. W. (1994). Pre-resettlement preparation: Needs and issues of refugees. *Proceedings of the conference of East African refugee service providers.* Arlington, VA: Ethiopian Community Development Council and Center for Applied Linguistics. (ERIC Document Retrieval No. ED 407480)

Li, G. (2003). Literacy, culture, and politics of schooling: Counter narratives of a Chinese Canadian family. *Anthropology and Education Quarterly, 34,* 184–206.

Li, G. (2005). *Culturally Contested Pedagogy: Battles of Literacy and Schooling Between Mainstream Teachers and Asian Immigrant Parents.* Albany, NY: SUNY Press.

Lincoln, Y. S., & Guba, G. E. (1985). *Naturalist Inquiry.* Beverly Hills, CA: Sage.

Migration News. (2005). *Welfare, Licenses, Sudanese.* Retrieved March 1, 2005, from http://migration.ucdavis.edu/mn

Ruiz-de-Velasco, J., & Fix, M. (2001). *Overlooked and Underserved: Immigrant Children in U.S. Secondary Schools.* Washington, DC: Urban Institute.

Shandy, D. J. (2003). Transnational linkages between refugees in africa and in the diaspora. *Forced Migration Review, 16,* 7–8.

Valdés, G. (2001). *Learning and Not Learning English: Latino Students in American Schools.* New York: Teachers College Press.

Chapter 16

Refugee Families With Preschool Children: Adjustment to Life in Canada

Darcey M. Dachyshyn
University of Alberta, Canada

As a humanitarian gesture, Canada accepts approximately 30,000 refugees each year (Citizenship and Immigration Canada, 2005). The provinces of Ontario, Quebec, British Columbia, and Alberta, in that order, receive the largest numbers of refugees to the country. Alberta, the province under consideration here, has approximately 2,000 refugees settle within its borders annually. Edmonton, the capital city of Alberta, receives approximately 30% of the refugees destined for Alberta. More than 25% of newcomers to Alberta are younger than 20, and most significantly, two thirds of this group arrive with little or no English language skills.

One of the defining characteristic of refugees is their need for protection because of a well-founded fear of persecution for reasons of "race, religion, nationality, membership of a particular social group, or political opinion" (Office of the United Nations High Commissioner for Refugees, 1996, p. 16). As such, refugees are people who had not intended to leave their country of origin. Given the forced and unsettled nature of their departure, many adult refugees struggle to parent their children as they find themselves displaced from home, climate, surroundings, and family members.

The research described in this chapter begins to map the complexities faced by refugee families with preschool children as they adapt to life in a new country.

RESEARCH CONTEXT

Refugee families arriving in the city of Edmonton face a multitude of factors that impinge on their ability to integrate into local society. The Multicultural Family Connections Program, funded through the Early Childhood Development Initiative, offers cultural brokering support to these families. Cultural brokers, those who share the same cultural and linguistic background as the families they work with, are key to the success of this approach. A primary component of the program mandate is to develop culturally and linguistically relevant parenting information and facilitate parenting groups, particularly for those families with preschool children. The main concern is supporting these families as they struggle to parent within two often-conflicting cultural frameworks.

Staff and volunteers working with refugee families through the Multicultural Family Connections Program labor from crisis to crisis. Small successes with individual family members serve as touchstones. The intensity of the work, however, leaves minimal time for reflection, analysis, and evaluation of the factors contributing to the stress and difficulties that refugee families face every day.

The lived experiences of refugees heard in this research help educators, settlement workers, and cultural brokers identify factors that influence the ability of these families to integrate into the Edmonton community and to parent their preschool children in their new location. Such knowledge is leading to greater understanding, awareness, compassion, and meaningful assistance being offered to these parents and children.

METHODOLOGY

Mapping the Life Experiences of Refugee and Immigrant Families With Preschool Children (Multicultural Family Connections Program, 2004), ethnographic research undertaken in Edmonton, Canada, involved 41 refugee parents, representing 62 children under 6 years of age, and 128 children 6 years of age or older. Seven focus groups and seven one-on-one conversational interviews were conducted. Afghan, African French-speaking (from Democratic Republic of Congo, Rwanda, Burundi, and Djibouti), Cambodian, Eritrean, Kurdish, Somali, and Sudanese refugees participated. Cultural brokers, who already have established relationships with the communities, served as group facilitators and interpreters, thus allowing all participants to communicate in the languages in which they felt most competent. All interviews and focus group conversations were taped, transcribed into English, and analyzed for common themes. Cultural brokers served to verify the translations and the interpretation of the data.

UNDERSTANDING THE REFUGEE FAMILIES' EXPERIENCES

The situation of each refugee family is unique; some may have been able to escape before unrest in their country arose, whereas others have faced severe atrocities before being able to flee their home country. The following recollections provided by refugees now living in Edmonton describe the variety of ways families experience unrest and resettlement.

Many refugees endured years of hardship and waiting in a refugee camp.

> You cannot imagine how we spent our whole life in a refugee camp. To be a Kurd from a mountain, a very beautiful cool weather country with water everywhere and then go to the desert where even we do not have water to drink. We were kicked out and moved from a heaven to a hell. (Kurdish refugee)

Not all refugee families relocate to camps. This Sudanese mother spoke of her situation after fleeing to Egypt.

> There is no security. One day I was not well and did not go to work so I went to the medical clinic. It happened that on that day people were caught and taken back to Sudan. They were put in a goods train with their children. They were just caught on the street. I was very, very lucky. Those that went back, I am sure that one hundred percent of them were killed. (Sudanese refugee)

Many Afghan refugees who participated in a focus group had fled to Iran shortly after the Taliban came to power.

> It was very difficult when the Taliban came. I made it to Iran all by myself with my children. After my husband was murdered we hid in the mountains for 40 days; the Taliban constantly threatened us. We made a caravan that fit seven families and we left for Iran.

Many refugee family members are left separated from one another for extended periods. A Somali father, who gained refugee status as a refugee claimant in Canada, was away from his wife and children for 4 years before he was in a financial position to sponsor them to come to Canada. Preschool children parented under such unstable and fear-filled circumstances often lack the experiences needed to prepare them for formal schooling. Canadian educators are then faced with the task of supporting families as they "make up for" those lost years.

Literature describing the refugee situation commonly identifies three phases of influence: premigration or preflight, transmigration or flight, and postmigration or resettlement (Beiser, Dion, Gotowiec, Hyman, & Vu, 1995; Frazel & Stein, 2002; Hamilton & Moore, 2004; Lustig et al., 2004). In considering the socio-cultural and historical background influencing refugee families, it is necessary to understand all three phases of the refugee experience. Following is a brief summary of key issues (premigration, transmigration, and postmigration) that affect resettlement.

FACTORS THAT AFFECT RESETTLEMENT

From the focus group and interview conversations I had with refugee parents living in Edmonton, it is possible to outline eight common issues influencing resettlement. Following are the main themes that emerged through the data analysis. A human voice is brought to these issues through the narrative comments provided by research participants.

Decreased Socioeconomic Status

Before the circumstances of displacement, many refugees were living peaceful and fruitful lives. Now in Canada, hoping for a better life, refugees I spoke with made it clear that they are thankful for the opportunity to live safely in Canada. They are grateful, but at the same time, this experience can be tinged with bitterness because of the financial pressure they feel.

On arrival in Canada, refugee families are provided with financial assistance from the federal government, at a social assistance rate, for 1 or 2 years depending on their circumstances. This year of settlement support income presents numerous barriers for refugees. "Finances are a problem, it is not enough, but if you go and work part-time then in April when you do your tax return they say you worked a lot so they cut your money" (Sudanese refugee). After this initial period of government financial support, refugees are expected to be self-sufficient. The thought of this brings fear to this Congolese mother.

> I am afraid because after two years my sponsorship will be cut off. This is worrying because I do not speak English, but I will have to look for a job. The daycare will be very expensive for me. Therefore, I will have to stay at home and look after the children, because I cannot move and leave the children alone.

In addition to the expectation of financial self-sufficiency after 1 or 2 years, it is expected that any travel expenses the federal government of Canada incurred in bringing the family or the individual to Canada will start to be repaid. This sum of money can vary from a few hundred dollars to several thousand dollars, depending on the size of the family. Along with the many financial obligations encountered in Canada, many refugees feel an obligation to provide financial assistance to family members "back home."

Once relocated to Canada for resettlement, the socioeconomic status of refugee families continues to be below that of their premigration situation. The lack of recognition given to work qualifications and experience, along with a lack of affordable housing makes resettlement difficult. The Edmonton Social Planning Council (2004) reported that children in visible minority and immigrant families are "two to three times as likely as the general population to be living in poverty." A study conducted in another Western Canadian province (British Columbia) examined poverty among immigrants and refugees living in that province and identified three key factors that result in high rates of poverty among this group: (a) unemployment and underemployment, (b) limited access to supports and services, and (c) government policies that create and tolerate poverty (Spigelman, 1998).

Although it is problematic to label "low-income" refugees as "disadvantaged" or "at-risk," parents involved in this research pointed out the inequities and barriers that exist for them because of their financial circumstances. Not being able to afford quality preschool learning opportunities for their children was discussed repeatedly.

Lack of Community and Family Support

Many refugees coming to Canada are ready and able to get on with their lives without the help of professional intervention; what they lack is the extended family and community support they had relied on in their home country.

> Here you are with your partner and there is no other person. The guidance that you would need from other members of your family like your mom is not here so it is very difficult for many of us. So now we are just raising our children the way we think it is right. (Eritrean refugee)

Instead of the close supportive community they are used to, many refugees struggle alone. "Here people are isolated and lonely, and it is very difficult for newcomers to integrate. They expect the same closeness with their neighbor just like it is in Africa, but it is not the case" (African French-speaking refugee). A Congolese single mother with five children under the age of 7, because of her isolation at home with her children, feels like she is in a prison. Children as well as parents feel the loss of extended family.

> The little one [daughter] misses her grandmother. Whenever she sees an older woman, she calls her "grandma." I sometimes feel bad, because my children do not really know their grandparents. (Sudanese refugee)

The fact that refugee families are bereft of extended family support is highly problematic, especially after childbirth. In their home countries, female relatives would provide 40 days of postpartum care.

> The next day after my baby was born in Canada, I was back in the kitchen. I had no choice. I felt bad, sad, and lonely. There is nobody here. I think if I was back home my sister, my aunty, my mom, everyone would be there, but now here we do not have a choice. (Sudanese refugee)

Refugee families previously accustomed to the support of community and extended family, now relocated to the independent and nuclear family social system of Canada, could derive great support through the preschool and school settings their children attend. Wenger (1998) described schools as places where learning, meaning, and identity are derived. Hamilton and Moore (2004) suggested that schools offer social support and acceptance. As institutions that have tremendous influence on families for a significant number of years, it is imperative that schools play a role in the social fabric of the community.

Unfamiliar Childrearing Practices

Along with struggling to raise their children without the help of family and neighbors, refugee parents are confused about how to guide and discipline their children in their host country. One African French-speaking father stated, while the other fathers laughed in knowing agreement, "The recommendation here in Canada is the only way to discipline your child is to be a friend with your child." One Cambodian mother expressed the viewpoint I heard repeatedly in focus group discussions, "Here it is harder to discipline the children. Back home, we can discipline the children by spanking them but here we cannot do that."

Fear of the authorities and the government intervening in their childrearing is another concern of refugees. "Back home, if the child is sick and dies, you do not even have to contact anybody. You just go make a grave and you bury your child. It is your child. You are the one who has the pain and the problem" (Somali refugee). This same mother goes on to express confusion about the Western view of protecting children from abusive parents. "If you speak loudly, calling your children, there is suspicion outside the door there, which makes us very uncomfortable even when we are in our own homes."

The nature of child guidance in Canadian culture can be very confusing for refugee families. At the same time, Canadians often do not understand or appreciate the child guidance strategies used by refugee families. Canadian educators hearing about or witnessing the use of physical punishment, shaming, and ostracism by parents of children in their class may have difficulty knowing how to respond. In Canada, people are legally bound to report to the child welfare authorities if they believe a child is being abused or neglected. Unfortunately, this can set up an adversarial stance between refugee parents and teachers. Teachers feel they must watch for signs of what they consider abuse or neglect, whereas parents feel they must hide, in case their actions are misinterpreted.

Changing Roles and Responsibilities of Family Members

Refugee families experience many challenges to the rhythm of family life when they relocate to Canada. "Back home, when our children are seven years old, they are grown" (Somali parent). Now in Canada, children under the age of 12 are believed to require the surveillance of a more mature person. The predominance of "learning through play" in Western cultures presents a challenge for fathers from other cultures. "We have to keep some distance. To compare with here, there is a gap. The father is the chief in the family, even when playing there is a gap" (African father). In describing the roles of men, women, and children in her culture, an African French-speaking woman related, "In our culture, the man is in charge of bringing money to the family, he has to go to work, and most of the wives stay at home doing household tasks." Knowing that this familiar pattern becomes challenged in Canadian society, her male counterpart declared, "People here know how to cope, but immigrant women when they get this freedom they tell the men to take off." Children in the midst of these changing roles and responsibilities are at one and the same time set adrift, while also often quicker to adapt to Canadian ways than their parents.

Dealing With Racism and Discrimination

Refugee parents express concern that their children are being subjected to racism and discrimination. They do not want to see their children hurt and unaccepted. Somali women described the racism and discrimination their children experience in Edmonton schools.

> My daughter was told by one of the children at school, your mom is ugly and she is always dressing up like Halloween.

> At school, the teachers are suspicious of our children. They think maybe their hair is not combed or not proper because they have it covered. They are suspicious. I do not like it.

An Eritrean mother shared this from her daughter's experiences.

> At school, the teacher does not give her attention or give her answers sometimes. When she asks questions she does not get answers, she does not get any attention. Now it is already recorded in her mind that there is discrimination.

Coping With Mental Health Issues

In addition to the complex and interrelated issues faced by all immigrants, because of the forced nature of migration, refugees will undoubtedly have experienced many losses: their homes, possessions, careers, finances, and, most significantly, loved ones. As a result, "unlike those who freely and deliberately choose to start a new life in Canada, their thoughts on arrival may be focused more on what they have left behind than on their future here" (Canadian Council for Refugees, 1998, p. 13). Virtually all refugees have left family and friends in the home country. They are often burdened by worry for those still living in difficult circumstances. "Right now, we do not know where exactly our family members are, we do not know whether they are alive or have been killed. At times when that comes back to mind, it brings sorrow and pain" (Congolese refugee). Children too are left with feelings of fear and uncertainty regarding life in the "home country."

> My son says if there is fighting or violence in Africa "I do not want to go there." I do not want him to grow up thinking our country is bad. I try to tell him that there is not only war in Sudan, that there can also be good things there. (Sudanese mother)

Depression is commonplace among male refugees struggling to find work and provide for their families. Women often suffer from postpartum depression when confronted with the reality of caring for their newborn and other family members without the help of extended family and community.

Knowing you cannot return "home," fearing for loved ones left behind to suffer, dealing with the effects of having witnessed and experienced traumatic events, and coping in a foreign context without the support of family and friends, these and other factors can lead to emotional and physical ill health. A government task force looking into the mental health issues affecting immigrants and refugees in Canada drew these conclusions:

> Negative public attitudes, separation from family and community, inability to speak English or French, and failure to find employment are among the most powerful causes of emotional distress. Persons whose pre-migration experience has been traumatic, women from traditional cultures, adolescents and the elderly also are at high risk for experiencing difficulties during resettlement. (Canadian Task Force on Mental Health Issues Affecting Immigrants and Refugees, 1988, p. 91)

Maintaining Home Language and Culture

Refugee parents want their children to have Canadian peers, while at the same time maintaining their home language and culture. "It is good for our children to be with other Canadian children and with children from our own culture. It will give them more chances to learn about both Canadian culture and our community" (Kurdish parent). Schooling in Canada however offers little support of the retention of home language and culture; this creates a distance between children and parents. "When my daughter first started school she did not speak much English, but now she wants to only speak English. I really want her to keep speaking Khmer otherwise I cannot talk with her" (Cambodian parent).

Unfortunately, the importance of young children maintaining their home language and culture is not always appreciated in schools, as is exemplified in the experience of a Congolese 7-year-old.

> When I started school, I met some people who speak Swahili, who have been living here for a long time. We started to play together. After a few days, a teacher told us that we could not speak Swahili, and we stopped talking to each other.

Understanding the Canadian Education System

The desire to have their children receive an education is a consistent theme running through the comments made by refugee parents. "We hope for education for our children so they can serve Canada, so they can become positive members of this society" and "School is important. We hope they can get good jobs, become teachers, doctors" (Afghan parents). When asked what is most important for the future of her children this Sudanese mother stated

> Their education, because with education they can do anything they want to do and they will know everything and they will know what is good to do and what is bad. Education is the key. They can go anywhere and do anything.

This Kurdish mother appealed for a better life for her children than she has.

> I want a greater sense of learning for my young children, because I do not want my children to be like I am right now, I want a better life for them, better learning, better education, more support from school, when they go to school in the future; a more open-minded school system.

With respect to the school system in Canada, many refugees have mixed feelings. They are thankful for access to quality public education, but struggle with the perceived lack of moral training provided in schools. "The only thing children get from education here is knowledge but not good behavior or respect" (African French-speaking parent). Parents want to be supportive of their children's educational experiences, but find the system here different from what they are familiar with.

> The difference between education here and back home is, if children do not do well they have to repeat a grade until they do well. Here they put children in the class

with the children the same age even if they do not know the English alphabet. The children are given assignments and the parents are expected to help even if they are not educated. Then if children do not do well in school the parents are blamed which is not their fault. (Sudanese mother)

DISCUSSION

Refugee parents live in the tension between hope and reality. They have high expectations for the futures of their children, especially with respect to education. Unfortunately, refugee families are seldom in a position to access culturally and linguistically appropriate preschool experiences that would help prepare their children for school success. Information gathered during an interview with a Congolese mother illustrates the difficulty refugees have accessing early years care and education. In the case of this single mother, forcefully separated from her husband by rebel factions while in a refugee camp, now relocated to Edmonton with her five children, ranging in age from infancy to 7 years; she experiences great difficulty making sure her school-age child safely gets on the school bus before trundling the other four children off with her on public transit to two different preschool settings in hopes of arriving to her English as a second language class before she is penalized for being late.

Preschool care and education can play a pivotal role in the settlement of refugee families. For example, the development of racist attitudes (Harris, 1998; Van Ausdale & Feagin, 2001) and prejudice (Aboud, 1988) are found to begin during the preschool years. As preschool settings rise to the challenge of a commitment to antibias and antiracist models of learning and living, I believe peace and acceptance will become the norm rather than the exception in our society. Furthermore, mentorship, caring, safety, acceptance of cultural differences, counseling, and support networks within preschools and schools will help ensure these settings become a "resilience factor" not another "risk factor" in refugee children's lives (Hamilton & Moore, 2004, p. 63). Finally, research into second language development and the retention of first languages has shown that heritage language and culture, if given greater prominence in the day-to-day life of preschool and school age children will result in many benefits: (a) newcomer children will experience a sense of pride and acceptance that leads to a feeling of belonging; (b) competence in one's first language will allow the learning of a second and subsequent languages to proceed more fluidly; (c) communication and relationships between home, school, and community will be strengthened; and (d) equal access to education will be ensured (Dei, James, Karumanchery, James-Wilson, & Zine, 2000).

While being in greater need, refugee families are among the least likely to receive the preschool support they need. Causes for this lack of access to preschool settings, according to Rutter (1998), include meager finances as a result of insufficient government assistance or the inability to secure suitable jobs, high mobility because of the inadequacy of housing, a lack of information regarding existing preschool services, unwillingness to place children in the care of people they do not know and who do not speak their home language, and the high cost of services including transportation to get the children to the preschool setting. Steps must be taken to eliminate these barriers.

The Multicultural Family Connections Program in Edmonton is working to address the lack of access to culturally and linguistically appropriate preschool experiences refugee families face. Although there are a multitude of aspects to address in the practical delivery of such programming, of paramount importance to this coalition of agencies is hearing the voices of refugee families. Newcomers are not seen as people in need of intervention, but rather people who have much to offer. Families are addressed as units with strengths and capabilities, not merely deficits. Both newcomers and Canadian-born persons share in a relationship so they can learn from one another. It is on this basis that relationships are established. The philosophy is that educational opportunities offered to refugee families with preschool children must not be so dominated by Canadian ways and expectations as to overshadow the hopes and desires of the families involved. Families need to feel part of the school preparation experiences of their children.

While it is true that refugee families have much to learn about life in Canada, we also have much to learn from them. Canadian educators would do well to consider the value other cultures place on sharing community and family support, fostering values and morals, strengthening cultural identity, and encouraging bilingualism and biculturalism. By doing this, education in Canada may open up to other ways of being in the world with young children.

Preschools and schools play a significant role in the resettlement of refugees and must be accessible in every sense of the word: financially affordable, conveniently located, community focused, supportive of integration, culturally and linguistically appropriate, free of racism and discrimination, offering support and referral for mental health issues, encouraging of bilingualism and biculturalism, and providing what is necessary for successful integration into Canadian schooling.

REFERENCES

Aboud, F. (1988). *Children and Prejudice.* Oxford, UK: Basil Blackwell.

Beiser, M., Dion, R., Gotowiec, A., Hyman, I., & Vu, N. (1995). Immigrant and refugee children in Canada. *Canadian Journal of Psychiatry, 40*(2), 67–72.

Canadian Council for Refugees. (1998). *Best Settlement Practice: Settlement Services for Refugees and Immigrants in Canada.* Montréal, QC: Canadian Council for Refugees.

Canadian Task Force on Mental Health Issues Affecting Immigrants and Refugees. (1988). *After the Door Has Been Opened: Mental Health Issues Affecting Immigrants and Refugees in Canada.* Ottawa, ON: Department of the Secretary of State of Canada, Multiculturalism Sector.

Citizenship and Immigration Canada. (2005). *Facts and figures 2004: Immigration overview.* Ottawa, ON, Canada: Author.

Dei, S. G. J., James, I. M., Karumanchery, L. L., James-Wilson, S., & Zine, J. (2000). *Removing the Margins: the Challenges and Possibilities of Inclusive Schooling.* Toronto, ON: Canadian Scholars' Press.

Edmonton Social Planning Council. (2004). *Child and family poverty in Alberta 2004* [Fact Sheet]. Edmonton, AB: Author.

Frazel, M., & Stein, A. (2002). The mental health of refugee children. *Archives of Disease in Childhood, 87*(5), 366–370.

Hamilton, R., & Moore, D. (2004). *Educational Interventions for Refugee Children: Theoretical Perspectives and Implementing Best Practice.* London: RoutledgeFalmer.

Harris, J. R. (1998). *The Nurture Assumption: Why Children Turn Out the Way They Do.* New York: Touchstone.

Lustig, S. L., Kia-Keating, M., Knight, W. G., Geltman, P., Ellis, H., Kinzie, J. D., Keane, T., & Saxe, G. N. (2004). Review of child and adolescent refugee mental health. *Journal of the American Academy of Child and Adolescent Psychiatry, 43*(1), 24–36.

Multicultural Family Connections Program. (2004). [Mapping the life experiences of refugee and immigrant families with preschool children]. Unpublished raw data.

Office of the United Nations High Commissioner for Refugees. (1996). *Convention and protocol relating to the status of refugees.* Geneva, Switzerland: Author.

Rutter, J. (1998). Refugee children in the early years. *Multicultural Teaching, 17*(1), 23–26.

Spigelman, M. (1998). *Unfulfilled Expectations, Missed Opportunities: Poverty Among Immigrants and Refugees in British Columbia.* Victoria, BC: British Columbia Policy, Planning and Research Division.

Van Ausdale, D., & Feagin, J. R. (2001). *The First R: How Children Learn Race and Racism.* Lanham, MD: Rowman & Littlefield.

Wenger, E. (1998). *Communities of Practice: Learning, Meaning, and Identity.* New York: Cambridge University Press.

Introduction to Part V

Searching for New Ways to Belong

Cottrell (1999) emphasized the importance of acknowledging when there are several constituent cultures in an individual's life. She suggested that many groups may share the elements of complex identity and worldview, including children who live in more than one country during the formative years; children of mixed race, ethnic, or national heritage; and children who live in border areas.

The studies included in part V examine the effects of two types of migration on children's identities and sense of belonging: transnational migration because of career assignments and rural-to-urban migration in one country. Chapters 17 and 18 describe educational issues that concern families that move to another country but are considered temporary migrants (i.e., migrant children in international schools in Singapore) and those who move repeatedly and might be considered what Ender (2002) called "global nomads" (i.e., children of military personnel, Friedmann, 2002).

Chapters 17 and 18 describe how the social capital from the network of families in a similar situation may be a positive force in the lives of children. Chapter 17 describes children who may be labeled as the experiences of third-culture kids (TCKs) because they have spent limited, if any, time in their parents' home country and who may be facing a number of quandaries in forging a personal identity. They are not raised entirely in their parents' home country or as citizens of the country or countries where they live and attend school. Thus, they are likely to build relationships to all the cultures while having no ownership in any.

Adaptation to a new culture is viewed as necessary for all children who migrate from one place to another. However, needing to fit in, yet feeling that there is little point in doing so because this is once again a temporary location, is unique to the children of armed forces personnel (chapter 18). Ender (2002) claimed that it is common knowledge that after World War II, first-world countries expanded their political, military, corporate, and humanitarian responsibilities beyond their national borders. Agencies place demands on their personnel, their spouses, and their children for out-of-country service and residence. Sometimes called TCKs or military brats, a nickname derived from the acronym for British

Regiment Attached Travelers, millions of children have grown up in these families. Furthermore, Ender pointed out that it is estimated that approximately 2% of the United States population grew up in such families living abroad and that millions of people worldwide are coming of age in the shadows of military and service organizations, living outside their country of origin.

The frustrations that the children in these families may feel when it comes to schooling may be based on inconsistencies in the curriculum, not having one's friends moving to the new location, and the feeling of loss from leaving their old home. However, the children and their parents identify some valuable learning experiences and benefits such as gaining a wider network of friends, appreciation for relationships, developing a sense of realism and the importance of *now,* and becoming adept at achieving closure. The studies in chapters 17 and 18 demonstrate that children are resilient and can be agents in the process of overcoming the challenges associated with the continual change of their family's place of residence.

Chapters 19 and 20 address educational issues concerning children whose families move within the national boundaries but find urban living significantly different from the rural home left behind. As countries like Turkey become more industrialized, thousands of people migrate from rural to urban regions of the country in search of better employment and educational opportunities for themselves and their children. However, regardless of the increased demand for workers in urban areas, rural migrants are seen as non–city-dwellers who need to be "integrated" into society. The authors of chapter 19 assert that children, who because of their young age cannot protect themselves from external factors, may suffer more from the migration process than their parents and that the sociocultural disadvantages that they experience after migration may permanently affect their personalities and development of identity. Although the families in these studies had moved hoping for a better economic situation, the struggles faced by these migrant families involve working long hours, living in poor housing conditions, and possibly holding several low-paying jobs that city dwellers do not choose to accept. As a result, their children grow up with limited supervised care and possibly without public education. In addition, the families may live in isolation from society, because as new arrivals, they may face rejection by local residents. Incorporation into the community may be slow and arduous, and they may remain on the edge of society for the foreseeable future. The authors offer suggestions for changes in state policy, nongovernmental organizations, and teacher preparation programs that can address concerns for appropriate education of the children of rural migrants.

Among the issues considered in research on the global movement of people is the effect of living in close proximity in migrant social communities. The pattern can be identified in countries around the world where these interpersonal networks provide migrants with social capital. This social capital in the migrant network may have a positive effect on income for men but may not do so for women. Ogdul (2000) argued that the existence of social cohesion in a neighborhood is not necessarily an advantage and that the community may constitute a closed "island." Although the migrant populations may have strong community ties, chapter 19 reveals that such urban communities in a city (e.g., Istanbul) can have both negative and positive aspects. Erman (2001) stated that in migrant communities in Turkey, traditional patriarchal control is reproduced in the urban context. Among the results are that women's economic contributions are devalued and the labor market offers only low-level jobs to migrant women. Concern is also growing about moral corruption (in urban settings), and this causes women to stay at home and inside their communities. Erman's observations substantiate the findings in chapter 19 that a low percentage of newly migrated mothers work outside the home. The isolation of mothers in an immigrant social community may not encourage acculturation, particularly acquisition of the host nation's language. This in turn can affect the ability of the parents to communicate with the school and thus the child's adaptation to the school (Children Now, 2004.)

Chapter 20 describes the multiple problems for children in China, where a large number of families migrate from rural to urban areas. Ma (2002) suggested that although providing employment opportunities in rural areas might stem the flow, the reality is that such a action will not be taken quickly, if ever, in China or in other countries with a high level of rural–urban migration. Meanwhile, young rural–urban migrant children with their need for education are often left outside the mainstream educational system. The community-based approach of providing informal education in the form of a playgroup offered in a migrant community in China, as described in chapter 20, brought positive outcomes for both the children and the parents. This might be seen as a possible form of early education for children of migrant families. The unique features of the program included appropriateness to local conditions, flexibility, relevance, and tapping into various sources of assistance. As a result, parents became the main actors in the community education effort, improving their own education and increasing their chances of being accepted into city life. Thus, the program became a center for lifelong learning and building a learning community.

All four chapters in part V invite the reader to consider what it means for a young child to feel that he or she does not belong in a given place. The implication is that the notion of *home* for children who experience multiple moves in their lives could be reinstated through fostering closer family and peer relationships.

REFERENCES

Children Now. 2004. *California Report Card: Focus on Children in Immigrant Families*. Oakland, CA: Author. Retrieved August 26, 2005 from http://publications.childrennow.org/publications/invest/reportcard2004.cfm

Cottrell, A. B. (1999). *Personal Manifestations of Childhood Border Crossings: Identity and Personality Traits of Adult TCKs.* Paper presented at the Phi Beta Delta Annual Conference, San Diego, CA.

Ender, M. (Ed.) (2002). Introduction. In M. G. Ender (Eds.) *Military Brats and Other Global Nomads: Growing Up in Organization Families* (pp. xxv–xxxi). Westport, CT: Praeger.

Erman. T. (2001). Rural migrants and patriarchy in Turkish cities. *International Journal of Urban and Regional Research, 25*(2), 118.

Friedmann, J. (2002). *The Prospect of Cities.* Minneapolis, MN: University of Minnesota Press.

Ma, Z. (2002). Social capital mobilization and income returns to entrepreneurship: The case of return migration in rural China. *Environment and Planning, 34*(10), 1763–1784.

Ogdul, H. (2000). Social cohesion: Is it sufficient? Migrant communities in two disadvantaged neighborhoods in Istanbul. *GeoJournal, 51*(4), 321–328.

Chapter 17

The Experiences of Third-Culture Children

Marjory Ebbeck
Valerie Reus
University of South Australia, Australia

This research was conducted in Singapore, a highly developed country with a relatively wealthy economy. The population of close to 5 million is multiracial, with Chinese, Indian, and Malay as the major ethnic groups. A large number of people live in Singapore on an *immigration permit*, which must be renewed annually. These people work in Singapore because of their particular employment, which has economic or other advantages to Singapore. The Singapore government has long recognized that it has limited natural resources and that its human resources are of prime importance. In 2001, some 16,414 children were enrolled in approximately 32 private foreign schools (Zoetmulder, 2003). These children are the focus of the research reported here.

THIRD-CULTURE CHILDREN

Children who are neither raised entirely in their parents' home country nor as citizens of the country in which they currently reside are called third-culture children

(TCC) and are also sometimes referred to as third-culture kids (TCKs). Pollock and Van Reken (2001) give the following definition of third-culture children.

> A Third Culture Kid (TCK) is a person who has spent a significant part of his or her developmental years outside the parents' culture. The TCK builds relationships to all of the cultures, while not having full ownership in any. Although elements from each culture are assimilated into the TCK's life experience, the sense of belonging is in relationship to others of similar background. (p. 19)

It is useful and important to remember that although culture can be thought of as the way of life of a group of people, TCC are members of several cultural groups: their family (which might be biracial), their country of origin, their host country, their school, and their peers.

TCC are not the only children who move around and experience cross-cultural or multicultural experiences. Often children of the same culture as the school experience difficulties when they move from one school to another. The difference between TCC and non-TCC lies in the fact that TCC do not have the opportunity to experience diversity in a rooted locality as a non-TCC experiences it. TCC frequently find themselves in transition between many places: country, school, grade level, teacher, and friends.

Although studies have shown that "international exposure at an early age appears to have an enduring impact that positively shapes both children and adults" (Glicksberg-Skipper 2000, n.p.), Berk (2002) commented that the psychological and other stresses placed on TCC as well as on nonmobile children require them to cope with challenging and sometimes threatening situations.

As Pollock and Van Reken (2001) stated, "It is vital that highly mobile families learn to deal well with the entire process of transition" (p. 199), as this process can affect the child's ability to cope and to make friends. Children have difficulties in foreseeing themselves in a different environment. They see what they are losing and leaving behind, and "in addition parents feel helpless because they realize that their decision to relocate has caused the stress their children are experiencing" (Roman 2001, n.p.).

Miller (2003), for example, reported the following comment from a now-adult TCC.

> [I] grew up in the Philippines and also lived in California and Singapore, but decided that Indianapolis would be home. If I lived in the same house for 50 years, I could be happy. I have been everywhere, and I don't want to go anywhere else … He [her husband], to me, means stability … he's from here and always lived here, and that's what I was looking for." (n.p.)

Van Reken (2001, p. 4) highlighted six emotional stages TCC face when they enter a new environment:

1. Feeling vulnerable
2. Feeling ambivalent
3. Feeling different
4. Feeling angry
5. Feeling depressed
6. Feeling to begin to live again. (p. 4)

This framework was used as a basis to categorize children's qualitative responses, that is, responses to questions and documentation after 1 week and 8 weeks (see Appendix I).

Parents and teachers need to remind themselves that becoming familiar with a new country or a new school can take time, often up to 6 months (Pollock & Van Reken, 2001). Teachers' and parents' roles in observing TCC's actions and reactions to transition are major roles as they can guide and help TCC entering a new environment. "Parents, educators … who interact with TCKs first need to realize that there are definite, recognized patterns in a TCK upbringing that can help parents and others give the right sort of support" (Global Assignment Abroad, 2001, n.p.).

The importance of parental support cannot be denied or overlooked as "Siblings and parents may become each other's best friends" (McCaig, 1994, n.p.). However, parental support needs to be positive and significant.

It's important that parents … explain to their children that they are moving, including the reasons why. Children should know that the entire family will be working together to realize a positive relocation experience. Parents need to listen very carefully when questions are raised by children and address each issue in a meaningful way. (Roman, 2003, n.p.)

Children are remarkably resilient. Newman and Blackburn (2002) used the term *resilience* to explain how children overcome difficulties. "Resilient children are better equipped to resist stress and adversity, cope with change and uncertainty, and to recover faster and more completely from traumatic events or episodes" (Newman and Blackburn, 2002, n.p.).

Leo (2003) mentioned the importance of attachment and how children deal with transition.

How well children cope with change, stress, loss and uncertainty depends greatly on how securely bonded they are, what we teach them to believe about themselves, how connected they feel, and how much safety they are given to release and heal their emotional hurts. (n.p.)

TCC experience many separations during their developmental years (Pollock & Van Reken. 2001). Therefore, for emotional stability that comes through sound attachments, they need a strong, continuing relationship with their parents.

Feelings of displacement and rejection are normal, even in TCC who are comfortable with transition. Age has a relative influence in how TCC feel when they are relocated. To keep the effects of international assignments on children as positive as possible, their socioemotional needs must be sensitively considered, especially by their parents.

According to Leo (2003), "We nurture our children's resilience when we focus on their strengths, spend enough time with them to stay connected to them, and to create safe space for them to work through their fears and feelings" (n.p.). O'Connell (2003) described the reactions of children aged from 6 to 12 years old when they relocate.

> Elementary-aged children are at the point where they are worried about losing friends, making friends, everyday routines and activities, and attending a new school. In addition to discussing these fears, parents should research the host area prior to the move in order to inform their children about new recreational activities, schools and communities. Allowing children to accompany their parents on a pre-assignment trip will also allow them to explore the new area on their own, see where they will be living and possibly meet some new friends. (n.p.)

When children enter school they search for more information about themselves; they often refer "to social groups in their self-descriptions" (Livesley & Bromley, cited in Berk, 2002, p. 484).

The self-concept of children at the end of early childhood and at the beginning of middle childhood changes considerably. They start to make social comparisons (Berk, 2002), they watch television, attend movies, and widen their circle of friends and adults outside the family. They also become more aware of similarities and differences in others' behavior and feelings, thus enabling them to strengthen their identification to a social, racial, religious, or national group (Ames & Haber, 1990). This generalization of 8-year-old children enhances the importance of belonging to a group and is an important challenge for TCC. Peer relationships become the beginning of a major socioemotional developmental stage. Children's friendships are extremely important, as they follow them through the developmental stages from early childhood to adolescence.

Pollock and Van Reken (2001) pointed out some of the challenges faced by TCC with respect to relationships.

> Because TCKs often cope with high mobility by defining their sense of rootedness in terms of relationships, rather than geography, many TCKs will go to greater lengths than some people might consider normal to nurture relational ties with others— be they family members, friends with whom the TCKs have shared boarding school years, or other important members of their third culture community. Unfortunately, that same mobility can result in relationships being a source of great conflict and pain as well. (p. 131)

These sources of pain, conflict, and external changes can cause significant feelings of grief and loss. "Unresolved grief ranks as the second greatest challenge TCC face" (p. 165) in their journey. TCC experience feelings of loss for many reasons. As globally mobile children acquiring knowledge and experiences in their daily life, they have more to lose than their counterparts who stay in one location. They lose homes, schools, friends, and relatives.

> The problem is that in these types of losses, no one actually died or was divorced, and nothing was physically stolen. Contrary to obvious losses, there are no markers, no rites of passage recognizing them as they occur—no recognized way to mourn. (p. 172)

Current literature on TCC clearly shows that these children experience many social and emotional challenges as they move through their early development in varying cultural contexts. These challenges are not necessarily negative and can and should be positive, thereby enriching the children's development in ways that non-TCC cannot experience. For young children beginning their lives as TCC, the home and the school play a crucial role in enabling their sound development to occur as normally as possible. No studies had been carried out to date in Singapore, and research was needed to define this is problem there.

THE RESEARCH PROJECT

We investigated some aspects of TCC's adaptation to their new school during a specific period of 8 weeks, which was considered the minimum time for any change in children's transitions. We intended to investigate the following questions: (a) What are TCC's feelings when they enter an overseas school? and (b) What are TCC's feelings about the school after a transition period of 8 weeks?

Research Setting and Sample

The research sample consisted of a group of eleven 8-year-old children newly arrived in Singapore and beginning their transition to a foreign school system. The group was selected because the principal investigator had access and permission to study the group. The children were enrolled in an international school in Singapore that implemented a U.S.-based curriculum and had an international group of teachers.

Methodology

A qualitative approach was adopted to "understand individuals' perception of the world" (Bell, 2002, p. 7), in this case to discover the feelings of children during transition to a new foreign school in Singapore. The frequency of mentioned feelings also was taken into account and necessitated a quantitative approach be included. Interviews of approximately 30–45 min involving participation in two written tasks were conducted with 11 children in Week 1 of their admission and again at Week 8.

The interviews were designed to collect information from the children and to offer them a certain frame and liberty to express their feelings. The first interview in Week 1 of school was designed to determine the children's comfort level and ability to answer and to document how they felt at this early stage of entering a new school. We asked questions of the children and invited them to discuss and write down some comments about their feelings. We used the same process in a second interview conducted after 8 weeks to document any changes in the children's feelings in the intervening time. A different format was used for documenting the children's feelings for Week 8 (see appendix I). However, the tasks were structured in keeping with the teaching approaches used in Singapore with children in this age group.

Pilot Study

We decided to implement a pilot study with three TCC not included in the main study to evaluate the proposed questions and forms of documentation to see if the children would feel comfortable and have no difficulty in understanding the questions. Some changes to the questions were made as a result of feedback from the pilot study

When both interviews were completed, we categorized the data. A subcategorization of the "*positive and negative feelings*" was needed; to achieve this, "negative feelings" were divided into five subcategories: *after shock, insecure, outcast, extreme, and passive. Positive feelings* were divided into *well-adjusted passive and well-adjusted active.* Again, this subcategorization was in agreement with Van Reken's (2001) stage except for the addition of the *well-adjusted passive* subcategory (see Table 1).

RESULTS AND IMPLICATIONS

Rich data were gathered from the children, as shown in the following samples of their qualitative responses. These are grouped into themes as follows to answer the research questions.

Question 1: What are TCC's feelings when they enter an overseas school?

In Week 1, common themes were scared, bored, nervous, shy, and different:

- "I feel scared, because I don't know anybody. I feel bored in the bus ride."
- "I feel nervous; it's such a big school. I thought I would get lost. I felt scared because I got lost on the first day."

TABLE 1
Comparative Categorization of Feelings From Van Reken (2001) and the Current Study

Van Reken's Stages	Study Classification
1. Feeling vulnerable	**After Shock** Disappointed–anxious–shocked–tired Homesick–nervous—sleepy
2. Feeling ambivalent	**Insecure** Insecure–unsure–reluctant– bored Weird
3. Feeling different	**Outcast** Displaced–shy–lost–uncomfortable Bewildered–isolated–lonely–outcast Different–behind–unsuccessful
4. Feeling angry	**Extreme** Horrible–overwhelmed–stressed–mad Angry
5. Feeling depressed	**Passive** Concerned–upset–apprehensive– tearful–sad–scared–worried
6. Feeling in the present again	**Well Adjusted Passive** Happy–positive–good–fine–settled Comfortable–satisfied–surprised–relaxed– OK——adjusted
No stage	**Well Adjusted Active** Involved–included–busy–excited Ahead–outgoing–confident–curious brace

- "I felt shy; I did not know anybody, and I did not think I would meet my teacher."
- "I felt scared: I thought I would not have fun at recess because I did not know anyone."
- "I felt nervous; I have never been in a big school and I felt shy; I never met the people here."
- "I felt shy. I am always that way. I was scared; I did not know who my teacher was."
- "I felt nervous; I did not know anything about the school."
- "I felt different, everybody else was not new."

At the end of 8 weeks, the qualitative responses were grouped into themes of positive and negative.

Question 2: What are TCC's feelings after a transition period of 8 weeks in the new international school?

Common themes (negative feelings) that children expressed included feeling stressed, tired, scared, different, and behind.

- "I feel stressed; school day needs to be shorter. I have lots of homework and after school activities to do. I get tired of school sometimes. I am anxious to end school and have a long break."
- I am tired."
- "I feel tired. I have to get up soooo early!"
- "I feel very tired; we are busy all the time."
- "I feel scared. I am new so I still don't know well the teachers and when they talk to me I am scared."
- "I feel different; each day different things happen and it affects how I feel."
- "I feel behind; I messed up on my spelling words."

Some of the children's comments in Week 8 were more negative than in Week 1, indicating tiredness, boredom, too much work, and anxiety about tests. Inferences drawn from this include the possibility that some of the excitement of starting a new school had worn off.

The emotional toll exacted by the transition affected some children physically and emotionally in their expressions of feeling tired and enduring long days. However, positive feelings also emerged and countered some of the negative. These showed that the transitional stage was ending and that children were more settled. Common themes (positive feelings) of feeling relaxed or excited also emerged. The experience of making friends and being accepted by teachers showed the importance of the social elements of transition. In addition, being able to achieve academically was viewed positively by four of the children.

- "I feel happy; my teacher is a great teacher."
- "I feel excited, I like to go to recess and play."
- I feel relaxed; I can find my way to the bathroom without getting lost. I feel excited; I have been in school for so long now."
- "I feel excited; I find new surprises."
- "I am happy; my friends can be nice and helpful."
- "I feel good; I have made a lot of good friends."
- "I feel happy; I have made new friends."
- "I am surprised how smart I am and I learn so fast."
- "I feel excited; I have a science test soon. I feel happy; I have never been to a school this big."
- "I am happy, I am learning cursive writing."
- "I feel ahead; I am very good at math. I am smart. I have a photographic memory."

Subcategorization of the *positive and negative feelings* was carried out according to adaptations made using Van Reken's (2001) model. Nine of the 11 children were categorized as *well-adjusted passive*, and two were categorized as *well-adjusted active*. This showed a considerable growth in being satisfied and positive about the school environment.

CONCLUSION AND IMPLICATIONS

The results from this small sample showed that children did indeed feel vulnerable, different, and nervous about starting a new foreign school in an unknown country. The sense of belonging was not there initially, but it did emerge in the children's initial responses. The loss of their friends and a new cultural context created emotional challenges and anxieties that the children readily expressed in their oral and written comments. Forging new friendships, being accepted by understanding teachers, and experiencing academic success were important for many of the 11 children. Again, children were able and willing to document freely how they felt at the end of 8 weeks.

The emotional needs of TCC must not be underestimated, because they have additional challenges to overcome. They need to belong and become part of a new culture whether in school or in their new home location. If children are successful in overcoming these challenges, the resilience they have shown should help them to continue to accept change and ultimately become part of the new cultural context in which they live.

Although the outcomes of this small study confirm the commonly held view of international schools where most of the children are TCC, the same results might not be obtained in noninternational school situations. Thus, it is even more crucial that teachers (and parents) appreciate the situations experienced by their TCC and understand their subsequent behavior. Children who relocate bring (and take) with them attributes of their own and other cultures, and so the process of acculturation continues. Although the sample size in this study was small and the results cannot be generalized, the findings are interesting and do provide a database that could be extended in the future.

REFERENCES

Adams Report 2001: Third Culture Kids. Retrieved December 25, 2002 from http://www.globalas signment.com/10-04-01/thirdculturekids.html

Allan, M. (2002). Cultural borderlands: A case study of cultural dissonance in an international school. *Journal of Research in International Education, 1*(1), 63–90.

Ames, L. B., & Haber, C. C. (1990). *Your Eight-Year Old, Lively and Outgoing.* New York: Dell.

Bell, B. (2002). *Doing Your Research Project: a Guide for First-Time Researchers in Education and Social Science.* Milton Keynes, UK: Open University Press.

Berk, L. E. (2002). *Infants, Children, and Adolescents.* Boston, MA: Allyn and Bacon.

Glicksberg-Skipper, R. (2000). Growing up abroad offers advantages. *Transition Abroad Magazine, 24*(2). Retrieved December 10, 2003, from http://www.transitionsabroad.com/publications/magazine/0009/third_culture_kids_ Research.shtml

Global Assignment Americans Abroad—The Adams Report 2001: Third Culture Kids. Retrieved December 25, 2002, from http://www.echointernational.com/Adams_Report/JAdams%20Newsletter%2010.2pdf

Leo, P. (2003). *Nurturing Our Children's Resilience.* Retrieved December 15, 2003, from http://www.connectionparenting.com/parenting_articles/resilience.html

McCaig, N. M. (1994, September). Growing up with a world view: Nomad children develop multicultural skills. *Foreign Service Journal,* 32-41. Retrieved December 26, 2003, from http://www.kaiku.com/nomads.html

Miller, E. (2003). Faces of many places: "Growing up in another culture has its benefits and pitfalls—And lessons for stay-at-home." *Indianapolis Star* [online]. Retrieved June 23, 2003, from http://www.figt.org/incEngine/inc_uploads/figt/Faces%20of%20many%20places%20-%20Indystar%2020121902.pdf

Newman, T., & Blackburn, S. (2002). Transitions in the lives of children and young people: resilience factors. *Interchange, 78* [online]. Retrieved October 8, 2003, from http://www.scotland.gov.uk/library5/education/ic78-00.asp

O'Connell, J. (2003). Helping expat kids bridge the culture gap. *National Relocation and Real Estate Magazine.* Retrieved April 26, 2006, from http://www.rismedia.com/index.php/article/article-view/4052/1/383/

Pollock, D. C., & Van Reken, R. E. (2001). *Third Culture Kids: The Experience of Growing Up Among Worlds.* Yarmouth, ME: Intercultural Press.

Roman, B. D. (2003). Relocating our small movers. *Families in Global Transitions,* [online]. Retrieved December 6, 2003, from Adams Report 2001, Third Culture Kids.

Van Reken, R. (2001, March). *Third Culture Kids—Raising Children in a Cross-Cultural World and Making the Most of the Journey.* Paper presented at the Supportive Parents and Resource Conferences, Singapore.

Zoetmulder, E. J. (2003, May). Making sense of education—For professionals. *Teach!* 20–21.

APPENDIX I

Instruction for Open Ended Interview

I would like you to write a story about yourself. Please write about the feelings you had when you started school here in Singapore. You can write more than one feeling, and it would be better if you could tell why this person had such feelings. Do not worry about spelling mistakes. This is not a test. What counts here is that you write about your feelings. There will be no right or wrong answers. Are there any questions?

Now let's have a look at the sheet

THIS IS MY STORY

My name is

_____

___. I am ___years old. I was born in

_____, but I have a

_____

passport. I lived in

_____

_____

_____ before I

came to Singapore.

My father is from _____ and

my mother is from

_____. I live with

_____

_____

_____and at home we speak

_____.

When I first came to this school I felt:

MY FEELINGS AFTER 8 WEEKS IN SCHOOL

My name is

_____

After being in school for eight weeks I feel:

_____
_____
_____

because

_____
_____.

_____
_____

because

_____
_____.
_____
_____
_____

because

_____

_____.

My friends' names are

_____

_____

_____

In class I would love to sit with

_____

_____

_____

_____

_____

Chapter 18

Children in Transition: Learning to Become Global Citizens

Hilary Fabian
North East Wales Institute of Higher Education, United Kingdom

Cari Roberts
Service Children's Education, Germany

There is little doubt that frequent changes of school and country can bring both benefits and challenges to children as they weave together living in a number of varying cultures with a high-mobility lifestyle (Pollock & Van Reken, 2001). Children whose parents are in the armed forces may experience multiple international changes because of their parents' careers, but they often move with the same group of people. Although they might be moving with friends, they still go through the process of settling into their new school in terms of getting to know the people and the environment, and they expect some curriculum continuity (Fabian, 2002b). In this chapter, we suggest that children's agency is key to the success of their transfer and that they will gain greater benefits from each move if they are involved in the decision-making processes.

FACTORS IN MOBILITY FOR CHILDREN OF FORCES PERSONNEL

Just as teachers take time to know their students, children take time to "build a picture" of their new school, adapt to any change in culture, and make sense of their new surroundings (Bruner, 1996). Ballinger (2001) suggested that they also need to explore the depth of their connection to the new country and consider how they are going to fit in or not bother to fit in if they believe that they will have to move again soon. Much of the ease of settling in has to do with high self-esteem, but this might be difficult to achieve if children have negative feelings about the new school (Fabian, 2002a). Negativity could arise from lack of curriculum continuity or because friendships, which play a significant role in transfer, may have been broken in the move (Noyes, 2004).

Mobility does not necessarily have a negative effect on children. Pollock and Van Reken (2001) pointed out that many students also gain valuable learning experiences and benefits. Students can become adaptable and flexible, become confident with change, gain a wide network of friends and value relationships, develop a sense of realism and the importance of now, and become adept at closure.

Many schools devote energy to efforts to smooth the emotional and social transfer process (Galton, Gray, & Rudduck, 1999). Nevertheless, it could be argued that preoccupation with social factors makes it difficult for students to focus on learning. The Office for Standards in Education (OFSTED, 2002) did not include service children in their survey about mobility because the study was less concerned with large-scale planned movement, such as military postings, than with individual transfers. Nevertheless, curriculum continuity was raised as a key concern. Not all armed forces personnel move as a large group. Some move as individual families, which continues to be of major concern to the Service Children's Authority (Chislett, 2001). Tracking individual students' movements, particularly those with special educational needs (SENs), has implications for the education service as a whole (Mott, 2002). Mott suggested that collecting data to track students be given priority in order for them to remain known to the system.

Children who move from one country to another might have particular difficulties during transfer. Whatever the circumstances of the change, there is "a widespread assumption that pupil mobility is disruptive to education, either directly, by disrupting curriculum continuity and progression, or indirectly, through domestic stress or poor social adjustment" (Strand, 2002, pp. 63–64).

The current focus on citizenship in the curriculum in the United Kingdom might help to begin to address the issue of disruption during transfer. By having a voice in the planning for each move, children learn how they can influence their lives; empathize with others; and acquire the knowledge, skills, and values to equip them to participate in decision making. Thus, they gain a sense of self-esteem and a belief that people can make a difference.

DESIGN OF THE STUDY

Ballinger (2000) documented three steps in the transfer process for children of armed forces personnel: a disengagement phase, an interim stage, and a reintegration phase. If the move is made at short notice, Ballinger suggested that the disengagement phase would be brief. For those who know about their posting some months in advance, the disengagement phase is characterized by spending more time and energy preparing to leave the current situation than in trying to live in it. However, she also suggested that once a family is relocated, it can take up to 12 months before the members have fully engaged with the new situation. The aim of this study was to identify the views of children and their parents about their moves from one country to another, to explore how teachers and parents seek ways to make the continuity of learning between transitions meaningful, and to consider how those in transition themselves make decisions that help them settle into their new school.

The participants were children who had moved between a number of countries, including Germany, Australia, Cyprus, and the UK in the course of their parents' work. Parents and teachers at a forces school in Germany also took part.

Listening to children and working with them to develop their ideas into strategies to address their anxieties and expectations is an important dimension of the transition process. "There is now increasing recognition and acceptance that children's views and perspectives need to be heard both as an ethical imperative and also as a matter of practical utility and efficacy" (Davie & Galloway, 1996, p. 3).

This study has three key areas of questioning and recognizes that children's ideas, approaches to life, choices, and relationships are viewed in their own right (James & Prout, 1997). In particular, these are the level of social and emotional well-being surrounding transition; strategies for dealing with change; and strategies for supporting continuity of curriculum.

CONTEXT, PARTICIPANTS, AND RESEARCH PROCEDURES

The forces community outside the United Kingdom is interesting because of the absence of the extended family—grandparents, uncles and aunts, and so forth—and the predominance of homemaker parents. Although the number of service-women who are the main wage earners and service wives who have been able to find a job has risen, in many families, the father is still the wage earner and the mother stays at home.

The research was conducted in a Service Children's Education (SCE) primary school in Germany. Six classes of years 4, 5, and 6 students (122 children in all, aged between 8 and 11 years) each used one of their regular class discussion lessons to talk with one of the researchers, who also teach at the school, about their views on the lives they lead. These sessions often focused on personal and social issues to help give students the knowledge, skills, and understanding they need to lead confident, healthy, independent lives and to become informed, active, and responsible citizens.

Most children in the school came from one close-knit Scottish regiment, and most had moved four times. A few children had moved five or six times, and one, whose father was part of a small unit and not part of the regiment, had moved seven times. The main moves were undertaken as a whole regiment and were between the United Kingdom and Cyprus, Cyprus and the United Kingdom, England and Scotland, and the United Kingdom and Germany. A small number of parents (28) were invited to an informal social after-school gathering organized by the researcher. The parents were asked the same questions as the children about their experience of moving. Two teachers were also interviewed after school to triangulate the data. The discussion section that follows shows the richness of the discussions that took place.

All names of parents, teachers, and children have been changed to preserve anonymity. Participants were informed that their comments would be used in a small-scale research project that was aimed at supporting children's learning in a mobile community. All were satisfied with this and gave their consent.

FINDINGS

This section shows the questions followed by the key findings and an informal account of the responses. The quotes included here represent issues about the move, friendships, school, the curriculum, and activities to support the transfer. Although the questions were asked at different times, by presenting the responses in this way, we can see the thoughts of parents, children, and teachers juxtaposed so that the varying perspectives become clear. The common themes are explored further in the key findings and discussion section.

Do You and Your Children Enjoy the Experience of Moving Around?

The key issues highlighted here were that moving can be stressful, that some children would prefer to stay in one place, that moving can create opportunities for developing new friends, and that although problems may follow them to the next school and teaching methods vary, the curriculum stays the same.

Andrea is the mother of a 10-year-old boy who attends a primary school in Germany close to where the family is quartered and a 14-year-old girl who is a weekly boarder at another school in Germany. Her husband is currently away on duty and will be returning soon.

> For my son the moving about has been a good thing. It's made him more sociable. He's only moved as part of a big thing—the whole regiment moving. He always knows that his mates will be there when he gets to the next place.

> My daughter is getting a bit sick of moving. She wants her own bedroom at home to come home to and I have to admit that we do chuck stuff away—stuffed toys and so on—every time we move, so there's not a lot left from when she was really little. I think she'll be glad when we get posted back to the UK. We'll be going to Scotland and staying. He [the husband] can do the next one unaccompanied.

Lucinda lives in Germany and is the mother of two boys who are in a boarding school in the United Kingdom. She has worked in an SCE school but no longer does so.

> That's one of the reasons we sent the boys off to school. They didn't like all the packing up and moving, and I do think it affects the standards in schools. I think the children miss a lot in all the packing up at one end and settling down at the next. I do think the children are less committed to a school because they know they're not going to be there for long.

Sheila lives in Germany and is the mother of a 14-year-old girl who is a weekly boarder at an SCE school in Germany. Her husband works for NATO, and the family has moved six times.

> The moving about was a nightmare for my daughter when she was little. She kept having to start different systems. It was all phonic stuff in one place and then it would be learning flashcards at another and so on. Mind you, I work in school, and I can see that the National Curriculum and all the planning that the teachers do means that the children are studying the same things wherever they are in the world. I was very concerned about her reading, but in terms of whether she was happy or not, I would say she was quite relaxed about it. She doesn't much like it now because she has discovered boys and also the friendships you make when you're a teenager are much more intense, aren't they? It's getting harder to keep saying goodbye to them.

Justin (10 years old) said, "I don't mind moving. We all stick together. I mean, you get some new ones and some people leave if their dad leaves the army—but usually we're together." Jo (10) said, "I've got a bit sick of it. Stuff gets thrown out but it's normally just baby stuff that I don't play with."
Holly (10) said,

> I get nervous when I go to a new place because we don't move like everyone else; I mean we move a lot! I get scared sometimes. When we move I stay out of the way because my mum gets in a real stress and shouts at my dad because he doesn't do anything to help.

Kate is a teacher who has taught in SCE schools in Germany and worked with forces families in various welfare roles since 1977.

I think it's remarkable how well children seem to adapt to moving about. I've met a few nervous ones, one who was genuinely school phobic but he was the son of a civilian worker and it was a whole new experience for him. I'm always amazed by how a new unit or regiment arrives and the children turn up, usually on a bus from the quartering area, check out the new place, hang their coats up and get on with it. I don't think the children are less committed to a school because they're moving. I don't think children think in those terms anyway, but I'm always impressed by how children make a school their own really quickly and develop a sense of pride in the place. I think our children are resourceful and sociable and I'm almost certain that life with the military has helped them develop that part of their character. Often I think it depends on how the parents present the move to them. Some, it has to be said it's the mothers usually, get rather stressed and I don't think that helps. It's an unbalanced community in a way as, over here, most mothers are at home—there's not a lot of work available—and the extended family, grannies and aunties and so on, are back in the UK and not around the corner.

How Far Ahead Do You or Your Children Like to Know About a Move? Is It Easier to Know at the Last Minute? If You Know a Long Time in Advance, Do You or Your Children Think About It a Lot? Does Knowing About a Move Affect How You or Your Children Think About Schoolwork?

The findings here indicate that people have varying coping strategies when they learn that they are moving. These range from shutting out the knowledge of the move until the last minute to wanting more time to say goodbye to the place and the people.

Andrea (parent) said,

> The thought of moving doesn't seem to worry my son. We never tell him more than a couple of months in advance, even if we know, but I think it's as important for him as it is for me that he has a chance to say Cheerio to people.

Sheila (parent) said,

> I dread telling her now because she gives me that look. I feel so guilty. I am wondering whether she'd be better off in a boarding school in the UK, near her granny but then I'd never see her at weekends.

The following exchange took place between Justin and Andrew in the group interview.

> Andrew (10): I don't think about it. I get told and then I put it at the back of my mind until I have to do something about it. I'm too busy in school to think about it but I suppose we talk about it on the bus and the playground, you know, like where we're going and stuff.

Justin (10): I'm leaving today. I'm not in the regiment here. I'm feeling a bit upset because I got on with people here. I've known for a few weeks. I suppose I prefer to know for a while but it has been on my mind. I don't work any differently, no really, don't laugh, Andrew. My books are going to my new school so my Mum says that they shouldn't look like a mess or they'll think I'm, you know, dumb.

Jamie (10): I didn't know we were going to Australia until just before we went. [Jamie's father took the family to Australia for a year as part of a military exchange program], but I didn't have to say goodbye really because we'd be coming back. But when we got back to the regiment, everyone here had moved. The Australian school was okay, a bit different, but everyone was friendly. I tried to keep up. In some lessons we were doing stuff that I'd already done and some stuff I'd never heard of. I'd missed a bit here when we came back but Miss X showed me what to do and I'm all right now.

Chris (9): I like to know about it at the last minute because I do think about it, you know, what the new place is going to be like and if someone is bullying you here you think will they be there again when you move.—It did happen to me at one place, not here, but his dad got chucked out of the army and he had to leave, ha ha!"

Kate (teacher) said,

I think most of them cope really well but I've known a few children who have just switched off as soon as they knew they were leaving and some, the older ones mainly, who've been really sad. We get one or two behavioral problems but they're usually the children who would react in the same way no matter what the change in their lifestyle was, you know, in the UK it would be mother's new boyfriend or something similar.

Could the School Do Anything to Help Make Moving Easier? Have You Been Anywhere That Was a Really Good Move for Some Reason? Is the Whole Business of Settling in Easier If the Next School Is an SCE School Rather Than a Civilian One?

Responses to this question indicate that seeing pictures of the next school is important, and this can be facilitated with information and communication technology (ICT); friendships and memories can ease the transfer, and information about students that is passed to the next teacher is not always recognized as relevant.

Sheila (parent) said, "Now that we've got all this ICT, computers and the Internet, the children could go on their next school's Web site and find out about it." Andrea (parent) said, "Those little movie cameras that Mr. M (ICT coordinator) has just bought would be great for putting moving images on."

George (9): We went to this brilliant school in Ireland. [Brilliant is a term for something very good.]

Chris (9): Oh yeah! That was really brilliant. It had an adventure playground and everything.—it wasn't an army school but we did all go there.

George: It was brilliant because the teachers were a bit strict but we did lots of interesting things as well. No one really cared about what your dad did or anything.—I made new friends by seeing where the footballs were kept and then I just went and got one and said, "Do you want to play?" to people.

Chris: I didn't. I just sort of watched and then someone came and kicked me and I said "don't" and then George came and said, "don't kick my friend," and then a teacher came.—When we knew we were leaving, our teacher let us all make scrapbooks—memories, you know, like pictures of places we'd been and everyone in the class signed each other's. I've still got mine.

George: I don't know where mine is. I think my mum put it in a box for moving and it got lost.

Tom (10): It would be good if the school you were leaving got information about the next school, wherever it was.

Justin (10): You could get brochures, like the one here [the School Council in this school helped to put together the school brochure], and you could do it on disk.

Tom: And you could put pictures and—

Justin: Movies, like the little ones did. [Foundation Stage children had shown their pictures using the new moving picture recorders at a recent assembly]

Jo (10): We got the one from the boarding school and that had a disc with it and it had pictures of the classrooms on it. That makes me feel better, just looking at where we're going to be.

When the teachers were asked about how the they could make the transition between schools easier for children, Kate replied,

Teachers do a lot to try to make a smooth transition. We send all the current books and the usual mountain of paperwork with all the statistics. I'm not sure people really read it all. These days they just want to know what level they are.

Do You Think Moving Around Affects the Education of Children With Special Needs?

Results here demonstrate that children with particular needs might be disadvantaged by moving, because of the lack of continuity of relationships and support staff, and children with SENs might be a disadvantage for their parent's career.

James (9): I have a lady that helps me. I like her. She lives in our road. I've always had help in every school and I like that, because I get things wrong a lot. I don't mind moving about but I think I might remember things better if I didn't.

Tally (James' learning support assistant): I haven't known James very long but I think we get along all right. James has a problem with remembering things and he has some difficulties relating to other people. His teacher suspects that he may be autistic. If he is autistic, then moving about is going to be the worst thing for him. He's all right if he knows his routine. But then, if he is diagnosed as autistic his father will be sent back to the UK and there'll be a block on him being posted and that'll mean he won't get promoted, so you can see that the parents aren't keen for us to find anything "wrong" with him.

Kate (teacher) said,

I don't know if I think that moving affects the children's education. I thought we had a disproportionate number of children with special needs until I spent a few years in schools in the UK, and now I think our children are pretty well behaved and motivated and do rather well although, in terms of all the tests we have to do they are performing below the national average in almost everything. I don't have a lot of faith in tests—any tests—for young children.

Jane (SEN teacher in an SCE primary school in Germany) said,

I don't think we have any more SEN problems than in the UK and those we do don't really have to do with the children moving, although for some children it's frustrating because you just get them started with something and they form a relationship with the helper and then one of them leaves. We do have a problem with the time it takes to put strategies in place. There's a big shortage of speech therapists, for example, and I have real problems getting Ed Psych consultations because of the pressure on the department. There's a big problem with funding. No one understands that you can't just magic up extra hours of help. But that's not to do with the children moving; it's to do with the organization of things at the top in education.

KEY FINDINGS AND DISCUSSION

Opinions about the effect of turbulence on the education of service children vary widely. Even the children themselves hold differing views, although most children in this admittedly small and informal sample who expressed views appeared fairly sanguine about their lifestyle. One teacher, Kate, appeared to think that the attitude of the parents was a contributing factor to the children's viewing movement as a positive experience.

Many of the children appeared to think that moving in the forces was a straightforward experience and because of how the services take the culture with them, this may well be so. Wherever the children go in the world, they can still buy their familiar treats and the parents can buy many of their favorite foods in the Navy, Army and Airforce Institutes (NAAFI) chain of shops. For some children, a move appears to be no more than an inconvenience. A few younger children appeared to be unhappy about moving, but more of the older children—primarily girls—were tired of the mobile lifestyle. Most followed Justin's attitude and did not mind moving because they moved with friends. However, the making and breaking of friendships is a major factor in transitions. Penn (2005) referring to Dunn's (1913) work, considered,

> Friendships can offer warmth and security, perspective taking, conflict resolution, moral understanding and a sense of self. Some young children have considerable powers of understanding, sensitivity and intimacy. Friends may quarrel more, but life with friends is more distinctive and more exciting. (p. 53)

Children are less likely to learn well and profit from school without the support of friends. In addition, how children feel about themselves in relation to their peers lays the emotional foundations for them to gain confidence for learning. Most of the children in this study had the advantage of moving with friends as the regiment usually moved as a whole, but they also took the opportunity to make new friends. However, children of attached personnel may find transfer more difficult as they usually move individually and at a different time from most of their friends, as witnessed by Jamie who found on his return that everyone had moved.

There appeared to be almost no anecdotal evidence of the children undergoing any noticeable period of disengagement or reengagement in moving, such as that outlined in Ballinger's (2000) study. This may be because the children were familiar with the process by which books and records are transferred from school to school, which gives an impression of continuity. It also may be connected with how they perceive themselves as belonging to a community that moves within a defined area: that collection of places in the world where the forces serve accompanied by their families. Jamie, whose family went to Australia for a year on an exchange program, was clear about this being an excursion. He talked about taking part in the life of the Australian school, but it was clear that he saw it as time out from the familiar system.

There was no doubt in the minds of teachers and parents that the introduction of the National Curriculum, and lately the availability of standardized planning for mathematics, English, and science, has been of benefit to the education of service children. The children know that when they transfer within the education system, the work will be familiar and that they will know how to do it. They also know that their progress is tracked and that they will take the same tests wherever they are.

A key factor that arose from this study was the finding that when children were consulted about transferring schools, they took a mature attitude to supporting others and dealing with issues. Recognizing children's competence to deal with their own lives can help adults reflect on the limitations of their understanding of children's lives (Clark & Moss, 2001). They appeared to enjoy the experience of discussing their lifestyle and sometimes became quite animated. When the children were told that their views would be considered seriously and included in a wider work examining the effect of moving on education, they were keen to extend some of the points raised by making notes for the School Council to consider, particularly about making information brochures for new students in the school. They considered it important to recognize and acknowledge the feelings of others. Involving children in making choices and decisions in factors that affect their lives helps them to recognize their rights and responsibilities. The theme that arose continually was the potential use of ICT. It was clear that the children and their parents saw themselves now as part of a global community. It has become routine for them to exchange e-mails with friends and with family they do not see often. As much of the curriculum for 7- to 11-year-olds in the United Kingdom includes the chance to use ICT skills, perhaps this might form a basis for future development.

This study indicates that a fundamental shift in the relationship between children and adults takes place if children are consulted about issues that affect them. Adults were once the assumed holders of knowledge, wisdom, and power, and children were seen as passive recipients in the transitions that they made. Today the relationship has more to do with negotiation and with children being given an increasing say in their lives. This is demonstrated by some children deciding that they would prefer to stay in one place and attend boarding school rather than continually move homes. By recognizing that others need their support, some children were able to take issues to the School Council to negotiate a better future for others.

The examples outlined in this study in which children were consulted with genuine intentions and a whole-school commitment are bringing great benefits. They help to offset the adult bias in the educational agenda and place issues such as curriculum continuity and emotional well-being much higher on the list of priorities. They also give young people a real experience of democratic processes through the School Council. Citizenship learning is developmental. It starts with children understanding themselves, leads to them understanding their role in their immediate community, and finally leads to them considering their role in society as a whole. Providing meaningful opportunities for children to make decisions that will help them settle into their new school and develop structures and processes will help them gain much-needed skills for their role as citizens.

WHAT CAN WE LEARN FROM THIS STUDY?
WHERE DO WE GO FROM HERE?

It can be seen from this study that most of the children developed resilience in dealing with change. If they had prior knowledge of the next school, moving with friends gave them the emotional foundations needed for them to gain confidence for learning and to feel in control of their lives.

It is clear that children's participation in discussions and decisions about real-life problems can encourage them to listen to one another, consider the needs of others, and begin to solve problems. However, this requires teachers and parents allowing children to take responsibility. The study raises a number of questions for future research including the following.

- How else can children be helped to make decisions about transfer to the next school?
- How can learners' differences be catered for during transfer?
- What place might ICT have in enhancing transitions?
- How can transitions help citizenship skills be developed further?

REFERENCES

Ballinger, A. (2000, July). *Psychological dimensions to transition.* Paper presented at the Wiltshire County Council Smoothing out Turbulence conference, Bradford-on-Avon, Bath, UK.

Ballinger, A. (2001, July). *Mobility: information for teachers and other staff who work with service children.* Paper presented at the Shropshire Service Schools' conference Pupil Mobility: What does it mean?/What can we do? Albrighton, UK.

Bruner, J. (1996). *The Culture of Education.* Cambridge, MA: Harvard University Press.

Chislett, M. (2001, July). *Turbulence and mobility.* Paper presented at the Shropshire Service Schools' conference Pupil Mobility: What does it mean?/What can we do? Albrighton, UK.

Clark, A., & Moss, P. (2001). *Listening to Young Children: The Mosaic Approach.* London: National Children's Bureau and Joseph Rowntree Foundation.

Davie, R., & Galloway, D. (1996). The voice of the child in education. In R. Davie & D. Galloway (Eds.), *Listening to Children in Education* (pp. 1–14). London: David Fulton.

Fabian, H. (2002a). *Children Starting School.* London: David Fulton.

Fabian, H. (2002b). Empowering children for transitions. In H. Fabian & A.-W. Dunlop (Eds.), *Transitions in the Early Years.* London: RoutledgeFalmer.

Galton, M., Gray, J., & Rudduck, J. (1999). *The Impact of School Transitions and Transfers on Pupil Progress and Attainment: Research Report RR131.* London: DfEE, HMSO.

James, A., & Prout, A. (Eds.). (1997). *Constructing and Reconstructing Childhood: Contemporary Issues in the Sociological Study of Childhood.* London: Falmer.

Mott, G. (2002). *Children on the Move: Helping High Mobility Schools and Their Pupils.* Slough, UK: National Foundation for Educational Research.

Noyes, A. (2004). Learning landscapes. *British Educational Research Journal, 30*(1), 27–41.

Office for Standards in Education (OFSTED). (2002). *Managing Pupil Mobility* (Reference No. HMI 403). Retrieved July 24, 2004 from http://www.ofsted.gov.uk/public/docs2/managingmobility.pdf

Penn, H. (2005). *Understanding Early Childhood.* Maidenhead, UK: Open University Press.

Pollock, D. C., & Van Reken, R. E. (2001). *Third Culture Kids: The Experience of Growing Up Among Worlds.* Yarmouth, ME: Intercultural Press.

Strand, S. (2002). Pupil mobility, attainment and progress during key stage 1: A study in cautious interpretation. *British Educational Research Journal, 28*(1), 63–78.

Chapter 19

The Social Adaptation and Skills of Migrant Children Attending Primary School in Turkey

Esra Ömeroğlu
Adalet Kandir
Gazi University, Turkey
Leah D. Adams
Eastern Michigan University, USA

Societal life emerged from people's need to solve their common problems together. Interactions among the people make it possible for a society to meet their economic, social, cultural, and administrative needs. Societies are dynamic constitutions and structures and change is their own most important characteristic; migration can be considered as one of the indications of societal change (Kağitçibaşi, 2003b; Yalçin, 2004). The urbanization process that started concurrently with the industrialization process can be seen clearly through the changes in a society's economic and social structure. The main reason behind migration that occurs from small town to large cities is the rising demand for the work force in the urban areas. Migration from villages to metropolitan centers can be considered as one of the requirements of industrialization, as well as a symbol of modernization process (Kağitçibaşi 2003a; Tezcan, 2000). In Turkey, rural to urban migrants are generally seen as a group of non–city dwellers, and their integration into urban society is considered to be the only way to solve the problems that arise from the migration process. It also could be said that migrants' integration into the cities are directly connected with their adaptation skills (Tezcan, 1996).

The migrant family members' social surroundings and relationships that they are accustomed to do not exist in the new place, and they lose their previous social roles. They are disengaged from the feelings of belonging, adequacy, and locus of control (Kalaycioglu & Rittersberger, 2000). The problems in the adaptation process especially affect the children's development and social adaptations (Gökçe, 1996). The social adaptation of a migrant family's children plays an important role in a family's integration into the city setting.

RESEARCH OBJECTIVES

Little is known about the families who move into large cities in Turkey and enroll their children in the public schools. Migrant children are brought face to face with a new social environment that is unfamiliar and often unaccepting of them and their families. Because the children are not capable of protecting themselves from external effects, they suffer more from the migration process. The sociocultural disadvantages that they experience after migration could permanently affect their personality development. The new problems the migration causes for the children are added to any prior problems. The feelings of insecurity, anxiety, and helplessness that the children experience play an important role in their social adaptation process, but limited research has focused on this subject of social adaptation and personality development of migrant children. This descriptive study aimed to learn of parents' and primary school teachers' opinions about social adaptation and skills of migrant children attending primary school and to consider new ways to overcome challenges to the development of healthy personality traits.

METHODS

Data were gathered by a questionnaire distributed to parents and teachers, using the survey method in accordance with the aim of the study (Sümbüloğlu & Sümbüloğlu, 1997) and working in cooperation with the Ministry of Education for permission and support to gather the data. Specialists in survey methods were consulted in the development of the questionnaire. The questionnaire consisted of two sections: demographic information about the family and information related to children's social adaptation and skills. The questionnaire had two forms. Form A gathered information about teachers' perceptions of the children's social adaptations and skills, and Form B was designed to ask parents similar questions. A pilot study was conducted to examine the reliability and validity of the questionnaire.

Data Collection

Bursa, one of the largest industrialized cities in Turkey and the recipient of many rural–urban migrants, was selected as the site for gathering data from parents and teachers of children in Grades 1, 3, and 5. Determining the number and location of primary schools to include from the Bursa city center and its districts was the first step. Because no data were available for the number of children enrolled in the schools who were rural–urban migrants, the Directorate of National Education in Bursa was asked to identify the primary schools in the districts estimated to have the highest percentage of migrant residents. The parents and teachers in those schools were informed of the study. Once the schools were identified, it was learned that the number of migrant children attending third grade and fourth grade was about equal, with a smaller number enrolled in fifth grade. The decision was made to include parents and teachers of children at fourth grade level in the data collection, along with those from Grades 1, 3, and 5 (Çingi, 1994, Table 1).

Several researchers familiar with the purpose of the study and trained in how the survey was to be conducted met with the principals in the selected schools to inform them about the study and the procedures. The sample for the parent survey consisted of those parents who volunteered to participate and the teachers of their children. Because it would be difficult for teacher to fill out the scales for all of the children because of the size of the classes, teachers filled out the scales only for the children whose parents had voluntarily agreed to complete a questionnaire. The teachers collated their own Form A for a child with the Form B that child's parents had submitted and sent them to the Directorate of National Education in Bursa as a set.

Data Analysis

A t-test was run to analyze whether there were differences between the parents' and teachers' perceptions about the migrant children's social adaptation and skills according to the frequency distribution of responses.

A Kruskal–Wallis test was run to analyze the effects such as the location from which the parents migrated, parents' age, and their education levels on the children's social adaptation and skills. Mann–Whitney test was run to determine whether the family structure, frequency of visiting the home community, level of families' perceptions of themselves as urban dwellers, or family regret about migrating affects the children's social adaptation and skills (Köklü & Büyüköztürk, 2000).

Factor Analysis of the Scale

The Rotated Principal Component Analysis (PCA) was used to examine the factorial structure of the scale of 35 items developed to study children's social adaptation and skills. Before using PCA, the data were tested for their appropriateness to

TABLE 1
The Cronbach Alpha Reliability Coefficients for the Scale
of Social Adaptation and Skills

Scale/Factor	Number of Items	Cronbach Alpha
Factor 1	16	.90
Factor 2	11	.77
Factor 3	5	.54
Total	32	.90

the factor analysis, and correlations between the items were examined. The correlation was generally around .30. Kaiser–Meyer–Olkin value was accounted for .82. The result of Barlett test was also significant ($\chi^2 = 2214, 76, p \ll .001$). These tests showed that the items on the scale were appropriate for factor analysis.

The PCA determined that the scale has three factors, with only three items loaded low on the factors. After removing those three items, PCA was used again and showed 16 items of the scale were loaded on Factor 1. The items with the highest loaded value were as follows: "Success in communication with friends," "Making friends easily," "Having empathy with others," and "Good at understanding others' feelings." Factor 1 was then labeled as *Social Adaptation and Skills.* Factor 1 explained 20.17 % of the total variance.

Of the 11 items of the scale loaded on Factor 2, the highest loaded values were "Being regretful for his/her unwanted behavior," "Taking pains to comply with the rules," and "Engaging in fights with friends." Factor 2 was therefore labeled as *Socially Anadaptation* (lacking social adaptation). Factor 2 explained 12.36% of the total variance.

Loaded on Factor 3 were "Being affected by friends who do not comply with the rules," "Prefer being alone instead of making friends," "Being shy for a long time in unknown environment," "Making friends based on their gender," "Visiting friends' homes," and "Preferring being with the same friends." It was thought that those items assess the behaviors of children who show social adaptation skills in a particular environment but do not transfer these behavioral patterns into a new environment. Thus, Factor 3 was labeled as *Limited Social Adaptation.* Factor 3 explained 7.39 % of the total variance. The three factors together explained 40% of total variance. The Cronbach alpha reliability coefficients for each factor were found as follows: Factor 1, .90; Factor 2, .77; Factor 3 .54; and for overall scale .90 (Table 2).

The internal consistency reliability analysis was run for parents' responses, and the result was approximately the same with Cronbach alpha reliability coefficients (internal consistency reliability for Factor 1, .80; for Factor 2, .77; for Factor 3, .14 and for overall scale, .86). Internal consistency reliability for the

TABLE 2
Grade Levels for Children of Parents Completing Survey

Grade	Migrants		Non-migrants		Total	
	n	%	n	%	n	%
1st	41	35,7	21	40,4	62	37,1
2nd						
3rd	36	31,3	19	36,5	55	32,9
4th	31	27	5	9,6	36	21,6
5th	7	6,1	7	13,5	14	8,4

overall scale and for Factor 1 and Factor 2 was quite high. Internal consistency reliability for Factor 3 was low in teachers' responses and significantly low in parents' responses.

RESULTS

Demographic Information About Migrant and Nonmigrant Families

Turkey's Ministry of Education was well aware of increasing rural–urban migration but did not have sufficient data about migrant children enrolled in the public schools. These survey results from the Bursa Province provided the ministry with some information about the demographics of the families newly migrated into the school district community and ways in which they are similar to or different from those of the nonmigrant families. The demographic data also enabled the researchers to consider the effect of family demographics on the social adaptation and skills of the children.

Both migrant and nonmigrant parents were asked about the size and composition of their family unit, the age of the parents, the length of marriage, the educational level of the parents, and the parental employment. It was learned that the average family size of migrant and nonmigrant families was similar (4–5 persons), but the migrant families were more likely to have an extended family unit living in the household (29.2% versus 22% for nonmigrant households). The migrant parents tended to be slightly older and to have been married for more years than the nonmigrant families, had slightly higher levels of education than the nonmigrant families, and were more somewhat more likely to be employed (Table 3).

The parents reported their perceptions of their children's performance in school. Overall, the migrant parents perceived their children as having a higher level of academic success, higher levels of participation in extracurricular activities, generally

TABLE 3

Migrant and Non-migrant Family Demographics

Variable	Group	Migrant		Non-migrant		Total	
		n	%	n	%	n	%
Mother's age	29 yrs and below	22	19.1	18	36	40	24.2
	30–34	55	47.8	22	44	77	46.7
	35 and above	38	33	10	20	48	29.1
Father's age	29 and below	12	10.5	5	10.4	17	10.5
	30–34	50	43.9	21	43.8	71	43.8
	35 and above	52	45.6	22	45.8	74	45.7
Mother's education level	Primary school and below	56	50	31	62	87	53.7
	Junior high School	23	20.5	5	10	28	17.3
	High School and above	33	29.5	14	28	47	29
Father's education level	Primary school and below	33	30.3	17	34.7	50	31.6
	Junior high School	21	19.3	12	24.5	33	20.9
	High School and above	55	50.5	20	40.8	75	47.5
Parent's working	Mother Working	52	53.6	16	34.8	68	47.6

TABLE 4
The Result of T-test for Differences of Teachers' and Parents' Perception About the
Children Social Adaptation and Skills

Scale	Group	n	$\overline{X}$	SS	sd	T	p
Factor 1	Teacher	167	40.03	5.96	166	.04	.968
	Parent		40.01	5.44			
Factor 2	Teacher	167	25.97	3.96	166	.46	.646
	Parent		25.88	3.47			
Factor 3	Teacher	167	10.28	1.80	166	.54	.585
	Parent		10.20	1.43			
Total	Teacher	167	76.29	9.60	166	.32	.747
	Parent		76.09	8.14			

more positive relationships with friends, more positive relationships with the teachers, and more satisfactory relationships with their parents than the nonmigrant families' perceptions of their children (Table 4.)

Findings About Children's Social Adaptation and Skills

There were no significant differences between the teachers' and parents' overall perceptions of the children's social adaptation and skills for the sample as a whole. However, significant differences appeared between the two groups—migrant and nonmigrant families—in terms of agreement between the teacher and parent perceptions of the children's social adaptation and skills. On both the positive social behaviors factored under Factor 1 (Social Adaptation and Skills) and the more negative behaviors showing a lack of social skills that are factored under Factor 2 (Socially Anadaptation) there were significant differences between the migrant and nonmigrant parents and the degree to which their perceptions matched those of the teacher (t parent (165) = 3.38, $p \ll .05$; t teacher (165) = 3.61, $p \ll .05$). There were no significant differences between parent and teacher perceptions on Factor 3 (Limited Social Adaptation and Skills).

The relationship between mother's age and the parents' perception of their children's social adaptation and skills was examined. A Kruskal–Wallis test determined that the mothers aged 30 to 34 reported that their children have higher, though limited, social adaptation and skills compared with the perceptions of mothers ages 35 and older (χ^2 (2) = 6.90, $p \ll .05$). In other words, the mothers aged between 30 and 34 reported that their children have higher social adaptation and skills in particular environment, but they have difficulty transferring those adaptations and skills to a new environment. A similar analysis for age of fathers did not show any significant differences between age groups. Kruskal–Wallis analysis showed no significant relationship between children's social adaptation and skills and the number of children in the family, total family size, or household composition.

Significant differences in the reported children's social adaptation and skills emerged from data analysis based on the migrant parents' level of education. In migrant families, mothers who graduated from junior high school reported that their children had higher social adaptation and skills compared with the mothers who graduated from primary school, high school or other higher educational institutions (χ^2 (2) = 15.93, $p \ll .05$). Conversely, teachers reported that the children whose mothers graduated form high school or other higher educational institutions had higher social adaptation and skills (χ^2 (2) = 11.51, $p \ll .05$). These findings are significant for both Factor 1 and 2. Regarding the differences between the teachers' and parents' perceptions of their children's social adaptation and skills, it could be claimed that the mothers who graduated from high school or other higher educational institutions have high criteria in the evaluation process of their children. However, in nonmigrant families, there was no significant relationship between the education level of mothers and the parents' perception of their children social adaptation and skills.

The relationship between the education level of the fathers and the children's social adaptation and skills in both migrant and nonmigrant families also was considered. The results showed that the education level of the fathers had a significant effect on children's social adaptation and skills, as reported in the surveys. The fathers who graduated from high school or higher educational institutions reported higher social adaptation and skills for their children compared with the fathers who had lower education levels (χ^2 (2) = 17.63, $p \ll .05$). The significance test on father's education also showed that the fathers who graduated from junior high school reported that their children have better social adaptation and skills (χ^2 (2) = 12.12, $p \ll .05$). The teachers concurred in that their ratings of social adaptations and skills were higher for migrant children whose fathers graduated from high school or higher (χ^2 (2) = 13.18, $p \ll .05$).

The data were examined for a possible link between the migration situation of the family and the social adaptation and skills of the children, including the family's reason for migrating, the frequency of visits to the home community, feelings toward migration, and the degree to which family members consider themselves city dwellers. The families were asked the reason for their migration, and the responses were grouped under two categories: "for better life conditions" and "for finding a job." According to the results of Mann–Whitney U test, the reasons behind a family's migration have an effect on children's social adaptation and skills. The teachers and parents reported that the children of the families that migrated for finding a proper job have lower social adaptation and skills.

The families visiting their home community were asked the frequency of those visits. The responses were generally "more than once in a year" or "once in a year or less than once a year." The frequency of visiting homeland had no significant effect on the children's social adaptation and skills.

To determine whether the locations from which the parents migrated had an effect on the children's social adaptation and skills, a Kruskal–Wallis test was used. The results showed that the children of families that migrated from the village had lower social adaptation and skills than the children of families that migrated from other cities or from abroad. The results were significant for both parents' and teachers' scores (χ^2 (2) = 10.50, $p \ll .05$ for parents' scores) (χ^2 (2) = 9.56, $p \ll .05$ for teachers' score).

The parents were asked whether they perceive themselves as urban dwellers; the relationship between the families' perception of themselves as urban dwellers and the children's social adaptation and skills was examined. The results of Mann–Whitney test validated that families that perceive themselves as urban dwellers reported that their children have a higher level of social adaptation and skills (U = 815.50, $p \ll .05$).

The migrant families were asked whether they feel regret for having migrated. The relationship between the level of regret and the children's social adaptation and skills was examined through Mann–Whitney test. The results showed that the children of families that have no regret for migration were evaluated as more positive by the teachers than the children of families that have regret (U = 171, $p \ll .05$) and parents (U = 179, $p \ll .05$).

Discussion

Many of the findings in this study ran counter to expectations, considering the existing awareness of the abundant challenges facing rural–urban migrant families (Tacoli, 1998). Although the data analysis failed to reveal numerous and important significant differences between the migrant and nonmigrant participants that would cry out for prompt action from authorities at all levels, there are many points that bear consideration. It is also possible to draw parallels between some of the findings and related prior research.

Howard and Hodes (2000) scanned the files of 30 migrant children and their families and 30 British children and their families who had applied to the clinic for health problems. They found that the migrant children had psychosocial problems rather than neurological problems. The majority of migrant parents in this study reported that most of their children were doing well in school and that the majority were following rules and participating in extracurricular activities. Although this is basically consistent with the teacher's perceptions, it still indicates that there may be underlying social adaptation issues that deserve attention for the overall ongoing development of the child and were not uncovered in this survey process.

The results of the current study show that the immigrant mothers who aged between 30 and 34 years reported that their children have higher social adaptation and skills. This result is similar to the age range of mothers in a study by Coll and his colleagues (2002) in which 85% of the mothers were around 30 years of age. In that study, it was found that the immigrant families with children attending second and fifth grade showed lower interest in their children, which affects the children's social adaptation and skills. The sample for this study consisted of parents who voluntarily completed a survey. It is possible, of course, that the more confident parents and those of the more socially adept children are the parents who elected to participate. However, it also could be possible that the parents were not keenly aware of details of their child's behavior or that migrant children are adaptive and may not have lingering and obvious psychosocial issues.

This may be particularly true if, as found in this study, the family is comfortable with the migration and has adapted to the point of thinking of themselves as urban dwellers. The social adaptation and skills of migrant children need to be studied further, with special attention on the contrasting or similar view of parents and teachers on what is socially accepted behavior and whether the inevitable changes in a migrant child's life affects his or her social adaptation.

Kolaitis and his colleagues (2003) conducted a study with the families who had migrated from Greece to former Soviet Union and then remigrated to Greece at the beginning of 1980s. They examined that social adaptation and academic skills of the immigrant families' children ages 8 to 12 years using a sample of 65 immigrant families and 41 local families. The immigrant families lived in the suburb area of Athens where generally the high socioeconomic level families settled. The teachers reported that immigrant children were more anxious and inattentive compared with the children of local families. The immigrant families also reported that their children had immature behavior.

The results of the current study showed that the rural–urban migrant parents who graduated from high school or college had higher criteria to evaluate their children's social adaptation and skills; this result is consistent with the results of the Kolaitis and his colleagues. It also should be noted that the parents of this rural–urban migrant sample were employed at a higher rate than the nonimmigrant parents (Table 3), which might make for a less stressful situation in the home than for some of the nonimmigrant families living in the same school attendance area.

The teachers in this sample perceived the children of those families that had migrated to find work, those who had some regret about migration, and those who did not consider themselves as city dwellers to rate lower on social adaptation and skills than the children from other migrant families. Sir, Bayram, and Özkan (1998) conducted interviews with 100 families that had migrated into Diyarbakir. The researchers utilized the posttraumatic stress disorder scale developed by Blake et al (1990), and found that 66% of the migrant group had suffered from posttraumatic stress disorder. The current study did not specifically investigate the possibility of such a problem. However, that does not mean that the issue was not there, only that it did not come to the surface with these data. In addition, the voluntary participation of both migrant and nonmigrant families may have skewed the sample membership toward those who were more resilient and who had made a more satisfactory acculturation than some other migrants. At the same time, the results of this study support the notion that the differences between the perception of migrant children's social adaptation and skills compared with the perception of nonmigrant children's social adaptation and skills may be unfairly seen in terms of social factors, rather than in the actual competencies displayed in school.

In his study about the women who migrate from rural areas to urban for economic reasons, Erman (1997) concluded that the women who migrated to urban areas wanted their children to live in the cities. The women have a chance to live as a nuclear family in the city, which enhances their independence. The women also could support their children's social adaptation and skills.

Conversely, in his study about the families that migrated from Chile to the United States, Eastmond (1993, cited in İkkaraca & İkkaraca, 1998) reported that the life standards of immigrant women decreased dramatically after migration. Living in the nuclear family caused the women to be isolated from public life and affected their social adaptation. İkkaraca and İkkaraca (1998) showed that 54.5 % of the immigrant women reported that they would want to migrate to big city (İtanbul) if they have any choice. They explained that living in a big city provided them social opportunities. This study did not explore such details of the migrant mothers' situation, but the overall ratings of the mothers for their children's social adaptation and skills—as well as the positive relationships with the school, the teacher, and the parents—suggest that many migrants can, and do, make a satisfactory transition to urban living.

This study revealed that the families migrated to reach "better life conditions" in new settings (mean rank was 52.15 for teacher and 51.36 for parents). This result is consistent with the results of the study by İkkaraca and İkkaraca (1998) in which they asked the reasons of the migration for women (aged between 15 and 64 years old) who had migrated from the east part ($N = 599$) and west part ($N = 530$) of Turkey. The results showed that the main reason for migration was economic factors. Economic stability in the home situation can help a child to feel confident and to be able to learn in school, and the families in this study had high levels of employment (92.3% of the fathers and 53.6% of the mothers employed). The limited reports of frequent visits to the home community also hint at a stable migratory experience for the families in this study.

In a major study considering emotional and behavioral problems in migrant children, Diler, Avci, and Seydaoglu (2003) concluded that there were significantly more emotional (e.g., depression, anxiety, self-esteem) problems but not behavioral problems in Turkish migrant children than in Turkish nonmigrant children. They also found increased problems in migrant children with a longer duration of residence after migration and suggested that migrant children appeared to experience a greater degree of social hardship than did their nonmigrant peers. However, both the Diler et al. study and this study relied on survey data rather than in-depth interviews or other data collection approaches. The current study did not attempt to differentiate between short- and long-term migrant residents, but the lack of significant difference in reported behavior problems is consistent with our findings from the teachers or parents as to maladjustment of the migrant children.

An overview of the literature suggests that adaptation problems arise after rural-to-urban migration (Diler et al., 2003; Kağitçibaşi, 1987; Tacoli, 1998). It was not easy to provide proper life conditions in new settings and to become city dwellers. Urbanization is a process that dramatically changes people's behavior, relationships with others, morality, and family life. (Keleş, 1983). At the same time, the results of this study support the notion that some negative perceptions of differences between migrant children's social adaptation and skills compared with the perception of nonmigrant children's social adaptation and skills may be unfairly seen in terms of social factors rather than in the actual competencies the migrant children display in school.

Implications

The main objectives of this study were to gather information for the National Ministry of Education about migrant families with children in school and to gain knowledge of teachers' and parents' opinions about social adaptation and skills of the migrant children who are attending first, third, fourth and fifth grade. Rural–urban migration in Turkey is not likely to come to a halt, and urban areas will continue to need to absorb migrants. The migrants arriving in the large cities will continue to face challenges as they attempt to acculturate to the realities of urban life. At the very highest level of state policy, those facts suggest that the government should consider trying to lessen some of the forces behind rural–urban migration, such as lack of employment or economic opportunity in the rural regions, to make it feasible for families to avoid rural–urban migration in search of work and a better way of life. Industrialized cities with large numbers of rural migrants continuing to flow in could arrange for public programs that aim to help adults, youths, and children with their social and cultural adaptation. Further, vocational training courses for migrant adults and youths should be explored to assist the families with acquiring employment that will meet the family needs in the urban setting.

The Ministry of Education could initiate research projects in large cities to determine the educational needs of migrant children. Activities could be arranged for families and their children to help them with overcoming difficulties related to urban social adaptation. Previous studies about immigration generally focused on the reasons for migration and its effects on migrant adults. However, it is apparent that more research is needed about the effects of migration on the children, their development, and education.

In-service training for teachers is needed to help them become more aware of the social adaptation need of migrant children and families. The training should focus on the problems that the migrant families and their children experience related to acculturation to urban life, as well as teaching strategies for working with migrant children in the schools.

The information gathered in this study is only a beginning step toward identifying the educational needs of Turkey's rural-to-urban migrant children. There is a need for additional data on the many factors that affect migrant families and their adaptation to the urban setting. There is a need to identify the stressors in migrant family households and the role of the schools in making the education of the child as successful as possible. The adaptation of migrant families is of importance to the schools to ensure parental involvement and support for the child's education and to maximize home-school communication. As long as the rural–urban flow continues, it is imperative that all concerned with the education of children from the Ministry of Education down to the classroom teachers, work together to make high-quality education available to all migrant children.

REFERENCES

Blake, D. D., Weathers, F. W., & Nagy, L. M. ve Ark. (1990). A Clinician Rating Scale for Assessing Current and Lifetime PTSD. The CAPS-I. *Behaviour Therapist, 13,* 187–188.

Çingi, H. (1994). *Sampling Theory.* Beytepe, Ankara, Turkey: Hacettepe University Arts and Science School Publication.

Coll, C. G., Akiba, D., Palacios, N., Bailey, B., Silver, R., Dimartino, L. & Chin, C. (2002). Parental involvement in children's education: Lessons from three immigrant groups. *Parenting: Science and Practice, 2*(3), 303–304.

Diler, R. S., Aci, A., & Seydaoglu, G. (2003). Emotional and behavioural problems in migrant children. *Swiss Medical Weekly, 133,* 16–21. Retrieved October 17, 2005 from http://www.smw.ch

Erman, T. (1997). The Meaning of City Living for Rural Migrant Women and Their Role in Migration: The Case of Turkey. *Women's Studies International Forum, 20*(2), 263–273.

Gökçe, B. (1996). Göç ve metodolojik tart:Mmalar (Discussion about migration and methodology). II. Ulusal Sosyoloji Kongresi (Toplum ve Göç) (2nd National Congress of Sociology: The Society and Migration) T. C. Devlet 9statistik Enstitüsü, Mersin, Turkey.

Howard, M. & Hodes, M. (2000). Psychopathology, adversity, and service utilization of young refugees. *Journal of the American Academy of Child and Adolescent Psychiatry, 39*(3), 368–377.

İkkaraca, P. & İkkaraca, 9. (1998). *1990'lar Türkiye'sinde Kadin ve Göç (Turkish Women and Migration in the Era of 1990's)* Tarih Vakf: Yayinlar:, İstanbul: Bilanço 98: 75 Y:lda Köylerden Lehirlere, 305–322.

Kağitçibaşi, Ç. (1987). Alienation of the outsider: the plight of migrants. *International Migration, 25* (2), 195–210.

Kağitçibaşi, Ç. (2003a). *Kültürel Psikoloji.* (*Books on Social Psychology, 2*) 9stanbul, Turkey: Sosyal Psikoloji Dizisi 2, Evrim Publication.

Kağitçibaşi, Ç. (2003b). *Yeni 9nsan ve 9nsanlar.* (*Books on Social Psychology, 1*) 9stanbul, Turkey: Sosyal Psikoloji Dizisi 1, Evrim Publication.

Kalaycioglu, S., & Rittersberger-Tiliç, H. (2000). Intergenerational solidarity networks of instrumental and cultural transfers within migrant families in Turkey. *Ageing & Society, 20,* 523–542.

Keleş, R. (1983). *Türkiye'de Sehirlesme, Konut ve Gecekondu (Urbanization, Dwelling, and Gecekondu).* Ankara, Turkey: Gerçek Publications.

Köklü, N. & Büyüköztürk, S. (2000). *Sosyal Bilimler 9çin 9statistige GiriM (Introduction to Statistics for Social Sciences).* Ankara, Turkey: Pegem Publication.

Kolaitis, G., Tsiantis, J., Madianos, M., & Kotsopoulos, S. (2003). Psychosocial Adaptation of Immigrant Greek Children from The Former Soviet Union. *European Child and Adolescent Psychiatry, 12,* 67–74.

Sir, A., Bayram, Y., & Özkan, M. (1998). Zorunlu Iç Göç Yasamis Bir Grupta Travma Sonrasi Stres Bozuklugu Üzerine Ön Çalisma. *Türk Psikiyatri Dergisi (Journal of Turkish Psychiatry), 9,* 173–180.

Sümbüloğlu, K., & Sümbüloğlu, V. (1997). *Biyoistatistik.* Ankara, Turkey: Hatiboglu Publication.

Tacoli, C. (1998). Rural–Urban Interactions: A Guide to the Literature. *Environment and Urbanization, 10*(1), 147–166.

Tezcan, M. (1996). Göç ve Egitim (Migration and Education) II. Ulusal Sosyoloji Kongresi (Toplum ve Göç) (2nd National Congress of Sociology-The Society and Migration) T.C. Devlet Istatistik Enstitüsü, Mersin, Turkey.

Tezcan, M. (2000). *Dis Göç ve Egitim (Migration to Abroad and Education).* Ankara, Turkey: Ani Publication.

Yalçin, C. (2004). *Göç Sosyolojisi (Sociology of Migration).* Ankara, Turkey: Ani Publication.

Chapter 20

Community-Based Education for Children of Migrant Peasant Workers

Zhang Yan and Wei-Xiao Bing
Beijing Normal University, China

A large-scale movement of unskilled workers from rural to urban areas across China has created some urgent and unavoidable social problems. One such problem is the lack of accessibility to education for the young children of low-income peasant workers who have migrated to the cities. Recognizing this urgent situation, a playgroup was set up in a market area where there were many peasant workers with young children who had recently arrived from rural areas. The goals of the pilot playgroup project were to (a) explore ways that an educational setting for the preschool children of peasant vendors might be provided in the market and (b) to see if the playgroup program might serve as a worthy model that could be used elsewhere. If so, such playgroup efforts could help address the need to further early childhood education in the heavily populated cities of mainland China.

Background of the Study

As China becomes more urbanized, increasing numbers of peasants move from the countryside to work in cities. Currently 140 million peasant workers now work in cities in China, and it is estimated that this number will continue to grow.

The migrants are not granted "urban citizenship" and are treated as "outsiders" (Fan, 2002). Providing education for their children has thus emerged as a challenge for society. For example, rural migrants in Beijing number 4.09 million and represent one third of the population (Zhang & Zhao, 2003). Some studies have shown that migrant peasants moving to cities with their families often have young preschool children in their households (Zhou, 2004). Official statistics for Beijing report that the population of migrant children eligible for compulsory education at close to 240,000, but the actual number of migrant children of preschool age may be more than 300,000 (Wang, Zhou, & Zhi, 2004).

An analysis of the occupations of peasant workers revealed that almost all work long hours under poor working conditions and are poorly paid. They work in jobs that city residents would rarely choose, such as construction workers, sanitation workers, or vegetable peddlers. Approximately 40.7% are peddlers in agricultural markets (Han, 2002). Because the parents must work long hours and have no means for finding nonworking adults to look after their children, the preschool-aged children grow up with little supervision. Many children of peasant workers do not participate in public education, partly because they do not speak Mandarin Chinese, the language used in the Beijing schools. In each of the 1,241 small-scale agricultural markets in Beijing, often 10 or more preschool children wander aimlessly about (Luo-ailin, 2004). Their parents, busy earning their meager wages, have little time to care for the children. The children, therefore, become vulnerable to unexpected dangers like accidental injury or childnapping.

Although their work is essential to city life, it is as if peasant workers are living on an island separated from and rejected by city society (Fan, 2002.) In recent years, as the central government has paid more attention to agriculture, rural areas, and peasants, the migrant population has begun to be seen as a problem of society as a whole. Education authorities at all levels are implementing policies to address the education for migrant children. For example, the school entrance fee that some local governments formerly levied for parents who were not registered as permanent residents has been cancelled. Education authorities have pointed out emphatically that local government must shoulder the main responsibility for providing education for migrant children. However, until recently, the government had no accurate statistics on the population of migrant children, and educational provisions for them remain weak. The government is a long way from taking such problems seriously. Because of their separation from city society and the hardship of their lives, few migrant parents show an awareness of their preschool children's educational needs.

THE PILOT SURVEY

Nonformal education in early years has been taken into great consideration by many other counties, including developed countries and developing countries.

For example, the Sure Start approach in the United Kingdom (2005) is taking the form of nonformal community education to offer a variety of programs, including early education, child care, health, and family support for people across the country and particularly people with disadvantaged young children (Sure Start, 2005), whereas middle class parents use playgroups to meet their individual family needs (e.g., nursing). Thailand and India have provided help for disadvantaged groups by means of nonformal education, as well. Since the last decade of the 20th century, some rural regions in China have provided nonformal early childhood education for local children, such as child activity station, family support station, and moving caravan in grassland (Liang-zhishen, 1992).

Peasant workers in the city usually live together in the same area, for instance, the boundary between city and country or the neighborhood near agricultural goods markets. Therefore, the community they live in could serve as a platform for early childhood education. Research both in China and elsewhere indicates that when the community is the platform for early childhood education, the community may provide rich resources in terms of human capital and supportive interest. It was decided that the pilot study would investigate whether the community could be interested in and supportive of nonformal community-based education for their young children. A playgroup as a kind of nonformal education has its own characteristics and values. Because community education is tied to the area it serves, the supply of and demand for education are closely linked and can be developed efficiently and appropriately. Nonformal education is established according to the local environment and conditions and can offer high benefits at a low cost. Nonformal education is also open, close to the community, and invites the participation of the community.

Drawing on the perspectives mentioned here, we can see that community as the platform of early childhood education is rich in educational resources. To solve the problem of migrant children's education in a practical and realistical manner requires appropriate forms and approaches. The pilot survey was established to answer the following: Can we provide a kind of early childhood education in the form of nonformal community education?

We selected Beijing Si Huan market as our pilot survey subject. Through interviews (see appendix I, Research Protocol), we tried to determine the educational needs of migrant children around Si Huan and find some ways to, provide a community-based program that was both practical and realistic. From the beginning we were aware that we had limited resources with which to implement a program. However, we had a firm commitment to help the peasant workers and their children in the Si Huan area with integrating into urban living. We were committed to helping both parents and their children shake off their isolated status and become a part of the city life. For the sake of healthy development of Si Huan children we wanted to build a strong and friendly community. Activities of Si Huan play group promote the self-improvement of parents and children but it's not enough. Starting from the beginning, we wanted go on to build a strong market community that could be self sustaining. The syrvey was to identify the needs and ways in which we could take the first steps toward those goals. At the same time, we would be providing a place in which students who plan to become teachers could gain from onsite experiences and increase their ability to work effectively with families. The project would provide students with personal experience in helping parents find ways to educate their children within their own community and at the same time assist with their integration into urban living.

FINDINGS OF THE SURVEY

Si Huan market is near the old city zone De Sheng Men. It is a large integrated market where more than 500 peddlers' stands are operated by peasant workers, most of whom have worked here for more than 3 years. Of the approximately 60–70 preschool children of these workers, few attend kindergarten and more than 80% do not attend school. They saunter through the market all day or remain in the booth with their parents. For the parents, making a living is the most important thing in their lives. They do not consider preschool education to be essential for their children, nor can they afford it. Survey results showed that most peddlers hoped their children could receive some kind of education and some expressed willingness to join in educational activities as volunteers. The survey indicated that although this floating population does not see early childhood education as a pressing need, the parents hope that their children will receive appropriate education. To this end, we attempted to set up a nonformal playgroup.

The Si Huan Playgroup: Nonformal Community Education

The research design applied in the study was community-based participatory action research (Stringer, 1999). Research methods used were a needs assessment survey, interviews, and participant observation.

After considerable effort on our part, the idea of using a small courtyard for a playgroup eventually gained the support of the local market management. Undergraduate and graduate students volunteered to come to the market for 2 h every day and organized games and other educational activities for the children. The Si Huan playgroup had taken its first step. Although we lacked materials, human resources, and especially experience, volunteers were enthusiastic. The volunteers tried their best to find appropriate ways to meet the educational needs of the children and did not believe that as researchers they should simply stand by. Rather, a researcher should be immersed in the social reality and explore how to improve the situation. With their work and activities, our volunteers earned the trust of the parents, and increasing numbers of children and parents joined in the activities provided.

Reflective Thinking and Adjusting Research Action. Out thinking became clear during practice. The Si Huan playgroup was intended to provide a center where young children could play, where parents could share experiences and help one another, and where young volunteers could contribute to society and carry out some action research. To ensure the smooth operation and improvement of the playgroup, we quickly learned that rules needed to be established. For example, regulations for volunteers, a handbook for parents, rules for children's behavior, and so forth were needed. We called the gathering a playgroup because we wished to emphasize play as the main activity for children and to show that nonformal education can be implemented by parents. We set our criteria of playgroup as follows:

- A happy place for children to play and grow
- A place for parents to learn, share, and help each other
- A base where volunteers could turn theory into practice

Because situations in any country vary, our playgroup has its own special characteristics and philosophy. We established a research approach to provide supportive help to the parents with child care. We hoped to stimulate and enhance the content knowledge and child care ability of parents. We want to develop early childhood education from the bottom up within the community, so it could flourish without outside leadership. The emblem we designed for the playgroup consists of a bud inside four circles, indicating that it is a local community that provides education for children and where volunteers, parents, and the community (e.g., local residents, council) cooperate.

Participation and Training of Parents. As nonformal education, a mission of the playgroup is to find educational means appropriate for this special group of children by organizing games and other educational activities for them. At the same time, we try to build a strong relationship between volunteers and parents; this is more important and more difficult. By attracting parents to join in, to promote the activity, and take part in related training, we can help them in several ways. The parents can gain more confidence in child care, enhance their knowledge about child development, and increase their skills for teaching and interacting with their children. The final objective is to help the parents to become the educational power of the Si Huan playgroup and assume the leadership. In this way, we hope to encourage all parents to join the activity and form an interdependent child-care group that can be self-determining and self-managed.

When organizing educational activities, we use varying means to promote playgroups and to direct parents' educational ideas and practice. We use means such as providing on-site consultation, training participants, delivering child development information sheets, telling the parents about sound child rearing practices, lending books, talking with parents, holding parents' meetings, exchanging experiences of educating children, and so forth. We also established a parents' leadership group and sought appropriate parents as leaders.

Support From Different Agencies

The Si Huan playgroup emerged from recognition of an unmet need and was built from almost nothing. After a few months, it gained the support of the local community, society, and other sectors. There have been many volunteers: undergraduate students, graduate students, kindergarten teachers (in service and retired), and so forth. More than 60 people are active in the project, and a retired kindergarten teacher who lives nearby comes every day. Her frequent presence helps to provide stability to the program. The volunteer team has grown continually.

The Si Huan playgroup continues to gain support from various providers of materials. Some kindergartens have sent toys, and neighbors and workers have donated used toys and books. To persuade parents to make use of whatever is at hand and embrace the slogan that "educational resources never run out in the explorative eye," we make good use of second hand and handmade toys. After 7 weeks the market management was so impressed by our project that they cleared a storeroom for the playgroup. The volunteers were applauded and encouraged, and it was noted that the children were benefiting. The local industrial and commercial regulation office also donated some tables and chairs. Since that time, the Si Huan playgroup has had its own classroom and outdoor space.

The acquisition of a designated space for the playgroup has increased the number of people joining the group. Besides graduates, undergraduates, kindergarten teachers, and retired teachers, early childhood education professionals from Taiwan and Japan have come to visit and observe. The attention and participation by outside educational community increases the pool of volunteers. The general support and positive responses to what we are doing gives all volunteers confidence that they are doing something worthwhile.

Gains of the Si Huan Playgroup

It has been more than 1 year since the Si Huan playgroup was founded. During this time, the playgroup has provided 2 h of educational activities every day, and our hard work has borne fruit. The results are based on the careful observations and reports from the student volunteers and others involved in the day-to-day operation of the playgroup.

Observed Changes in Children.   After joining in the playgroup activities, the children became cleaner, happier, and more polite. They seldom fought and became friendlier with one another. They learned how to express themselves better. They also quickly learned Mandarin Chinese, the language of instruction in the Beijing schools, and now can speak it fluently.

Yang-Chen Jie was a child from He Nan province who did not speak Mandarin but a local dialect. His mother accompanied him in our activities. Because of the language barrier, Yang-Chen was shy and self-conscious and dared not take part in any activity in spite of his mother's encouragement. One month latter, although he still did not take part in activities alone, he became more confident and willing to play with other children.

When XuQi-teng first took part in the playgroup, she did not pay much attention to the other children and was listless. Her attitude changed as a result of the teachers' supportive help and the interesting activities available in the playgroup. Now when XuQi-teng comes into the room she says "Hello" to the teacher without her mother reminding her to do so.

Last summer, some of the children's brothers and sisters came to Beijing and joined us. Licao-huimin, sister of Licao-huikai, an 11-year-old in Grade 2, and other older children became capable assistants in the playgroup.

Approximately 60 children benefited from our work and continue to show further positive changes. For example, Liuv-zhihai was aggressive at first, often fighting with others, and was rejected by his peers. After taking part in the playgroup for some time, he learned how to express himself properly through friendly words and actions, and his peer relationships gradually improved.

Observed Benefits for Parents.   Parents have begun to understand and accept the Si Huan playgroup, and increasing numbers of parents now wish to join. Many came to realize that play is a form of education, and they understood more about childhood learning and how to support it. By participating in the playgroup, many children participate in activities and learn games and songs. They go home and tell about what they have learned. Their families are glad to know that their children learn through play. Some help their children to review what the teacher taught them in playgroup. Li-xiaolong's father said,

> I've been in Beijing for more than 10 years. Thank you for coming here to organize these activities for our children. They are growing up day by day and need to have some education, but there are few cheap kindergartens nearby, and we parents have to stay here to make a living. We could not pay too much attention on our kids' education. We hope the Si Huan playgroup can last all the time.

Every day, many parents joined in and helped with the educational activities. More than 50 have taken part in the parents' meeting. Some active parents came forward and joined the Si Han playgroup to organize activities in the afternoons. Parents were invited by the teachers to learn how to play games with the children, how to teach them to play ball, how to help them to color pictures and so forth.

By participating in such activities, the parents' confidence in their child-care abilities grew.

During the last national holiday and 2 weeks before the Chinese Spring Festival this year, it was the turn of the "mom–teachers" to come to the Si Huan playgroup to organize activities for the children. Xu-xiaoxiao's grandmother was one of our mom–teachers, and she had plenty of experience of folk paper-cutting, so she taught the children how to make simple paper cuts-outs. Dear Grandma, as we called her, sent us a beautiful paper-cut rooster as a gift.

The parents' participation extended our volunteer team for working with the children. Some volunteer organizations, such as Son of Peasants from Beijing Normal University, also joined us. Recently through our activities, we tried to spread the word about what we are doing. We want to convey the idea to others to "build a playgroup and a civilized market together." The effort has attracted much attention and support, and we hope that many other playgroups will emerge in other locations.

DISCUSSION

Early childhood education for preschool children should be provided in multiple forms to meet various educational needs of children. Early childhood education should not be limited to one form of formal kindergarten or preschool education but should be organized according to varying standards to provide choices. The Si Huan playgroup is a pilot project to provide one form of early childhood education as an option to fill the needs of peasant workers' children apart from formal education. For China to carry out systematic development in the field of education, it is important to emphasize the humanistic, diverse, balanced, and sustained development of education. In fact, when the Chinese ministry of education promulgated its *Implement Opinions About Development of National Early Childhood Education During the Ninth Five-Year Plan* in 1997, it pointed out that "the development orientation of early childhood education should be in the form of relying on the community, adapting to the local economy and social development, including formal and non-formal ones." This is to provide early childhood education at lower cost and higher efficiency, to protect every child's right to education and to realize educational equality, and to emphasize full use of the abundant educational resources available because of the resource shortage of the whole country. Because great potential educational power and enthusiasm exist in the community, it is feasible to develop educational services appropriate to local needs from the bottom up.

What Is Quality Early Childhood Education for Young Migrant Children?

The months of practice of operating the Si Huan playgroup verify that what is appropriate can provide a high-quality experience for children. First, high-quality early childhood education should be appropriate to young children's developmental needs. The educational activities in the Si Huan playgroup have an explicit focus, especially on *learning to be,* which is mainly based on play, so young children are learning happily. The open and informal features of the Si Huan playgroup engaged parents in learning with their children in the same process. The educational concepts and child-care habits of parents appear to be changing as a result of their participation in the playgroup. We observed that some former inappropriate bad habits of parents are being corrected. Nonformal education "both facing children and parents and developing synchronously, can radically improve the growing environment of the child" (Tang, 1996, p. 10).

Second, early childhood education should be appropriate to the needs and real situation of the local people. As nonformal education, the Si Huan playgroup was set up according to the status of the market, and it is appropriate for the characteristics of peasant workers and their special needs. The activities it provides are now extended from 2 h every morning to 2 h each morning and afternoon, which parents welcomed and better satisfies their needs. The Si Huan playgroup is committed to exploring the provision of education with low investment and high benefit to ensure the education rights of children of migrant workers. "Exploring kinds of non-formal education forms … and making good use of any kind of education resources in community, provides more chances for children receiving early childhood education" (Zhang, 1997, p. 301). All our current activities are free of charge, and in the first year of operation, investment has been limited. Implementation of a playgroup depends on finding and organizing available educational resources in the community. In addition to volunteer resources, we make good use of community resources, parents, used materials, and folk nursery resources. For example, as we follow the seasons, we teach the children to recognize various vegetables and commodities and to learn our country's customs. Although Si Huan market is noisy, it is near the beautiful western lake country, so we take the children there on regular monthly field trips.

The success of the Si Huan playgroup shows that high-quality education does have to be costly and that enhancing the lives of children takes little investment.

Coordination of the Development of Early Childhood Education, the Community Building, and Social Development

Since implementation of the open policy 20 years ago, political and economic developments in our society have challenged the traditional binary city–countryside structure. The Si Huan playgroup effort has tried to integrate city residents and peasant workers, operating with the belief that early childhood education in a community can be of mutual benefit to the education system and to society. In addition, it fosters unity in both human and social development (Zhang, 1997). The problem of the providing high-quality education for the children of migrant workers needs more attention. We need to help peasant workers and their children to avoid isolation and to participate in city life. For the healthy development of Si Huan children, we must build a strong and friendly community. The activities of the Si Huan playgroup not only promote self-improvement among parents but also help the work of the market management. After talking with people from the market management office and the community committee, we agreed to build the playgroup and to try to build a civilized market.

REFLECTIONS AND FUTURE DIRECTIONS

Value of Nonformal Education and the Future Direction of the Si Huan Playgroup

Unlike kindergarten, the Si Huan playgroup as nonformal education has unique features and value. The main features are appropriateness to local conditions, openness, flexibility, relevance, and involvement of various resources. Nonformal early childhood education is indispensable in its provision of diverse choices and satisfaction of varying social needs.

Expected Results and Future Direction of the Si Huan Playgroup

The playgroup was started when researchers went to the site to establish the preliminary demonstration and facilitation model. Researchers and parents worked together, then parents became interested in autonomy. The researchers helped them understand their need to develop social partnerships to enable them to solve the educational problems of their children and to strive for local support to protect their rights. As residents of the Si Huan community, parents are not only beneficiaries but also supervisors and main actors in community education. As children's first teachers, parents' knowledge of their role and duty in their children's learning could be awakened only through participation in the educational activities. They could become the real actors in education only through this, which would have long-term positive effects on the development of young children. In this process, parents also could improve their own education and gradually be accepted into city life. This is one purpose of lifelong learning and building a learning community. Thus, it can be seen that the value of nonformal community education goes beyond the education itself.

Although the Si Huan playgroup has achieved a great deal, difficult tasks remain. First, the quality of the educational activities offered to the children needs improvement. Second, we need to improve communication with parents and help them to organize themselves and to assume leadership, which is the focus of our future efforts. In addition, the Si Huan playgroup has shown us the need to pay more attention to studying the characteristics of children of migrant workers and how appropriately to reach them and meet their educational needs. There is a need to further refine the curriculum and make use of rural culture toys and materials. The management of the playgroup needs to coordinate with community organizations for formal and nonformal education and with policymakers who have and effect on the education of migrant children. We see a need to seek amendments to policies at the city level.

Through our action and research, we hope to promote playgroups as a kind of nonformal community education to make education accessible to more migrant children. At the same time, we wish to advance reform in early childhood education programs and management systems in cities in China

REFERENCES

China Preschool Education Research Association. (1999). Implementation opinions about the Development of National Early Childhood Education during the Nineth Five-year Plan. *Important Document Collection of People's Republic of China's Early Childhood Education.* Beijing, China: Beijing Normal University Press.

Fan, C. C. (2002). The Elite, the Natives, and the Outsiders: Migration and Labor Market Segmentation in Urban China. *Annals of the Association of American Geographers, 92*, 103–124.

Han, J. (Ed.). (2002). *Matters Concerning Education of Children of Migrant Population.* Beijing, China: Forum of Party Cadre in China.

Han-jialing. (Eds.) (2002). *Matters Concerning Education of Children of Migrant Population.* Beijing, China: Forum of Party Cadre in China.

Liang-zhishen. (1992). *The Flourishing Development of Community Early Childhood Education in China.* Beijing, China: Beijing Normal University Press.

Luo-ailin. (2004, April 1). How long will the Fairyland for vegetable peddlers' kids last? *Early Childhood Education Weekly.*

Stringer, E. T. (1999). *Action Research* (2nd ed.). Thousand Oaks, CA: Sage.

Sure Start. (2005). *Welcome to sure start.* Retrieved May 19, 2005, from http://www.surestart.gov.uk/

Tang, S. (1996). Many kinds of nursery ways to adapt to different needs. *Early Childhood Education, 10*, 23–24.

Wang, D., Zhou, L., & Zhi, P. (Eds.). (2004). *Basic Education for the Children of Rural–Urban Migrant Workers: Policies and Innovations* (UNESCO-sponsored publication). Zhejiang, China: Zhejiang University Press.

Zhang, Y. (1997). *Management of Kindergarten.* Beijing, China: Normal University Press.

Zhang, Y. (Ed.). (2002). *Report on the Investigation of the Management System Reform of Kindergartens in Beijing.* Unpublished manuscript. Beijing, China: School of Education, Beijing Normal University.

Zhang, Y.(2004a). The development of private early childhood education in the mainland of China. In Chen (Ed.) *Private Early Childhood Education in the Mainland of China and Taiwan* (pp. 345–357).Taibei, China: Wunan Book Co.

Zhang, Y. (2004b). Problems and solutions of community early childhood education in the Mainland of China, *Preschool Education, 6*, 38–39.

Zhang, L., & Zhao, S. (2003). *Let Us Share Sunshine Together—The Report of Migrant Children in Nine Cities of China.* Beijing, China: Renmin Education Press.

Zhou, Y. (Ed.). (2004). *Observation: One Hundred of Poor Migrant Peasant Families.* Beijing, China: China Youth Press.

APPENDIX I

Research Protocol of Migrant Workers' Education Needs in Si Huan (March 2004)

Information About Parents

How old are you and your wife/husband?
What's the educational level of you and your wife/husband?
Do you and your wife/husband both work in the market? How long have you been in Beijing?
Do you live nearby? Is it a fixed housing?
Would you mind telling us the monthly income of your family? How much of it do you spend on your kids, and spend on what usually?

Information About Child and His/Her Education

Does your kid live with you? Do you have just one kid? If not, please introduce some thing about your children.
The sex of your kid and his/her age.
How about your kid's health? Does he/she join in the immunity web of community? How do you get information about this?
Do you agree that children should receive some education? Why?
Do you send your kid to kindergarten? If not, why? Who takes care of the kid usually?
(If parents send their kid to kindergarten, go on to ask these questions: which kindergarten does your kid go to? How much does it cost every month? Do you need to pay the extra fees? Did you hear of a statute issue for enforcement this year banning asking for extra payment to the migrant worker, when their children go to school to receive education? Who takes care of your kid during weekends?)
How do you solve the snack and meal problems about your kid? Can this bite and sup ensure his/her nutrition or not? Is the bite and sup hygienic enough? How do you solve the problem of his/her noon break? Does your kid stay along with you all day? Does he/she have time going out the market? Does any accident ever happen to your kid? Does your kid have his/her own playmate? What does your kid fond of?
Where does your information about nursery come from? (from eldership, communication with other parents, etc.)
Which kind of nursery information would you love to know? (safety, education, psychology, etc.) What kind of things would you worry the most about your kid?
Do you find it hard to take care of your kid when you are working? What's the biggest problem you've ever met when you are taking care of the kid?

Opinion About Volunteer Teacher

Do you hear of Fairyland for Vegetable Chapmen's Childs? (If not, interviewer should try to give some brief information.)

Which kind of public education forms would you love to join in: person especially assigned for taking care of children; fixed time going to kindergarten to have some activities; baby-watching service; interdependent group of parents; book and toys lending; hot-line consultation about nursery; health service, etc.

What's your opinion about the proper time and frequency of these activities? What other needs do you have?

If some one can provide these services for you for free or just cost a little money, are you willing to receive some of them? How much could you afford them?

Are you willing to be volunteer joining in the services, e.g. taking care of children in the market, interdependent group of parents? How many times would you like to be a volunteer teacher every week? What is the best time for you to join in?

Are you willing to receive some consultations about early childhood education held by volunteer teachers? Do you have some good ideas for this kind of activity?

Are you willing to let your kid to join in some activities we hold in Si Huan market? Do you have some good ideas about what the activities should be?

Chapter 21

Lessons Learned and Implications for the Future

Anna Kirova
University of Alberta, Canada

Leah D. Adams
Eastern Michigan University, USA

The gathering of studies presented in this volume has been an extraordinary journey. It started with our commitment to understanding and improving the educational experiences of immigrant children in their new host countries. We have had first-hand experiences both with teaching newly arrived children and with preparing the future teachers of such children. We believed that to prepare future teachers better to work in an increasingly diverse global world, we needed a better understanding of the daily struggles of the newly arrived families, their children, and their teachers as they tried to learn about one another and to negotiate the complex issues related to the education of the young. The official statistics indicating an increased diversification of the student population in the receiving countries as a result of the new global mobility were no longer just numbers to us as we worked in various capacities in classrooms in our respective countries, Canada and the United States. These were real children from around the world. We have observed over the years that the efforts of individual schools to support newly arrived children academically and socially have had various degrees of success, and we have evaluated programs and initiatives implemented by local school authorities or local governments that have not always achieved anticipated outcomes. We have also observed many dedicated teachers who have made a difference in the lives of newly arrived children and their families.

As we began to talk with colleagues about why we could not always grasp the reasons for success or failure of seemingly "good initiatives," it became clear that not only the children in the classroom but also we ourselves were part of a global world. This is the global world of educators, teacher educators, and educational researchers, who, like us, face the ups and downs of work with immigrant families, children, and their teachers. We wondered if providing space for the international teaching communities to share their struggles, successes, programs, and practices would enable us to examine the similarities in the process of educating newly arrived children, as well as the differences among educational practices in addressing the unique contexts and the characteristics of the children involved. This volume is an extension of our professional discussions with early childhood colleagues from around the world who work with families who have recently arrived in their respective countries and who are concerned with issues related to the education of children.

What have we learned from the works included in this volume? First, the works included confirm that hardly any nation in the world remains unaffected by the process of globalization. The education systems in the 14 immigrant-receiving nations on five continents represented here have been greatly affected by global migration trends. Increasing diversity in school populations in some of these countries is a relatively recent phenomenon; for others it is a common practice. In either case, as almost all chapters point out, immigrant families have a significant effect on school enrollments. Many countries are experiencing a burgeoning immigrant population accompanied by a declining birth rate in the native population. This has implications for both present and future school practices as the populations served continue to change. Working with parents in the community, an essential part of a quality educational system, calls for flexibility on the part of school personnel. The flow of newcomers into a given locality may be from a particular region in a given sending nation or may be from many countries and may represent a broad spectrum of ethnic groups and nationalities. The flow into a certain locality may or may not be melded into an existing pocket of immigrants and their ethnic community. Whatever the situation in the specific locality, the schools must adjust to the needs of the newcomers and offer the children the best possible education.

However, the studies collected in this volume reveal that educators are experiencing a number of challenges in meeting the needs of all students in their classrooms. The expectation that global migration trends are likely to continue in the future suggests that changes are needed in teacher preparation programs if teachers are to begin their careers with the knowledge, skills, attitudes, and beliefs needed to provide the quality education to which all children are entitled. In addition, the need for continual support for teachers who are already in school systems is emphasized by many of the teachers and school administrators who participated in the studies. Availability of appropriate curriculum resources, sufficient funding for children who need to learn the language of instruction, or adequate psychological and counseling services for victims of violence and trauma before they entered the host country are among the most commonly described areas of pressing need.

Second, because these studies include participants who have migrated from all six inhabited continents, they represent a wide range of ethnic, cultural, racial, and linguistic groups. This has allowed us to appreciate the unique and complex amalgamation of circumstances and experiences that make each family and child unique. The more we learned about the individual families' and children's approaches to coping with multiple losses and adjusting to the new culture, as well as solving problems and creating new ways of living, the less meaningful the labels such as *immigrant, refugee, migrant, asylum seeker, newcomer,* or *TCKs* (third culture kids) became. These categories were helpful in providing information about the status of the persons involved in the various studies, about the general reasons for their migration, and perhaps to some extent about their experiences during the premigration period. However, the variations among the experiences of the individual families in these categories clearly show that no generalizations could or should be made based solely on the label given to the family. Diversity exists in every group, whether refugees or nations, whether of a single ethnic or cultural group or of a multicultural group. The labels not only reduce the diversity in each group to a single category but also are intangible as the schools do not always know the legal status of children who enter the system. In some cases presented here, teachers were not aware of where the newcomers in their classrooms came from or what they had experienced before entering the school. The studies suggest that the lack of information about children in the mainstream classrooms can be a two-edged sword. On one hand, it can free teachers from any preconceived notions about what the child might be like based on the label given to him or her. On the other hand, it can prevent teachers from being as helpful as they might be if a child's unique circumstances warrant particular attention.

Third, because the numerous pedagogical approaches explored and described here by the authors provide strong evidence in support of each child's unique circumstances, it is evident that there is no single right way of teaching the immigrant, migrant, refugee, or internationally mobile student. However, too heavy of an emphasis on the uniqueness of individual children's circumstances should not lead to an individualized view that ignores the cultural resources present in all ethnic groups. Some authors warn that a strong emphasis on the individual child's background can reproduce the asymmetrical dichotomy of "us" and "*them*" used by dominant ethnic majorities in the host countries as a framework to interpret interethnic and intercultural relationships. Such an emphasis can lead to the social construction of "*them*" as having individual family problems associated with specific ethnic identities. The authors make us aware that whatever labels are or are not used for migrant families and their children, prejudice against new arrivals exists. It is a documented fact of life in the societies represented here. The prejudices and biases that exist in the general communities are not left outside the door of the school building. Most authors address this issue and emphasize the need for teachers to work conscientiously against their own biases and those of the students. They call for actively addressing and rigorously contesting the issues of racism, prejudice, discrimination, and exclusion in schools.

Fourth, the works in this volume demonstrate that educational communities around the world can be a leading force in educational reform to ensure the right of all children to high-quality education. The educators and educational researchers in the countries represented here ask critical questions about the goals of education, the philosophy of education, the practices in their respective communities, and what future directions might be. As the most "national" of institutions, schools are caught in the tension between their traditional role in reproducing national culture and national identity, which is seen as a way of stabilizing society, and the expectation that by preparing society's future adults, they will be the force of change.

The realization that the future of education depends on critical analysis of the state of today's education policies and practices makes crucial the debates on multiculturalism and pluralism both in schools and in the broader society. The authors raise their voices strongly in this regard. This in itself demonstrates the vigor and dedication in the international education community that is not only struggling and coping with the influx of immigrants in their countries but also trying to conceptualize this change. One way to conceptualize the future of education systems worldwide is to see the current changes in the makeup of the student population as an advantage, an opportunity for learning, and an overall enrichment of educational opportunities for all involved: children, parents, teachers, communities, and societies. Thus, global migration could be interpreted, as it is by many authors, not only as an opportunity to challenge the existing education system but also as an impetus for positive educational change.

Fifth, a number of studies on children's experiences of immigration included here indicate that educators acknowledge the difficulties that immigrant and refugee children may experience after the many losses in their lives and the many changes they face as they enter education systems in their host countries. However, the educators do not see children as helpless victims of these changes. Rather, they recognize the children as agents who actively negotiate their new identities between their home culture and the dominant culture. Researchers describe children's strategies: actively learning the new language to establish and maintain meaningful peer relationships at school, using television shows to learn about life in the new country and to engage in conversations with their majority-group peers, working hard to achieve in school, and actively seeking information about the new school location before arrival. As some of the studies also suggest, the fact that children are prepared to advise other children who are also new to the school and country shows that children understand the strategies they use to cope with the pressures in school and are capable of assessing their effectiveness.

Sixth, the parents' views captured by the researchers speak to the complex and sometimes opposing forces affecting both parents and children in shaping their new identities. Parents' determination to succeed in the host country can result in high expectations for their children's education and a desire for them to function successfully in the larger society. Some parents in these studies are critical of the education system in their new host country and express concerns about their children's opportunities to move upward in society as a result of their education. Some parents feel powerless to help their children succeed in school and fear they may face rejection, discrimination, and marginalization in school and in the larger society. Others actively confront the system in protecting their children's rights to equal participation and quality education.

Parents are also concerned with preserving their own cultural values and lifestyles and wish to raise their children according to their cultural expectations. However, children's quicker adaptation to mainstream culture and the language of the host country leads, in some cases, to a reversal of family roles and increases the parents' feelings of loss of control. The interplay between these conflicting forces, paired with the strong influence of the peer group, affects the individual child's sense of self and belonging to either, both, or neither of the cultures.

Seventh, the numerous research approaches to the study of educational life experiences of immigrant, migrant, refugee, and internationally mobile children and their families demonstrate that various research methods allow varying types of questions about these experiences to be addressed. An array of research methods and approaches is represented here. Although each study reveals an important aspect of the effects of globalization on either children, their families, their schools, or a combination of all three, the use of multiple- or mixed-method designs in addressing the complex issues related to these experiences could be fruitful for future studies. There is also a need for more longitudinal studies of families and children of immigrant and internationally mobile backgrounds, especially of those who have experienced family separation or violence before migration. Interdisciplinary studies that allow for the educational, psychological, health, and economic factors that shape the experiences of immigrant and refugee families with young children to be understood should be considered if a comprehensive picture of the complex interrelationship between them is to be achieved. Multidisciplinary studies on acculturation and the rights of all immigrants and newly arrived minorities are urgently needed.

Studies that explore the strengths of families with immigrant and refugee backgrounds, as well as their children's agency in the process of acculturation and development of their new identities, are extremely important. Educators can approach the work with these students and their families not from the point of view of deficiency, but from the point of view of building on their already existing strengths. The adversity that almost all transitional–migrant families experience brings out these strengths. However, unless they are recognized as strengths, the deficit models of educational interventions may continue to be a force in the field of education.

Eighth, advocacy for newly arrived children can take many forms. In Part 1, it takes the form of advocating for all children's right to accessible, quality education and for their right to have teachers who are adequately prepared to teach in multicultural, multiethnic, and multilingual classrooms. In Part 2, advocacy includes understanding the varying cultural expectations immigrant and refugee children need to meet at home and in school and the need to use specific strategies to support them in their adjustment to the expectations of schools in the host countries. Part 3 provides a description of challenging government policies in educating displaced children. In Part 4, advocacy builds on children's agency in the acculturation process. In Part 5, advocacy is for community-based education with a high level of parental involvement and control.

By pointing to the efforts made by educators worldwide and by identifying future directions in the development of these efforts, the authors become strong advocates for the right of all children to protection from bias, fear, and misinterpretation and for their right to quality education. Advocacy includes learning more about the many and changing needs of immigrant children as they move through each stage of their acculturation process, knowing that there is no universal timeline or pathway for acculturation and that acculturation is a complex and multidimensional process. It also involves raising educators' awareness of cultural misunderstandings based on lack of accurate information about culturally acceptable and relevant behavioral patterns and differences in cognitive norms in various cultures. The advocacy of teachers for "slow bilingual approaches" to learning the language of instruction and retaining children's native language to maintain cultural and family relationships is crucial to immigrant and refugee children's successful acculturation. The development of bicultural identities and dual loyalties are, among others, the anticipated and desired outcomes of this process. Recognizing that achieving such outcomes for all children is far from being a reality makes the need for advocacy at all levels and in all forms a primary task for educators and educational researchers around the world. We hope that all readers of this volume will find a renewed commitment to the world's children and especially to those who are new arrivals—wherever they may be.

Author Index

A

Aboud, F., 260
Aci, A., 303, 304
Ackers, H. L., 185, 187
Adams, L., 9
Adjukovic, D., 206
Adjukovic, M., 206
Adkins, M. A., 232
Aitken, S. C., 156
Akiba, D., 302
Alexander, R., 192
Al-Haj, M., 106
Alvin, N., 70
Ames, L. B., 270
Andersen, L. F., 71
Anderson, A., 220
Anderson, B., 170
Andreoni, H., 212
Ani, C., 70
Antonsen, R., 70, 72, 74
Appadurai, A., 170
Archer, D., 152, 153
Armour-Hileman,
    V. L., 205, 206
Arney, F., 207
Arshad, R., 153
Arsky, G. H., 70, 72, 73
Artelt, C., 41
Asendorpf, J. B., 45
Axelsson, M., 31
Azuma, H., 104, 116

B

Bachmair, B., 174
Bærug, A., 71
Baghurst, P., 207
Baider, L., 106
Bailey, B., 302
Baines, E., 152, 156
Bakhtin, M., 196
Baldassar, L., 207
Ballinger, A., 280, 281, 288
Bandura, A., 136, 165
Banks, J. A., 18
Bankston III, C. L., 8, 9
Barber, M., 195
Barrere, L., 83
Barrett G., 129
Bartolome, L. I., 5, 8, 135
Baruth, L., 100
Bar-Yosef, R. W., 107
Bastien, D. T., 209
Batelaan, P., 18
Bauman, A., 205
Baumeister, R. F., 99, 152
Baumert, J., 41
Baungaard Rasmussen, L., 21
Bayram, Y., 302
Beard, J. L., 70
Beavin, J. H., 153
Beck, U., 204
Beekman, T., 186, 187
Beiser, M., 88, 205, 206, 254

Belenky, M., 195
Bell, B., 271
Bemak, F., 205
Ben Ezer, G., 105, 106, 109
Ben-Ari, A. T., 106
Ben-David, A., 106, 107
Ben-Eliezer, U., 106
Benita, E., 107
Berk, L. E., 268, 270
Berman, H., 154
Bernstein, B., 130
Berry, J. W., 4, 5, 10, 45
Bhavnagri, N. P., 142, 147
Biarnes, J., 129
Biderman, P., 107
Biklen, S. K., 108
Birman, D., 204
Bjørnebo, G. E., 71
Blackburn, S., 269
Blake, D. D., 302
Blanco, G. R., 53, 56, 64
Blatchford, P., 152, 156, 174
Bogdan, R. C., 108
Bolea, P. T., 238
Borch-Iohnsen, B., 70, 72, 74
Boulton, M., 156
Bourdieu, P., 19, 122
Boyd-Barrett, O., 180
Boyden, J., 4
Boyle, M., 123, 129
Brah, A., 182
Brekke, O. L., 70, 72, 74
Brisk, M. E., 18
Brittain, C., 6
Brkic, N., 206, 209
Bronfenbrenner, U., 41, 123, 124, 130
Brooker, L., 124
Brox, O., 31
Bruner, J., 280
Brunvand, L., 70, 71, 73, 79
Brunvatne, R., 70
Brustad, M., 71
Bryceson, D., 6, 7
Buckingham, D., 170
Buki, L. P., 104
Burgess, M., 238

Burgess-Pinoto, E., 8
Burgner, D., 207
Burris, M. A., 154
Büyüköztürk, S., 295

C

Cain, C., 188, 192, 196
Camerota, S. A., 6
Capra, F., 195
Cattanach, A., 186
Caufield, C., 8
Cekic S., 154
Cha, C. S., 2
Chan, R. M. C., 140, 141, 147
Chan, S., 148
Cheung, H. Y., 147
Chin, C., 302
Chislett, M., 280
Christie, P., 206, 209, 210, 211
Chui, Y., 8
Chung, R. C., 205
Çingi, H., 295
Clark, A., 289
Clark, J., 207
Class, A., 153
Claussen, A. H., 70
Clayton, J., 99
Clinchy, B., 195
Cocking, R., 105, 107
Cohen, R., 105
Cole, E., 232
Coleman, H. L. K., 4
Coll, C. G., 302
Collier, V., 31
Comerford, S. A., 205, 206
Commins, N. L., 18, 27
Conrad, D., 14, 154
Cook, J. D., 70
Coomans, F., 18
Corson, D., 2, 201
Cottrell, A. B., 263
Creamer, M., 232
Creswell, J., 108
Creswell, J. W., 239
Cronen, V. E., 152
Curato, S., 64

Curiel, F., 153
Cushner, K., 137
Custrini, R. J., 136, 153, 165
Cutler, N., 207

D
Dalen, I., 76
Danby, S., 204
Dasen, P., 10
Dauber, S., 130
Davidson, N., 207
Davie, R., 281
Davies, L., 207
Dawes, T., 69
de Berry, J., 4
de Block, L., 170, 182
De Vos, G., 8
DeCorby, E., 152
Deegan, J., 152
Dei, S. G. J., 14, 260
Delgado-Gaitan, C., 105
Deliyanni, K., 84, 85
Deliyanni-Kouimtzi, V., 122
DeNour, A., 106
Derwing, M. T., 152
Dewey, J., 215
Dhirad, A., 69, 77
Diler, R. S., 303, 304
Dimakos, I., 132
Dimartino, L.,   302
Dion, R., 88, 254
Djuric-Bejdic, Z., 206, 209
Dolev-Gindelman, Z., 105, 106
Dossetor, D., 207
Dubrow, N., 205, 206
Dudley, M., 204, 205, 206, 211
Dunn, B., 232
Duran, B. J., 135

E
Eden, M. D., 70
Efron, D., 153
Egelund, N., 24
Ek, J., 70, 72, 74
Ekblad, S., 206

Ekman, P., 153
Elbedour, S., 209
Ells, H., 154
Emme, M., 153, 154, 155
Ender, M., 263, 264
Engen, T. O., 31
Entzinger, H., 5
Epstein J., 130
Epstein, D., 172, 176
Erel, U., 6
Erman. T., 265, 303
Escudero, P., 199
Ever-Hadani, P., 106

F
Fabian, H., 129, 132,
      133, 279, 280
Fagerli, R., 70, 72, 74
Fairweather-Tait, S. J., 70
Fakiolas, R., 85
Fan, C. C., 308
Farnier, M. A., 69
Farrell, A., 204
Feagin, J. R., 260
Feeny, T., 4
Feldman, R. S., 136, 153, 165
Fend, H., 41
Field, A., 206
Field, J., 207
Filer A., 122
Fine, M., 248
Fink, A., 199
Fisher, C. T., 186
Fix, M., 3, 87, 248
Fleming, D., 8
Fong, R., 7
Ford, D. Y., 83
Ford-Gilboe M., 154
Frankel, D. G., 104, 105
Franson, C., 231
Frater-Mathieson, K., 220, 232
Frazel, M., 254
Freire, P., 190
Friedlander, M., 87
Friedmann, D., 106

G

Gadamer, H., 190, 191
Galati P., 122
Gale, F., 204, 205, 206, 211
Galin, P., 69
Gallimore, L. R., 105
Galloway, D., 281
Galton, M., 280
Garbarino, J., 205, 206
Gerton, J., 4
Ghaemii-Ahmadi, S., 15
Giangounidis, P., 122, 131
Gibson, M. A., 5
Giddens, A., 204
Gillespie, M., 170, 180
Gimbel, J., 26
Giorgi, A., 186
Gitelman, Z., 105
Glicksberg-Skipper, R., 268
Godkin, M. A., 188
Gökçe, B., 294
Goldberger, N., 195
Goldenberg, E., 206
Goldman, L., 105, 114
Gonzalez-Ramos, G., 135
Gordon, M. M., 5
Gorst-Unsworth, C., 206
Gossetti, P. P., 14
Gotowiec, A., 88, 254
Gottesberg, M., 105
Gracey, M., 15
Graetz, B., 207
Grant, G., Jr., 238
Grantham-McGregor, S., 70
Gray, J., 280
Greenfield, P. M., 105, 107
Gregory E., 129
Grugeon, E., 175
Guba, G. E., 239
Guery, M. F., 69
Gümen, S., 45

H

Haber, C. C., 270
Hagemann-White, C., 43
Hagendoorn, L., 5

Hall, E., 153
Hall, J. A., 153
Hamilton, R., 220, 233, 254, 256, 260
Han, J. L., 308
Hanna, J. L., 136, 165
Hannover, B., 44
Hansen, E. J., 30
Harding, R. K., 205
Harris, J. R., 260
Hart, C. H., 156
Hart, J., 4
Hatziprokopiou, P., 132
Haug, E., 73, 79
Hayward, P. W., 238, 241
Hazan, H., 105
Heidegger, M., 186, 188, 189,
    190, 192, 193, 195, 196
Helmke, A., 41
Henriksen, C., 73
Hercberg, S., 69
Hernandez, D., 83, 85, 87
Herwartz-Emden, L., 35, 36, 37, 41, 45
Herzberg, B., 207
Heslin, R., 153
Hess, D. R., 104, 116
Hodes, M., 301
Hofstede, G., 44
Holick, M. F., 71
Holland, D., 188, 192, 196
Holland, P., 176
Holloway, S., 156
Holmboe-Ottesen, G., 68, 69, 76, 77
Holmen, A., 26, 27
Holvik, K., 73, 79
Hones, D. F., 2, 14
Honig, A. S., 105
Horowitz, R. T., 105
Horst, C., 18, 23, 27
Hou, F., 206
Howard, M., 301
Hubbard, N., 123, 129
Huberman, A. M., 108
Hui, S. K. F., 147
Hunger, U., 35
Hvenekilde, A., 31
Hydon, C., 213

Hyltenstam, K., 18, 31
Hyman, I., 88, 254

I

Ichikawa, J., 152
Igoa, C., 99
Ilatov, Z., 84, 85
Inces, R. Q., 193
Ip, K.Y., 140, 141, 147
Izuhara, M., 6

J

Jackson, D. D., 153
Jacobs, L., 2, 6, 9, 13, 14
James, A., 152, 205, 281, 287
James, I. M., 14, 260
James-Wilson, S., 14, 260
Jamieson, K., 152
Jasinskaja-Lahti, I., 105
Jaycox, L. H., 199
Jenks, C., 152, 205
Jimenez, E., 70
Jones, C., 212
Jørgensen, J. N., 26
Jozajtis, K., 173

K

Kagitcibasi, C., 10, 293, 304
Kahane, R., 105
Kalaycioglu, S., 294
Kalesnik, J., 123
Kamau, O., 155
Kanno, Y., 136
Karabenick, S. A., 9
Karumanchery, L. L., 14, 260
Kasimis, C., 83, 85, 122
Kassimi, C., 83, 85, 122
Kataoka, S. I. H., 199
Katsikas, C., 122
Keles, R., 304
Kelly, P., 207
Kendon, A., 152, 154
Kentaro, K., 152, 156
Kim, E., 105
Kirova, A., 4, 8, 88, 89, 142, 152, 153,
    154, 155, 187, 188, 190, 193, 194

Kirova-Petrova, A., 130, 136, 152, 153,
    156, 187, 194
Kirton, E., 2, 6, 9, 13, 14
Kitayama, S., 43
Klafki,W., 19, 20
Knoff, H., 123
Köklü, N., 295
Kolaitis, G., 302
Köller, O., 41
Kosanovich, S., 155
Kosky, R., 207
Kostelny, K., 205, 206
Kotsionis, P., 122
Kotsopoulos, S., 302
Kramer, L., 83
Krieger, E. H., 70
Kristjansdottir, B., 23
Kroesen, K., 105
Krohne, J. A., 35
Küffner, D., 36, 37, 41
Kuhn, A., 176
Kühnen, U., 44
Kumar, B. N., 68, 69, 76, 77, 78

L

Lachicotte Jr., W., 188, 192, 196
Ladson-Billings, G., 14
Læssøe, J., 21
Lafromboise, T., 4
Lakasas, A., 121
Lande, B., 71
Langeveld, M., 192
Langford, M., 1
Larsson, M., 73
Lau, P. S.Y., 140, 141, 147, 148
Lazin, F. A., 107
Leach, E., 153
Leary, M. R., 99, 152
Lee, S., 6, 14
Lennartson-Hokkanen, I., 31
Leo, P.   , 269, 270
Leshem, E., 105, 106
Leshem, L., 106
Leung, C., 231
Li, G., 248
Li, P., 4

Liang, Z. S., 309
Lie, B., 68
Liebkind, K., 105
Lincoln, Y. S., 239
Linschoten, K., 8
Loewen, S., 220, 231, 232
Loomba, A., 189
Looney, J. G., 205
Lopez, G. R., 105
Lorimer, C., 210, 211
Lozoff, B., 70
Lüdtke, O., 41
Lukmann, T., 186
Lund-Larsen, K., 71
Luo, A. L., 308

M
Ma, T. C., 104
Ma, Z., 265
Madar, A., 70, 72, 74
Madianos, M., 302
Major, P., 70
Malcuit, G., 104
Mana, A., 105
Mana, Y., 105
Mandell, N., 187
Manicavasagar, V., 206
Manning, M. L., 100
Mares, S., 204, 205, 206, 211
Markowitz, F., 205
Markus, H. R., 43
Masten, A., 88
Mathiesen, A., 21
McBrien, J. L., 4, 5, 6, 14, 136, 231, 233
McCaig, N. M., 269
McCallin, M., 205, 206
McClelland, A., 137
McGorry, P., 205, 206
McKelvey, R., 207
McLennan, W., 205
Mead, G. H., 195
Mehrabian, A., 153
Meier, U., 35
Mellin-Olsen, T., 77
Melville, F., 205

Menuchin-Isickson, S., 105
Merkens, H., 39
Meyer, H. E., 73, 76, 79
Middelthon, A. O., 69
Miles, M. B., 108
Miller, E., 268
Miller, K. E., 206
Miller, L., 206, 209
Milner, H. R.,83
Mir, M. D.,70
Miramontes, O.,18, 27
Mohammad, A.,70
Mohan, P.,205, 206
Moore, D.,220, 254, 256, 260
Moosa, S.,9
Moreau, G.,4
Morley, D.,170, 182
Mortimore, P.,26
Moss, P., 289
Mosselson, J., 8
Mott, G., 280
Moutrey B., 154
Mummendey, H. D., 41
Murray, E., 186

N
Nadeau, A., 18, 27
Nagy, L. M. ve Ark., 302
Natland Sannan, S. T., 75
Nauck, B., 4
Newman, L., 204, 205, 206, 211
Newman, T., 269
Ninio, A., 104
Noam, G., 107
Nordshus, T., 71
Norris, C., 153
Norton Peirce, B., 136
Norton, B., 136
Noyes, A., 280
Nurcombe, B., 207
Nuttall, E. V., 123

O
O'Connell, J., 270
O'Sullivan, K., 208

Oakley, A., 205
Offer, S., 106
Ogbu, J. U., 104
Ogdul, H., 265
Ogilvie, L., 8
Ojanuga, D. N., 106
Olsen, P. T., 70, 72, 74
Opie, I., 175
Opie, P., 175
Oppedal, B., 88
Ormrod, J. E., 43
Orr, E., 105
Osterman, K. F., 152, 153
Özden, C., 1, 3
Ozdowski, S., 209
Øzerk, K., 18
Özkan, M., 302

P

Palacios, N., 302
Pandey, J., 10
Papoz, L., 69
Parekh, B., 19
Passel, J., 3, 87
Patterson, M. L., 153
Patton, G., 207
Patton, M., 107
Pearce, W. B., 152
Pelligrini, A. D., 152, 156
Penn, H., 288
Phalet, K., 4, 5, 6
Phan, T., 205
Philippot, P., 136, 153, 165
Phillips, J., 210, 211
Pile, S., 7
Plasa, O., 238
Politou, E., 122
Politt, E., 70
Pollard, A., 122
Pollock, D. C., 268, 269, 270, 279, 280
Pomerleau, A., 104
Poortinga, Y. H., 10
Portes, A., 9, 42
Powell, J., 88
Poyatos, F., 153

Preissle, J., 1, 100, 199
Prior, G., 207
Prout, A., 152, 205, 281, 287
Psalti, A., 84, 85, 122

R

Råberg, M., 79
Raman, S., 207
Ramic, A., 206, 209
Ramirez, A. Y., 105
Rao, M. S. A., 68
Rao, N., 140, 141
Raphael, B., 207
Rayner, M., 205
Reason, P., 21
Reed, J. L., 153, 154
Reese, L., 105
Richman, N., 181
Rittersberger-Tiliç, H., 294
Roberts, L., 207
Robins, K., 170
Roer-Bornstein, D., 104, 105
Roer-Strier, D., 04, 105, 114, 115
Roessingh, H., 152
Roman, B. D., 268, 269
Romero, I., 123
Rong, X. L., 1, 100, 199
Rosen, H., 105
Rosenthal, M. K., 104, 105
Rossignol, C., 69
Rubin, L., 142, 147
Rudduck, J., 280
Ruiz-de-Velasco, J., 248
Rumbaut, R. G., 9, 42
Rusch, E., 14
Rutter, J., 212, 220, 231, 232, 260
Ryan, G. W., 105

S

Sabatier, C., 104
Safford, P. L., 137
Sam, D. L., 4, 5, 88
Sammons, P., 26
Sanches-Nester, M., 135
Sandberg, A. S., 73

Sander, J., 70
Sandmeier, A., 43
Sang, D., 207
Santamaria, U., 106
Saraswathi, T. S., 10
Sattles, B. H., 4
Sawyer, M., 207
Schauder, T., 41, 45
Schiff, M., 1, 3
Schmitz, P. G., 147
Schneewind, J., 39
Schneider, S., 36, 37, 41
Schneller, R., 153
Schrader, F. W., 41
Schümer, G., 70
Schutz, A., 186
Schwartz, A. E., 14
Schweitzer, R., 205
Scott, K. G., 70
Searless, H. F., 188
Segal, A., 3, 6, 15, 199
Segall, M., 10
Sellgren, M., 31
Seydaoglu, G., 303, 304
Shamai, S., 84, 85
Shandy, D. J., 238
Shibata, H., 6
Sidhu, R., 206, 209, 210, 211
Silove, D., 204, 205, 206, 207, 208
Silver, R., 302
Sinnerbrink, I., 206
Sir, A., 302
Skinner, D., 188, 192, 196
Skull, S., 207
Sluckin, A., 175
Smajkic, A., 206, 209
Smith, M., 207
Smith, P. K., 156
Sobel, D. M., 83
Solem, I. H., 70
Solheim, E., 105
Soto, L. D., 193
Spence, J., 176
Spigelman, M., 255
Spurling, L., 193
Sreberny, A., 182

Sroufe, L. A., 156
Städtler, T., 41
Stainback, S., 105, 107
Stainback, W., 105, 107
Stalford, H., 185, 187
Stanat, P., 41
Stead, J., 153
Steel, Z., 204, 205, 206, 207
Steele, T., 14
Stein, A., 254
Stein, B. D., 199
Steinberg, D., 172
Stiefel, L., 14
Stöckli, G., 41
Strand, S., 280
Stringer, E. T., 310
Strom, R. D., 104
Strom, S. K., 104
Suárez-Orozco, C., 2, 88, 103, 104, 135
Suárez-Orozco, M. M., 2, 6, 9, 14, 88, 103, 104, 135
Sultan, A., 208
Sümbüloğlu, K., 294
Sümbüloğlu, V., 294
Sutton-Smith, B., 156
Szwarc, J., 205

T

Tacoli, C., 301, 304
Takanishi, R., 100
Tang, S., 315
Tarule, J., 195
Tasiopoulou, K., 132
Tate, W. F., 14
Taylor, S. V., 83
ten Bensel, R., 209
Tezcan, M., 293, 294
Thomas, S., 26
Thomas, W., 31
Thorne, B., 175
Thorstensen, K., 70, 72, 74
Thränhardt, D., 5
Thrift, N., 7
Tillmann, K. J., 35
Timm, J. T., 9
Tollefson, J., 4

Tomkins, A., 15
Toohey, K., 136
Trickett, E. J., 204
Trueba, E. T., 2, 5, 6, 8, 9, 13, 14, 135
Trygg, K. U., 71
Tse, L., 85
Tsiantis, J., 302

V

Valdés, G., 248
Valencia, A., 55
Valentine, G., 156
van Aken, M. A. G., 45
Van Ausdale, D., 260
van de Vijver, F. J. R., 4, 5, 6
Van den Berg, J. H., 189
Van Lotringen, C., 5
van Manen, M., 186, 191
van Ngo, H., 152
Van Reken, R. E., 268, 269, 270,
    272, 273, 275, 279, 280
Veierød, M. B., 71
Veikou, C., 122
Vidali, L. E., 122, 131
Vinokurova, A., 204
Viruru, R., 194
von Raffler-Engel, W., 153
Vora, R., 207
Vu, N., 88, 254
Vuorela, U., 6, 7

W

Wacquant, L., 19
Waites, L., 207
Waller, S. R., 205, 206
Walter, T., 70
Wandel, M., 68, 70, 72, 74, 76. 77
Wang, C., 154
Wang, D., 308
Waniganayake, M., 212, 213
Ward, C. J., 83
Ward, M. J., 83
Waters, E., 156

Watt, D., 152
Watters, C., 204
Watzlawick, P., 153
Weathers, F. W., 302
Weffer, R. E., 135
Weil, S., 106
Weine, S., 206, 209
Weiner, M., 153
Weisner, T., 105
Wells, P., 173
Wenger, E., 256
Wenkart, A., 188
Willes, M., 123
Winicott, D. W., 152
Winning, A., 188, 191, 194, 195
Woehrer, C. E., 45
Wolf, A. W., 70
Wong, M., 199
Wong, S., 205
Woods, P., 123, 129
Woolfolk Hoy, A., 83
Wu, J., 88, 89, 136, 152, 187, 194
Wu, S.W., 140, 141, 147

Y

Yalçin, C., 293
Yitzhak, R., 105
Yuen, M., 140, 141, 147, 148

Z

Zaragoza, C., 199
Zegeye, A., 106
Zhang, L., 308
Zhang, Y., 315
Zhao, S., 308
Zhi, P., 308
Zhou, L., 308
Zhou, M., 8, 9
Zhou, Y., 308
Zine, J., 14, 260
Zoetmulder, E. J., 267
Zubrick, S., 207
Zwi, K., 207

Subject Index

A

Academic achievement, 35, 41, 85, 100, 145, 147, *See also* Education, Educational achievement, School achievement, Educational attainment

Acculturation, *See also* Acculturation continuum, Acculturation process, and educational achievement, 35, 40, 44, 85
environment and, 36, 130
feeling lonely as predictor of, 147, 194
gender and, 14, 48
language proficiency and, 36, 103, performance of, 40–41
self-concept and, 14, 35, 41, 44
self-esteem and, 14, 35, 41, 44

Acculturation continuum, 7

Acculturation process, 35, 48, 99, 136, 147, 326

Action research, 310, 311, *See also* Dialogue research

Adaptation, *See also* Limited social adaptation
adapting to
new social environment, 294
early childhood settings in the Greek context, 123

Adaptive adult image,
adaptability in cultures undergoing transitions and, 104
honesty, integrity, and respect for others and, 113

preserving cultural cohesion and, 105

Adaptive adult in working with home and school and, 115–116

Adjustment,
friendships and, 127, 132
refugee families with preschool children and, 220, 225, 238, 248
to Greek schools, 123
to language, 243, 247
to changes in family ecologies, 141-142
to life in Canada, 251
to new education system, 6, 141
to school, 7, 97, 131, 248

Advocacy, 212, 213, 326, *See also* Advocates

Advocates, 213, 248, 326

Afghan parents, 259

African French-speaking parents, 201, 256, 257, 259

Age-appropriate school placement, 140-141

Armed conflicts,
refugees and, 3

Arts-based methodology, 153, 154

Aspirations,
immigrant parents' high aspirations, 201

Assessment,
grade placement and, 8
and lack of appropriate assessment, 8, 214, 223, 226, 231
placement of immigrant children, 8

337

Assimilation, 3, 5, 42, *See also*
    Segmented assimilation
Asylum seekers,
Australia's mandatory detention
    laws and, 212
    definition of, 2, 200
    economic hardship and, 179
    mandatory detention and, 200, 204
Attitudes,
    host country and parents' attitudes, 7
Australia's mandatory detention laws,
    asylum seekers and, 200
Australian curriculum
    and appropriate resources, 210
    special needs of detainee children
        and, 210
Autobiographical histories
    and media, 137, 176

B

Belong,
    searching for news ways
        to, 263–266
Belonging
    children's feelings of, 124, 126,
        142, 167, 272
    children's sense of, 152, 189,
        194, 263, 268, 275
    peer relationships and, 130, 136,
        152, 165, 265, 270, 313, 324
Bicultural background,
    children and, 42
    identity and, 40
Bilingual children,
    Danish schools and, 18, 22, 24
        26, 30, 31
    insufficient support of, 30
    language acquisition and, 28, 40
    underachievement of, 13, 17, 20, 30
Bilingualism,
    school leaving age and, 31, 261
Body language,
    cultural differences and, 165
    intercultural misunderstanding and, 165
    miscommunication and, 165
Bronfenbrenner's ecological model, 123

C

Cambodian parents, 201, 256, 259
Case study,
    of a Sudanese refugee family, 237–262
Children of forces personnel, 279
    factors in mobility of, 279–280
Child interviews, 89, 97, 124, 125,
    126, 142, 143, 147, 171, 187, 272
Children's competence, 289
Children's feelings,
    of loneliness and isolation in
        school, 124, 126, 142,
Children's participation, 290
Children's rights,
    to early childhood education,
        211–213, 325
Choice of school,
    refugee parents and, 245
    working the system through, 245
Circle of poverty, 53–54
Civil war,
    refugees and, 3, 200, 237
Coding, 92, 108, 143
Cognitive representation
    self-concept and, 40, 43
Collaboration between teachers
    and parents,
communications skills and, 130
    inadequate communication and, 130
Community,
    immigrant, 15, 169, 171, 199
    resources, 7, 315
    support, 255
Community-based education, 326, *See
    also* Nonformal Community
    Education
    for migrant peasant workers, 307–319
Content analysis methods, 125
Convention refugees,
    definition of, 200
Cultural brokering, 252
Cultural brokers, *See also* Cultural
    brokering,
children of immigrants and, 5
    ethnic communities and, 252
    refugee families and, 252

Cultural diversity,
  teacher preparation and, 14, 18,
    20, 23, 92, 122, 169
Cultural expectations, 14
Cultural heterogeneity,
children with an immigrant
    background and, 39
  native-born school children and, 39
Cultural ideologies,
  image of the adaptive adult
    and, 84, 104
Cultural lag,
  definition of, 105
  teachers' understanding of,
    84, 114, 116
Cultural logic,
  definition of, 104
  socialization agents and, 115, 116
  teacher understanding of, 84
Cultural transition,
  adaptive adult logic and, 104, 107
Culturally homogeneous society,
  transformation of, 19, 20, 25,
    27, 28, 29
Curriculum differences, 243
Curriculum materials,
  education of immigrant
    children and, 8
  lack of, 8

D

Declaration of Education for all,
  children's right to education and, 13
  high quality education and, 54
Democratic values,
  multicultural society and, 20
Dialogue research, 21
Dietary changes, 67, 69, 78
  role of children in, 77–78
Diet-related chronic diseases,
  diabetes and immigrant adolescents
    in Norway and, 68, 69, 78
  gender differences and, 76
  intake of sugar and fat, and, 74
  iron deficiency and, 68–74
  iron supplementation and, 73, 74

obesity and overweight in Norway
    and, 68, 69, 73, 78
  vitamin D deficiency and,
    68, 70–76, 79
Discrimination,
  immigrants and, 14, 42, 54–65
  immigrant children and,
    136, 241, 242
  refugees and, 200, 257
Displaced children,
  education of, 54, 57, 200,
    203, 206-208, 209–213
  ethical responsibilities to, 215
  future directions for, 213–214
  health and well-being of, 215
Displaced people,
  definition of, 2
Dominant culture,
  acculturation and, 4, 5, 18, 324
  adaptation and, 4, 5, 18, 324
  adjustment and, 4, 5, 18, 324
  assimilation and, 4, 5, 18, 324

E

Eating habits,
  school children of immigrants
    and, 68, 75, 77, 79
Education,
  achievement and, 145, 151
  preschool and, 85, 107, 256, 260
  primary schools and, 37, 139–141,
    145, 295
Education for all, 13, 54, 56,
    57, 58, 60, 65
Education of displaced children,
  curriculum resources and,
    200, 210, 323
  (ESL) programs and, 201, 209,
    239, 241, 243, 245, 247, 248
  future directions for, 213
  literacy programs and, 63, 209
  mental health issues and, 203, 211,
  standard Australian
    curriculum and, 210
  trauma counselling and, 209
Education system

Canadian education system,
    schooling in Canada, 155, 259
Greek education system, 121
Israeli education system, 113, 115
Educational achievement, 35, 36, 44
Educational attainment, 14
Educational inequalities,
    Caribbean countries and, 55
    ethnic origin and, 49, 68
    geographic location and, 60, 76, 104
    Latin America and, 53–55, 64
    public and private schools and, 55
    socioeconomic origins and, 55
Educational needs,
    assessment and, 8, 99, 101
    displaced children and, 54, 57,
        200, 203, 206, 209–213
    Haitian immigrants and refugees
        and, 60, 231
English as a Second Language (ESL)
    programs, 201, 209, 239, 241,
        243, 245, 247, 248
Epidemiological transition,
    immigrants and, 67
Eritrean parents, 201, 255, 257
Ethnic cleansing,
    refugees and, 3
Ethnic minority children,
    Danish schools and, 17, 20
    underachievement of, 20, 26
Ethnographic design, 171, 252
Exclusion, *See also* Social exclusion,
    immigrant children and, 4, 15,
        55, 56, 64, 65
    "Life of the playground"
        fotonovela and, 158
Expectations of teachers,
    immigrant children and, 13, 57
    immigrant parents and, 13, 57
Expressive values,
    image of the 'Adaptive adult' and,
        103, 104
External education,
    refugee and immigrant children's
        access to language and social
        network and, 209, 210

F
Family background,
    school achievement and, 19, 24,
        25, 27, 28, 30, 39
Family ecologies,
    mainland Chinese immigrant
        children and adjustment to, 139
Family issues,
    immigrant families and, 9,
        124, 238, 302
    refugee families and, 200, 219–221
Family language,
    and influence on school
        performance, 48, 49, 116
Fathers' roles,
    adaptive adult image and, 109
    Ethiopian immigrants and, 84, 85, 107
    Russian immigrants and, 84, 106, 107,
Focus groups,
    interviews and, 107, 223, 252
Food habits, 68
    among immigrant mothers
        and preschoolers, 71–75
    and nutritional challenges in
        schoolchildren and
        adolescents, 75–77
    immigrant mothers and
        breast-feeding, 71
    immigrant mothers and weaning
        traditions, 71
Food patterns, 68
Food values,
    change of dietary environment
        and, 68
Foreign-language-speaking children,
    Danish schools and, 17
Fotonovela,
    developing the "Getting into
        Basketball", 154
    storyboard and, 154
    tableau and, 154
    visual narrative and, 136, 153-156, 165
Friendships, *See also* Making friends
    adjustment to school and, 97
    children's adaptation process
        and, 126, 130

immigrant children and, 5, 13, 38,
71, 71, 116, 124, 132, 157
peer relationships and, 130, 136,
152, 165, 265, 270, 313, 324

G

Gains,
of the Si Huan Playgroup, 312–314
Gained possibilities, 195–196
Games,
group histories and, 176
school playground and, 156, 175
television programs and, 172
television shows and, 137, 324
Gender,
academic achievement and, 30, 55, 65
societal models of femininity and,
acculturation and, 43
societal models of masculinity and, 43
Gesture,
body language and, 158, 162, 165
nonverbal behavior (NVB) and,
136, 152, 154, 159, 165
nonverbal communication and,
136, 152, 153, 165
Globalization, xi, 8, 13, 67, 121,
124, 322, 325,
media and, 170
television viewing and, 170
Global citizens,
children of forces personnel as, 3, 215
learning to become, 279
Global migration, 1, 2, 6, 44, 322, 324

H

Haitian immigrant children, 15
Health outcomes,
socioeconomic differences and
ethnicity and, 76
socioeconomic differences and
lifestyle of various ethic
groups and, 76
Health policy,
implications for, 78–79
and nutrition education, 78–79
Hermeneutic phenomenology,

immigrant children's lived
experiences and, 186
High-mobility families, *See also* High
mobility lifestyle, Third-Culture
Children (TCC) and, Third Culture
Kids TCK and,
High mobility lifestyle, 279
High-quality education, 57, 305, 315, 324
Home,
concept of, 187
far from, 199–202
immigrant children's sense of
"at-home-ness", 187, 188
language of, 137, 186, 187, 193, 196
sense of belonging and, 152, 188,
194, 263, 265, 275
the space of, 188
Host country language,
academic achievement and, 14, 40
Host culture,
acculturation and, 2, 4, 5, 8, 68, 84
adaptation and, adjustment to,
2, 4, 5, 8, 68, 84, 201
assimilation and, 5, 31
Humanitarian-designated refugees,
definition of, 200

I

Images of fathers,
and expectations of an adaptive adult
image for the Ethiopian
fathers, 108–109
and expectations of an adaptive adult
image for Russian fathers, 110–111
Immigrant children, *See also* Bilingual
children, Children of immigrants,
Ethic minority children,
Foreign-language speaking
children, Haitian immigrant
children, Minority students
academic achievement of, *See also*
Academic underachievement of
academic underachievement of, 13
achievement tests of, 35, 40, 44, 85
adjustment to
school environment, 7, 97, 131, 248

changing family ecologies, 140, 141
new education system, 6
age appropriate school placement
    of, 88, 140
agency and, 279, 325, 326
assessment of, 8, 99, 101
bicultural identity of, 40, 42
children's rights and, 211, 213, 325
competence and, 289
diet of, 15, 16, 75
educational attainment level of, 14
emotional adjustment of, 8
exclusion of, 4, 64, *See also*
    Social exclusion of
friendships and, 5, 13, 38, 71, 71,
    116, 124, 132, 157
global issues for, 13–16
grade placement of, 8
health education of, 15, 69, 78
identity formation of, 8, 175
inclusion movement and, 56, 57
inclusions of, *See* Inclusion
    movement and
individual needs assessment of,
    8, 214, 223, 226, 231
instrumental skills and success in
    the host culture and, 103
integration of, *See* Integration
    movement and
integration movement and, 56, 57
intercultural competence and, 20
intercultural understanding and,
    136, 158, 162, 165
nonverbal behaviors (NVB) and,
    136, 152, 154, 159, 165
nonverbal communication and,
    130, 136, 152, 165, 265, 270, 324
nutrition of, 67–70, 74, 75, 78, 79
peer relationships and, 130, 136,
    152, 165, 265, 270, 324
performance level of, 9
posttraumatic stress disorder and,
    201, 208, 227, 232, 302, 303
right to education and, *See* Education
    for all, High-quality education,
right to participation and, 57

school placement of, 140, *See also* Age
    appropriate school placement of
school issues, 144–145
self-concept of, 43–48, 125, 188,
    189, 196, 270, 288, 325
self-esteem of, 41–43, 45–48,
    142, 280, 303
socialization of, 43, 84, 103–119
social adjustment of, 101, 135,
    148, 227, 294, 295, 299–304
social competence of, 30, 88
social exclusion of, 15, 64, 65
trauma and, 206, 209, 212, 213,
    224, 227, 232, *See also*
    Posttraumatic stress disorder and
views and voices of, 135–138
voices of, 135–138, 139–150
Immigrant parents,
    adaptive adult images, 105, 109, 111
    attitudes towards the host culture
        and, 85, 105
    beliefs of, 9
    expectations of, 108, 110, 115
    expressive values and, 104
    fathers' roles, 109, 111
    images of fathers and, 108–113
    parental image of an "adaptive
        adult", 84, 105, 115
    parent-teacher conferences, 9, 229, 230
    preserving culture and traditions
        and, 114
    values of, 111, *See also* Cultural
        values of
    voice of, 213
Immigrants,
    assimilation of, 3, 5, 31, 42, 58, 85
    diet of, 15, 16, 75
    discrimination, 14, 15, 42, 54–59,
        64–66, 106, 136, 141, 200,
        241, 242, 257, 261, 324, 325,
        See also Racial discrimination
        and ethnic discrimination of
    exclusion of, 3, 14, 15, 55, 56, 64,
        65, 106, 158, *See also* Political
        exclusion of
    from Ethiopia, 106–107

from Mainland China, 139
challenges for, 140–142
human rights and, 13, 16, 59, 85,
    205, 209, 211
inclusion of, 53, 56, 57, 60, 65
marginalization of, 4, 14, 15, 30,
    135, 140, 141, 325
mental health of, 10, 15, 18, 203,
    206, 211, 227
recent waves of immigration to
    Israel, 105–106
rejection of, 13, 159
Russian immigrants from the
    Former Soviet Union, 106-107
segregation of, 5, 20, 135, 140, 245
Immigration detention facilities,
    unauthorized-arrival children and
        families and, 205
Inclusion in schools,
    in Latin America, 53–56
    inclusion versus integration, 56–57
    negotiating, 169–184
    significance of, 57–58
In-depth interviews, 107, 238, 304
Inequalities of educational opportunities,
    Latin America and, 53, 64
Integral policies of inclusion,
    need for, 56
Intercultural competence,
    students, teachers and principals and, 20
Intercultural didactics,
    respect of cultural diversity and, 20
Intercultural education,
    challenges of globalization
        and, 19, 25, 123, 124
    in-service teachers training and,
        20, 22, 23, 25, 96, 101
    preservice teachers training
        and, 83, 96, 101
Intercultural misunderstanding
    body language and, 158, 162, 165
    nonverbal cultural differences
        and, 136, 165
    peer relationships and, nonverbal
        communication and, 130,
        136, 152, 165, 265, 270, 324

social competence and, 30, 88
Intercultural validation,
    process of, 44, 45
Interculturality,
    primary school population and, 40
Internal education,
    detention centers and, 209
    education of displaced children, 209
Internalization of schools,
    Denmark and, 42
Interviews, 107, 108, 124-129, 187,
    221, 223,, 238, 239, 252, 309,
    318 *See also* Child interviews,
Parent interviews, Teacher interviews

L

Language(s),
    home of, 137, 186, 187,
        193, 196, 198
    between, 189–191
    new, 7, 135, 186, 189, 191–196,
        200, 324
    problems with, 49, 131
    school achievement and, 27, 31
Language adjustment, 243
Language proficiency,
    acculturation and, 209, 233
    German language proficiency and, 38
Limited social adaptation, 296, 299
Linguistic facility,
    primary language spoken at
        home and, 37
Linguistic heterogeneity,
    schoolchildren in Germany and, 40
Literacy programs,
    Haitian children in the Dominican
        Republic and, 63, 209
Lived experiences of immigration,
    children and, 154, 186
    phenomenology and the study of, 252
Loneliness,
    "Getting into Basketball", fotonovela
        and, 136, 153–161, 163, 165–167
    immigrant children and, 4, 11, 99,
        128, 133, 138, 141, 142, 148,
        152, 158, 167, 187, 197

Loss of first language,
    breakdown of family relations and, 210
    loss of feelings of self-worth
        and, 195, 210
    loss of motivation to learn and, 210
Lost possibilities, 193–195

M

Majority culture,
    ethic minority children and
        proficiency in, 9, 153
    proficiency in, 9, 153
Majority language,
    ethnic minority children and
        proficiency in, 20, 23, 26
    proficiency in, 20, 38, 42, 103
Making friends, 126, 146-147, 270, 296
Media,
    news media as a social
        reference, 179–180
    revived memories and personal
        connections, and, 180–182
Migrant children,
    Limited social adaptation of, 296, 299
    observed changes in, 312
    preschool education of, 85, 107,
        256, 260
    social adaptation and skills
        of, 299–306
    social anadaptation of, 296, 299
Migrant parents,
    child-care group and, 311
    child-rearing practices and, 311
    handbook for, 311
    leadership groups and, 311, 312, 316
    mom-teachers and, 314
    observed benefits for, 313
    parent volunteers and, 252
    participation of, 303, 309
    playgroup project and, 307
Migrants, *See also* Rural migrants
        in Beijing,
    industrialization and, 293
    low-income peasant workers,
        307–310, 314–316

modernization, and 293
    urbanization and, 67, 293, 304
Migration, *See also* Global migration,
    postmigratory dietary changes, 77
    pre-migration experiences, 293
    transnational migration, 121
    trends of, 322
Minority students,
    linguistic and cultural
        backgrounds of, 13
Mother tongue,
    Danish schools and teaching of, 17
    language policy and, 27, 28
    minority children and, 23, 27,
        31, 37, 42, 190
Multicultural education,
    global (US) media products
        and, 183
    and interaction between educational
        tradition and national
        identity, 18-19
    developing multicultural education
        in schools, 20–21
    policy for the future, 30–31
Multicultural society,
    politics of, 19, 20, 26–29, 32
Multilingualism,
    schoolchildren in Germany
        and, 38, 40

N

Naming,
    children's play and, 192, 193
Negative feelings,
    of children, 152, 274, 280
    of TCC/TCK, 274
Negotiating,
    identity and, 122
    inclusions and exclusion and,
        169, 175, 177, 183
Neighborhood,
    children's adjustment and,
        127, 130, 175, 180
    determining children's friendships
        and, 126, 146, 175, 180

development of the host country's
   language and, 130
immigrant clusters and, 126
New arrival children (NAC), 88, 89,
   92, 99, 100, 101, 139, 140
family and neighbourhood issues
   and, 145-146
hopes and worries of, 145
likes and dislikes of, 146-147
school issues and, 144
strategies for providing social
   emotional support for, 93–94
strategies for supporting the cognitive
   development of, 95-96
teachers' advice for new teachers with
   NAC in the classroom, 97-98
Newcomers,
   definition of, 2
News media,
   social reference and, 179
Nonformal community education,
   Si Huan Playgroup and, 310-311
   gains of, 312
   observed changes in children, 312–313
   observed changes in parents, 313–314
   participation and training of
      parents and, 311-312
   support from different agencies
      and, 312
Nonverbal behavior (NVB),
   cultural differences in, 136, 152,
      154, 159, 165
   interpersonal relationships and,
      136, 152, 154, 159, 165
   miscommunication and
      misunderstanding and,
      136, 152, 154, 159, 165
Nonverbal communication,
   peer acceptance and, 136,
      152, 153, 165
Nonverbal peer interaction,
   understanding of, 136, 152, 153, 165
Nutritional challenges,
   among immigrant children and
      youth in Norway, 67–81

among preschoolers, 69–71
iron deficiency, 69–70
vitamin D deficiency, 70–71
and food habits in schoolchildren
   and adolescents, 74–76
Nutritional transition,
   children of immigrants and, 67–70,
      74, 75, 78, 79
   immigrants and, 67–70, 74, 75, 78

O-P
Official school language, 42
Parent interviews, 125, 126,
   131, 224, 231
Parents, *See* Immigrant parents, Migrant
   Parents, Refugee parents, Sudanese
   parents
Parental expectations, 241–242
Pedagogical possibilities,
   gained possibilities for immigrant
      children, 137, 193, 196
   lost possibilities for immigrant
      children, 137, 193, 196
Peer acceptance,
   immigrant children and, 130,
      136, 152, 165, 265, 270, 324
   interpersonal relationships, 153
   nonverbal behaviour (NVB) and,
      136, 152, 154, 159, 165
   nonverbal communication and,
      130, 136, 152, 165,
      265, 270, 324
peer conflict and, miscommunication
   and, 152
   social competence and, 30, 88
   TV talk and, 172–175, 178, 182
Peer group,
   immigrant children and, 130, 136,
      152, 165, 265, 270, 324
   nonverbal behaviour (NVB) and,
      136, 152, 154, 159, 165
   nonverbal communication and,
      130, 136, 152, 165, 265, 270, 324
   social competence and, 30, 88
   TV talk and, 172–175, 178, 182

Peer relationships,
    body language and, 158, 162, 165
    and friendships, 126, 146, 175, 180
    immigrant children and, 130, 136,
        152, 165, 265, 270, 324
    loneliness and, 13, 152, 159, 161,
        264, 270
    nonverbal translation and, 136, 165
    rejection and, 152, 153, 159, 161
    social isolation and, 99, 152
    verbal exchange and, 159
Performance level,
    immigrant children and, 9
    parents' concerns and, 84, 85
Performative research,
    developing of fotonovelas and, 154
Phenomenology,
    human lived experiences and, 186
Photography,
    eliciting children's opinions and, 154
    research with children and,
        30, 153, 165
Playground,
    cultural transmission and, 175
    development of social skills
        and, 129, 175
    games on the, 175–177
    peer social interaction and, 130,
        136, 152, 165, 265, 270, 324
    playing media games and, 178
    visual documentation of, 156
Pluralistic education system,
    immigrant parents and, 116
Pluralistic integration,
    social policy of, 31
Positive discrimination,
    access to education and retention
        of children at risk and, 54
Postmigratory dietary changes,
    health of immigrant population
        and, 68, 69, 71, 73, 75, 77–79
Poverty, See also Circle of poverty
    education and, 225
    Latin America and the Caribbean,
        53–55, 59, 64

Preschool environment,
    children's experiences of
        transition and, 126, 129, 132
Public health education,
    health policy and, 78, 79
    health prevention and, 69
    health promotion and, 69
    nutrition improvements and, 15, 69
Purposeful sampling, 107

R

Re-authoring self,
    learning new language and, 196
Refugee children,
    academic enrichment opportunities
        for, 229
    academic support, 226, 228,
        231, 232, 234
    adjustment to schools and, 7, 97,
        131, 248
    (in)appropriate academic
        assessment of, 223, 225, 231, 234
    counselling services for, 227,
        232, 234, 323
    ESL services for, 201, 209, 239,
        241, 243, 245, 247, 248
    experiences of trauma and horror
        and, 227, 232, 302, 303
    lack of biographical information
        and, 137, 176
    meaningful family or home
        partnerships and, 229, 231,
        233, 234
    needs of, 219–235
    prior educational experiences of,
        8, 225, 229
    social-emotional skill-building
        activities and, 227
    social-emotional support of, 92–94,
        96, 99, 101, 221, 223,
        226, 227, 231
Refugee parents, See also Afghan
    parents, African French-speaking
    parents, Cambodian Parents,
    Eritrean parents, Sudanese parents,

adjustment experiences, 220, 225,
    238, 248
beliefs and values of, 9
changing family roles and, 201
changing responsibilities of family
    members and, 257
decreased socioeconomic status
    and, 76, 83, 135, 254, 255
discrimination against and, 200, 257
expectations of, 241, 260, 261
feeling of belonging and, 294
heritage language and culture, and, 261
hopes of, 241, 60, 261
lack of community support and,
    255, 256, 261
lack of family support and,
    255, 256, 261
maintaining home culture and,
    126, 324
maintaining home language and,
    137, 186, 187, 193, 196
mental health issues of, 203, 211
perceptions of the U.S. urban
    schools and, 238, 241, 247
postmigration experiences and, 77
premigration experiences
    and, 258, 293
preschool care and, 220, 225, 238, 248
racism and, 256, 257, 260
refugee camp experiences and,
    253, 260
relationships between home school
    and community, and, 260
resettlement and,
factors that influence, 254, 255
sacrifices of, 242, 247
transmigration experiences
    and, 253, 254
unequal power relationship
    and, 247, 248
unfamiliar childrearing practices
    and, 256
Refugees,
    definition of, 204
    wave of African, 237, 238, 241

Rejection,
    loneliness and, 13, 152, 159,
        161, 264, 270
    of the new child, 13, 152,
        159, 161, 264, 270
Resettlement,
    of children in Australia, 209–218
    factors that affect, 254–259
    changing roles and responsibilities
        of family members, 257
    coping with mental health issues, 258
    dealing with racism and
        discrimination, 257
    decreased socioeconomic
        status, 254-255
    lack of community and family
        support, 255–256
    maintaining home language and
        culture, 258–259
    understanding the Canadian
        education system, 259–260
    unfamiliar childrearing
        practices, 256–257
Resilience, *See also* Resilient children,
    TCC (TCK) and, 203, 204,
        206, 269, 270, 275
Resilient children, 269
Rural migrants in Beijing, 308

S

Safe havens for children,
    government agencies and
        non-government organizations
        and, 212
School achievement,
    family background and, 27-28
    immigrant background and 31, 35, 40
    role of language and, 27
    minority students' cultural
        backgrounds and, 35
    positions on, 24
    teacher positions on, 26, 27, 31, 35, 40
    well-being and, 26–27
Second language acquisition,
    deficits in, 22, 219, 231

language policy and, 22, 28, 94, 209, 231
learning process and, 31, 44
self-esteem and well-being and,
        31, 44, 219
Segmented assimilation, 42
Self-concept,
    acculturation and, 43–48, 125,
        188, 189, 196, 270, 288, 325
    culture-specific influences and, 43
    factors that influence, 42–44
    gender-specific influences and, 43
    scales for, 46
Self-efficacy,
    depression and, 130
    parents' sense of, 130
    parents' perception of children's
        difficulties and, 130
Self-esteem,
    acculturation and, 41–43,
        45–48, 142, 280, 303
    factors that influence, 42–44
    scales for, 47
Semistructured interviews, 142, 239
Social adaptation, 293–297, 299–305
    and skills of migrant children
        attending primary school in
        Turkey, 293–306
    findings about, 299–301
    in primary school, 303–304
Social competence,
    nonverbal behaviors (NVB) and,
        136, 152, 154, 159, 165
    student-centered approach and, 29
Social exclusion, 64–65
Social inequalities,
    circle of poverty and, 53, 54
    Latin America and, 53–55, 64–66
Social mirroring,
    self-concept and, 44
    self-esteem and, 41, 42
Socialization of children, 43, 108
    role of home and school in, 103–119
Societal models of femininity,
    gender and, 43
    self-concept and, 41, 42
    self-esteem and, 44

Societal models of masculinity,
    gender and, 43
    self-concept and, 41, 42
    self-esteem and, 44
Special education needs (SEN),
    of forces personnel's children,
        22, 55–58, 231, 280
Still photography,
    visual data collection and, 153, 154
Structured interview protocol, 239
Student-centered approach,
    reform movement in Denmark and, 29
Sudanese parents, 237–238
Survey,
    children survey,
    parent survey,
    teacher survey,

T
Teacher interviews, 92
Teacher qualifications,
    minority children and, 24
Teacher training,
    data on, 22–24
    perceived helpfulness of, 95–96
Teachers,
    and their roles in children's social
        adjustment, 101, 135, 148,
        227, 294, 295, 299–304
Teaching materials,
    manipulative materials and helping
        NAC, 20, 24, 59, 63, 94
Teaching strategies,
    adjusting standards and, 94
    dealing with language barriers and,
        93, 94, 96, 101, 126, 175, 230
    demonstrating, 94, 99, 114
    engaging NAC in non-language
        activities and, 96
    helping NAC learn and, 94, 99, 114
    influence on, 36, 89, 92, 93, 95,
        98, 99, 101, 305
    repeating instructions and, 94
    social-emotional support and, 92–94,
        96, 99, 101, 221, 223,
        226, 227, 231

time and patience and, 101
using gesture and, 94
Television shows,
    access to experiences and, 174
    autobiographical memories or
        histories and, 176
    children's, 136, 152, 154, 159, 165
    creating continuities and, 174-175, 180
    establishing location and belonging
        and, 178–179
    games and chats and, 137, 172,
        175,-176, 324
    learning about family and, 172–174
Third Culture Children (TCC), *See also*
    Third Culture Kids (TCK),
    academic success and, 268
    adaptation and, 268
    definition of, 267–268
    experiences of, 267–278
    feelings of loss and, 269–272, 274, 275
    international school in Singapore
        and, 263, 268, 271, 272
    interviews with, 107, 223, 252
    negative feelings of, 269–272, 274, 275
    positive feelings of, 269–272, 274, 275
    sense of belonging and, 268
    social and emotional challenges
        and, 268
Third Culture Kids (TCK), 268
Traditional dietary beliefs and practices,
    cultural identity and, 68
Transnational displacement of children,
    an Australian perspective, 203–217

Trauma,
    acculturation and migration-related
        trauma, 206, 209
    counselling and, 8,209, 227,
        232, 234, 260, 323
    forced migration and, 182, 200
    posttraumatic stress disorder and,
        227, 232, 302, 303
    pre-migration and, 258
TV talk,
    shared space and, 172, 173
    social inclusion and, 174

U-V
United Nations Declaration of
    Human Rights,
    rights of immigrants and, 13
Visual narratives,
    fotonovelas as, 158

W
Waves of immigration,
    Ethiopian immigration to
        Israel and, 84, 106, 107
    Israel and recent waves of,
        84, 105, 106
    Russian immigration to Israel
        and, 84, 106
Well-being,
    school achievement and, 26